A BOOK OF GOLDEN DEEDS

ALSO AVAILABLE FROM
LIVING BOOK PRESS

The Burgess Animal Book for Children (in color)
The Burgess Bird Book for Children (in color)
The Burgess Flower Book for Children (in color)
Home Geography—C.C. Long
Elementary Geography—Charlotte Mason
Viking Tales—Jeannie Hall
Parables From Nature*—Margaret Gatty
Fifty Famous Stories Retold*—James Baldwin
The Blue Fairy Book* —Andrew Lang
The Red Fairy Book —Andrew Lang
Beautiful Stories of Shakespeare* —Edith Nesbit
Tales from Shakespeare* —Charles and Mary Lamb
    * in AO reading order

Richard Halliburton's Marvels of the Orient
Richard Halliburton's Marvels of the Occident

Charlotte Mason's Home Education Series
1.   Home Education
2.   Parents and Children
3.   School Education
4.   Ourselves
5.   Formation of Character
6.   A Philosophy of Education
And many, many more!

All Living Book Press titles are complete and unabridged, and (when possible) presented with the original illustrations, sometimes from several sources, to bring these great books even more to life.

To see a complete list of all our releases or if you wish to leave us any feedback please visit www.livingbookpress.com

A Book of
Golden Deeds

CHARLOTTE M. YONGE

This edition published 2019
By Living Book Press
Copyright © Living Book Press, 2019

ISBN: 978-1-925729-76-4

 A catalogue record for this
book is available from the
National Library of Australia

GREATER LOVE HATH NO MAN THAN THIS, THAT

HE LAY DOWN HIS LIFE FOR HIS FRIEND.

"I HAVE DONE THAT WHICH WAS MY DUTY TO DO"

Contents

Preface

As the most striking lines of poetry are the most hackneyed, because they have grown to be the common inheritance of all the world, so many of the most noble deeds that earth can show have become the best known, and enjoyed their full meed of fame. Therefore it may be feared that many of the events here detailed, or alluded to, may seem trite to those in search of novelty; but it is not for such that the collection has been made. It is rather intended as a treasury for young people, where they may find minuter particulars than their abridged histories usually afford of the soul-stirring deeds that give life and glory to the record of events; and where also other like actions, out of their ordinary course of reading, may be placed before them, in the trust that example may inspire the spirit of heroism and self-devotion. For surely it must be a wholesome contemplation to look on actions, the very essence of which is such entire absorption in others that self is forgotten; the object of which is not to win promotion, wealth, or success, but simple duty, mercy, and lovingkindness. These are the actions wrought, "hoping for nothing again", but which most surely have their reward.

The authorities have not been given, as for the most part the narratives lie on the surface of history. For the description of the Colisæum, I have, however, been indebted to the Abbé Gerbet's *Rome Chrétienne;* for the Housewives of Löwenburg, and St. Stephen's Crown, to Freytag's *Sketches of German Life;* and for the story of George the Triller, to Mr. Mayhew's *Germany.* The Escape of Attalus is narrated (from Gregory of Tours) in Thierry's *Lettres sur l'Histoire de France;* the Russian officer's adventures, and those of Prascovia Lopouloff, the true Elisabeth of Siberia, are from M. le Maistre; the shipwrecks chiefly from Gilly's *Shipwrecks of the British Navy;* the Jersey Powder Magazine from the *Annual Registrer*, and that at Ciudad Rodrigo, from the traditions of the 52nd Regiment.

There is a cloud of doubt resting on a few of the tales, which it may be honest to mention, though they were far too beautiful not to tell. These are the details of the Gallic occupation of Rome, the Legend of St. Geneviève, the Letter of Gertrude von der Wart, the stories of the Keys of Calais, of the Dragon of Rhodes, and we fear we must add, both Nelson's plan of the Battle of the Nile, and likewise the exact form of the heroism of young Casabianca, of which no two accounts agree. But it was not possible to give up such stories as these, and the thread of truth there must be in them has developed into such a beautiful tissue, that even if unsubstantial when tested, it is surely delightful to contemplate.

Some stories have been passed over as too devoid of foundation, in especial that of young Henri, Duke of Nemours, who, at ten years old, was said to have been hung up with his little brother of eight in one of Louis XI's cages at Loches, with orders that two of the children's teeth should daily be pulled out and brought to the king. The elder child was said to have insisted on giving the whole supply of teeth, so as to save his brother; but though they were certainly imprisoned after their father's execution, they were released after Louis's death in a condition which disproves this atrocity.

The Indian mutiny might likewise have supplied glorious instances of Christian self-devotion, but want of materials has compelled us to stop short of recording those noble deeds by which delicate women and light-hearted young soldiers showed, that in the hour of need there was not wanting to them the highest and deepest "spirit of self-sacrifice."

At some risk of prolixity, enough of the surrounding events has in general been given to make the situation comprehensible, even without knowledge of the general history. This has been done in the hope that these extracts may serve as a mother's storehouse for reading aloud to her boys, or that they may be found useful for short readings to the intelligent, though uneducated classes.

NOVEMBER 17, 1864.

What is a Golden Deed?

WE all of us enjoy a story of battle and adventure. Some of us delight in the anxiety and excitement with which we watch the various strange predicaments, hair-breadth escapes, and ingenious contrivances that are presented to us; and the mere imaginary dread of the dangers thus depicted, stirs our feelings and makes us feel eager and full of suspense.

This taste, though it is the first step above the dulness that cannot be interested in anything beyond its own immediate world, nor care for what it neither sees, touches, tastes, nor puts to any present use, is still the lowest form that such a liking can take. It may be no better than a love of reading about murders in the newspaper, just for the sake of a sort of startled sensation; and it is a taste that becomes unwholesome when it absolutely delights in dwelling on horrors and cruelties for their own sake; or upon shifty, cunning, dishonest stratagems and devices. To learn to take interest in what is evil is always mischievous.

But there is an element in many of such scenes of woe and violence that may well account for our interest in them. It is that which makes the eye gleam and the heart throb, and bears us through the details of suffering, bloodshed, and even barbarity,–feeling our spirits moved and elevated by contemplating the courage and endurance that they have called forth. Nay, such is the charm of brilliant valour, that we often are tempted to forget the injustice of the cause that may have called forth the actions that delight us. And this enthusiasm is often united with the utmost tenderness of heart, the very appreciation of suffering only quickening the sense of the heroism that risked the utmost, till the young and ardent learn absolutely to look upon danger as an occasion for evincing the highest qualities.

> "O Life, without thy chequer'd scene
> Of right and wrong, of weal and woe,
> Success and failure, could a ground
> For magnanimity be found?"

The true cause of such enjoyment is perhaps an inherent consciousness that there is nothing so noble as forgetfulness of self. Therefore it is that

3

we are struck by hearing of the exposure of life and limb to the utmost peril, in oblivion, or recklessness of personal safety, in comparison with a higher object.

That object is sometimes unworthy. In the lowest form of courage it is only avoidance of disgrace; but even fear of shame is better than mere love of bodily ease, and from that lowest motive the scale rises to the most noble and precious actions of which human nature is capable–the truly golden and priceless deeds that are the jewels of history, the salt of life.

And it is a chain of Golden Deeds that we seek to lay before our readers; but, ere entering upon them, perhaps we had better clearly understand what it is that to our mind constitutes a Golden Deed.

It is not mere hardihood. There was plenty of hardihood in Pizarro when he led his men through terrible hardships to attack the empire of Peru, but he was actuated by mere greediness for gain, and all the perils he so resolutely endured could not make his courage admirable. It was nothing but insensibility to danger, when set against the wealth and power that he coveted, and to which he sacrificed thousands of helpless Peruvians. Daring for the sake of plunder has been found in every robber, every pirate, and too often in all the lower grade of warriors, from the savage plunderer of a besieged town up to the reckless monarch making war to feed his own ambition.

There is a courage that breaks out in bravado, the exuberance of high spirits, delighting in defying peril for its own sake, not indeed producing deeds which deserve to be called golden, but which, from their heedless grace, their desperation, and absence of all base motives–except perhaps vanity–have an undeniable charm about them, even when we doubt the right of exposing a life in mere gaiety of heart.

Such was the gallantry of the Spanish knight who, while Fernando and Isabel lay before the Moorish city of Granada, galloped out of the camp, in full view of besiegers and besieged, and fastened to the gate of the city with his dagger a copy of the Ave Maria. It was a wildly brave action, and yet not without service in showing the dauntless spirit of the Christian army. But the same can hardly be said of the daring shown by the Emperor Maximilian when he displayed himself to the citizens of Ulm upon the topmost pinnacle of their cathedral spire; or of Alonso de Ojeda, who figured in like manner upon the tower of the Spanish cathedral. The same daring afterwards carried him in the track of Columbus, and there he stained his name with the usual blots of rapacity and cruelty. These deeds, if not tinsel, were little better than gold leaf.

A Golden Deed must be something more than mere display of fearlessness. Grave and resolute fulfilment of duty is required to give it the true weight. Such duty kept the sentinel at his post at the gate of Pompeii, even when the stifling dust of ashes came thicker and thicker from the volcano, and the liquid mud streamed down, and the people fled and struggled on, and still the sentry stood at his post, unflinching, till death had stiffened his limbs; and his bones, in their helmet and breastplate, with the hand still raised to keep the suffocating dust from mouth and nose, have remained even till our own times to show how a Roman soldier did his duty. In like manner the last of the old Spanish infantry originally formed by the Great Captain, Gonzalo de Cordova, were all cut off, standing fast to a man, at the battle of Rocroy, in 1643, not one man breaking his rank. The whole regiment was found lying in regular order upon the field of battle, with their colonel, the old Count de Fuentes, at their head, expiring in a chair, in which he had been carried, because he was too infirm to walk, to this his twentieth battle. The conqueror, the high-spirited young Duke d'Enghien, afterwards Prince of Condé, exclaimed, "Were I not a victor, I should have wished thus to die!" and preserved the chair among the relics of the bravest of his own fellow countrymen.

Such obedience at all costs and all risks is, however, the very essence of a soldier's life. An army could not exist without it, a ship could not sail without it, and millions upon millions of those whose "bones are dust and good swords are rust" have shown such resolution. It is the solid material, but it has hardly the exceptional brightness, of a Golden Deed.

And yet perhaps it is one of the most remarkable characteristics of a Golden Deed that the doer of it is certain to feel it merely a duty; "I have done that which it was my duty to do" is the natural answer of those capable of such actions. They have been constrained to them by duty, or by pity; have never even deemed it possible to act otherwise, and did not once think of themselves in the matter at all.

For the true metal of a Golden Deed is self-devotion. Selfishness is the dross and alloy that gives the unsound ring to many an act that has been called glorious. And, on the other hand, it is not only the valour, which meets a thousand enemies upon the battlefield, or scales the walls in a forlorn hope, that is of true gold. It may be, but often it is a mere greed of fame, fear of shame, or lust of plunder. No, it is the spirit that gives itself for others—the temper that for the sake of religion, of country, of duty, of kindred, nay, of pity even to a stranger, will dare all things, risk all things, endure all things, meet death in one moment, or wear life away in slow, persevering tendance and suffering.

Such a spirit was shown by Leæna, the Athenian woman at whose house the overthrow of the tyranny of the Pisistratids was concerted, and who, when seized and put to the torture that she might disclose the secrets of the conspirators, fearing that the weakness of her frame might overpower her resolution, actually bit off her tongue, that she might be unable to betray the trust placed in her. The Athenians commemorated her truly golden silence by raising in her honour the statue of a lioness without a tongue, in allusion to her name, which signifies a lioness.

Again, Rome had a tradition of a lady whose mother was in prison under sentence of death by hunger, but who, at the peril of her own life, visited her daily, and fed her from her own bosom, until even the stern senate were moved with pity, and granted a pardon. The same story is told of a Greek lady, called Euphrasia, who thus nourished her father; and in Scotland, in 1401, when the unhappy heir of the kingdom, David, Duke of Rothesay, had been thrown into the dungeon of Falkland Castle by his barbarous uncle, the Duke of Albany, there to be starved to death, his only helper was one poor peasant woman, who, undeterred by fear of the savage men that guarded the castle, crept, at every safe opportunity, to the grated window on a level with the ground, and dropped cakes through it to the prisoner, while she allayed his thirst from her own breast through a pipe. Alas! the visits were detected, and the Christian prince had less mercy than the heathen senate. Another woman, in 1450, when Sir Gilles of Brittany was savagely imprisoned and starved in much the same manner by his brother, Duke François, sustained him for several days by bringing wheat in her veil, and dropping it through the grated window, and when poison had been used to hasten his death, she brought a priest to the grating to enable him to make his peace with Heaven. Tender pity made these women venture all things; and surely their doings were full of the gold of love.

So again two Swiss lads, whose father was dangerously ill, found that they could by no means procure the needful medicine, except at a price far beyond their means, and heard that an English traveller had offered a large price for a pair of eaglets. The only eyrie was on a crag supposed to be so inaccessible, that no one ventured to attempt it, till these boys, in their intense anxiety for their father, dared the fearful danger, scaled the precipice, captured the birds, and safely conveyed them to the traveller. Truly this was a deed of gold.

Such was the action of the Russian servant whose master's carriage was pursued by wolves, and who sprang out among the beasts, sacrificing his own life willingly to slake their fury for a few minutes in order that the horses might be untouched, and convey his master to a place of safety. But his act of self-devotion has been so beautifully expanded in the story of "Eric's Grave", in "Tales of Christian Heroism", that we can only hint at it, as at that of the "Helmsman of Lake Erie", who, with the steamer on fire around him, held fast by the wheel in the very jaws of the flame, so as to guide the vessel into harbour, and save the many lives within her, at the cost of his own fearful agony, while slowly scorched by the flames.

Memorable, too, was the compassion that kept Dr. Thompson upon the battlefield of the Alma, all alone throughout the night, striving to alleviate the sufferings and attend to the wants, not of our own wounded, but of the enemy, some of whom, if they were not sorely belied, had been known to requite a friendly act of assistance with a pistol shot. Thus to remain in the darkness, on a battlefield in an enemy's country, among the enemy themselves, all for pity and mercy's sake, was one of the noblest acts that history can show. Yet, it was paralleled in the time of the Indian Mutiny, when every English man and woman was flying from the rage of the Sepoys at Benares, and Dr. Hay alone remained because he would not desert the patients in the hospital, whose life depended on his care—many of them of those very native corps who were advancing to massacre him. This was the Roman sentry's firmness, more voluntary and more glorious. Nor may we pass by her to whom our title page points[1] as our living type of Golden Deeds—to her who first showed how woman's ministrations of mercy may be carried on, not only within the city, but on the borders of the camp itself—"the lady with the lamp", whose health and strength were freely devoted to the holy work of softening the after sufferings that render war so hideous; whose very step and shadow carried gladness and healing to the sick soldier, and who has opened a path of like shining light to many another woman who only needed to be shown the way. Fitly, indeed, may the figure of Florence Nightingale be shadowed forth at the opening of our roll of Golden Deeds.

Thanks be to God, there is enough of His own spirit of love abroad in the earth to make Golden Deeds of no such rare occurrence, but that they are of "all time". Even heathen days were not without them, and how much more should they not abound after the words have been spoken, "Greater love hath no man than this, that he lay down his life for his friend", and after the one Great Deed has been wrought that has consecrated all other deeds of self-sacrifice. Of martyrdoms we have scarcely spoken. They were truly deeds of the purest gold; but they are too numerous to be dwelt on here: and even as soldiers deem it each man's simple duty to face death unhesitatingly, so the "glorious army of martyrs" had, for the most part, joined the Church with the expectation that they should have to confess the faith, and confront the extremity of death and torture for it.

What have been here brought together are chiefly cases of self-devotion that stand out remarkably, either from their hopelessness, their courage, or their patience, varying with the character of their age; but with that one essential distinction in all, that the dross of self was cast away.

Among these we cannot forbear mentioning the poor American soldier, who, grievously wounded, had just been laid in the middle bed, by far the most comfortable of the three tiers of berths in the ship's cabin in which the wounded were to be conveyed to New York. Still thrilling with the suffering of being carried from the field, and lifted to his place, he saw a comrade in even worse plight brought in, and thinking of the pain it must

---

1   See the title page for an engraving of Florence Nightingale.

cost his fellow soldier to be raised to the bed above him, he surprised his kind lady nurses (daily scatterers of Golden Deeds) by saying, "Put me up there, I reckon I'll bear hoisting better than he will".

And, even as we write, we hear of an American Railway collision that befell a train on the way to Elmira with prisoners. The engineer, whose name was William Ingram, might have leapt off and saved himself before the shock; but he remained in order to reverse the engine, though with certain death staring him in the face. He was buried in the wreck of the meeting train, and when found, his back was against the boiler–he was jammed in, unable to move, and actually being burnt to death; but even in that extremity of anguish he called out to those who came round to help him to keep away, as he expected the boiler would burst. They disregarded the generous cry, and used every effort to extricate him, but could not succeed until after his sufferings had ended in death.

While men and women still exist who will thus suffer and thus die, losing themselves in the thought of others, surely the many forms of woe and misery with which this earth is spread do but give occasions of working out some of the highest and best qualities of which mankind are capable. And oh, young readers, if your hearts burn within you as you read of these various forms of the truest and deepest glory, and you long for time and place to act in the like devoted way, bethink yourselves that the alloy of such actions is to be constantly worked away in daily life; and that if ever it be your lot to do a Golden Deed, it will probably be in unconsciousness that you are doing anything extraordinary, and that the whole impulse will consist in the having absolutely forgotten self.

The Stories of Alcestis and Antigone

IT has been said, that even the heathens saw and knew the glory of self-devotion; and the Greeks had two early instances so very beautiful that, though they cannot in all particulars be true, they must not be passed over. There must have been some foundation for them, though we cannot now disentangle them from the fable that has adhered to them; and, at any rate, the ancient Greeks believed them, and gathered strength and nobleness from dwelling on such examples; since, as it has been truly said, "Every word, look or thought of sympathy with heroic action, helps to make heroism". Both tales were presented before them in their solemn religious tragedies, and the noble poetry in which they were recounted by the great Greek dramatists has been preserved to our time.

Alcestis was the wife of Admetus, King of Pheræ, who, according to the legend, was assured that his life might be prolonged, provided father, mother, or wife would die in his stead. It was Alcestis alone who was willing freely to give her life to save that of her husband; and her devotion is thus exquisitely described in the following translation, by Professor Anstice, from the choric song in the tragedy by Euripides:–

> "Be patient, for thy tears are vain–
> They may not wake the dead again:
> E'en heroes, of immortal sire
> And mortal mother born, expire.
>   Oh, she was dear
>   While she linger'd here;
> She is dear now she rests below,
>   And thou mayst boast
>   That the bride thou hast lost
> Was the noblest earth can show.
>
> "We will not look on her burial sod
>   As the cell of sepulchral sleep,
> It shall be as the shrine of a radiant god,
> And the pilgrim shall visit that blest abode

To worship, and not to weep;
And as he turns his steps aside,
  Thus shall he breathe his vow:
'Here sleeps a self-devoted bride,
Of old to save her lord she died.
    She is a spirit now.
Hail, bright and blest one! grant to me
  The smiles of glad prosperity.'
Thus shall he own her name divine,
Thus bend him at Alcestis' shrine."

The story, however, bore that Hercules, descending in the course of one of his labours into the realms of the dead, rescued Alcestis, and brought her back; and Euripides gives a scene in which the rough, jovial Hercules insists on the sorrowful Admetus marrying again a lady of his own choice, and gives the veiled Alcestis back to him as the new bride. Later Greeks tried to explain the story by saying that Alcestis nursed her husband through an infectious fever, caught it herself, and had been supposed to be dead, when a skilful physician restored her; but this is probably only one of the many reasonable versions they tried to give of the old tales that were founded on the decay and revival of nature in winter and spring, and with a presage running through them of sacrifice, death, and resurrection. Our own poet Chaucer was a great admirer of Alcestis, and improved upon the legend by turning her into his favourite flower–

"The daisie or els the eye of the daie,
The emprise and the floure of flouris all".

Another Greek legend told of the maiden of Thebes, one of the most self-devoted beings that could be conceived by a fancy untrained in the knowledge of Divine Perfection. It cannot be known how much of her story is true, but it was one that went deep into the hearts of Grecian men and women, and encouraged them in some of their best feelings; and assuredly the deeds imputed to her were golden.

Antigone was the daughter of the old King Oedipus of Thebes. After a time heavy troubles, the consequence of the sins of his youth, came upon him, and he was driven away from his kingdom, and sent to wander forth a blind old man, scorned and pointed at by all. Then it was that his faithful daughter showed true affection for him. She might have remained at Thebes with her brother Eteocles, who had been made king in her father's room, but she chose instead to wander forth with the forlorn old man, fallen from his kingly state, and absolutely begging his bread. The great Athenian poet Sophocles began his tragedy of "Oedipus Coloneus" with showing the blind old king leaning on Antigone's arm, and asking–

"Tell me, thou daughter of a blind old man,
Antigone, to what land are we come,
Or to what city? Who the inhabitants
Who with a slender pittance will relieve
Even for a day the wandering Oedipus?"

POTTER.

The place to which they had come was in Attica, hear the city of Colonus. It was a lovely grove–

"All the haunts of Attic ground,
Where the matchless coursers bound,
Boast not, through their realms of bliss,
Other spot so fair as this.
Frequent down this greenwood dale
Mourns the warbling nightingale,
Nestling 'mid the thickest screen
Of the ivy's darksome green,
Or where each empurpled shoot
Drooping with its myriad fruit,
Curl'd in many a mazy twine,
Droops the never-trodden vine."

ANSTICE.

This beautiful grove was sacred to the Eumenides, or avenging god-desses, and it was therefore a sanctuary where no foot might tread; but near it the exiled king was allowed to take up his abode, and was protected by the great Athenian King, Theseus. There his other daughter, Ismene, joined him, and, after a time, his elder son Polynices, arrived.

Polynices had been expelled from Thebes by his brother Eteocles, and had been wandering through Greece seeking aid to recover his rights. He had collected an army, and was come to take leave of his father and sisters; and at the same time to entreat his sisters to take care that, if he should fall in the battle, they would prevent his corpse from being left unburied; for the Greeks believed that till the funeral rites were performed, the spirit went wandering restlessly up and down upon the banks of a dark stream, unable to enter the home of the dead. Antigone solemnly promised to him that he should not be left without these last rites. Before long, old Oedipus was killed by lightning, and the two sisters returned to Thebes.

The united armies of the seven chiefs against Thebes came on, led by Polynices. Eteocles sallied out to meet them, and there was a terrible battle, ending in all the seven chiefs being slain, and the two brothers, Eteocles and Polynices, were killed by one another in single combat. Creon, the uncle, who thus became king, had always been on the side of Eteocles, and therefore commanded that whilst this younger brother was entombed with all due solemnities, the body of the elder should be left upon the battlefield to be torn by dogs and vultures, and that whosoever durst bury it should be treated as a rebel and a traitor to the state.

This was the time for the sister to remember her oath to her dead brother. The more timid Ismene would have dissuaded her, but she answered,–

> "To me no sufferings have that hideous form
> Which can affright me from a glorious death".

And she crept forth by night, amid all the horrors of the deserted field of battles, and herself covered with loose earth the corpse of Polynices. The barbarous uncle caused it to be taken up and again exposed, and a watch was set at some little distance. Again Antigone

> "Was seen, lamenting shrill with plaintive notes,
> Like the poor bird that sees her lonely nest
> Spoil'd of her young".

Again she heaped dry dust with her own hands over the body, and poured forth the libations of wine that formed an essential part of the ceremony. She was seized by the guard, and led before Creon. She boldly avowed her deed, and, in spite of the supplications of Ismene, she was put to death, a sufferer for her noble and pious deeds; and with this only comfort:–

> "Glowing at my heart
> I feel this hope, that to my father, dear
> And dear to thee, my mother, dear to thee,
> My brother, I shall go."
>
>   POTTER.

Dim and beautiful indeed was the hope that upbore the grave and beautiful Theban maiden; and we shall see her resolution equalled, though hardly surpassed, by Christian Antigones of equal love and surer faith.

The Cup of Water

NO touch in the history of the minstrel king David gives us a more warm and personal feeling towards him than his longing for the water of the well of Bethlehem. Standing as the incident does in the summary of the characters of his mighty men, it is apt to appear to us as if it had taken place in his latter days; but such is not the case, it befell while he was still under thirty, in the time of his persecution by Saul.

It was when the last attempt at reconciliation with the king had been made, when the affectionate parting with the generous and faithful Jonathan had taken place, when Saul was hunting him like a partridge on the mountains on the one side, and the Philistines had nearly taken his life on the other, that David, outlawed, yet loyal at the heart, sent his aged parents to the land of Moab for refuge, and himself took up his abode in the caves of the wild limestone hills that had become familiar to him when he was a shepherd. Brave captain and Heaven-destined king as he was, his name attracted around him a motley group of those that were in distress, or in debt, or discontented, and among them were the "mighty men" whose brave deeds won them the foremost parts in that army with which David was to fulfill the ancient promises to his people. There were his three nephews, Joab, the ferocious and imperious, the chivalrous Abishai, and Asahel the fleet of foot; there was the warlike Levite Benaiah, who slew lions and lionlike men, and others who, like David himself, had done battle with the gigantic sons of Anak. Yet even these valiant men, so wild and lawless, could be kept in check by the voice of their young captain; and, outlaws as they were, they spoiled no peaceful villages, they lifted not their hands against the persecuting monarch, and the neighbouring farms lost not one lamb through their violence. Some at least listened to the song of their warlike minstrel:–

> "Come, ye children, and hearken to me,
> I will teach you the fear of the Lord.
> What man is he that lusteth to live,
> And would fain see good days?
> Let him refrain his tongue from evil

> And his lips that they speak no guile,
> Let him eschew evil and do good,
> Let him seek peace and ensue it."

With such strains as these, sung to his harp, the warrior gained the hearts of his men to enthusiastic love, and gathered followers on all sides, among them eleven fierce men of Gad, with faces like lions and feet swift as roes, who swam the Jordan in time of flood, and fought their way to him, putting all enemies in the valleys to flight.

But the Eastern sun burnt on the bare rocks. A huge fissure, opening in the mountain ridge, encumbered at the bottom with broken rocks, with precipitous banks, scarcely affording a foothold for the wild goats—such is the spot where, upon a cleft on the steep precipice, still remain the foundations of the "hold", or tower, believed to have been the David's retreat, and near at hand is the low-browed entrance of the galleried cave alternating between narrow passages and spacious halls, but all oppressively hot and close. Waste and wild, without a bush or a tree, in the feverish atmosphere of Palestine, it was a desolate region, and at length the wanderer's heart fainted in him, as he thought of his own home, with its rich and lovely terraced slopes, green with wheat, trellised with vines, and clouded with grey olive, and of the cool cisterns of living water by the gate of which he loved to sing—

> "He shall feed me in a green pasture,
> And lead me forth beside the waters of comfort".

His parched longing lips gave utterance to the sigh, "Oh that one would give me to drink of the water of the well of Bethlehem that is by the gate!" Three of his brave men, apparently Abishai, Benaiah, and Eleazar, heard the wish. Between their mountain fastness and the dearly loved spring lay the host of the Philistines; but their love for their leader feared no enemies. It was not only water that he longed for, but the water from the fountain which he had loved in his childhood. They descended from their chasm, broke through the midst of the enemy's army, and drew the water from the favourite spring, bearing it back, once again through the foe, to the tower upon the rock! Deeply moved was their chief at this act of self-devotion—so much moved that the water seemed to him to be too sacred to be put to his own use. "May God forbid it me that I should do this thing. Shall I drink the blood of these men that have put their lives in jeopardy, for with the jeopardy of their lives they brought it?" And as a hallowed and precious gift, he poured out unto the Lord the water obtained at the price of such peril to his followers.

In later times we meet with another hero, who by his personal qualities inspired something of the same enthusiastic attachment as did David, and who met with an adventure somewhat similar, showing the like nobleness of mind on the part of both leader and followers.

It was Alexander of Macedon, whose character as a man, with all its dark shades of violence, rage, and profanity, has a nobleness and sweetness that win our hearts, while his greatness rests on a far broader basis than that of his conquests, though they are unrivalled. No one else so gained the love of the conquered, had such wide and comprehensive views for the amelioration of the world, or rose so superior to the prejudice of race; nor have any ten years left so lasting a trace upon the history of the world as those of his career.

It is not, however, of his victories that we are here to speak, but of his return march from the banks of the Indus, in B. C. 326, when he had newly recovered from the severe wound which he had received under the fig tree, within the mud wall of the city of the Malli. This expedition was as much the expedition of a discoverer as the journey of a conqueror: and, at the mouth of the Indus, he sent his ships to survey the coasts of the Indian Ocean and Persian Gulf, while he himself marched along the shore of the province, then called Gedrosia, and now Mekhran. It was a most dismal tract. Above towered mountains of reddish-brown bare stone, treeless and without verdure, the scanty grass produced in the summer being burnt up long before September, the month of his march; and all the slope below was equally desolate slopes of gravel. The few inhabitants were called by the Greeks fish-eaters and turtle-eaters, because there was apparently, nothing else to eat; and their huts were built of turtle shells.

The recollections connected with the region were dismal. Semiramis and Cyrus were each said to have lost an army there through hunger and thirst; and these foes, the most fatal foes of the invader, began to attack the Greek host. Nothing but the discipline and all-pervading influence of Alexander could have borne his army through. Speed was their sole chance; and through the burning sun, over the arid rock, he stimulated their steps with his own high spirit of unshrinking endurance, till he had dragged them through one of the most rapid and extraordinary marches of his wonderful career. His own share in their privations was fully and freely taken; and once when, like the rest, he was faint with heat and deadly thirst, a small quantity of water, won with great fatigue and difficulty, was brought to him, he esteemed it too precious to be applied to his own refreshment, but poured it forth as a libation, lest, he said, his warriors should thirst the more when they saw him drink alone; and, no doubt, too, because he felt the exceeding value of that which was purchased by loyal love.

A like story is told of Rodolf of Hapsburg, the founder of the greatness of Austria, and one of the most open-hearted of men. A flagon of water was brought to him when his army was suffering from severe drought. "I cannot," he said, "drink alone, nor can all share so small a quantity. I do not thirst for myself, but for my whole army."

Yet there have been thirsty lips that have made a still more trying renunciation. Our own Sir Philip Sidney, riding back, with the mortal hurt in his broken thigh, from the fight at Zutphen, and giving the draught from his own lips to the dying man whose necessities were greater than his own, has long been our proverb for the giver of that self-denying cup of water that shall by no means lose its reward.

A tradition of an act of somewhat the same character survived in a Slesvig family, now extinct. It was during the wars that ranged from 1652 to 1660, between Frederick III of Denmark and Charles Gustavus of Sweden, that, after a battle, in which the victory had remained with the Danes, a stout burgher of Flensborg was about to refresh himself, ere retiring to have his wounds dressed, with a draught of beer from a wooden bottle, when an imploring cry from a wounded Swede, lying on the field, made him turn, and, with the very words of Sidney, "Thy need is greater than mine," he knelt down by the fallen enemy, to pour the liquor into his mouth. His requital was a pistol shot in the shoulder from the treacherous Swede. "Rascal," he cried, "I would have befriended you, and you would murder me in return! Now I will punish you. I would have given you the whole bottle; but now you shall have only half." And drinking off half himself, he gave the rest to the Swede. The king, hearing the story, sent for the burgher, and asked him how he came to spare the life of such a rascal.

"Sire," said the honest burgher, "I could never kill a wounded enemy."

"Thou meritest to be a noble," the king said, and created him one immediately, giving him as armorial bearings a wooden bottle pierced with an arrow! The family only lately became extinct in the person of an old maiden lady.

How One Man has Saved a Host

B. C. 507

THERE have been times when the devotion of one man has been the saving of an army. Such, according to old Roman story, was the feat of Horatius Cocles. It was in the year B.C. 507, not long after the kings had been expelled from Rome, when they were endeavouring to return by the aid of the Etruscans. Lars Porsena, one of the great Etruscan chieftains, had taken up the cause of the banished Tarquinius Superbus and his son Sextus, and gathered all his forces together, to advance upon the city of Rome. The great walls, of old Etrurian architecture, had probably already risen round the growing town, and all the people came flocking in from the country for shelter there; but the Tiber was the best defence, and it was only crossed by one wooden bridge, and the farther side of that was guarded by a fort, called the Janiculum. But the vanguards of the overwhelming Etruscan army soon took the fort, and then, in the gallant words of Lord Macaulay's ballad–

> "Thus in all the Senate
>   There was no heart so bold
> But sore it ached, and fast it beat,
>   When that ill news was told.
> Forthwith uprose the Consul,
>   Up rose the Fathers all,
> In haste they girded up their gowns,
>   And hied them to the wall.
>
> "They held a council standing
>   Before the River Gate:
> Short time was there, ye well may guess,
>   For musing or debate.
> Out spoke the Consul roundly,
>   'The bridge must straight go down,
> For, since Janiculum is lost,

Nought else can save the town.'
"Just then a scout came flying,
  All wild with haste and fear:
'To arms! To arms! Sir Consul,
  Lars Porsena is here.'
On the low hills to westward
  The Consul fixed his eye,
And saw the swarthy storm of dust
  Rise fast along the sky.

. . . .

"But the Consul's brow was sad,
  And the Consul's speech was low,
And darkly looked he at the wall,
  And darkly at the foe.
'Their van will be upon us
  Before the bridge goes down;
And if they once may win the bridge
  What hope to save the town?'

"Then out spoke brave Horatius,
  The Captain of the Gate,
'To every man upon this earth
  Death cometh soon or late;
And how can man die better
  Than facing fearful odds,
For the ashes of his fathers,
  And the temples of his gods?

"'And for the tender mother
  Who dandled him to rest,
And for the wife who nurses
  His baby at her breast?
And for the holy maidens
  Who feed the eternal flame,
To save them from false Sextus,
  That wrought the deed of shame?

"'Hew down the bridge, Sir Consul,
  With all the speed ye may,
I, with two more to help me,
  Will hold the foe in play.
In yon strait path a thousand

> May well be stopp'd by three:
> Now who will stand on either hand,
> And keep the bridge with me?'

> "Then out spake Spurius Lartius,
>   A Ramnian proud was he,
> 'Lo, I will stand at thy right hand,
>   And keep the bridge with thee.'
> And out spake strong Herminius,
>   Of Titian blood was he,
> 'I will abide on thy left side,
>   And keep the bridge with thee.'"

So forth went these three brave men, Horatius, the Consul's nephew, Spurius Lartius, and Titus Herminius, to guard the bridge at the farther end, while all the rest of the warriors were breaking down the timbers behind them.

> "And Fathers mixed with commons,
>   Seized hatchet, bar, and crow,
> And smote upon the planks above,
>   And loosen'd them below.

> "Meanwhile the Tuscan army,
>   Right glorious to behold,
> Came flashing back the noonday light,
> Rank behind rank, like surges bright,
>   Of a broad sea of gold.
> Four hundred trumpets sounded
>   A peal of warlike glee,
> As that great host, with measured tread,
> And spears advanced, and ensigns spread,
> Roll'd slowly towards the bridge's head,
>   Where stood the dauntless three.

> "The three stood calm and silent,
>   And look'd upon the foes,
> And a great shout of laughter
>   From all the vanguard rose."

They laughed to see three men standing to meet the whole army; but it was so narrow a space, that no more than three enemies could attack them at once, and it was not easy to match them. Foe after foe came forth against them, and went down before their swords and spears, till at last—

> "Was none that would be foremost
>   To lead such dire attack;
> But those behind cried "Forward!"
>   And those before cried 'Back!' "

. . . .

However, the supports of the bridge had been destroyed.

> "But meanwhile axe and lever
>   Have manfully been plied,
> And now the bridge hangs tottering
>   Above the boiling tide.
> 'Come back, come back, Horatius!'
>   Loud cried the Fathers all;
> 'Back, Lartius! Back, Herminius!
>   Back, ere the ruin fall!'
>
> "Back darted Spurius Lartius,
>   Herminius darted back;
> And as they passed, beneath their feet
>   They felt the timbers crack;
> But when they turn'd their faces,
>   And on the farther shore
> Saw brave Horatius stand alone,
>   They would have cross'd once more.
>
> "But with a crash like thunder
>   Fell every loosen'd beam,
> And, like a dam, the mighty wreck
>   Lay right athwart the stream;
> And a long shout of triumph
>   Rose from the walls of Rome,
> As to the highest turret-tops
>   Was splash'd the yellow foam."

The one last champion, behind a rampart of dead enemies, remained till the destruction was complete.

> "Alone stood brave Horatius,
>   But constant still in mind,
> Thrice thirty thousand foes before

And the broad flood behind."

A dart had put out one eye, he was wounded in the thigh, and his work was done. He turned round, and–

> "Saw on Palatinus,
>   The white porch of his home,
> And he spake to the noble river
>   That rolls by the walls of Rome:
> 'O Tiber! father Tiber!
>   To whom the Romans pray,
> A Roman's life, a Roman's arms
>   Take thou in charge this day.'"

And with this brief prayer he leapt into the foaming stream. Polybius was told that he was there drowned; but Livy gives the version which the ballad follows:–

> "But fiercely ran the current,
>   Swollen high by months of rain,
> And fast his blood was flowing,
>   And he was sore in pain,
> And heavy with his armour,
>   And spent with changing blows,
> And oft they thought him sinking,
>   But still again he rose.
>
> "Never, I ween, did swimmer,
>   In such an evil case,
> Struggle through such a raging flood
>   Safe to the landing place.
> But his limbs were borne up bravely
>   By the brave heart within,
> And our good father Tiber
>   Bare bravely up his chin.
>
>   . . . .
> "And now he feels the bottom,
>   Now on dry earth he stands,
> Now round him throng the Fathers,
>   To press his gory hands.
> And now with shouts and clapping,
>   And noise of weeping loud,
> He enters through the River Gate,
>   Borne by the joyous crowd.

"They gave him of the corn land,
  That was of public right,
As much as two strong oxen
  Could plough from morn to night.
And they made a molten image,
  And set it up on high,
And there it stands unto this day,
  To witness if I lie.

"It stands in the Comitium,
  Plain for all folk to see,
Horatius in his harness,
  Halting upon his knee:
And underneath is written,
  In letters all of gold,
How valiantly he kept the bridge
  In the brave days of old."

Never was more honourable surname than his, of Cocles, or the one-eyed; and though his lameness prevented him from ever being a Consul, or leading an army, he was so much beloved and honoured by his fellow citizens, that in the time of a famine each Roman, to the number of 300,000, brought him a day's food, lest he should suffer want. The statue was shown even in the time of Pliny, 600 years afterwards, and was probably only destroyed when Rome was sacked by the barbarians.

Nor was the Roman bridge the only one that has been defended by one man against a host. In our own country, Stamford Bridge was, in like manner, guarded by a single brave Northman, after the battle fought A.D. 1066, when Earl Tostig, the son of Godwin, had persuaded the gallant sea king, Harald Hardrada, to come and invade England. The chosen English king, Harold, had marched at full speed from Sussex to Yorkshire, and met the invaders marching at their ease, without expecting any enemy, and wearing no defensive armour, as they went forth to receive the keys of the city of York. The battle was fought by the Norsemen in the full certainty that it must be lost. The banner, "Landwaster", was planted in the midst; and the king, chanting his last song, like the minstrel warrior he had always been, stood, with his bravest men, in a death ring around it. There he died, and his choicest warriors with him; but many more fled back towards the ships, rushing over the few planks that were the only way across the River Ouse. And here stood their defender, alone upon the bridge, keeping back the whole pursuing English army, who could only attack him one at a time; until, with shame be it spoken, he died by a cowardly blow by an enemy, who had crept down the bank of the river, and under the bridge, through the openings between the timbers of which he thrust up his spear, and thus was able to hurl the brave Northman into the river, mortally wounded, but not till great numbers of his countrymen had reached their ships, their lives saved by his gallantry.

In like manner, Robert Bruce, in the time of his wanderings, during the year 1306, saved his whole band by his sole exertions. He had been defeated by the forces of Edward I. at Methven, and had lost many of his friends. His little army went wandering among the hills, sometimes encamping in the woods, sometimes crossing the lakes in small boats. Many ladies were among them, and their summer life had some wild charms of romance; as the knightly huntsmen brought in the salmon, the roe, and the deer that formed their food, and the ladies gathered the flowering heather, over which soft skins were laid for their bedding. Sir James Douglas was the most courtly and graceful knight of all the party, and ever kept them enlivened by his gay temper and ready wit; and the king himself cherished a few precious romances, which he used to read aloud to his followers as they rested in their mountain home.

But their bitter foe, the Lord of Lorn, was always in pursuit of them, and, near the head of the Tay, he came upon the small army of 300 men with 1000 Highlanders, armed with Lochaber axes, at a place which is still called Dalry, or the King's Field. Many of the horses were killed by the axes; and James Douglas and Gilbert de la Haye were both wounded. All would have been slain or fallen into the hand of the enemy, if Robert Bruce had not sent them all on before him, up a narrow, steep path, and placed himself, with his armour and heavy horse, full in the path, protecting the retreat with his single arm. It was true, that so tall and powerful a man, sheathed in armour and on horseback, had a great advantage against the wild Highlanders, who only wore a shirt and a plaid, with a round target upon the arm; but they were lithe, active, light-footed men, able to climb like goats on the crags around him, and holding their lives as cheaply as he did.

Lorn, watching him from a distance, was struck with amazement, and exclaimed, "Methinks, Marthokson, he resembles Gol Mak Morn protecting his followers from Fingal;" thus comparing him to one the most brilliant champions a Highland imagination could conceive. At last, three men, named M'Androsser, rushed forward, resolved to free their chief from this formidable enemy. There was a lake on one side, and a precipice on the other, and the king had hardly space to manage his horse, when all three sprang on him at once. One snatched his bridle, one caught him by the stirrup and leg, and a third leaped from a rising ground and seated himself behind him on his horse. The first lost his arm by one sweep of the king's sword; the second was overthrown and trampled on; and the last, by a desperate struggle, was dashed down, and his skull cleft by the king's sword; but his dying grasp was so tight upon the plaid that Bruce was forced to unclasp the brooch that secured it, and leave both in the dead man's hold. It was long preserved by the Macdougals of Lorn, as a trophy of the narrow escape of their enemy.

Nor must we leave Robert the Bruce without mentioning that other Golden Deed, more truly noble because more full of mercy; namely, his halting his little army in full retreat in Ireland in the face of the English host under Roger Mortimer, that proper care and attendance might be given to one sick and suffering washerwoman and her new-born babe. Well may his old Scotch rhyming chronicler remark:–

> "This was a full great courtesy
> That swik a king and so mighty,
> Gert his men dwell on this manner,
> But for a poor lavender."

We have seen how the sturdy Roman fought for his city, the fierce Northman died to guard his comrades' rush to their ships after the lost battle, and how the mail-clad knightly Bruce perilled himself to secure the retreat of his friends. Here is one more instance, from far more modern times, of a soldier, whose willing sacrifice of his own life was the safety of a whole army. It was in the course of the long dismal conflict between Frederick the Great of Prussia and Maria Theresa of Austria, which was called the Seven Years' War. Louis XV. of France had taken the part of Austria, and had sent an army into Germany in the autumn of 1760. From this the Marquis de Castries had been despatched, with 25,000 men, towards Rheinberg, and had taken up a strong position at Klostercamp. On the night of the 15th of October, a young officer, called the Chevalier d'Assas, of the Auvergne regiment, was sent out to reconnoitre, and advanced alone into a wood, at some little distance from his men. Suddenly he found himself surrounded by a number of soldiers, whose bayonets pricked his breast, and a voice whispered in his ear, "Make the slightest noise, and you are a dead man!" In one moment he understood it all. The enemy were advancing, to surprise the French army, and would be upon them when night was further advanced. That moment decided his fate. He shouted, as loud as his voice would carry the words, "Here, Auvergne! Here are the enemy!" By the time the cry reached the ears of his men, their captain was a senseless corpse; but his death had saved the army; the surprise had failed, and the enemy retreated.

Louis XV was too mean-spirited and selfish to feel the beauty of this brave action; but when, fourteen years later, Louis XVI came to the throne, he decreed that a pension should be given to the family as long as a male representative remained to bear the name of D'Assas. Poor Louis XVI had not long the control of the treasure of France; but a century of changes, wars, and revolutions has not blotted out the memory of the self-devotion of the chevalier; for, among the new war-steamers of the French fleet, there is one that bears the ever-honoured name of *D'Assas*.

The Pass of Thermopylæ

B. C. 480

THERE was trembling in Greece. "The Great King", as the Greeks called the chief potentate of the East, whose domains stretched from the Indian Caucasus to the Ægæus, from the Caspian to the Red Sea, was marshalling his forces against the little free states that nestled amid the rocks and gulfs of the Eastern Mediterranean. Already had his might devoured the cherished colonies of the Greeks on the eastern shore of the Archipelago, and every traitor to home institutions found a ready asylum at that despotic court, and tried to revenge his own wrongs by whispering incitements to invasion. "All people, nations, and languages," was the commencement of the decrees of that monarch's court; and it was scarcely a vain boast, for his satraps ruled over subject kingdoms, and among his tributary nations he counted the Chaldean, with his learning and old civilization, the wise and steadfast Jew, the skilful Phoenician, the learned Egyptian, the wild, free-booting Arab of the desert, the dark-skinned Ethiopian, and over all these ruled the keen-witted, active native Persian race, the conquerors of all the rest, and led by a chosen band proudly called the Immortal. His many capitals–Babylon the great, Susa, Persepolis, and the like–were names of dreamy splendour to the Greeks, described now and then by Ionians from Asia Minor who had carried their tribute to the king's own feet, or by courtier slaves who had escaped with difficulty from being all too serviceable at the tyrannic court. And the lord of this enormous empire was about to launch his countless host against the little cluster of states, the whole of which together would hardly equal one province of the huge Asiatic realm! Moreover, it was a war not only on the men but on their gods. The Persians were zealous adorers of the sun and of fire, they abhorred the idol worship of the Greeks, and defiled and plundered every temple that fell in their way. Death and desolation were almost the best that could be looked for at such hands–slavery and torture from cruelly barbarous masters would only too surely be the lot of numbers, should their land fall a prey to the conquerors.

True it was that ten years back the former Great King had sent his best troops to be signally defeated upon the coast of Attica; but the losses at Marathon had but stimulated the Persian lust of conquest, and the new King Xerxes was gathering together such myriads of men as should crush down the Greeks and overrun their country by mere force of numbers.

The muster place was at Sardis, and there Greek spies had seen the multitudes assembling and the state and magnificence of the king's attendants. Envoys had come from him to demand earth and water from each state in Greece, as emblems that land and sea were his, but each state was resolved to be free, and only Thessaly, that which lay first in his path, consented to yield the token of subjugation. A council was held at the Isthmus of Corinth, and attended by deputies from all the states of Greece to consider of the best means of defence. The ships of the enemy would coast round the shores of the Ægean sea, the land army would cross the Hellespont on a bridge of boats lashed together, and march southwards into Greece. The only hope of averting the danger lay in defending such passages as, from the nature of the ground, were so narrow that only a few persons could fight hand to hand at once, so that courage would be of more avail than numbers.

The first of all these passes was called Tempe, and a body of troops was sent to guard it; but they found that this was useless and impossible, and came back again. The next was at Thermopylæ. Look in your map of the Archipelago, or Ægean Sea, as it was then called, for the great island of Negropont, or by its old name, Euboea. It looks like a piece broken off from the coast, and to the north is shaped like the head of a bird, with the beak running into a gulf, that would fit over it, upon the main land, and between the island and the coast is an exceedingly narrow strait. The Persian army would have to march round the edge of the gulf. They could not cut straight across the country, because the ridge of mountains called Oeta rose up and barred their way. Indeed, the woods, rocks, and precipices came down so near the seashore, that in two places there was only room for one single wheel track between the steeps and the impassable morass that formed the border of the gulf on its south side. These two very narrow places were called the gates of the pass, and were about a mile apart. There was a little more width left in the intervening space; but in this there were a number of springs of warm mineral water, salt and sulphurous, which were used for the sick to bathe in, and thus the place was called Thermopylæ, or the Hot Gates. A wall had once been built across the western-most of these narrow places, when the Thessalians and Phocians, who lived on either side of it, had been at war with one another; but it had been allowed to go to decay, since the Phocians had found out that there was a very steep narrow mountain path along the bed of a torrent, by which it was possible to cross from one territory to the other without going round this marshy coast road.

This was, therefore, an excellent place to defend. The Greek ships were all drawn up on the farther side of Euboea to prevent the Persian vessels from getting into the strait and landing men beyond the pass, and a division of the army was sent off to guard the Hot Gates. The council at the Isthmus did not know of the mountain pathway, and thought that all would be safe as long as the Persians were kept out of the coast path.

The troops sent for this purpose were from different cities, and amounted to about 4000, who were to keep the pass against two millions. The leader of them was Leonidas, who had newly become one of the two kings of Sparta, the city that above all in Greece trained its sons to be hardy soldiers, dreading death infinitely less than shame. Leonidas had already made up his mind that the expedition would probably be his death, perhaps because a prophecy had been given at the Temple of Delphi that Sparta should be saved by the death of one of her kings of the race of Hercules. He was allowed by law to take with him 300 men, and these he chose most carefully, not merely for their strength and courage, but selecting those who had sons, so that no family might be altogether destroyed. These Spartans, with their helots or slaves, made up his own share of the numbers, but all the army was under his generalship. It is even said that the 300 celebrated their own funeral rites before they set out, lest they should be deprived of them by the enemy, since, as we have already seen, it was the Greek belief that the spirits of the dead found no rest till their obsequies had been performed. Such preparations did not daunt the spirits of Leonidas and his men, and his wife, Gorgo, who was not a woman to be faint-hearted or hold him back. Long before, when she was a very little girl, a word of hers had saved her father from listening to a traitorous message from the King of Persia; and every Spartan lady was bred up to be able to say to those she best loved that they must come home from battle "with the shield or on it"–either carrying it victoriously or borne upon it as a corpse.

When Leonidas came to Thermopylæ, the Phocians told him of the mountain path through the chestnut woods of Mount Oeta, and begged to have the privilege of guarding it on a spot high up on the mountain side, assuring him that it was very hard to find at the other end, and that there was every probability that the enemy would never discover it. He consented, and encamping around the warm springs, caused the broken wall to be repaired, and made ready to meet the foe.

The Persian army were seen covering the whole country like locusts, and the hearts of some of the southern Greeks in the pass began to sink. Their homes in the Peloponnesus were comparatively secure–had they not better fall back and reserve themselves to defend the Isthmus of Corinth? But Leonidas, though Sparta was safe below the Isthmus, had no intention of abandoning his northern allies, and kept the other Peloponnesians to their posts, only sending messengers for further help.

Presently a Persian on horseback rode up to reconnoitre the pass. He could not see over the wall, but in front of it, and on the ramparts, he saw the Spartans, some of them engaged in active sports, and others in combing their long hair. He rode back to the king, and told him what he had seen. Now, Xerxes had in his camp an exiled Spartan Prince, named Demaratus, who had become a traitor to his country, and was serving as counsellor to the enemy. Xerxes sent for him, and asked whether his countrymen were mad to be thus employed instead of fleeing away; but Demaratus made answer that a hard fight was no doubt in preparation, and that it was the custom of the Spartans to array their hair with special care when they were about to enter upon any great peril. Xerxes would, however, not believe that so petty a force could intend to resist him, and waited four days, probably expecting his fleet to assist him, but as it did not appear, the attack was made.

The Greeks, stronger men and more heavily armed, were far better able to fight to advantage than the Persians, with their short spears and wicker shields, and beat them off with great ease. It is said that Xerxes three times leapt off his throne in despair at the sight of his troops being driven backwards; and thus for two days it seemed as easy to force a way through the Spartans as through the rocks themselves. Nay, how could slavish troops, dragged from home to spread the victories of an ambitious king, fight like freemen who felt that their strokes were to defend their homes and children!

But on that evening a wretched man, named Ephialtes, crept into the Persian camp, and offered, for a great sum of money, to show the mountain path that would enable the enemy to take the brave defenders in the rear! A Persian general, named Hydarnes, was sent off at nightfall with a detachment to secure this passage, and was guided through the thick forests that clothed the hillside. In the stillness of the air, at daybreak, the Phocian guards of the path were startled by the crackling of the chestnut leaves under the tread of many feet. They started up, but a shower of arrows was discharged on them, and forgetting all save the present alarm, they fled to a higher part of the mountain, and the enemy, without waiting to pursue them, began to descend.

As day dawned, morning light showed the watchers of the Grecian camp below a glittering and shimmering in the torrent bed where the shaggy forests opened; but it was not the sparkle of water, but the shine of gilded helmets and the gleaming of silvered spears! Moreover, a Cimmerian crept over to the wall from the Persian camp with tidings that the path had been betrayed, that the enemy were climbing it, and would come down beyond the Eastern Gate. Still, the way was rugged and circuitous, the Persians would hardly descend before midday, and there was ample time for the Greeks to escape before they could be shut in by the enemy.

There was a short council held over the morning sacrifice. Megistias, the seer, on inspecting the entrails of the slain victim, declared, as well he might, that their appearance boded disaster. Him Leonidas ordered to retire, but he refused, though he sent home his only son. There was no disgrace to an ordinary tone of mind in leaving a post that could not be held, and Leonidas recommended all the allied troops under his command to march away while yet the way was open. As to himself and his Spartans, they had made up their minds to die at their post, and there could be no doubt that the example of such a resolution would do more to save Greece than their best efforts could ever do if they were careful to reserve themselves for another occasion.

All the allies consented to retreat, except the eighty men who came from Mycenae and the 700 Thespians, who declared that they would not desert Leonidas. There were also 400 Thebans who remained; and thus the whole number that stayed with Leonidas to confront two million of enemies were fourteen hundred warriors, besides the helots or attendants on the 300 Spartans, whose number is not known, but there was probably at least one to each. Leonidas had two kinsmen in the camp, like himself, claiming the blood of Hercules, and he tried to save them by giving them letters and messages to Sparta; but one answered that "he had come to fight, not to carry letters"; and the other, that "his deeds would tell all that Sparta wished to know". Another Spartan, named Dienices, when told that the enemy's archers were so numerous that their arrows darkened the sun, replied, "So much the better, we shall fight in the shade." Two of the 300 had been sent to a neighbouring village, suffering severely from a complaint in the eyes. One of them, called Eurytus, put on his armour, and commanded his helot to lead him to his place in the ranks; the other, called Aristodemus, was so overpowered with illness that he allowed himself to be carried away with the retreating allies. It was still early in the day when all were gone, and Leonidas gave the word to his men to take their last meal. "To-night," he said, "we shall sup with Pluto."

Hitherto, he had stood on the defensive, and had husbanded the lives of his men; but he now desired to make as great a slaughter as possible, so as to inspire the enemy with dread of the Grecian name. He therefore marched out beyond the wall, without waiting to be attacked, and the battle began. The Persian captains went behind their wretched troops and scourged them on to the fight with whips! Poor wretches, they were driven on to be slaughtered, pierced with the Greek spears, hurled into the sea, or trampled into the mud of the morass; but their inexhaustible numbers told at length. The spears of the Greeks broke under hard service, and their swords alone remained; they began to fall, and Leonidas himself was among the first of the slain. Hotter than ever was the fight over his corpse, and two Persian princes, brothers of Xerxes, were there killed; but at length word

"Eurytus put on his armor and commanded his
helot to lead him to his place in the ranks."

was brought that Hydarnes was over the pass, and that the few remaining men were thus enclosed on all sides. The Spartans and Thespians made their way to a little hillock within the wall, resolved to let this be the place of their last stand; but the hearts of the Thebans failed them, and they came towards the Persians holding out their hands in entreaty for mercy. Quarter was given to them, but they were all branded with the king's mark as untrustworthy deserters. The helots probably at this time escaped into the mountains; while the small desperate band stood side by side on the hill still fighting to the last, some with swords, others with daggers, others even with their hands and teeth, till not one living man remained amongst them when the sun went down. There was only a mound of slain, bristled over with arrows.

Twenty thousand Persians had died before that handful of men! Xerxes asked Demaratus if there were many more at Sparta like these, and was told there were 8000. It must have been with a somewhat failing heart that he invited his courtiers from the fleet to see what he had done to the men who dared to oppose him! and showed them the head and arm of Leonidas set up upon a cross; but he took care that all his own slain, except 1000, should first be put out of sight. The body of the brave king was buried where he fell, as were those of the other dead. Much envied were they by the unhappy Aristodemus, who found himself called by no name but the "Coward", and was shunned by all his fellow citizens. No one would give him fire or water, and after a year of misery, he redeemed his honour by perishing in the forefront of the battle of Plataea, which was the last blow that drove the Persians ingloriously from Greece.

The Greeks then united in doing honour to the brave warriors who, had they been better supported, might have saved the whole country from invasion. The poet Simonides wrote the inscriptions that were engraved upon the pillars that were set up in the pass to commemorate this great action. One was outside the wall, where most of the fighting had been. It seems to have been in honour of the whole number who had for two days resisted–

> "Here did four thousand men from Pelops' land
> Against three hundred myriads bravely stand".

In honour of the Spartans was another column–

> "Go, traveller, to Sparta tell
> That here, obeying her, we fell".

On the little hillock of the last resistance was placed the figure of a stone lion, in memory of Leonidas, so fitly named the lion-like, and Simonides, at his own expense, erected a pillar to his friend, the seer Megistias–

"The great Megistias' tomb you here may view,
Who slew the Medes, fresh from Spercheius fords;
Well the wise seer the coming death foreknew,
Yet scorn'd he to forsake his Spartan lords".

The names of the 300 were likewise engraven on a pillar at Sparta.

Lions, pillars, and inscriptions have all long since passed away, even the very spot itself has changed; new soil has been formed, and there are miles of solid ground between Mount Oeta and the gulf, so that the Hot Gates no longer exist. But more enduring than stone or brass—nay, than the very battlefield itself—has been the name of Leonidas. Two thousand three hundred years have sped since he braced himself to perish for his country's sake in that narrow, marshy coast road, under the brow of the wooded crags, with the sea by his side. Since that time how many hearts have glowed, how many arms have been nerved at the remembrance of the Pass of Thermopylæ, and the defeat that was worth so much more than a victory!

The Rock of the Capitol
B. C. 389

THE city of Rome was gradually rising on the banks of the Tiber, and every year was adding to its temples and public buildings.

Every citizen loved his city and her greatness above all else. There was as yet little wealth among them; the richest owned little more than a few acres, which they cultivated themselves by the help of their families, and sometimes of a few slaves, and the beautiful Campagna di Roma, girt in by hills looking like amethysts in the distance, had not then become almost uninhabitable from pestilential air, but was rich and fertile, full of highly cultivated small farms, where corn was raised in furrows made by a small hand plough, and herds of sheep, goats, and oxen browsed in the pasture lands. The owners of these lands would on public days take off their rude working dress and broad-brimmed straw hat, and putting on the white toga with a purple hem, would enter the city, and go to the valley called the Forum or Marketplace to give their votes for the officers of state who were elected every year; especially the two consuls, who were like kings all but the crown, wore purple togas richly embroidered, sat on ivory chairs, and were followed by lictors carrying an axe in a bundle of rods for the execution of justice. In their own chamber sat the Senate, the great council composed of the patricians, or citizens of highest birth, and of those who had formerly been consuls. They decided on peace or war, and made the laws, and were the real governors of the State, and their grave dignity made a great impression on all who came near them. Above the buildings of the city rose steep and high the Capitoline Hill, with the Temple of Jupiter on its summit, and the strong wall in which was the chief stronghold and citadel of Rome, the Capitol, the very centre of her strength and resolution. When a war was decided on, every citizen capable of bearing arms was called into the Forum, bringing his helmet, breast plate, short sword, and heavy spear, and the officers called tribunes, chose out a sufficient number, who were formed into bodies called legions, and marched to battle under the command of one of the consuls. Many little States or Italian tribes, who had nearly the same customs as Rome, surrounded the Campagna, and so many disputes arose that every year, as soon as the crops were saved, the armies marched out, the flocks were driven to folds on the hills, the women and children were placed in the walled cities, and a battle was fought, sometimes followed up by the siege of the city of the defeated. The Romans did not always obtain the victory, but there was a staunchness about them that was sure to prevail in the long run; if beaten one year, they came back to the charge the next, and thus they gradually mastered one of their neighbors after another, and spread their dominion over the central part of Italy.

They were well used to Italian and Etruscan ways of making war, but after nearly 400 years of this kind of fighting, a stranger and wilder enemy came upon them. These were the Gauls, a tall strong, brave people, long limbed and red-haired, of the same race as the highlanders of Scotland. They had gradually spread themselves over the middle of Europe, and had for some generations past lived among the Alpine mountains, whence they used to come down upon the rich plans of northern Italy for forays, in which they slew and burnt, and drove off cattle, and now and then, when a country was quite depopulated, would settle themselves in it. And thus, the Gauls conquering from the north and the Romans from the south, these two fierce nations at length came against one another.

The old Roman story is that it happened thus: The Gauls had an unusually able leader, whom Latin historians call Brennus, but whose real name was most likely Bran, and who is said to have come out of Britain. He had brought a great host of Gauls to attack Clusium, a Tuscan city, and the inhabitants sent to Rome to entreat succour. Three ambassadors, brothers of the noble old family of Fabius, were sent from Rome to intercede for the Clusians. They asked Brennus what harm the men of Clusium had done the Gauls, that they thus made war on them, and, according to Plutarch's account, Brennus made answer that the injury was that the Clusians possessed land that the Gauls wanted, remarking that it was exactly the way in which the Romans themselves treated their neighbors, adding, however, that this was neither cruel nor unjust, but according–

> "To the good old plan
> That they should take who have the power
> And they should keep who can."[2]

The Fabii, on receiving this answer, were so foolish as to transgress the rule, owned by the savage Gauls, that an ambassador should neither fight nor be fought with; they joined the Clusians, and one brother, named Quintus, killed a remarkably large and tall Gallic chief in single combat. Brennus was justly enraged, and sent messengers to Rome to demand that

---

2   These lines of Wordsworth on Rob Roy's grave almost literally translate the speech Plutarch gives the first Kelt of history, Brennus.

the brothers should be given up to him for punishment. The priests and many of the Senate held that the rash young men had deserved death as covenant-breakers; but their father made strong interest for them, and prevailed not only to have them spared, but even chosen as tribunes to lead the legions in the war that was expected.[3] Thus he persuaded the whole nation to take on itself the guilt of his sons, a want of true self-devotion uncommon among the old Romans, and which was severely punished.

The Gauls were much enraged, and hurried southwards, not waiting for plunder by the way, but declaring that they were friends to every State save Rome. The Romans on their side collected their troops in haste, but with a lurking sense of having transgressed; and since they had gainsayed the counsel of their priests, they durst not have recourse to the sacrifices and ceremonies by which they usually sought to gain the favour of their gods. Even among heathens, the saying has often been verified, "a sinful heart makes failing hand", and the battle on the banks of the River Allia, about eleven miles from Rome, was not so much a fight as a rout. The Roman soldiers were ill drawn up, and were at once broken. Some fled to Veii and other towns, many were drowned in crossing the Tiber, and it was but a few who showed in Rome their shame-stricken faces, and brought word that the Gauls were upon them.

Had the Gauls been really in pursuit, the Roman name and nation would have perished under their swords; but they spent three day in feasting and sharing their plunder, and thus gave the Romans time to take measures for the safety of such as could yet escape. There seems to have been no notion of defending the city, the soldiers had been too much dispersed; but all who still remained and could call up something of their ordinary courage, carried all the provisions they could collect into the stronghold of the Capitol, and resolved to hold out there till the last, in hopes that the scattered army might muster again, or that the Gauls might retreat, after having revenged themselves on the city. Everyone who could not fight, took flight, taking with them all they could carry, and among them went the white-clad troop of vestal virgins, carrying with them their censer of fire, which was esteemed sacred, and never allowed to be extinguished. A man named Albinus, who saw these sacred women footsore, weary, and weighted down with the treasures of their temple, removed his own family and goods from his cart and seated them in it–an act of reverence for which he was much esteemed–and thus they reached the city of Cumae. The only persons left in Rome outside the Capitol were eighty of the oldest senators and some of the priests. Some were too feeble to fly, and would not come into the Capitol to consume the food that might maintain fighting men; but most of them were filled with a deep, solemn thought that, by offering

---

3   These events happened during an experiment made by the Romans of having six military tribunes instead of two consuls.

themselves to the weapons of the barbarians, they might atone for the sin sanctioned by the Republic, and that their death might be the saving of the nation. This notion that the death of a ruler would expiate a country's guilt was one of the strange presages abroad in the heathen world of that which alone takes away the sin of all mankind.

On came the Gauls at last. The gates stood open, the streets were silent, the houses' low-browed doors showed no one in the paved courts. No living man was to be seen, till at last, hurrying down the steep empty streets, they reached the great open space of the Forum, and there they stood still in amazement, for ranged along a gallery were a row of ivory chairs, and in each chair sat the figure of a white-haired, white-bearded man, with arms and legs bare, and robes either of snowy white, white bordered with purple, or purple richly embroidered, ivory staves in their hands, and majestic, unmoved countenances. So motionless were they, that the Gauls stood still, not knowing whether they beheld men or statues. A wondrous scene it must have been, as the brawny, red-haired Gauls, with freckled visage, keen little eyes, long broad sword, and wide plaid garment, fashioned into loose trousers, came curiously down into the marketplace, one after another; and each stood silent and transfixed at the spectacle of those grand figures, still unmoving, save that their large full liquid dark eyes showed them to be living beings. Surely these Gauls deemed themselves in the presence of that council of kings who were sometimes supposed to govern Rome, nay, if they were not before the gods themselves. At last, one Gaul, ruder, or more curious than the rest, came up to one of the venerable figures, and, to make proof whether he were flesh and blood, stroked his beard. Such an insult from an uncouth barbarian was more than Roman blood could brook, and the Gaul soon had his doubt satisfied by a sharp blow on the head from the ivory staff. All reverence was dispelled by that stroke; it was at once returned by a death thrust, and the fury of the savages wakening in proportion to the awe that had at first struck them, they rushed on the old senators, and slew each one in his curule chair.

Then they dispersed through the city, burning, plundering, and destroying. To take the Capitol they soon found to be beyond their power, but they hoped to starve the defenders out; and in the meantime they spent their time in pulling down the outer walls, and such houses and temples as had resisted the fire, till the defenders of the Capitol looked down from their height on nothing but desolate black burnt ground, with a few heaps of ruins in the midst, and the barbarians roaming about in it, and driving in the cattle that their foraging parties collected from the country round. There was much earnest faith in their own religion among the Romans: they took all this ruin as the just reward of their shelter of the Fabii, and even in their extremity were resolved not to transgress any sacred rule. Though food daily became more scarce and starvation was fast approaching, not one of the sacred geese that were kept in Juno's Temple was touched; and one Fabius Dorso, who believed that the household gods of his family required yearly a sacrifice on their own festival day on the Quirinal Hill, arrayed himself in the white robes of a sacrificer, took his sacred images in his arms, and went out of the Capitol, through the midst of the enemy, through the ruins to the accustomed alter, and there preformed the regular rites. The Gauls, seeing that it was a religious ceremony, let him pass through them untouched, and he returned in safety; but Brennus was resolved on completing his conquest, and while half his forces went out to plunder, he remained with the other half, watching the moment to effect an entrance into the Capitol; and how were the defenders, worn out with hunger, to resist without relief from without? And who was there to bring relief to them, who were themselves the Roman State and government?

Now there was a citizen, named Marcus Furius Camillus, who was, without question, at that time, the first soldier of Rome, and had taken several of the chief Italian cities, especially that of Veii, which had long been a most dangerous enemy. But he was a proud, haughty man, and had brought on himself much dislike; until, at last, a false accusation was brought against him, that he had taken an unfair share of the plunder of Veii. He was too proud to stand a trial; and leaving the city, was immediately fined a considerable sum. He had taken up his abode at the city of Ardea, and was there living when the plundering half of Brennus' army was reported to be coming thither. Camillus immediately offered the magistrates to undertake their defense; and getting together all the men who could bear arms, he led them out, fell upon the Gauls as they all lay asleep and unguarded in the dead of night, made a great slaughter of them, and saved Ardea. All this was heard by the many Romans who had been living dispersed since the rout of Allia; and they began to recover heart and spirit, and to think that if Camillus would be their leader, they might yet do something to redeem the houour of Rome, and save their friends in the Capitol. An entreaty was sent to him to take the command of them; but, like a proud, stern man as he was, he made answer, that he was a mere exile, and could not take upon himself to lead Romans without a decree from the Senate giving him authority. The Senate was—all that remained of it—shut up in the Capitol; the Gauls were spread all round; how was that decree to be obtained?

A young man, named Pontius Cominius, undertook the desperate mission. He put on a peasant dress, and hid some corks under it, supposing that he should find no passage by the bridge over the Tiber. Traveling all day on foot, he came at night to the bank, and saw the guard at the bridge; then, having waited for darkness, he rolled his one thin light garment, with the corks wrapped up in it, round his head, and trusted himself to the stream of Father Tiber, like "good Horatius" before him; and he was safely borne along to the foot of the Capitoline Hill. He crept along, avoiding every place where he saw lights or heard noise, till he came to a rugged precipice, which he suspected would not be watched by the enemy, who would suppose it too steep to be climbed from above or below. But the resolute man did not fear the giddy dangerous ascent, even in the darkness; he swung himself up by the stems and boughs of the vines and climbing plants, his naked feet clung to the rocks and tufts of grass, and at length he stood on the top of the rampart, calling out his name to the soldiers who came in haste around him, not knowing whether he were friend or foe. A joyful sound must his Latin speech have been to the long-tried, half starved garrison, who had not seen a fresh face for six long months! The few who represented the Senate and people of Rome were hastily awakened from their sleep, and gathered together to hear the tidings brought them at so much risk. Pontius told them of the victory at Ardea, and that Camillus and the Romans collected at Veii were only waiting to march to their succour till they should give him lawful power to take the command. There was little debate. The vote was passed at once to make Camillus Dictator, an office to which Romans were elected upon great emergencies, and which gave them, for the time, absolute kingly control; and then Pontius, bearing the appointment, set off once again upon his mission, still under shelter of night, clambered down the rock, and crossed the Gallic camp before the barbarians were yet awake.

There was hope in the little garrison; but danger was not over. The sharp-eyed Gauls observed that the shrubs and creepers were broken, the moss frayed, and fresh stones and earth rolled down at the crag of the Capitol: they were sure that the rock had been climbed, and, therefore, that it might be climbed again. Should they, who were used to the snowy peaks, dark abysses, and huge glaciers of the Alps, be afraid to climb where a soft dweller in a tame Italian town could venture a passage? Brennus chose out the hardiest of his mountaineers, and directed them to climb up in the dead of night, one by one, in perfect silence, and thus to surprise the Romans, and complete the slaughter and victory, before the forces assembling at Veii would come to their rescue.

Silently the Gauls climbed, so stilly that not even a dog heard them; and the sentinel nearest to the post, who had fallen into a dead sleep of exhaustion from hunger, never awoke. But the fatal stillness was suddenly broken by loud gabbling, cackling, and flapping of heavy wings. The sacred geese of Juno, which had been so religiously spared in the famine, were frightened by the rustling beneath, and proclaimed their terror in their own noisy fashion. The first to take the alarm was Marcus Manlius, who started forward just in time to meet the foremost climbers as they set foot on the rampart. One, who raised an axe to strike, lost his arm by one stroke of Manlius' short Roman sword; the next was by main strength hurled backwards over the precipice, and Manlius stood along on the top, for a few moments, ready to strike the next who should struggle up.

The whole of the garrison were in a few moments on the alert, and the attack was entirely repulsed; the sleeping sentry was cast headlong down the rock; and Manlius was brought, by each grateful soldier, that which was then most valuable to all, a little meal and a small measure of wine. Still, the condition of the Capitol was lamentable; there was no certainty that Pontius had ever reached Camillus in safety; and, indeed, the discovery of his path by the enemy would rather have led to the supposition that he had been seized and detected. The best hope lay in wearying out the besiegers; and there seemed to be more chance of this since the Gauls often could be seen from the heights, burying the corpses of their dead; their tall, bony forms looked gaunt and drooping, and, here and there, unburied carcasses lay amongst the ruins. Nor were the flocks and herds any longer driven in from the country. Either all must have been exhausted, or else Camillus and his friends must be near, and preventing their raids. At any rate, it appeared as if the enemy was quite as ill off as to provisions as the garrison, and in worse condition as to health. In effect, this was the first example of the famous saying, that Rome destroys her conquerors. In this state of things one of the Romans had a dream that Jupiter, the special god of the Capitol, appeared to him, and gave the strange advice that all the remaining flour should be baked, and the loaves thrown down into the enemy's camp. Telling the dream, which may, perhaps, have been the shaping of his own thoughts, that this apparent waste would persuade the barbarians that the garrison could not soon be starved out, this person obtained the consent of the rest of the besieged. Some approved the stratagem, and no one chose to act contrary to Jupiter's supposed advice; so the bread was baked, and tossed down by the hungry men.

After a time, there was a report from the outer guards that the Gallic watch had been telling them that their leader would be willing to speak with some of the Roman chiefs. Accordingly, Sulpitius, one of the tribunes, went out, and had a conference with Brennus, who declared that he would depart, provided the Romans would lay down a ransom, for their Capital and their own lives, of a thousand pounds' weight of gold. To this Sulpitius agreed, and returning to the Capitol, the gold was collected from the treasury, and carried down to meet the Gauls, who brought their own weights. The weights did not meet the amount of gold ornaments that had been contributed for the purpose, and no doubt the Gauls were resolved to have all that they beheld; for when Sulpitius was about to try to arrange the balance, Brennus insultingly threw his sword into his own scale, exclaiming, Voe victis! "Woe to the conquered!" The Roman was not yet fallen so low as not to remonstrate, and the dispute was waxing sharp, when there was a confused outcry in the Gallic camp, a shout from the heights of the Capitol, and into the midst of the open space rode a band of Roman patricians and knights in armour, with the Dictator Camillus at their head.

He no sooner saw what was passing, than he commanded the treasure to be taken back, and, turning to Brennus, said, "It is with iron, not gold, that the Romans guard their country."

Brennus declared that the treaty had been sworn to, and that it would be a breach of faith to deprive him of the ransom; to which Camillus replied, that he himself was Dictator, and no one had the power to make a treaty in his absence. The dispute was so hot, that they drew their swords against one another, and there was a skirmish among the ruins; but the Gauls soon fell back, and retreated to their camp, when they saw the main body of Camillus' army marching upon them. It was no less than 40,000 in number; and Brennus knew he could not withstand them with his broken, sickly army. He drew off early the next morning: but was followed by Camillus, and routed, with great slaughter, about eight miles from Rome; and very few of the Gauls lived to return home, for those who were not slain in battle were cut off in their flight by the country people, whom they had plundered.

In reward for their conduct on this occasion, Camillus was termed Romulus, Father of his Country, and Second Founder of Rome; Marcus Manlius received the honourable surname of Capitolinus; and even the geese were honoured by having a golden image raised to their honour in Juno's temple, and a live goose was yearly carried in triumph, upon a soft litter, in a golden cage, as long as any heathen festivals lasted. The reward of Pontius Cominius does not appear; but surely he, and the old senators who died for their country's sake, deserved to be for ever remembered for their brave contempt of life when a service could be done to the State.

The truth of the whole narrative is greatly doubted, and it is suspected that the Gallic conquest was more complete than the Romans ever chose to avow. Their history is far from clear up to this very epoch, when it is said that all their records were destroyed; but even when place and period are misty, great names and the main outline of their actions loom through the cloud, perhaps exaggerated, but still with some reality; and if the magnificent romance of the sack of Rome be not fact, yet it is certainly history, and well worthy of note and remembrance, as one of the finest extant traditions of a whole chain of Golden Deeds.

The Two Friends of Syracuse

B. C. 380 (CIRCA)

MOST of the best and noblest of the Greeks held what was called the Pythagorean philosophy. This was one of the many systems framed by the great men of heathenism, when by the feeble light of nature they were, as St. Paul says, "seeking after God, if haply they might feel after Him", like men groping in the darkness. Pythagoras lived before the time of history, and almost nothing is known about him, though his teaching and his name were never lost. There is a belief that he had traveled in the East, and in Egypt, and as he lived about the time of the dispersion of the Israelites, it is possible that some of his purest and best teaching might have been crumbs gathered from their fuller instruction through the Law and the Prophets. One thing is plain, that even in dealing with heathenism the Divine rule holds good, "By their fruits ye shall know them". Golden Deeds are only to be found among men whose belief is earnest and sincere, and in something really high and noble. Where there was nothing worshiped but savage or impure power, and the very form of adoration was cruel and unclean, as among the Canaanites and Carthaginians, there we find no true self-devotion. The great deeds of the heathen world were all done by early Greeks and Romans before yet the last gleams of purer light had faded out of their belief, and while their moral sense still nerved them to energy; or else by such later Greeks as had embraced the deeper and more earnest yearnings of the minds that had become a "law unto themselves".

The Pythagoreans were bound together in a brotherhood, the members of which had rules that are not now understood, but which linked them so as to form a sort of club, with common religious observances and pursuits of science, especially mathematics and music. And they were taught to re-strain their passions, especially that of anger, and to endure with patience all kinds of suffering; believing that such self-restraint brought them nearer to the gods, and that death would set them free from the prison of the body. The souls of evil-doers would, they thought, pass into the lower and more degraded animals, while those of good men would be gradually purified, and rise to a higher existence. This, though lamentably deficient, and false in some points, was a real religion, inasmuch as it gave a rule of life, with a motive for striving for wisdom and virtue. Two friends of this Pythagorean sect lived at Syracuse, in the end of the fourth century before the Christian era. Syracuse was a great Greek city, built in Sicily, and full of all kinds of Greek art and learning; but it was a place of danger in their time, for it had fallen under the tyranny of a man of strange and capricious temper, though of great abilities, namely Dionysius. He is said to have been originally only a clerk in a public office, but his talents raised him to continually higher situations, and at length, in a great war with the Carthaginians, who had many settlements in Sicily, he became general of the army, and then found it easy to establish his power over the city.

This power was not according to the laws, for Syracuse, like most other cities, ought to have been governed by a council of magistrates; but Dionysius was an exceedingly able man, and made the city much more rich and powerful, he defeated the Carthaginians, and rendered Syracuse by far the chief city in the island, and he contrived to make everyone so much afraid of him that no one durst attempt to overthrow his power. He was a good scholar, and very fond of philosophy and poetry, and he delighted to have learned men around him, and he had naturally a generous spirit; but the sense that he was in a position that did not belong to him, and that everyone hated him for assuming it, made him very harsh and suspicious. It is of him that the story is told, that he had a chamber hollowed in the rock near his state prison, and constructed with galleries to conduct sounds like an ear, so that he might overhear the conversation of his captives; and of him, too, is told that famous anecdote which has become a proverb, that on hearing a friend, named Damocles, express a wish to be in his situation for a single day, he took him at his word, and Damocles found himself at a banquet with everything that could delight his senses, delicious food, costly wine, flowers, perfumes, music; but with a sword with the point almost touching his head, and hanging by a single horsehair! This was to show the condition in which a usurper lived!

Thus Dionysius was in constant dread. He had a wide trench round his bedroom, with a drawbridge that he drew up and put down with his own hands; and he put one barber to death for boasting that he held a razor to the tyrant's throat every morning. After this he made his young daughters shave him; but by and by he would not trust them with a razor, and caused them to singe of his beard with hot nutshells! He was said to have put a man named Antiphon to death for answering him, when he asked what was the best kind of brass, "That of which the statues of Harmodius and Aristogeiton were made." These were the two Athenians who had killed the sons of Pisistratus the tyrant, so that the jest was most offensive, but its boldness might have gained forgiveness for it. One philosopher, named Philoxenus, he sent to a dungeon for finding fault with his poetry, but he afterwards composed another piece, which he thought so superior, that he could not be content without sending for this adverse critic to hear it. When he had finished reading it, he looked to Philoxenus for a compliment; but the philosopher only turned round to the guards, and said dryly, "Carry me back to prison." This time Dionysius had the sense to laugh, and forgive his honesty.

All these stories may not be true; but that they should have been current in the ancient world shows what was the character of the man of whom they were told, how stern and terrible was his anger, and how easily it was incurred. Among those who came under it was a Pythagorean called Pythias, who was sentenced to death, according to the usual fate of those who fell under his suspicion.

Pythias had lands and relations in Greece, and he entreated as a favour to be allowed to return thither and arrange his affairs, engaging to return within a specified time to suffer death. The tyrant laughed his request to scorn. Once safe out of Sicily, who would answer for his return? Pythias made reply that he had a friend, who would become security for his return; and while Dionysius, the miserable man who trusted nobody, was ready to scoff at his simplicity, another Pythagorean, by name of Damon, came forward, and offered to become surety for his friend, engaging, if Pythias did not return according to promise, to suffer death in his stead.

Dionysius, much astonished, consented to let Pythias go, marveling what would be the issue of the affair. Time went on and Pythias did not appear. The Syracusans watched Damon, but he showed no uneasiness. He said he was secure of his friend's truth and honour, and that if any accident had cause the delay of his return, he should rejoice in dying to save the life of one so dear to him.

Even to the last day Damon continued serene and content, however it might fall out; nay even when the very hour drew nigh and still no Pythias. His trust was so perfect, that he did not even grieve at having to die for a faithless friend who had left him to the fate to which he had unwarily pledged himself. It was not Pythias' own will, but the winds and waves, so he still declared, when the decree was brought and the instruments of death made ready. The hour had come, and a few moments more would have ended Damon's life, when Pythias duly presented himself, embraced his friend, and stood forward himself to receive his sentence, calm, resolute, and rejoiced that he had come in time.

Even the dim hope they owned of a future state was enough to make these two brave men keep their word, and confront death for one another without quailing. Dionysius looked on more struck than ever. He felt that neither of such men must die. He reversed the sentence of Pythias, and calling the two to his judgment seat, he entreated them to admit him as a third in their friendship. Yet all the time he must have known it was a mockery that he should ever be such as they were to each other—he who had lost the very power of trusting, and constantly sacrificed others to secure his own life, whilst they counted not their lives dear to them in comparison with their truth to their word, and love to one another. No wonder that Damon and Pythias have become such a byword that they seem too well known to have their story told here, except that a name in everyone's mouth sometimes seems to be mentioned by those who have forgotten or never heard the tale attached to it.

The Devotion of the Decii

B. C. 339

THE spirit of self-devotion is so beautiful and noble, that even when the act is performed in obedience to the dictates of a false religion, it is impossible not to be struck with admiration and almost reverence for the unconscious type of the one great act that has hallowed every other sacrifice. Thus it was that Codrus, the Athenian king, has ever since been honoured for the tradition that he gave his own life to secure the safety of his people; and there is a touching story, with neither name nor place, of a heathen monarch who was bidden by his priests to appease the supposed wrath of his gods by the sacrifice of the being dearest to him. His young son had been seized on as his most beloved, when his wife rushed between and declared that her son must live, and not by his death rob her of her right to fall, as her husband's dearest. The priest looked at the father; the face that had been sternly composed before was full of uncontrolled anguish as he sprang forward to save the wife rather than the child. That impulse was an answer, like the entreaty of the mother before Solomon; the priest struck the fatal blow ere the king's hand could withhold him, and the mother died with a last look of exceeding joy at her husband's love and her son's safety. Human sacrifices are of course accursed, and even the better sort of heathens viewed them with horror; but the voluntary confronting of death, even at the call of a distorted presage of future atonement, required qualities that were perhaps the highest that could be exercised among those who were devoid of the light of truth.

In the year 339 there was a remarkable instance of such devotion. The Romans were at war with the Latins, a nation dwelling to the south of them, and almost exactly resembling themselves in language, habits, government, and fashions of fighting. Indeed the city of Rome itself was but an offshoot from the old Latin kingdom; and there was not much difference between the two nations even in courage and perseverence. The two consuls of the year were Titus Manlius Torquatus and Publius Decius Mus. They were both very distinguished men. Manlius was a patrician, or one of the high ancient nobles of Rome, and had in early youth fought a single combat with a gigantic Gaul, who offered himself, like Goliath, as a champion of his tribe; had slain him, and taken from him a gold torque, or collar, whence his surname Torquatus. Decius was a plebeian; one of the free though not noble citizens who had votes, but only within a few years had been capable of being chosen to the higher offices of state, and who looked upon every election to the consulship as a victory. Three years previously, when a tribune in command of a legion, Decius had saved the consul, Cornelius Cossus, from a dangerous situation, and enabled him to gain a great victory; and this exploit was remembered, and led to the choice of this well-experienced soldier as the colleague of Manlius.

The two consuls both went out together in command of the forces, each having a separate army, and intending to act in concert. They marched to the beautiful country at the foot of Mount Vesuvius, which was then a harmless mountain clothed with chestnut woods, with spaces opening between, where farms and vineyards rejoiced in the sunshine and the fresh breezes of the lovely blue bay that lay stretched beneath. Those who climbed to the summit might indeed find beds of ashes and the jagged edge of a huge basin or gulf; the houses and walls were built of dark-red and black material that once had flowed from the crater in boiling torrents: but these had long since cooled, and so long was it since a column of smoke had been seen to rise from the mountain top, that it only remained as a matter of tradition that this region was one of mysterious fire, and that the dark cool lake Avernus, near the mountain skirts, was the very entrance to the shadowy realms beneath, that were supposed to be inhabited by the spirits of the dead.

It might be that the neighbourhood of this lake, with the dread imaginations connected with it by pagan fancy, influenced even the stout hearts of the consuls; for, the night after they came in sight of the enemy, each dreamt the same dream, namely, that he beheld a mighty form of gigantic height and stature, who told him "that the victory was decreed to that army of the two whose leader should devote himself to the Dii Manes", that is, to the deities who watched over the shades of the dead. Probably these older Romans held the old Etruscan belief, which took these "gods beneath" to be winged beings, who bore away the departing soul, weighted its merits and demerits, and placed it in a region of peace or of woe, according to its deserts. This was part of the grave and earnest faith that gave the earlier Romans such truth and resolution; but latterly they so corrupted it with the Greek myths, that, in after times, they did not even know who the gods of Decius were.

At daybreak the two consuls sought one another out, and told their dreams; and they agreed that they would join their armies in one, Decius leading the right and Manlius the left wing; and that whichever found his troops giving way, should at once rush into the enemy's columns and die, to secure the victory to his colleague. At the same time strict commands were given that no Roman should come out of his rank to fight in single combat with the enemy; a necessary regulation, as the Latins were so like, in every respect, to the Romans, that there would have been fatal confusion had there been any mingling together before the battle. Just as this command had been given out, young Titus Manlius, the son of the consul, met a Latin leader, who called him by name and challenged him to fight hand to hand. The youth was emulous of the honour his father had gained by his own combat at the same age with the Gaul, but forgot both the present edict and that his father had scrupulously asked permission before accepting the challenge. He at once came forward, and after a brave conflict, slew his adversary, and taking his armour, presented himself at his father's tent and laid the spoils at his feet.

But old Manlius turned aside sadly, and collected his troops to hear his address to his son: "You have transgressed," he said, "the discipline which has been the support of the Roman people, and reduced me to the hard necessity of either forgetting myself and mine, or else the regard I owe to the general safety. Rome must not suffer by one fault. We must expiate it ourselves. A sad example shall we be, but a wholesome one to the Roman youth. For me, both the natural love of a father, and that specimen thou hast given of thy valour move me exceedingly; but since either the consular authority must be established by thy death, or destroyed by thy impunity, I cannot think, if thou be a true Manlius, that thou wilt be backward to repair the breach thou hast made in military discipline by undergoing the just meed of thine offence. He then placed the wreath of leaves, the reward of a victor, upon his son's head, and gave the command to the lictor to bind the young man to a stake, and strike off his head. The troops stood round as men stunned, no one durst utter a word; the son submitted without one complaint, since his death was for the good of Rome: and the father, trusting that the doom of the Dii Manes was about to overtake him, beheld the brave but rash young head fall, then watched the corpse covered with the trophies won from the Latins, and made no hindrance to the glorious obsequies with which the whole army honoured this untimely death. Strict discipline was indeed established, and no one again durst break his rank; but the younger men greatly hated Manlius for his severity, and gave him no credit for the agony he had concealed while giving up his gallant son to the wellbeing of Rome.

A few days after, the expected battle took place, and after some little time the front rank of Decius' men began to fall back upon the line in their rear. This was the token he had waited for. He called to Valerius, the chief priest of Rome, to consecrate him, and was directed to put on his chief robe of office, the beautiful toga proetexta, to cover his head, and standing on his javelin, call aloud to the "nine gods" to accept his devotion, to save the Roman legions, and strike terror into his enemies. This done, he commanded his lictors to carry word to his colleague that the sacrifice was accomplished, and then girding his robe round him in the manner adopted in sacrificing to the gods, he mounted his white horse, and rushed like lightning into the thickest of the Latins. At first they fell away on all sides as if some heavenly apparition had come down on them; then, as some recognized him, they closed in on him, and pierced his breast with their weapons; but even as he fell the superstition that a devoted leader was sure to win the field, came full on their minds, they broke and fled. Meanwhile the message came to Manlius, and drew from him a burst of tears—tears that he had not shed for his son—his hope of himself meeting the doom and ending his sorrow was gone; but none the less he nerved himself to complete the advantage gained by Decius' death. Only one wing of the Latins had fled, the other fought long and bravely, and when at last it was defeated, and cut down on the field of battle, both conqueror and conquered declared that, if Manlius had been the leader of the Latins, they would have had the victory. Manlius afterwards completely subdued the Latins, who became incorporated with the Romans; but bravely as he had borne up, his health gave way under his sorrow, and before the end of the year he was unable to take the field.

Forty-five years later, in the year 294, another Decius was consul. He was the son of the first devoted Decius, and had shown himself worthy of his name, both as a citizen and soldier. His first consulate had been in conjunction with one of the most high-spirited and famous Roman nobles, Quintus Fabius, surnamed Maximus, or the Greatest, and at three years' end they were again chosen together, when the Romans had been brought into considerable peril by an alliance between the Gauls and the Samnites, their chief enemies in Italy.

One being a patrician and the other a plebeian, there was every attempt made at Rome to stir up jealousies and dissensions between them; but both were much too noble and generous to be thus set one against the other; and when Fabius found how serious was the state of affairs in Etruria, he sent to Rome to entreat that Decius would come and act with him. "With him I shall never want forces, nor have too many enemies to deal with."

The Gauls, since the time of Brennus, had so entirely settled in northern Italy, that it had acquired the name of Cisalpine Gaul, and they were as warlike as ever, while better armed and trained. The united armies of Gauls, Samnites, and their allies, together, are said to have amounted to 143,330 foot and 46,000 horse, and the Roman army consisted of four legions, 24,000 in all, with an unspecified number of horse. The place of battle was at Sentinum, and here for the first time the Gauls brought armed chariots into use,—probably the wicker chariots, with scythes in the midst of the clumsy wooden wheels, which were used by the Kelts in Britain two centuries later. It was the first time the Romans had encountered these barbarous vehicles; they were taken by surprise, the horses started, and could not be brought back to the charge, and the legions were mowed down like corn where the furious Gaul impelled his scythe. Decius shouted in vain, and tried to gather his men and lead them back; but the terror at this new mode of warfare had so mastered them, that they paid no attention to his call. Then, half in policy, half in superstition, he resolved to follow his father in his death. He called the chief priest, Marcus Livius, and standing on his javelin, went through the same formula of self-dedication, and in the like manner threw himself, alone and unarmed, in the midst of the enemy, among whom he soon fell, under many a savage stroke. The priest, himself a gallant soldier, called to the troops that their victory was now secured, and thoroughly believing him, they let him lead them back to the charge, and routed the Gauls; whilst Fabius so well did his part against the other nations, that the victory was complete, and 25,000 enemies were slain. So covered was the body of Decius by the corpses of his enemies, that all that day it could not be found; but on the next it was discovered, and Fabius, with a full heart, pronounced the funeral oration of the second Decius, who had willingly offered himself to turn the tide of battle in favour of his country. It was the last of such acts of dedication—the Romans became more learned and philosophical, and perhaps more reasonable; and yet, mistaken as was the object, it seems a falling off that, 200 years later, Cicero should not know who were the "nine gods" of the Decii, and should regard their sacrifice as "heroic indeed, but unworthy of men of understanding".

Regulus

B.C. 249

THE first wars that the Romans engaged in beyond the bounds of Italy, were with the Carthaginians. This race came from Tyre and Zidon; and were descended from some of the Phoenicians, or Zidonians, who were such dangerous foes, or more dangerous friends, to the Israelites. Carthage had, as some say, been first founded by some of the Canaanites who fled when Joshua conquered the Promised Land; and whether this were so or not, the inhabitants were in all their ways the same as the Tyrians and Zidonians, of whom so much is said in the prophecies of Isaiah and Ezekiel. Like them, they worshipped Baal and Ashtoreth, and the frightful Moloch, with foul and cruel rites; and, like them, they were excellent sailors and great merchants trading with every known country, and living in great riches and splendour at their grand city on the southern shore of the Mediterranean. That they were a wicked and cruel race is also certain; the Romans used to call deceit Punic faith, that is, Phoenician faith, and though no doubt Roman writers show them up in their worst colours, yet, after the time of Hiram, Solomon's ally at Tyre, it is plain from Holy Scripture that their crimes were great.

The first dispute between Rome and Carthage was about their possession in the island of Sicily; and the war thus begun had lasted eight years when it was resolved to send an army to fight the Carthaginians on their own shores. The army and fleet were placed under the command of the two consuls, Lucius Manlius and Marcus Attilius Regulus. On the way, there was a great sea fight with the Carthaginian fleet, and this was the first naval battle that the Romans ever gained. It made the way to Africa free; but the soldiers, who had never been so far from home before, murmured, for they expected to meet not only human enemies, but monstrous serpents, lions, elephants, asses with horns, and dog-headed monsters, to have a scorching sun overhead, and a noisome marsh under their feet. However, Regulus sternly put a stop to all murmurs, by making it known that disaffection would be punished by death, and the army safely landed, and set up a fortification at Clypea, and plundered the whole country round. Orders here came from Rome that Manlius should return thither, but that Regulus should remain to carry on the war. This was a great grief to him. He was a very poor man, with nothing of his own but a little farm of seven acres, and the person whom he had employed to cultivate it had died in his absence; a hired labourer had undertaken the care of it, but had been unfaithful, and had run away with his tools and his cattle; so that he was afraid that, unless he could return quickly, his wife and children would starve. However, the Senate engaged to provide for his family, and he remained, making expeditions into the country round, in the course of which the Romans really did fall in with a serpent as monstrous as their imagination had depicted. It was said to be 120 feet long, and dwelt upon the banks of the River Bagrada, where it used to devour the Roman soldiers as they went to fetch water. It had such tough scales that they were obliged to attack it with their engines meant for battering city walls, and only succeeded with much difficulty in destroying it.

The country was most beautiful, covered with fertile cornfields and full of rich fruit trees, and all the rich Carthaginians had country houses and gardens, which were made delicious with fountains, trees, and flowers. The Roman soldiers, plain, hardy, fierce, and pitiless, did, it must be feared, cruel damage among these peaceful scenes; they boasted of having sacked 300 villages, and mercy was not yet known to them. The Carthaginian army, though strong in horsemen and in elephants, kept upon the hills and did nothing to save the country, and the wild desert tribes of Numidians came rushing in to plunder what the Romans had left. The Carthaginians sent to offer terms of peace; but Regulus, who had become uplifted by his conquests, made such demands that the messengers remonstrated. He answered, "Men who are good for anything should either conquer or submit to their betters;" and he sent them rudely away, like a stern old Roman as he was. His merit was that he had no more mercy on himself than on others.

The Carthaginians were driven to extremity, and made horrible offerings to Moloch, giving the little children of the noblest families to be dropped into the fire between the brazen hands of his statue, and grown-up people of the noblest families rushed in of their own accord, hoping thus to propitiate their gods, and obtain safety for their country. Their time was not yet fully come, and a respite was granted to them. They had sent, in their distress, to hire soldiers in Greece, and among these came a Spartan, named Xanthippus, who at once took the command, and led the army out to battle, with a long line of elephants ranged in front of them, and with clouds of horsemen hovering on the wings. The Romans had not yet learnt the best mode of fighting with elephants, namely, to leave lanes in their columns where these huge beasts might advance harmlessly; instead of which, the ranks were thrust and trampled down by the creatures' bulk, and they suffered a terrible defeat; Regulus himself was seized by the horsemen, and dragged into Carthage, where the victors feasted and rejoiced through half the night, and testified their thanks to Moloch by offering in his fires the bravest of their captives.

Regulus himself was not, however, one of these victims. He was kept a close prisoner for two years, pining and sickening in his loneliness, while in the meantime the war continued, and at last a victory so decisive was gained by the Romans, that the people of Carthage were discouraged, and resolved to ask terms of peace. They thought that no one would be so readily listened to at Rome as Regulus, and they therefore sent him there with their envoys, having first made him swear that he would come back to his prison if there should neither be peace nor an exchange of prisoners. They little knew how much more a true-hearted Roman cared for his city than for himself–for his word than for his life.

Worn and dejected, the captive warrior came to the outside of the gates of his own city, and there paused, refusing to enter. "I am no longer a Roman citizen," he said; "I am but the barbarian's slave, and the Senate may not give audience to strangers within the walls."

His wife Marcia ran out to greet him, with his two sons, but he did not look up, and received their caresses as one beneath their notice, as a mere slave, and he continued, in spite of all entreaty, to remain outside the city, and would not even go to the little farm he had loved so well.

The Roman Senate, as he would not come in to them, came out to hold their meeting in the Campagna.

The ambassadors spoke first, then Regulus, standing up, said, as one repeating a task, "Conscript fathers, being a slave to the Carthaginians, I come on the part of my masters to treat with you concerning peace, and an exchange of prisoners." He then turned to go away with the ambassadors, as a stranger might not be present at the deliberations of the Senate. His old friends pressed him to stay and give his opinion as a senator who had twice been consul; but he refused to degrade that dignity by claiming it, slave as he was. But, at the command of his Carthaginian masters, he remained, though not taking his seat.

Then he spoke. He told the senators to persevere in the war. He said he had seen the distress of Carthage, and that a peace would only be to her advantage, not to that of Rome, and therefore he strongly advised that the war should continue. Then, as to the exchange of prisoners, the Carthaginian generals, who were in the hands of the Romans, were in full health and strength, whilst he himself was too much broken down to be fit for service again, and indeed he believed that his enemies had given him a slow poison, and that he could not live long. Thus he insisted that no exchange of prisoners should be made.

It was wonderful, even to Romans, to hear a man thus pleading against himself, and their chief priest came forward, and declared that, as his oath had been wrested from him by force, he was not bound to return to his captivity. But Regulus was too noble to listen to this for a moment. "Have you resolved to dishonour me?" he said. "I am not ignorant that death and the extremest tortures are preparing for me; but what are these to the shame of an infamous action, or the wounds of a guilty mind? Slave as I am to Carthage, I have still the spirit of a Roman. I have sworn to return. It is my duty to go; let the gods take care of the rest."

The Senate decided to follow the advice of Regulus, though they bitterly regretted his sacrifice. His wife wept and entreated in vain that they would detain him; they could merely repeat their permission to him to remain; but nothing could prevail with him to break his word, and he turned back to the chains and death he expected so calmly as if he had been returning to his home. This was in the year B.C. 249.

"Let the gods take care of the rest," said the Roman; the gods whom alone he knew, and through whom he ignorantly worshipped the true God, whose Light was shining out even in this heathen's truth and constancy. How his trust was fulfilled is not known. The Senate, after the next victory, gave two Carthaginian generals to his wife and sons to hold as pledges for his good treatment; but when tidings arrived that Regulus was dead, Marcia began to treat them both with savage cruelty, though one of them assured her that he had been careful to have her husband well used. Horrible stories were told that Regulus had been put out in the sun with his eyelids cut off, rolled down a hill in a barrel with spikes, killed by being constantly kept awake, or else crucified. Marcia seems to have set about, and perhaps believed in these horrors, and avenged them on her unhappy captives till one had died, and the Senate sent for her sons and severely reprimanded them. They declared it was their mother's doing, not theirs, and thenceforth were careful of the comfort of the remaining prisoner.

It may thus be hoped that the frightful tale of Regulus' sufferings was but formed by report acting on the fancy of a vindictive woman, and that Regulus was permitted to die in peace of the disease brought on far more probably by the climate and imprisonment, than by the poison to which he ascribed it. It is not the tortures he may have endured that make him one of the noblest characters of history, but the resolution that would neither let him save himself at the risk of his country's prosperity, nor forfeit the word that he had pledged.

The Brave Brethren of Judah

B.C. 180

IT was about 180 years before the Christian era. The Jews had long since come home from Babylon, and built up their city and Temple at Jerusalem. But they were not free as they had been before. Their country belonged to some greater power, they had a foreign governor over them, and had to pay tribute to the king who was their master.

At the time we are going to speak of, this king was Antiochus Epiphanes, King of Syria. He was descended from one of those generals who, upon the death of Alexander the Great, had shared the East between them, and he reigned over all the country from the Mediterranean Sea even into Persia and the borders of India. He spoke Greek, and believed in both the Greek and Roman gods, for he had spent some time at Rome in his youth; but in his Eastern kingdom he had learnt all the self-indulgent and violent habits to which people in those hot countries are especially tempted.

He was so fierce and passionate, that he was often called the "Madman", and he was very cruel to all who offended him. One of his greatest desires was, that the Jews should leave their true faith in one God, and do like the Greeks and Syrians, his other subjects, worship the same idols, and hold drunken feasts in their honour. Sad to say, a great many of the Jews had grown ashamed of their own true religion and the strict ways of their law, and thought them oldfashioned. They joined in the Greek sports, played games naked in the theatre, joined in riotous processions, carrying ivy in honour of Bacchus, the god of wine, and offered incense to the idols; and the worst of all these was the false high priest, Menelaus, who led the King Antiochus into the Temple itself, even into the Holy of Holies, and told him all that would most desecrate it and grieve the Jews. So a little altar to the Roman god Jupiter was set up on the top of the great brazen altar of burnt offerings, a hog was offered up, and broth of its flesh sprinkled everywhere in the Temple; then all the precious vessels were seized, the shewbread table of gold, the candlesticks, and the whole treasury, and carried away by the king; the walls were thrown down, and the place made desolate.

SOME JEWS WERE STILL FAITHFUL TO THEIR GOD.

Some Jews were still faithful to their God, but they were horribly punished and tortured to death before the eyes of the king; and when at last he went away to his own country, taking with him the wicked high priest Menelaus, he left behind him a governor and an army of soldiers stationed in the tower of Acra, which overlooked the Temple hill, and sent for an old man from Athens to teach the people the heathen rites and ceremonies. Any person who observed the Sabbath day, or any other ordinance of the law of Moses, was put to death in a most cruel manner; all the books of the Old Testament Scripture that could be found were either burnt or defiled, by having pictures of Greek gods painted upon them; and the heathen priests went from place to place, with a little brazen altar and image and a guard of soldiers, who were to kill every person who refused to burn incense before the idol. It was the very saddest time that the Jews had ever known, and there seemed no help near or far off; they could have no hope, except in the promises that God would never fail His people, or forsake His inheritance, and in the prophecies that bad times should come, but good ones after them.

The Greeks, in going through the towns to enforce the idol worship, came to a little city called Modin, somewhere on the hills on the coast of the Mediterranean Sea, not far from Joppa. There they sent out, as usual, orders to all the men of the town to meet them in the marketplace; but they were told beforehand, that the chief person in the place was an old man named Mattathias, of a priestly family, and so much respected, that all the other inhabitants of the place were sure to do whatever he might lead them in. So the Greeks sent for him first of all, and he came at their summons, a grand and noble old man, followed by his five sons, Johanan, Simon, Judas, Jonathan, and Eleazar. The Greek priest tried to talk him over. He told him that the high priest had forsaken the Jewish superstition, that the Temple was in ruins, and that resistance was in vain; and exhorted him to obtain gratitude and honour for himself, by leading his countrymen in thus adoring the deities of the king's choice, promising him rewards and treasures if he would comply.

But the old man spoke out with a loud and fearless voice: "Though all the nations that are under the king's dominion obey him, and fall away every one from the religion of their fathers, and give consent to his commandments; yet will I and my sons and my brethren walk in the covenant of our fathers. God forbid that we should forsake the law and the ordinances! We will not hearken to the king's words, to go from our religion, either on the right hand or the left?"

As he spoke, up came an apostate Jew to do sacrifice at the heathen altar. Mattathias trembled at the sight, and his zeal broke forth. He slew the offender, and his brave sons gathering round him, they attacked the Syrian soldiers, killed the commissioner, and threw down the altar. Then, as they knew that they could not there hold out against the king's power, Mattathias proclaimed throughout the city: "Whosoever is zealous of the law, and maintaineth the covenant, let him follow me!" With that, he and his five sons, with their families, left their houses and lands, and drove their cattle with them up into the wild hills and caves, where David had once made his home; and all the Jews who wished to be still faithful, gathered around them, to worship God and keep His commandments.

There they were, a handful of brave men in the mountains, and all the heathen world and apostate Jews against them. They used to come down into the villages, remind the people of the law, promise their help, and throw down any idol altars that they found, and the enemy never were able to follow them into their rocky strongholds. But the old Mattathias could not long bear the rude wild life in the cold mountains, and he soon died. First he called all his five sons, and bade them to "be zealous for the law, and give their lives for the covenant of their fathers"; and he reminded them of all the many brave men who had before served God, and been aided in their extremity. He appointed his son Judas, as the strongest and mightiest, to lead his brethren to battle, and Simon, as the wisest, to be their counsellor; then he blessed them and died; and his sons were able to bury him in the tomb of his fathers at Modin.

Judas was one of the bravest men who ever lived; never dreading the numbers that came against him. He was surnamed Maccabeus, which some people say meant the hammerer; but others think it was made up of the first letters of the words he carried on his banner, which meant "Who is like unto Thee, among the gods, O Lord?" Altogether he had about six thousand men round him when the Greek governor, Apollonius, came out to fight with him. The Jews gained here their first victory, and Judas killed Apollonius, took his sword, and fought all his other battles with it. Next came a captain called Seron, who went out to the hills to lay hold of the bold rebels that dared to rise against the King of Syria. The place where Judas met him was one to make the Jews' hearts leap with hope and trust. It was on the steep stony broken hillside of Beth-horon, the very place where Joshua had conquered the five kings of the Amorites, in the first battle on the coming in of the children of Israel to Palestine. There was the rugged path where Joshua had stood and called out to the sun to stand still in Gibeon, and the moon in the valley of Ajalon. Miracles were over, and Judas looked for no wonder to help him; but when he came up the mountain road from Joppa, his heart was full of the same trust as Joshua's, and he won another great victory.

By this time King Antiochus began to think the rising of the Jews a serious matter, but he could not come himself against them, because his provinces in Armenia and Persia had refused their tribute, and he had to go in person to reduce them. He appointed, however, a governor, named

Lysias, to chastise the Jews, giving him an army of 40,000 foot and 7000 horse. Half of these Lysias sent on before him, with two captains, named Nicanor and Gorgias, thinking that these would be more than enough to hunt down and crush the little handful that were lurking in the hills. And with them came a great number of slave merchants, who had bargained with Nicanor that they should have ninety Jews for one talent, to sell to the Greeks and Romans, by whom Jewish slaves were much esteemed.

There was great terror in Palestine at these tidings, and many of the weaker-minded fell away from Judas; but he called all the faithful together at Mizpeh, the same place where, 1000 years before, Samuel had collected the Israelites, and after prayer and fasting, had sent them forth to free their country from the Philistines. Shiloh, the sanctuary, was then lying desolate, just as Jerusalem now lay in ruins; and yet better times had come. But very mournful was that fast day at Mizpeh, as the Jews looked along the hillside to their own holy mountain crowned by no white marble and gold Temple flashing back the sunbeams, but only with the tall castle of their enemies towering over the precipice. They could not sacrifice, because a sacrifice could only be made at Jerusalem, and the only book of the Scriptures that they had to read from was painted over with the hateful idol figures of the Greeks. And the huge army of enemies was ever coming nearer! The whole assembly wept, and put on sackcloth and prayed aloud for help, and then there was a loud sounding of trumpets, and Judas stood forth before them. And he made the old proclamation that Moses had long ago decreed, that no one should go out to battle who was building a house, or planting a vineyard, or had just betrothed a wife, or who was fearful and faint-hearted. All these were to go home again. Judas had 6000 followers when he made this proclamation. He had only 3000 at the end of the day, and they were but poorly armed. He told them of the former aid that had come to their fathers in extremity, and made them bold with his noble words. Then he gave them for their watchword "the help of God", and divided the leadership of the band between himself and his brothers, appointing Eleazar, the youngest, to read the Holy Book.

With these valiant men, Judas set up his camp; but tidings were soon brought him that Gorgias, with 5000 foot and 1000 horse, had left the main body to fall on his little camp by night. He therefore secretly left the place in the twilight; so that when the enemy attacked his camp, they found it deserted, and supposing them to be hid in the mountains, proceeded hither in pursuit of them.

But in the early morning Judas and his 3000 men were all in battle array in the plains, and marching full upon the enemy's camp with trumpet sound, took them by surprise in the absence of Gorgias and his choice troops, and utterly defeated and put them to flight, but without pursuing them, since the fight with Gorgias and his 5000 might be yet to come.

Even as Judas was reminding his men of this, Gorgias's troops were seen looking down from the mountains where they had been wandering all night; but seeing their own camp all smoke and flame, they turned and fled away. Nine thousand of the invaders had been slain, and the whole camp, full of arms and treasures, was in the hands of Judas, who there rested for a Sabbath of glad thanksgiving, and the next day parted the spoil, first putting out the share for the widows and orphans and the wounded, and then dividing the rest among his warriors. As to the slave merchants, they were all made prisoners, and instead of giving a talent for ninety Jews, were sold themselves.

The next year Lysias came himself, but was driven back and defeated at Bethshur, four or five miles south of Bethlehem. And now came the saddest, yet the greatest, day of Judas's life, when he ventured to go back into the holy city and take possession of the Temple again. The strong tower of Acra, which stood on a ridge of Mount Moriah looking down on the Temple rock, was still held by the Syrians, and he had no means of taking it; but he and his men loved the sanctuary too well to keep away from it, and again they marched up the steps and slopes that led up the holy hill. They went up to find the walls broken, the gates burnt, the cloisters and priests' chambers pulled down, and the courts thickly grown with grass and shrubs, the altar of their one true God with the false idol Jupiter's altar in the middle of it. These warriors, who had turned three armies to flight, could not bear the sight. They fell down on their faces, threw dust on their heads, and wept aloud for the desolation of their holy place. But in the midst Judas caused the trumpets to sound an alarm. They were to do something besides grieving. The bravest of them were set to keep watch and ward against the Syrians in the tower, while he chose out the most faithful priests to cleanse out the sanctuary, and renew all that could be renewed, making new holy vessels from the spoil taken in Nicanor's camp, and setting the stones of the profaned altar apart while a new one was raised. On the third anniversary of the great profanation, the Temple was newly dedicated, with songs and hymns of rejoicing, and a festival day was appointed, which has been observed by the Jews ever since. The Temple rock and city were again fortified so as to be able to hold out against their enemies, and this year and the next were the most prosperous of the life of the loyal-hearted Maccabee.

The great enemy of the Jews, Antiochus Epiphanes, was in the meantime dying in great agony in Persia, and his son Antiochus Eupator was set on the throne by Lysias, who brought him with an enormous army to reduce the rising in Judea. The fight was again at Bethshur, where Judas had built a strong fort on a point of rock that guarded the road to Hebron. Lysias tried to take this fort, and Judas came to the rescue with his little army, to meet the far mightier Syrian force, which was made more terrific by possessing thirty war elephants imported from the Indian frontier. Each of these creatures carried a tower containing thirty-two men armed with darts and javelins, and an Indian driver on his neck; and they had 1000 foot and 500 horse attached to the special following of the beast, who, gentle as he was by nature, often produced a fearful effect on the enemy; not so much by his huge bulk as by the terror he inspired among men, and far more among horses. The whole host was spread over the mountains and the valleys so that it is said that their bright armour and gold and silver shields made the mountains glisten like lamps of fire.

Still Judas pressed on to the attack, and his brother Eleazar, perceiving that one of the elephants was more adorned than the rest, thought it might be carrying the king, and devoted himself for his country. He fought his way to the monster, crept under it, and stabbed it from beneath, so that the mighty weight sank down on him and crushed him to death in his fall. He gained a "perpetual name" for valour and self-devotion; but the king was not upon the elephant, and after a hard-fought battle, Judas was obliged to draw off and leave Bethshur to be taken by the enemy, and to shut himself up in Jerusalem.

There, want of provisions had brought him to great distress, when tidings came that another son of Antiochus Epiphanes had claimed the throne, and Lysias made peace in haste with Judas, promising him full liberty of worship, and left Palestine in peace.

This did not, however, last long. Lysias and his young master were slain by the new king, Demetrius, who again sent an army for the subjection of Judas, and further appointed a high priest, named Alcimus, of the family of Aaron, but inclined to favour the new heathen fashions.

This was the most fatal thing that had happened to Judas. Though of the priestly line, he was so much of a warrior, that he seems to have thought it would be profane to offer sacrifice himself; and many of the Jews were so glad of another high priest, that they let Alcimus into the Temple, and Jerusalem was again lost to Judas. One more battle was won by him at Beth-horon, and then finding how hard it was to make head against the Syrians, he sent to ask the aid of the great Roman power. But long before the answer could come, a huge Syrian army had marched in on the Holy Land, 20,000 men, and Judas had again no more than 3000. Some had gone over to Alcimus, some were offended at his seeking Roman alliance, and when at Eleasah he came in sight of the host, his men's hearts failed more than they ever had done before, and, out of the 3000 at first collected, only 800 stood with him, and they would fain have persuaded him to retreat.

"God forbid that I should do this thing," he said, "and flee away from them. If our time be come, let us die manfully for our brethren, and let us not stain our honour."

Sore was the battle, as sore as that waged by the 800 at Thermopylæ, and the end was the same. Judas and his 800 were not driven from the field, but lay dead upon it. But their work was done. What is called the moral effect of such a defeat goes further than many a victory. Those lives, sold so dearly, were the price of freedom for Judea.

Judas's brothers Jonathan and Simon laid him in his father's tomb, and then ended the work that he had begun; and when Simon died, the Jews, once so trodden on, were the most prosperous race in the East. The Temple was raised from its ruins, and the exploits of the Maccabees had nerved the whole people to do or die in defence of the holy faith of their fathers.

The Chief of the Arverni

B. C. 52

WE have seen the Gauls in the heart of Rome, we have now to see them showing the last courage of despair, defending their native lands against the greatest of all the conquerors that Rome ever sent forth.

These lands, where they had dwelt for so many years as justly to regard them as their inheritance, were Gaul. There the Celtic race had had their abode ever since history has spoken clearly, and had become, in Gaul especially, slightly more civilized from intercourse with the Greek colony at Massilia, or Marseilles. But they had become borderers upon the Roman dominions, and there was little chance that they would not be absorbed; the tribes of Provence, the first Roman province, were already conquered, others were in alliance with Rome, and some had called in the Romans to help them fight their battles. There is no occasion to describe the seven years' war by which Julius Cæsar added Gaul to the provinces claimed by Rome, and when he visited Britain; such conquests are far from being Golden Deeds, but are far worthier of the iron age. It is the stand made by the losing party, and the true patriotism of one young chieftain, that we would wish here to dwell upon.

In the sixth year of the war the conquest seemed to have been made, and the Roman legions were guarding the north and west, while Cæsar himself had crossed the Alps. Subjection pressed heavily on the Gauls, some of their chiefs had been put to death, and the high spirit of the nation was stirred. Meetings took place between the warriors of the various tribes, and an oath was taken by those who inhabited the centre of the country, that if they once revolted, they would stand by one another to the last. These Gauls were probably not tall, bony giants, like the pillagers of Rome; their appearance and character would be more like that of the modern Welsh, or of their own French descendants, small, alert, and dark-eyed, full of fire, but, though fierce at the first onset, soon rebuffed, yet with much perseverance in the long run. Their worship was conducted by Druids, like that of the Britons, and their dress was of checked material, formed into a loose coat and wide trousers. The superior chiefs, who had

had any dealings with Rome, would speak a little Latin, and have a few Roman weapons as great improvements upon their own. Their fortifications were wonderfully strong. Trunks of trees were laid on the ground at two feet apart, so that the depth of the wall was their full length. Over these another tier of beams was laid crosswise, and the space between was filled up with earth, and the outside faced with large stones; the building of earth and stone was carried up to some height, then came another tier of timbers, crossed as before, and this was repeated again to a considerable height, the inner ends of the beams being fastened to a planking within the wall, so that the whole was of immense compactness. Fire could not damage the mineral part of the construction, nor the battering ram hurt the wood, and the Romans had been often placed in great difficulties by these rude but admirable constructions, within which the Gauls placed their families and cattle, building huts for present shelter. Of late, some attempts had been made at copying the regular streets and houses built round courts that were in use among the Romans, and Roman colonies had been established in various places, where veteran soldiers had received grants of land on condition of keeping the natives in check. A growing taste for arts and civilization was leading to Romans of inferior classes settling themselves in other Gallic cities.

The first rising of the Gauls began by a quarrel at the city we now call Orleans, ending in a massacre of all the Romans there. The tidings were spread through all the country by loud shouts, repeated from one to the other by men stationed on every hill, and thus, what had been done at Orleans at sunrise was known by nine at night 160 miles off among the mountains, which were then the homes of a tribe called by the Romans the Arverni, who have left their name to the province of Auvergne.

Here dwelt a young chieftain, probably really called Fearcuincedorigh, or Man who is chief of a hundred heads, known to us by Cæsar's version of his name, as Vercingetorix, a high-spirited youth, who keenly felt the servitude of his country, and who, on receiving these tidings, instantly called on his friends to endeavour to shake off the yoke. His uncle, who feared to provoke Roman vengeance, expelled him from the chief city, Gergovia, the remains of which may be traced on the mountain still called Gergoie, about six miles from Clermont; but he collected all the younger and more high-spirited men, forced a way into the city, and was proclaimed chief of his tribe. All the neighbouring tribes joined in the league against the common enemy, and tidings were brought to Cæsar that the whole country round the Loire was in a state of revolt.

In the heart of winter he hurried back, and took the Gauls by surprise by crossing the snows that lay thick on the wild waste of the Cebenna, which the Arverni had always considered as their impenetrable barrier throughout the winter. The towns quickly fell into his hands, and he was rapidly recovering all he had lost, when Vercingetorix, collecting his chief supporters, represented to them that their best hope would be in burning all the inhabited places themselves and driving off all the cattle, then lying in wait to cut off all the convoys of provisions that should be sent to the enemy, and thus starving them into a retreat. He said that burning houses were indeed a grievous sight, but it would be more grievous to see their wives and children dragged into captivity. To this all the allies agreed, and twenty towns in one district were burnt in a single day; but when they came to the city of Avaricum, now called Bourges, the tribe of Bituriges, to whom it belonged, entreated on their knees not to be obliged to destroy the most beautiful city in the country, representing that, as it had a river on one side, and a morass everywhere else, except at a very narrow entrance, it might be easily held out against the enemy, and to their entreaties Vercingetorix yielded, though much against his own judgment.

Cæsar laid siege to the place, but his army suffered severely from cold and hunger; they had no bread at all, and lived only on the cattle driven in from distant villages, while Vercingetorix hovered round, cutting off their supplies. They however laboured diligently to raise a mount against a wall of the town; but as fast as they worked, the higher did the Gauls within raise the stages of their rampart, and for twenty-five days there was a most brave defence; but at last the Romans made their entrance, and slaughtered all they found there, except 800, who escaped to the camp of Vercingetorix. He was not disconcerted by this loss, which he had always expected, but sheltered and clothed the fugitives, and raised a great body of archers and of horsemen, with whom he returned to his own territory in Auvergne. There was much fighting around the city of Gergovia; but at length, owing to the revolt of the Aedui, another Gallic tribe, Cæsar was forced to retreat over the Loire; and the wild peaks of volcanic Auvergne were free again.

But no gallant resolution could long prevail against the ever-advancing power of Rome, and at length the Gauls were driven into their fortified camp at Alesia, now called Alise[4], a city standing on a high hill, with two rivers flowing round its base, and a plain in front about three miles wide. Everywhere else it was circled in by high hills, and here Cæsar resolved to shut these brave men in and bring them to bay. He caused his men to begin that mighty system of earthworks by which the Romans carried on their attacks, compassing their victim round on every side with a deadly slowness and sureness, by those broad ditches and terraced ramparts that everywhere mark where their foot of iron was trod. Eleven miles round did this huge rampart extend, strengthened by three-and-twenty redoubts, or places of defence, where a watch was continually kept. Before the lines were complete, Vercingetorix brought out his cavalry, and gave battle, at one

---

4   In Burgundy, between Semur and Dijon.

time with a hope of success; but the enemy were too strong for him, and his horsemen were driven into the camp. He then resolved to send home all of these, since they could be of no use in the camp, and had better escape before the ditch should have shut them in on every side. He charged them to go to their several tribes and endeavour to assemble all the fighting men to come to his rescue; for, if he were not speedily succoured, he and 80,000 of the bravest of the Gauls must fall into the hands of the Romans, since he had only corn for thirty days, even with the utmost saving.

Having thus exhorted them, he took leave of them, and sent them away at nine at night, so that they might escape in the dark where the Roman trench had not yet extended. Then he distributed the cattle among his men, but retained the corn himself, serving it out with the utmost caution. The Romans outside fortified their camp with a double ditch, one of them full of water, behind which was a bank twelve feet high, with stakes forked like the horns of a stag. The space between the ditches was filled with pits, and scattered with iron caltrops or hooked spikes. All this was against the garrison, to prevent them from breaking out; and outside the camp he made another line of ditches and ramparts against the Gauls who might be coming to the rescue.

The other tribes were not deaf to the summons of their friends, but assembled in large numbers, and just as the besieged had exhausted their provisions, an army was seen on the hills beyond the camp. Their commander was Vergosillaunus (most probably Fearsaighan, the Man of the Standard), a near kinsman of Vercingetorix; and all that bravery could do, they did to break through the defences of the camp from outside, while within, Vercingetorix and his 80,000 tried to fill up the ditches, and force their way out to meet their friends. But Cæsar himself commanded the Romans, who were confident in his fortunes, and raised a shout of ecstasy wherever they beheld his thin, marked, eagle face and purple robe, rushing on the enemy with a confidence of victory that did in fact render them invincible. The Gauls gave way, lost seventy-four of their standards, and Vergosillaunus himself was taken a prisoner; and as for the brave garrison within Alesia, they were but like so many flies struggling in vain within the enormous web that had been woven around them. Hope was gone, but the chief of the Arverni could yet do one thing for his countrymen–he could offer up himself in order to obtain better terms for them.

The next day he convened his companions in arms, and told them that he had only fought for the freedom of their country, not to secure his private interest; and that now, since yield they must, he freely offered himself to become a victim for their safety, whether they should judge it best for themselves to appease the anger of the conqueror by putting him to death themselves, or whether they preferred giving him up alive.

It was a piteous necessity to have to sacrifice their noblest and bravest,

who had led them so gallantly during the long war; but they had little
choice, and could only send messengers to the camp to offer to yield
Vercingetorix as the price of their safety. Cæsar made it known that he
was willing to accept their submission, and drawing up his troops in battle
array, with the Eagle standards around him, he watched the whole Gallic
army march past him. First, Vercingetorix was placed as a prisoner in his
hands, and then each man lay down sword, javelin, or bow and arrows,
helmet, buckler and breastplate, in one mournful heap, and proceeded
on his way, scarcely thankful that the generosity of their chieftain had
purchased for them subjection rather than death.

Vercingetorix himself had become the property of the great man from
whom alone we know of his deeds; who could perceive his generous spirit
and high qualities as a general, nay, who honoured the self-devotion by
which he endeavoured to save his countrymen. He remained in captivity–six long years sped by–while Cæsar passed the Rubicon, fought out his
struggle for power at Rome, and subdued Egypt, Pontus, and Northern
Africa–and all the time the brave Gaul remained closely watched and
guarded, and with no hope of seeing the jagged peaks and wild valleys of
his own beautiful Auvergne. For well did he, like every other marked foe
of Rome, know for what he was reserved, and no doubt he yielded himself
in the full expectation of that fate which many a man, as brave as he, had
escaped by self-destruction.

The day came at last. In July, B.C. 45, the victorious Cæsar had leisure
to celebrate his victories in four grand triumphs, all in one month, and
that in honour of the conquest of Gaul came the first. The triumphal gate
of Rome was thrown wide open, every house was decked with hangings
of silk and tapestry, the household images of every family, dressed with
fresh flowers, were placed in their porches, those of the gods stood on the
steps of the temples, and in marched the procession, the magistrates first
in their robes of office, and then the trumpeters. Next came the tokens of
the victory–figures of the supposed gods of the two great rivers, Rhine and
Rhone, and even of the captive Ocean, made in gold, were carried along,
with pictures framed in citron wood, showing the scenes of victory–the
wild waste of the Cevennes, the steep peaks of Auvergne, the mighty camp
of Alesia; nay, there too would be the white cliffs of Dover, and the struggle
with the Britons on the beach. Models in wood and ivory showed the fortifications of Avaricum, and of many another city; and here too were carried
specimens of the olives and vines, and other curious plants of the newly
won land; here was the breastplate of British pearls that Cæsar dedicated
to Venus. A band of flute-players followed, and then came the white oxen
that were to be sacrificed, their horns gilded and flowers hung round them,
the sacrificing priests with wreathed heads marching with them. Specimens
of bears and wolves from the woods and mountains came next in order,

and after them waved for the last time the national ensigns of the many tribes of Gaul. Once more Vercingetorix and Vergosillaunus saw their own Arvernian standard, and marched behind it with the noblest of their clan: once more they wore their native dress and well-tried armour. But chains were on their hands and feet, and the men who had fought so long and well for freedom, were the captive gazing-stock of Rome. Long, long was the line of chained Gauls of every tribe, before the four white horses appeared, all abreast, drawing the gilded car, in which stood a slight form in a purple robe, with the bald head and narrow temples encircled with a wreath of bay, the thin cheeks tinted with vermilion, the eager aquiline face and narrow lips gravely composed to Roman dignity, and the quick eye searching out what impression the display was making on the people. Over his head a slave held a golden crown, but whispered, "Remember that thou too art a man." And in following that old custom, how little did the victor know that, bay-crowned like himself, there followed close behind, in one of the chariots of the officers, the man whose dagger-thrust would, two years later, be answered by his dying word of reproach! The horsemen of the army followed, and then the legions, every spear wreathed, every head crowned with bay, so that an evergreen grove might have seemed marching through the Roman streets, but for the war songs, and the wild jests, and ribald ballads that custom allowed the soldiers to shout out, often in pretended mockery of their own victorious general, the Imperator.

The victor climbed the Capitol steps, and laid his wreath of bay on Jupiter's knees, the white oxen were sacrificed, and the feast began by torchlight. Where was the vanquished? He was led to the dark prison vault in the side of Capitoline hill, and there one sharp sword-thrust ended the gallant life and long captivity.

It was no special cruelty in Julius Cæsar. Every Roman triumph was stained by the slaughter of the most distinguished captives, after the degradation of walking in chains had been undergone. He had spirit to appreciate Vercingetorix, but had not nobleness to spare him from the ordinary fate. Yet we may doubt which, in true moral greatness, was the superior in that hour of triumph, the conqueror who trod down all that he might minister to his own glory, or the conquered, who, when no resistance had availed, had voluntarily confronted shame and death in hopes to win pardon and safety for his comrades.

Withstanding the Monarch in His Wrath

A. D. 389

WHEN a monarch's power is unchecked by his people, there is only One to whom he believes himself accountable; and if he have forgotten the dagger of Damocles, or if he be too high-spirited to regard it, then that Higher One alone can restrain his actions. And there have been times when princes have so broken the bounds of right, that no hope remains of recalling them to their duty save by the voice of the ministers of God upon Earth. But as these ministers bear no charmed life, and are subjects themselves of the prince, such rebukes have been given at the utmost risk of liberty and life.

Thus it was that though Nathan, unharmed, showed David his sin, and Elijah, the wondrous prophet of Gilead, was protected from Jezebel's fury, when he denounced her and her husband Ahab for the idolatry of Baal and the murder of Naboth; yet no Divine hand interposed to shield Zachariah, the son of Jehoiada, the high priest, when he rebuked the apostasy of his cousin, Jehoash, King of Judah, and was stoned to death by the ungrateful king's command in that very temple court where Jehoiada and his armed Levites had encountered the savage usurping Athaliah, and won back the kingdom for the child Jehoash. And when "in the spirit and power of Elijah", St. John the Baptist denounced the sin of Herod Antipas in marrying his brother Philip's wife, he bore the consequences to the utmost, when thrown into prison and then beheaded to gratify the rage of the vindictive woman.

Since Scripture Saints in the age of miracles were not always shielded from the wrath of kings, Christian bishops could expect no special interposition in their favour, when they stood forth to stop the way of the sovereign's passions, and to proclaim that the cause of mercy, purity, and truth is the cause of God.

The first of these Christian bishops was Ambrose, the sainted prelate of Milan. It was indeed a Christian Emperor whom he opposed, no other than the great Theodosius, but it was a new and unheard-of thing for any voice to rebuke an Emperor of Rome, and Theodosius had proved himself

"THE CAUSE OF MERCY, PURITY, AND TRUTH, IS THE CAUSE OF GOD."

a man of violent passions.

The fourth century was a time when races and all sorts of shows were the fashion, nay, literally the rage; for furious quarrels used to arise among the spectators who took the part of one or other of the competitors, and would call themselves after their colours, the Blues or the Greens. A favourite chariot driver, who had excelled in these races at Thessalonica, was thrown into prison for some misdemeanour by Botheric, the Governor of Illyria, and his absence so enraged the Thessalonican mob, that they rose in tumult, and demanded his restoration. On being refused, they threw such a hail of stones that the governor himself and some of his officers were slain.

Theodosius might well be displeased, but his rage passed all bounds. He was at Milan at the time, and at first Ambrose so worked on his feelings as to make him promise to temper justice with mercy; but afterwards fresh accounts of the murder, together with the representations of his courtier Rufinus, made him resolve not to relent, and he sent off messengers commanding that there should be a general slaughter of all the race-going Thessalonicans, since all were equally guilty of Botheric's death. He took care that his horrible command should be kept a secret from Ambrose, and the first that the Bishop heard of it was the tidings that 7,000 persons had been killed in the theatre, in a massacre lasting three hours!

There was no saving these lives, but Ambrose felt it his duty to make the Emperor feel his sin, in hopes of saving others. Besides, it was not consistent with the honour of God to receive at his altar a man reeking with innocent blood. The Bishop, however, took time to consider; he went into the country for a few days, and thence wrote a letter to the Emperor, telling him that thus stained with crime, he could not be admitted to the Holy Communion, nor received into church. Still the Emperor does not seem to have believed he could be really withstood by any subject, and on Ambrose's return, he found the imperial procession, lictors, guards, and all, escorting the Emperor as usual to the Basilica or Justice Hall, that had been turned into a church.

Then to the door came the Bishop and stood in the way, forbidding the entrance, and announcing that there, at least, sacrilege should not be added to murder.

"Nay," said the Emperor, "did not holy King David commit both murder and adultery, yet was he not received again?"

"If you have sinned like him, repent like him," answered Ambrose.

Theodosius turned away, troubled. He was great enough not to turn his anger against the Bishop; he felt that he had sinned, and that the chastisement was merited, and he went back to his palace weeping, and there spent eight months, attending to his duties of state, but too proud to go through the tokens of penitence that the discipline of the Church had prescribed before a great sinner could be received back into the congregation of the faithful. Easter was the usual time for reconciling penitents, and Ambrose was not inclined to show any respect of persons, or to excuse the Emperor from a penance he would have imposed on any offender. However, Rufinus could not believe in such disregard, and thought all would give way to the Emperor's will. Christmas had come, but for one man at Milan there were no hymns, no shouts of "glad tidings!" no midnight festival, no rejoicing that "to us a Child is born; to us a Son is given". The Basilica was thronged with worshippers and rang with their Amens, resounding like thunder, and their echoing song–the *Te Deum* –then their newest hymn of praise. But the lord of all those multitudes was alone in his palace. He had not shown good will to man; he had not learnt mercy and peace from the Prince of Peace; and the door was shut upon him. He was a resolute Spanish Roman, a well-tried soldier, a man advancing in years, but he wept, and wept bitterly. Rufinus found him thus weeping. It must have been strange to the courtier that his master did not send his lictors to carry the offending bishop to a dungeon, and give all his court favour to the heretics, like the last empress who had reigned at Milan. Nay, he might even, like Julian the Apostate, have altogether renounced that Christian faith which could humble an emperor below the poorest of his subjects.

But Rufinus contented himself with urging the Emperor not to remain at home lamenting, but to endeavor again to obtain admission into the church, assuring him that the Bishop would give way. Theodosius replied that he did not expect it, but yielded to the persuasions, and Rufinus hastened on before to warn the Bishop of his coming, and represented how inexpedient it was to offend him.

"I warn you," replied Ambrose, "that I shall oppose his entrance, but if he chooses to turn his power into tyranny, I shall willingly let him slay me."

The Emperor did not try to enter the church, but sought Ambrose in an adjoining building, where he entreated to be absolved from his sin.

"Beware," returned the Bishop, "of trampling on the laws of God."

"I respect them," said the Emperor, "therefore I have not set foot in the church, but I pray thee to deliver me from these bonds, and not to close against me the door that the Lord hath opened to all who truly repent."

"What repentance have you shown for such a sin?" asked Ambrose.

"Appoint my penance," said the Emperor, entirely subdued.

And Ambrose caused him at once to sign a decree that thirty days should always elapse between a sentence of death and its execution. After this, Theodosius was allowed to come into the church, but only to the corner he had shunned all these eight months, till the "dull hard stone within him" had "melted", to the spot appointed for the penitents. There, without his crown, his purple robe, and buskins, worked with golden eagles, all laid aside, he lay prostrate on the stones, repeating the verse, "My soul cleaveth unto the dust; quicken me, O Lord, according to thy word." This was the place that penitents always occupied, and there fasts and other discipline were also appointed. When the due course had been gone through, probably at the next Easter, Ambrose, in his Master's name, pronounced the forgiveness of Theodosius, and received him back to the full privileges of a Christian. When we look at the course of many another emperor, and see how easily, where the power was irresponsible, justice became severity, and severity, bloodthirstiness, we see what Ambrose dared to meet, and from what he spared Theodosius and all the civilized world under his sway. Who can tell how many innocent lives have been saved by that thirty days' respite?

Pass over nearly 700 years, and again we find a church door barred against a monarch. This time it is not under the bright Italian sky, but under the grey fogs of the Baltic sea. It is not the stately marble gateway of the Milanese Basilica, but the low-arched, rough stone portal of the newly built cathedral of Roskilde, in Zealand, where, if a zigzag surrounds the arch, it is a great effort of genius. The Danish king Swend, the nephew of the well-known Knut, stands before it; a stern and powerful man, fierce and passionate, and with many a Danish axe at his command. Nay, only lately for a few rude jests, he caused some of his chief jarls to be slain without a trial. Half the country is still pagan, and though the king himself is baptized, there is no certainty that, if the Christian faith do not suit his taste, he may not join the heathen party and return to the worship of Thor and Tyr, where deeds of blood would be not blameworthy, but a passport to the rude joys of Valhall. Nevertheless there is a pastoral staff across the doorway, barring the way of the king, and that staff is held against him by an Englishman, William, Bishop of Roskilde, the missionary who had converted a great part of Zealand, but who will not accept Christians who have not laid aside their sins.

He confronts the king who has never been opposed before. "Go back," he says, "nor dare approach the alter of God—thou who art not a king but a murderer."

Some of the jarls seized their swords and axes, and were about to strike the bishop away from the threshold, but he, without removing his staff, bent his head, and bade them strike, saying he was ready to die in the cause of God. But the king came to a better frame of mind, he called the jarls away, and returning humbly to his palace, took off his royal robes, and came again barefoot and in sackcloth to the church door, where Bishop William met him, took him by the hand, gave him the kiss of peace, and led him to the penitents' place. After three days he was absolved, and for the rest of his life, the bishop and the king lived in the closest friendship, so much so that William always prayed that even in death he might not be divided from his friend. The prayer was granted. The two died almost at the same time, and were buried together in the cathedral at Roskilde, where the one had taught and other learnt the great lesson of mercy.

The Last Fight in the Colisæum
A. D. 404

AS the Romans grew prouder and more fond of pleasure, no one could hope to please them who did not give them sports and entertainments. When any person wished to be elected to any public office, it was a matter of course that he should compliment his fellow citizens by exhibitions of the kind they loved, and when the common people were discontented, their cry was that they wanted panem ac Circenses, "bread and sports", the only things they cared for. In most places where there has been a large Roman colony, remains can be seen of the amphitheatres, where the citizens were wont to assemble for these diversions. Sometimes these are stages of circular galleries of seats hewn out of the hillside, where rows of spectators might sit one above the other, all looking down on a broad, flat space in the centre, under their feet, where the representations took place. Sometimes, when the country was flat, or it was easier to build than to excavate, the amphitheatre was raised above ground, rising up to a considerable height.

The grandest and most renowned of all these amphitheatres is the Colisæum at Rome. It was built by Vespasian and his son Titus, the conquerors of Jerusalem, in a valley in the midst of the seven hills of Rome. The captive Jews were forced to labour at it; and the materials, granite outside, and softer travertine stone within, are so solid and so admirably built, that still at the end of eighteen centuries it has scarcely even become a ruin, but remains one of the greatest wonders of Rome.

Five acres of ground were enclosed within the oval of its outer wall, which outside rises perpendicularly in tiers of arches one above the other. Within, the galleries of seats projected forwards, each tier coming out far beyond the one above it, so that between the lowest and the outer wall there was room for a great space of chambers, passages, and vaults around the central space, called the arena, from the arena, or sand, with which it was strewn.

When the Roman Emperors grew very vain and luxurious, they used to have this sand made ornamental with metallic filings, vermilion, and even powdered precious stones; but it was thought better taste to use the scrapings of a soft white stone, which, when thickly strewn, made the whole arena look as if covered with untrodden snow. Around the border of this space flowed a stream of fresh water. Then came a straight wall, rising to a considerable height, and surmounted by a broad platform, on which stood a throne for the Emperor, curule chairs of ivory and gold for the chief magistrates and senators, and seats for the vestal virgins. Next above were galleries for the equestrian order, the great mass of those who considered themselves as of gentle station, though not of the highest rank; farther up, and therefore farther back, were the galleries belonging to the freemen of Rome; and these were again surmounted by another plain wall with a platform on the top, where were places for the ladies, who were not (except the vestal virgins) allowed to look on nearer, because of the unclothed state of some of the performers in the arena. Between the ladies' boxes, benches were squeezed in where the lowest people could seat themselves; and some of these likewise found room in the two uppermost tiers of porticoes, where sailors, mechanics, and persons in the service of the Colisæum had their post. Altogether, when full, this huge building held no less than 87,000 spectators. It had no roof; but when there was rain, or if the sun was too hot, the sailors in the porticoes unfurled awnings that ran along upon ropes, and formed a covering of silk and gold tissue over the whole. Purple was the favourite colour for this velamen, or veil; because, when the sun shone through it, it cast such beautiful rosy tints on the snowy arena and the white purple-edged togas of the Roman citizens.

Long days were spent from morning till evening upon those galleries. The multitude who poured in early would watch the great dignitaries arrive and take their seats, greeting them either with shouts of applause or hootings of dislike, according as they were favourites or otherwise; and when the Emperor came in to take his place under his canopy, there was one loud acclamation, "Joy to thee, master of all, first of all, happiest of all. Victory to thee for ever!"

When the Emperor had seated himself and given the signal, the sports began. Sometimes a rope-dancing elephant would begin the entertainment, by mounting even to the summit of the building and descending by a cord. Then a bear, dressed up as a Roman matron, would be carried along in a chair between porters, as ladies were wont to go abroad, and another bear, in a lawyer's robe, would stand on his hind legs and go through the motions of pleading a case. Or a lion came forth with a jewelled crown on his head, a diamond necklace round his neck, his mane plaited with gold, and his claws gilded, and played a hundred pretty gentle antics with a little hare that danced fearlessly within his grasp. Then in would come twelve elephants, six males in togas, six females with the veil and pallium; they took their places on couches around an ivory table, dined with great decorum, playfully sprinkled a little rosewater over the nearest spectators, and then received more guests of their unwieldy kind, who arrived in ball dresses, scattered flowers, and performed a dance.

Sometimes water was let into the arena, a ship sailed in, and falling to pieces in the midst, sent a crowd of strange animals swimming in all directions. Sometimes the ground opened, and trees came growing up through it, bearing golden fruit. Or the beautiful old tale of Orpheus was acted; these trees would follow the harp and song of the musician; but–to make the whole part complete–it was no mere play, but real earnest, that the Orpheus of the piece fell a prey to live bears.

For the Colisæum had not been built for such harmless spectacles as those first described. The fierce Romans wanted to be excited and feel themselves strongly stirred; and, presently, the doors of the pits and dens round the arena were thrown open, and absolutely savage beasts were let loose upon one another–rhinoceroses and tigers, bulls and lions, leopards and wild boars–while the people watched with savage curiosity to see the various kinds of attack and defence; or, if the animals were cowed or sullen, their rage would be worked up–red would be shown to the bulls, white to boars, red-hot goads would be driven into some, whips would be lashed at others, till the work of slaughter was fairly commenced, and gazed on with greedy eyes and ears delighted, instead of horror-struck, by the roars and howls of the noble creatures whose courage was thus misused. Sometimes indeed, when some especially strong or ferocious animal had slain a whole heap of victims, the cries of the people would decree that it should be turned loose in its native forest, and, amid shouts of "A triumph!–a triumph!" the beast would prowl round the arena, upon the carcasses of the slain victims. Almost incredible numbers of animals were imported for these cruel sports, and the governors of distant provinces made it a duty to collect troops of lions, elephants, ostriches, leopards–the fiercer or the newer the creature the better–to be thus tortured to frenzy, to make sport in the amphitheatre. However, there was daintiness joined with cruelty: the Romans did not like the smell of blood, though they enjoyed the sight of it, and all the solid stonework was pierced with tubes, through which was conducted the stream of spices and saffron, boiled in wine, that the perfume might overpower the scent of slaughter below.

Wild beasts tearing each other to pieces might, one would think, satisfy any taste of horror; but the spectators needed even nobler game to be set before their favourite monsters–men were brought forward to confront them. Some of these were at first in full armour, and fought hard, generally with success; and there was a revolving machine, something like a squirrel's cage, in which the bear was always climbing after his enemy, and then rolling over by his own weight. Or hunters came, almost unarmed, and gaining the victory by swiftness and dexterity, throwing a piece of cloth over a lion's head, or disconcerting him by putting their fist down his throat. But it was not only skill, but death, that the Romans loved to see; and condemned criminals and deserters were reserved to feast the lions, and to entertain the populace with their various kinds of death. Among these condemned was many a Christian martyr, who witnessed a good confession before the savage-eyed multitude around the arena, and "met the lion's gory mane" with a calm resolution and hopeful joy that the lookers-on could not understand. To see a Christian die, with upward gaze and hymns of joy on his tongue, was the most strange unaccountable sight the Colisæum could offer, and it was therefore the choicest, and reserved for the last part of the spectacles in which the brute creation had a part.

The carcasses were dragged off with hooks, and bloodstained sand was covered with a fresh clean layer, the perfume wafted in stronger clouds, and a procession came forward–tall, well-made men, in the prime of their strength. Some carried a sword and a lasso, others a trident and a net; some were in light armour, others in the full heavy equipment of a soldier; some on horseback, some in chariots, some on foot. They marched in, and made their obeisance to the Emperor; and with one voice, their greeting sounded through the building, *Ave, Caesar, morituri te salutant!* "Hail, Caesar, those about to die salute thee!"

They were the gladiators–the swordsmen trained to fight to the death to amuse the populace. They were usually slaves placed in schools of arms under the care of a master; but sometimes persons would voluntarily hire themselves out to fight by way of a profession: and both these, and such slave gladiators as did not die in the arena, would sometimes retire, and spend an old age of quiet; but there was little hope of this, for the Romans were not apt to have mercy on the fallen.

Fights of all sorts took place–the light-armed soldier and the netsman–the lasso and the javelin–the two heavy-armed warriors–all combinations of single combat, and sometimes a general *melee*. When a gladiator wounded his adversary, he shouted to the spectators, *Hoc habet!* "He has it!" and looked up to know whether he should kill or spare. If the people held up their thumbs, the conquered was left to recover, if he could; if they turned them down, he was to die: and if he showed any reluctance to present his throat for the deathblow, there was a scornful shout, Recipe ferrum! "Receive the steel!" Many of us must have seen casts of the most touching statue of the wounded man, that called forth the noble lines of indignant pity which, though so often repeated, cannot be passed over here:–

> "I see before me the Gladiator lie;
> He leans upon his hand–his manly brow
> Consents to death, but conquers agony.
> And his droop'd head sinks gradually low,
> And through his side the last drops, ebbing slow

From the red gash, fall heavy one by one,
Like the first of a thunder shower; and now
The arena swims around him—he is gone
Ere ceased the inhuman shout which
    hailed the wretch who won.

"He heard it, but he heeded not—his eyes
Were with his heart, and that was far away.
He reck'd not of the life he lost, nor prize,
But where his rude hut by the Danube lay,
There were his young barbarians all at play,
There was their Dacian mother—he their sire,
Butcher'd to make a Roman holiday.
All this rush'd with his blood—Shall he expire,
And unavenged? Arise ye Goths and glut your ire."

Sacred vestals, tender mothers, fat, good-humoured senators, all thought it fair play, and were equally pitiless in the strange frenzy for exciting scenes to which they gave themselves up, when they mounted the stone stairs of the Colisaeum. Privileged persons would even descend into the arena, examine the death agonies, and taste the blood of some specially brave victim ere the corpse was drawn forth at the death gate, that the frightful game might continue undisturbed and unencumbered. Gladiator shows were the great passion of Rome, and popular favour could hardly be gained except by ministering to it. Even when the barbarians were beginning to close in on the Empire, hosts of brave men were still kept for this slavish mimic warfare—sport to the beholders, but sad earnest to the actors.

Christianity worked its way upwards, and at least was professed by the Emperor on his throne. Persecution came to an end, and no more martyrs fed the beasts in the Colisaeum. The Christian emperors endeavoured to prevent any more shows where cruelty and death formed the chief interest and no truly religious person could endure the spectacle; but custom and love of excitement prevailed even against the Emperor. Mere tricks of beasts, horse and chariot races, or bloodless contests, were tame and dull, according to the diseased taste of Rome; it was thought weak and sentimental to object to looking on at a death scene; the Emperors were generally absent at Constantinople, and no one could get elected to any office unless he treated the citizens to such a show as they best liked, with a little bloodshed and death to stir their feelings; and thus it went on for full a hundred years after Rome had, in name, become a Christian city, and the same custom prevailed wherever there was an amphitheatre and pleasure-loving people.

Meantime the enemies of Rome were coming nearer and nearer, and

Alaric, the great chief of the Goths, led his forces into Italy, and threatened the city itself. Honorius, the Emperor, was a cowardly, almost idiotical, boy; but his brave general, Stilicho, assembled his forces, met the Goths at Pollentia (about twenty-five miles from where Turin now stands), and gave them a complete defeat on the Easter Day of the year 403. He pursued them into the mountains, and for that time saved Rome. In the joy of the victory the Roman senate invited the conqueror and his ward Honorius to enter the city in triumph, at the opening of the new year, with the white steeds, purple robes, and vermilion cheeks with which, of old, victorious generals were welcomed at Rome. The churches were visited instead of the Temple of Jupiter, and there was no murder of the captives; but Roman bloodthirstiness was not yet allayed, and, after all the procession had been completed, the Colisæum shows commenced, innocently at first, with races on foot, on horseback, and in chariots; then followed a grand hunting of beasts turned loose in the arena; and next a sword dance. But after the sword dance came the arraying of swordsmen, with no blunted weapons, but with sharp spears and swords—a gladiator combat in full earnest. The people, enchanted, applauded with shouts of ecstasy this gratification of their savage tastes. Suddenly, however, there was an interruption. A rude, roughly robed man, bareheaded and barefooted, had sprung into the arena, and, signing back the gladiators, began to call aloud upon the people to cease from the shedding of innocent blood, and not to requite God's mercy in turning away the sword of the enemy by encouraging murder. Shouts, howls, cries, broke in upon his words; this was no place for preachings—the old customs of Rome should be observed—"Back, old man!"—"On, gladiators!" The gladiators thrust aside the meddler, and rushed to the attack. He still stood between, holding them apart, striving in vain to be heard. "Sedition! Sedition!"—"Down with him!"—was the cry; and the man in authority, Alypius, the praefect, himself added his voice. The gladiators, enraged at interference with their vocation, cut him down. Stones, or whatever came to hand, rained down upon him from the furious people, and he perished in the midst of the arena! He lay dead, and then came the feeling of what had been done.

His dress showed that he was one of the hermits who vowed themselves to a holy life of prayer and self-denial, and who were greatly reverenced, even by the most thoughtless. The few who had previously seen him, told that he had come from the wilds of Asia on pilgrimage, to visit the shrines and keep his Christmas at Rome—they knew he was a holy man—no more, and it is not even certain whether his name was Alymachus or Telemachus. His spirit had been stirred by the sight of thousands flocking to see men slaughter one another, and in his simple-hearted zeal he had resolved to stop the cruelty or die. He had died, but not in vain. His work was done. The shock of such a death before their eyes turned the hearts of the people;

THE ARENA

they saw the wickedness and cruelty to which they had blindly surrendered themselves; and from the day when the hermit died in the Colisæum there was never another fight of the Gladiators. Not merely at Rome, but in every province of the Empire, the custom was utterly abolished; and one habitual crime at least was wiped from the earth by the self-devotion of one humble, obscure, almost nameless man.

The Shepherd Girl of Nanterre
A.D. 438

FOUR hundred years of the Roman dominion had entirely tamed the once wild and independent Gauls. Everywhere, except in the moorlands of Brittany, they had become as much like Romans themselves as they could accomplish; they had Latin names, spoke the Latin tongue, all their personages of higher rank were enrolled as Roman citizens, their chief cities were colonies where the laws were administered by magistrates in the Roman fashion, and the houses, dress, and amusements were the same as those of Italy. The greater part of the towns had been converted to Christianity, though some Paganism still lurked in the more remote villages and mountainous districts.

It was upon these civilized Gauls that the terrible attacks came from the wild nations who poured out of the centre and east of Europe. The Franks came over the Rhine and its dependent rivers, and made furious attacks upon the peaceful plains, where the Gauls had long lived in security, and reports were everywhere heard of villages harried by wild horsemen, with short double-headed battleaxes, and a horrible short pike, covered with iron and with several large hooks, like a gigantic artificial minnow, and like it fastened to a long rope, so that the prey which it had grappled might be pulled up to the owner. Walled cities usually stopped them, but every farm or villa outside was stripped of its valuables, set on fire, the cattle driven off, and the more healthy inhabitants seized for slaves.

It was during this state of things that a girl was born to a wealthy peasant at the village now called Nanterre, about two miles from Lutetia, which was already a prosperous city, though not as yet so entirely the capital as it was destined to become under the name of Paris. She was christened by an old Gallic name, probably Gwenfrewi, or White Stream, in Latin Genovefa, but she is best known by the late French form of Genevieve. When she was about seven years old, two celebrated bishops passed through the village, Germanus, of Auxerre, and Lupus, of Troyes, who had been invited to Britain to dispute the false doctrine of Pelagius. All the inhabitants flocked into the church to see them, pray with them, and receive their blessing; and here the sweet childish devotion of Genevieve so struck Germanus, that he called her to him, talked to her, made her sit beside him at the feast, gave her his special blessing, and presented her with a copper medal with a cross engraven upon it. From that time the little maiden always deemed herself especially consecrated to the service of Heaven, but she still remained at home, daily keeping her father's sheep, and spinning their wool as she sat under the trees watching them, but always with a heart full of prayer.

After this St. Germanus proceeded to Britain, and there encouraged his converts to meet the heathen Picts at Maes Garmon, in Flintshire, where the exulting shout of the white-robed catechumens turned to flight the wild superstitious savages of the north–and the Hallelujah victory was gained without a drop of bloodshed. He never lost sight of Genevieve, the little maid whom he had so early distinguished for her piety.

After she lost her parents she went to live with her godmother, and continued the same simple habits, leading a life of sincere devotion and strict self-denial, constant prayer, and much charity to her poorer neighbors.

In the year 451 the whole of Gaul was in the most dreadful state of terror at the advance of Attila, the savage chief of the Huns, who came from the banks of the Danube with a host of savages of hideous features, scarred and disfigured to render them more frightful. The old enemies, the Goths and the Franks, seemed like friends compared with these formidable beings whose cruelties were said to be intolerable, and of whom every exaggerated story was told that could add to the horrors of the miserable people who lay in their path. Tidings came that this "Scourge of God", as Attila called himself, had passed the Rhine, destroyed Tongres and Metz, and was in full march for Paris. The whole country was in the utmost terror. Everyone seized their most valuable possessions, and would have fled; but Genevieve placed herself on the only bridge across the Seine, and argued with them, assuring them in a strain that was afterwards thought of as prophetic, that, if they would pray, repent, and defend instead of abandoning their homes, God would protect them. They were at first almost ready to stone her for thus withstanding their panic, but just then a priest arrived from Auxerre, with a present for Genevieve from St. Germanus, and they were thus reminded of the high estimation in which he held her; they became ashamed of their violence, and she held them back to pray and to arm themselves. In a few days they heard that Attila had paused to besiege Orleans, and that Aetius, the Roman general, hurrying from Italy, had united his troops with those of the Goths and Franks, and given Attila so terrible a defeat at Chalons that the Huns were fairly driven out of Gaul. And here it must be mentioned that when the next year, 453, Attila with his murderous host came down into Italy, and after horrible devasation of all the northern provinces, came to the gates of Rome, no one dared to meet him but one venerable Bishop, Leo, the Pope, who, when his flock were in transports of despair, went forth only accompanied by one magistrate to meet the invader, and endeavour to turn his wrath side. The savage Huns were struck with awe by the fearless majesty of the unarmed old man. They conducted him safely to Attila, who listened to him with respect, and promised not to lead his people into Rome, provided a tribute should be paid to him. He then retreated, and, to the joy of all Europe, died on his way back to his native dominions.

But with the Huns the danger and suffering of Europe did not end. The happy state described in the Prophets as "dwelling safely, with none to make them afraid", was utterly unknown in Europe throughout the long break-up of the Roman Empire; and in a few more years the Franks were overrunning the banks of the Seine, and actually venturing to lay siege to the Roman walls of Paris itself. The fortifications were strong enough, but hunger began to do the work of the besiegers, and the garrison, unwarlike and untrained, began to despair. But Genevieve's courage and trust never failed; and finding no warriors willing to run the risk of going beyond the walls to obtain food for the women and children who were perishing around them, this brave shepherdess embarked alone in a little boat, and guiding it down the stream, landed beyond the Frankish camp, and repairing to the different Gallic cities, she implored them to send succour to the famished brethen. She obtained complete success. Probably the Franks had no means of obstructing the passage of the river, so that a convoy of boats could easily penetrate into the town, and at any rate they looked upon Genevieve as something sacred and inspired whom they durst not touch; probably as one of the battle maids in whom their own myths taught them to believe. One account indeed says that, instead of going alone to obtain help, Genevieve placed herself at the head of a forage party, and that the mere sight of her inspired bearing caused them to be allowed to enter and return in safety; but the boat version seems the more probable, since a single boat on a broad river would more easily elude the enemy than a troop of Gauls pass through their army.

But a city where all the valour resided in one woman could not long hold out, and in another inroad, when Genevieve was absent, Paris was actually seized by the Franks. Their leader, Hilperik, was absolutely afraid of what the mysteriously brave maiden might do to him, and commanded the gates of the city to be carefully guarded lest she should enter; but Geneviere learnt that some of the chief citizens were imprisoned, and that Hilperik intended their death, and nothing could withhold her from making an effort in their behalf. The Franks had made up their minds to settle, and not to destroy. They were not burning and slaying indiscriminately, but while despising the Romans, as they called the Gauls, for their cowardice, they were in awe of the superior civilization and the knowledge of arts. The country people had free access to the city, and Genevieve in her homely gown and veil passed by Hilperik's guards without being suspected of being more than an ordinary Gaulish village maid; and thus she fearlessly made her way, even to the old Roman halls, where the long-haired Hilperik was holding his wild carousal. Would that we knew more of that interview—one of the most striking that ever took place! We can only picture to ourselves the Roman tessellated pavement bestrewn with wine, bones, and fragments of the barbarous revelry. There were untamed Franks, their sunburnt hair tied up in a knot at the top of their heads, and falling down like a horse's tail, their faces close shaven, except two moustaches, and dressed in tight leather garments, with swords at their wide belts. Some slept, some feasted, some greased their long locks, some shouted out their favourite war songs around the table which was covered with the spoils of churches, and at their heads sat the wild, long-haired chieftain, who was a few years later driven away by his own followers for his excesses,—the whole scene was all that was abhorrent to a pure, devout, and faithful nature, most full of terror to a woman. Yet, there, in her strength, stood the peasant maiden, her heart full of trust and pity, her looks full of the power that is given by fearlessness of them that can kill the body. What she said we do not know—we only know that the barbarous Hilperik was overawed; he trembled before the expostulations of the brave woman, and granted all she asked—the safety of his prisoners, and mercy to the terrified inhabitants. No wonder that the people of Paris have ever since looked back to Genevieve as their protectress, and that in after ages she has grown to be the patron saint of the city.

She lived to see the son of Hilperik, Chlodweh, or, as he was more commonly called, Clovis, marry a Christian wife, Clotilda, and after a time became a Christian. She saw the foundation of the Cathedral of Notre-Dame, and of the two famous churches of St. Denys and of St. Martin of Tours, and gave her full share to the first efforts for bringing the rude and bloodthirsty conquerors to some knowledge of Christian faith, mercy, and purity. After a life of constant prayer and charity she died, three months after King Clovis, in the year 512, the eighty-ninth of her age.[5]

---

5   Perhaps the exploits of the Maid of Orleans were the most like those of Genevieve, but they are not here added to our collection of "Golden Deeds", because the Maid's belief that she was directly inspired removes them from the ordinary class. Alas! The English did not treat her as Hilperik treated Genevieve.

Leo the Slave

A. D. 533

THE Franks had fully gained possession of all the north of Gaul, except Brittany. Chlodweh had made them Christians in name, but they still remained horribly savage—and the life of the Gauls under them was wretched. The Burgundians and Visigoths who had peopled the southern and eastern provinces were far from being equally violent. They had entered on their settlements on friendly terms, and even showed considerable respect for the Roman-Gallic senators, magistrates, and higher clergy, who all remained unmolested in their dignities and riches. Thus it was that Gregory, Bishop of Langres, was a man of high rank and consideration in the Burgundian kingdom, whence the Christian Queen Clotilda had come; and even after the Burgundians had been subdued by the four sons of Chlodweh, he continued a rich and prosperous man.

After one of the many quarrels and reconciliations between these fierce brethren, there was an exchange of hostages for the observance of the terms of the treaty. These were not taken from among the Franks, who were too proud to submit to captivity, but from among the Gaulish nobles, a much more convenient arrangement to the Frankish kings, who cared for the life of a "Roman" infinitely less than even for the life of a Frank. Thus many young men of senatorial families were exchanged between the domains of Theodrik to the south, and of Hildebert to the northward, and quartered among Frankish chiefs, with whom at first they had nothing more to endure than the discomfort of living as guests with such rude and coarse barbarians. But ere long fresh quarrels broke out between Theodrik and Hildebert, and the unfortunate hostages were at once turned into slaves. Some of them ran away if they were near the frontier, but Bishop Gregory was in the utmost anxiety about his young nephew Attalus, who had been last heard of as being placed under the charge of a Frank who lived between Treves and Metz. The Bishop sent emissaries to make secret enquiries, and they brought word that the unfortunate youth had indeed been reduced to slavery, and was made to keep his master's herds of horses. Upon this the uncle again sent off his messengers with presents for the ransom of

Attalus, but the Frank rejected them, saying, "One of such high race can only be redeemed for ten pounds' weight of gold."

This was beyond the Bishop's means, and while he was considering how to raise the sum, the slaves were all lamenting for their young lord, to whom they were much attached, till one of them, named Leo, the cook to the household, came to the Bishop, saying to him, "If thou wilt give me leave to go, I will deliver him from captivity." The Bishop replied that he gave free permission, and the slave set off for Treves, and there watched anxiously for an opportunity of gaining access to Attalus; but though the poor young man—no longer daintily dressed, bathed, and perfumed, but ragged and squalid—might be seen following his herds of horses, he was too well watched for any communication to be held with him. Then Leo went to a person, probably of Gallic birth, and said, "Come with me to this barbarian's house, and there sell me for a slave. Thou shalt have the money, I only ask thee to help me thus far."

Both repaired to the Frank's abode, the chief among a confused collection of clay and timber huts intended for shelter during eating and sleeping. The Frank looked at the slave, and asked him what he could do.

"I can dress whatever is eaten at lordly tables," replied Leo. "I am afraid of no rival; I only tell thee the truth when I say that if thou wouldst give a feast to the king, I would send it up in the neatest manner."

"Ha!" said the barbarian, "the Sun's day is coming—I shall invite my kinsmen and friends. Cook me such a dinner as may amaze them, and make then say, 'We saw nothing better in the king's house.'"

"Let me have plenty of poultry, and I will do according to my master's bidding," returned Leo.

Accordingly, he was purchased for twelve gold pieces, and on the Sunday (as Bishop Gregory of Tours, who tells the story, explains that the barbarians called the Lord's day) he produced a banquet after the most approved Roman fashion, much to the surprise and delight of the Franks, who had never tasted such delicacies before, and complimented their host upon them all the evening. Leo gradually became a great favourite, and was placed in authority over the other slaves, to whom he gave out their daily portions of broth and meat; but from the first he had not shown any recognition of Attalus, and had signed to him that they must be strangers to one another. A whole year had passed away in this manner, when one day Leo wandered, as if for pastime, into the plain where Attalus was watching the horses, and sitting down on the ground at some paces off, and with his back towards his young master, so that they might not be seen together, he said, "This is the time for thoughts of home! When thou hast led the horses to the stable to-night, sleep not. Be ready at the first call!"

That day the Frank lord was entertaining a large number of guests, among them his daughter's husband, a jovial young man, given to jesting.

On going to rest he fancied he should be thirsty at night and called Leo to set a pitcher of hydromel by his bedside. As the slave was setting it down, the Frank looked slyly from under his eyelids, and said in joke, "Tell me, my father-in-law's trusty man, wilt not thou some night take one of those horses, and run away to thine own home?"

"Please God, it is what I mean to do this very night," answered the Gaul, so undauntedly that the Frank took it as a jest, and answered, "I shall look out that thou dost not carry off anything of mine," and then Leo left him, both laughing.

All were soon asleep, and the cook crept out to the stable, where Attalus usually slept among the horses. He was broad awake now, and ready to saddle the two swiftest; but he had no weapon except a small lance, so Leo boldly went back to his master's sleeping hut, and took down his sword and shield, but not without awaking him enough to ask who was moving. "It is I—Leo," was the answer, "I have been to call Attalus to take out the horses early. He sleeps as hard as a drunkard." The Frank went to sleep again, quite satisfied, and Leo, carrying out the weapons, soon made Attalus feel like a free man and a noble once more. They passed unseen out of the enclosure, mounted their horses, and rode along the great Roman road from Treves as far as the Meuse, but they found the bridge guarded, and were obliged to wait till night, when they cast their horses loose and swam the river, supporting themselves on boards that they found on the bank. They had as yet had no food since the supper at their master's, and were thankful to find a plum tree in the wood, with fruit, to refresh them in some degree, before they lay down for the night. The next morning they went on in the direction of Rheims, carefully listening whether there were any sounds behind, until, on the broad hard-paved causeway, they actually heard the trampling of horses. Happily a bush was near, behind which they crept, with their naked swords before them, and here the riders actually halted for a few moments to arrange their harness. Men and horses were both those they feared, and they trembled at hearing one say, "Woe is me that those rogues have made off, and have not been caught! On my salvation, if I catch them, I will have one hung and the other chopped into bits!" It was no small comfort to hear the trot of the horses resumed, and soon dying away in the distance. That same night the two faint, hungry, weary travellers, footsore and exhausted, came stumbling into Rheims, looking about for some person still awake to tell them the way to the house of the Priest Paul, a friend of Attalus' uncle. They found it just as the church bell was ringing for matins, a sound that must have seemed very like home to these members of an episcopal household. They knocked, and in the morning twilight met the Priest going to his earliest Sunday morning service.

Leo told his young master's name, and how they had escaped, and the

Priest's first exclamation was a strange one: "My dream is true. This very night I saw two doves, one white and one black, who came and perched on my hand."

The good man was overjoyed, but he scrupled to give them any food, as it was contrary to the Church's rules for the fast to be broken before mass; but the travellers were half dead with hunger, and could only say, "The good Lord pardon us, for, saving the respect due to His day, we must eat something, since this is the forth day since we have touched bread or meat." The Priest upon this gave them some bread and wine, and after hiding them carefully, went to church, hoping to avert suspicion; but their master was already at Rheims, making strict search for them, and learning that Paul the Priest was a friend of the Bishop of Langres, he went to church, and there questioned him closely. But the Priest succeeded in guarding his secret, and though he incurred much danger, as the Salic law was very severe against concealers of runaway slaves, he kept Attalus and Leo for two days till the search was blown over, and their strength was restored, so that they could proceed to Langres. There they were welcomed like men risen from the dead; the Bishop wept on the neck of Attalus, and was ready to receive Leo as a slave no more, but a friend and deliverer.

A few days after Leo was solemnly led to the church. Every door was set open as a sign that he might henceforth go whithersoever he would. Bishop Gregorus took him by the hand, and, standing before the Archdeacon, declared that for the sake of the good services rendered by his slave, Leo, he set him free, and created him a Roman citizen.

Then the Archdeacon read a writing of manumission. "Whatever is done according to the Roman law is irrevocable. According to the constitution of the Emperor Constantine, of happy memory, and the edict that declares that whosoever is manumitted in church, in the presence of the bishops, priests, and deacons, shall become a Roman citizen under the protection of the Church: from this day Leo becomes a member of the city, free to go and come where he will as if he had been born of free parents. From this day forward, he is exempt from all subjection of servitude, of all duty of a freed-man, all bond of clientship. He is and shall be free, with full and entire freedom, and shall never cease to belong to the body of Roman citizens."

At the same time Leo was endowed with lands, which raised him to the rank of what the Franks called a Roman proprietor—the highest reward in the Bishop's power for the faithful devotion that had incurred such dangers in order to rescue the young Attalus from his miserable bondage.

Somewhat of the same kind of faithfulness was shown early in the nineteenth century by Ivan Simonoff, a soldier servant belonging to Major Kascambo, an officer in the Russian army, who was made prisoner by one of the wild tribes of the Caucasus. But though the soldier's attachment to his master was quite as brave and disinterested as that of the Gallic slave, yet he was far from being equally blameless in the means he employed, and if his were a golden deed at all, it was mixed with much of iron.

Major Kascambo, with a guard of fifty Cossacks, was going to take the command of the Russian outpost of Lars, one of the forts by which the Russian Czars have slowly been carrying on the aggressive warfare that has nearly absorbed into their vast dominions all the mountains between the Caspian and Black seas. On his way he was set upon by seven hundred horsemen of the savage and independent tribe of Tchetchenges. There was a sharp fight, more than half his men were killed, and he with the rest made a rampart of the carcasses of their horses, over which they were about to fire their last shots, when the Tchetchenges made a Russian deserter call out to the Cossacks that they would let them all escape provided they would give up their officer. Kascambo on this came forward and delivered himself into their hands; while the remainder of the troops galloped off. His servant, Ivan, with a mule carrying his baggage, had been hidden in a ravine, and now, instead of retreating with the Cossacks, came to join his master. All the baggage was, however, instantly seized and divided among the Tchetchenges; nothing was left but a guitar, which they threw scornfully to the Major. He would have let it lie, but Ivan picked it up, and insisted on keeping it. "Why be dispirited?" he said; "the God of the Russians is great, it is the interest of the robbers to save you, they will do you no harm."

Scouts brought word that the Russian outposts were alarmed, and that troops were assembling to rescue the officer. Upon this the seven hundred broke up into small parties, leaving only ten men on foot to conduct the prisoners, whom they forced to take off their iron-shod boots and walk barefoot over stones and thorns, till the Major was so exhausted that they were obliged to drag him by cords fastened to his belt.

After a terrible journey, the prisoners were placed in a remote village, where the Major had heavy chains fastened to his hands and feet, and another to his neck, with a huge block of oak as a clog at the other end; they half-starved him, and made him sleep on the bare ground of the hut in which he lodged. The hut belonged to a huge, fierce old man of sixty named Ibrahim, whose son had been killed in a skirmish with the Russians. This man, together with his son's widow, were continually trying to revenge themselves on their captive. The only person who showed him any kindness was his little grandson, a child of seven years old, called Mamet, who often caressed him, and brought him food by stealth. Ivan was also in the same hut, but less heavily ironed than his master, and able to attempt a few alleviations for his wretched condition. An interpreter brought the Major a sheet of paper and a reed pen, and commanded him to write to his friends that he might be ransomed for 10,000 roubles, but that, if the whole sum were not paid, he would be put to death. He obeyed, but he knew that his friends could not possibly raise such a sum, and his only hope was in the government, which had once ransomed a colonel who had fallen into the hands of the same tribe.

These Tchetchenges professed to be Mahometans, but their religion sat very loose upon them, and they were utter barbarians. One piece of respect they paid the Major's superior education was curious–they made him judge in all the disputes that arose. The houses in the village were hollowed out underground, and the walls only raised three or four feet, and then covered by a flat roof, formed of beaten clay, where the inhabitants spent much of their time. Kascambo was every now and then brought, in all his chains, to the roof of the hut, which served as a tribunal whence he was expected to dispense justice. For instance, a man had commissioned his neighbour to pay five roubles to a person in another valley, but the messenger's horse having died by the way, a claim was set up to the roubles to make up for it. Both parties collected all their friends, and a bloody quarrel was about to take place, when they agreed to refer the question to the prisoner, who was accordingly set upon his judgment seat.

"Pray," said he, "if, instead of giving you five roubles, your comrade had desired you to carry his greetings to his creditor, would not your horse have died all the same?"

"Most likely."

"Then what should you have done with the greetings? Should you have kept them in compensation? My sentence is that you should give back the roubles, and that your comrade gives you a greeting."

The whole assembly approved the decision, and the man only grumbled out, as he gave back the money, "I knew I should lose it, if that dog of a Christian meddled with it."

All this respect, however, did not avail to procure any better usage for the unfortunate judge, whose health was suffering severely under his privations. Ivan, however, had recommended himself in the same way as Leo, by his perfections as a cook, and moreover he was a capital buffoon. His fetters were sometimes taken off that he might divert the villagers by his dances and strange antics while his master played the guitar. Sometimes they sang Russian songs together to the instrument, and on these occasions the Major's hands were released that he might play on it; but one day he was unfortunately heard playing in his chains for his own amusement, and from that time he was never released from his fetters.

In the course of a year, three urgent letters had been sent; but no notice was taken of them, and Ivan began to despair of aid from home, and set himself to work. His first step was to profess himself a Mahometan. He durst not tell his master till the deed was done, and then Kascambo was infinitely shocked; but the act did not procure Ivan so much freedom as he had hoped. He was, indeed, no longer in chains, but he was evidently distrusted, and was so closely watched, that the only way in which he could communicate with his master was when they were set to sing together, when they chanted out question and answer in Russ, unsuspected, to the tune of their national airs. He was taken on an expedition against the Russians, and very nearly killed by the suspicious Tchetchenges on one side, and by the Cossacks on the other, as a deserter. He saved a young man of the tribe from drowning; but though he thus earned the friendship of the family, the rest of the villagers hated and dreaded him all the more, since he had not been able to help proving himself a man of courage, instead of the feeble buffoon he had tried to appear.

Three months after this expedition, another took place; but Ivan was not allowed even to know of it. He saw preparations making, but nothing was said to him; only one morning he found the village entirely deserted by all the young men, and as he wandered round it, the aged ones would not speak to him. A child told him that his father had meant to kill him, and on the roof of her house stood the sister of the man he had saved, making signals of great terror, and pointing towards Russia. Home he went and found that, besides old Ibrahim, his master was watched by a warrior, who had been prevented by an intermitting fever from joining the expedition. He was convinced that if the tribe returned unsuccessful, the murder of both himself and his master was certain; but he resolved not to fly alone, and as he busied himself in preparing the meal, he sung the burden of a Russian ballad, intermingled with words of encouragement for his master:—

> The time is come;
>   Hai Luli!
> The time is come,
>   Hai Luli!
> Our woe is at an end,
>   Hai Luli!
> Or we die at once!
>   Hai Luli!
> To-morrow, to-morrow,
>   Hai Luli!
> We are off for a town,
>   Hai Luli!
> For a fine, fine town,
>   Hai Luli!
> But I name no names,
>   Hai Luli!
> Courage, courage, master dear,
>   Hai Luli!

Never, never, despair,
  Hai Luli!
For the God of the Russians is great,
  Hai Luli!

Poor Kascambo, broken down, sick, and despairing, only muttered, "Do as you please, only hold your peace!"

Ivan's cookery incited the additional guard to eat so much supper, that he brought on a severe attack of his fever, and was obliged to go home; but old Ibrahim, instead of going to bed, sat down on a log of wood opposite the prisoner, and seemed resolved to watch him all night. The woman and child went to bed in the inner room, and Ivan signed to his master to take the guitar, and began to dance. The old man's axe was in an open cupboard at the other end of the room, and after many gambols and contortions, during which the Major could hardly control his fingers to touch the strings, Ivan succeeded in laying his hands upon it, just when the old man was bending over the fire to mend it. Then, as Ibrahim desired that the music should cease, he cut him down with a single blow, on his own hearth. And the daughter-in-law coming out to see what had happened, he slew her with the same weapon. And then, alas! in spite of the commands, entreaties, and cries of his master, he dashed into the inner room, and killed the sleeping child, lest it should give the alarm. Kascambo, utterly helpless to save, fell almost fainting upon the bloody floor, and did not cease to reproach Ivan, who was searching the old man's pockets for the key of the fetters, but it was not there, nor anywhere else in the hut, and the irons were so heavy that escape was impossible in them. Ivan at last knocked off the clog and the chains on the wrist with the axe, but he could not break the chains round the legs, and could only fasten them as close as he could to hinder them clanking. Then securing all the provisions he could carry, and putting his master into his military cloak, obtaining also a pistol and dagger, they crept out, but not on the direct road. It was February, and the ground was covered with snow. All night they walked easily, but at noon the sun so softened it that they sank in at every step, and the Major's chains rendered each motion terrible labour. It was only on the second night that Ivan, with his axe, succeeded in breaking through the fastenings, and by that time the Major's legs were so swollen and stiffened that he could not move without extreme pain. However, he was dragged on through the wild mountain paths, and then over the plains for several days more, till they were on the confines of another tribe of Tchetchenges, who were overawed by Russia, and in a sort of unwilling alliance. Here, however, a sharp storm, and a fall into the water, completely finished Kascambo's strength, and he sank down on the snow, telling Ivan to go home and explain his fate, and give his last message to his mother.

"If you perish here," said Ivan, "trust me, neither your mother nor mine will ever see me again."

He covered his master with his cloak, gave him the pistol, and walked on to a hut, where he found a Tchetchenge man, and told him that here was a means of obtaining two hundred roubles. He had only to shelter the major as a guest for three days, whilst Ivan himself went on to Mosdok, to procure the money, and bring back help for his master. The man was full of suspicion, but Ivan prevailed, and Kascambo was carried into the village nearly dying, and was very ill all the time of his servant's absence. Ivan set off for the nearest Russian station, where he found some of the Cossacks who had been present when the major was taken. All eagerly subscribed to raise the two hundred roubles, but the Colonel would not let Ivan go back alone, as he had engaged to do, and sent a guard of Cossacks. This had nearly been fatal to the Major, for as soon as his host saw the lances, he suspected treachery, and dragging his poor sick guest to the roof of the house, he tied him up to a stake, and stood over him with a pistol, shouting to Ivan, "If you come nearer, I shall blow his brains out, and I have fifty cartridges more for my enemies, and the traitor who leads them."

"No traitor!" cried Ivan. "Here are the roubles. I have kept my word!"

"Let the Cossacks go back, or I shall fire."

Kascambo himself begged the officer to retire, and Ivan went back with the detachment, and returned alone. Even then the suspicious host made him count out the roubles at a hundred paces from the house, and at once ordered him out of sight; but then went up to the roof, and asked the Major's pardon for all this rough usage.

"I shall only recollect that you were my host, and kept your word," said Kascambo.

In a few hours more, Kascambo was in safety among his brother officers. Ivan was made a non-commissioned officer, and some months after was seen by the traveller who told the story, whistling the air of Hai Luli at his former master's wedding feast. He was even then scarcely twenty years old, and peculiarly quiet and soft in manners.

The Battle of the Blackwater
991

IN the evil days of King Ethelred the Unready, when the teaching of good King Alfred was fast fading away from the minds of his descendants, and self-indulgence was ruining the bold and hardy habits of the English, the fleet was allowed to fall into decay, and Danish ships again ventured to appear on the English coasts. The first Northmen who had ravaged England came eager for blood and plunder, and hating the sight of a Christian church as an insult to their gods, Thor and Odin; but the lapse of a hundred years had in some degree changed the temper of the North; and though almost every young man thought it due to his fame to have sailed forth as a sea rover, yet the attacks of these marauders might be bought off, and provided they had treasure to show for their voyage, they were willing to spare the lives and lands of the people of the coasts they visited.

King Ethelred and his cowardly, selfish Court were well satisfied with this expedient, and the tax called Danegeld was laid upon the people, in order to raise a fund for buying off the enemy. But there were still in England men of bolder and truer hearts, who held that bribery was false policy, merely inviting the enemy to come again and again, and that the only wise course would be in driving them back by English valour, and keeping the fleet in a condition to repel the "Long Serpent" ships before the foe could set foot upon the coast.

Among those who held this opinion was Brythnoth, Earl of Essex. He was of partly Danish descent himself, but had become a thorough Englishman, and had long and faithfully served the King and his father. He was a friend to the clergy, a founder of churches and convents, and his manor house of Hadleigh was a home of hospitality and charity. It would probably be a sort of huge farmyard, full of great barn-like buildings and sheds, all one story high; some of them serving for storehouses, and others for living-rooms and places of entertainment for his numerous servants and retainers, and for the guests of all degrees who gathered round him as the chief dispenser of justice in his East-Saxon earldom. When he heard the advice given and accepted that the Danes should be bribed, instead of being fought with, he made up his mind that he, at least, would try to raise up a nobler spirit, and, at the sacrifice of his own life, would show the effect of making a manful stand against them.

He made his will, and placed it in the hands of the Archbishop of Canterbury; and then, retiring to Hadleigh, he provided horses and arms, and caused all the young men in his earldom to be trained in warlike exercises, according to the good old English law, that every man should be provided with weapons and know the use of them.

The Danes sailed forth, in the year 991, with ninety-three vessels, the terrible "Long Serpents", carved with snakes' heads at the prow, and the stern finished as the gilded tail of the reptile; and many a lesser ship, meant for carrying plunder. The Sea King, Olaf (or Anlaff), was the leader; and as tidings came that their sails had been seen upon the North Sea, more earnest than ever rang out the petition in the Litany, "From the fury of the Northmen, good Lord, deliver us".

Sandwich and Ipswich made no defence, and were plundered; and the fleet then sailed into the mouth of the River Blackwater, as far as Maldon, where the ravagers landed, and began to collect spoil. When, however, they came back to their ships, they found that the tide would not yet serve them to re-embark; and upon the farther bank of the river bristled the spears of a body of warriors, drawn up in battle array, but in numbers far inferior to their own.

Anlaff sent a messenger, over the wooden bridge that crossed the river, to the Earl, who, he understood, commanded this small army. The brave old man, his grey hair hanging down beneath his helmet, stood, sword in hand, at the head of his warriors.

"Lord Earl," said the messenger, "I come to bid thee to yield to us thy treasure, for thy safety. Buy off the fight, and we will ratify a peace with gold."

"Hear, O thou sailor!" was Brythnoth's answer, "the reply of this people. Instead of Danegeld, thou shalt have from them the edge of the sword, and the point of the spear. Here stands an English Earl, who will defend his earldom and the lands of his King. Point and edge shall judge between us."

Back went the Dane with his message to Anlaff, and the fight began around the bridge, where the Danes long strove to force their way across, but were always driven back by the gallant East-Saxons. The tide had risen, and for some time the two armies only shot at one another with bows and arrows; but when it ebbed, leaving the salt-marshes dry, the stout old Earl's love of fair play overpowered his prudence, and he sent to offer the enemy a free passage, and an open field in which to measure their strength.

The numbers were too unequal; but the battle was long and bloody before the English could be overpowered. Brythnoth slew one of the chief Danish leaders with his own hand, but not without receiving a wound.

He was still able to fight on, though with ebbing strength and failing numbers. His hand was pierced by a dart; but a young boy at his side instantly withdrew it, and, launching it back again, slew the foe who had aimed it. Another Dane, seeing the Earl faint and sinking, advanced to plunder him of his ring and jewelled weapons; but he still had strength to lay the spoiler low with his battleaxe. This was his last blow; he gathered his strength for one last cheer to his brave men, and then, sinking on the ground, he looked up to heaven, exclaiming: "I thank thee, Lord of nations, for all the joys I have known on earth. Now, O mild Creator! have I the utmost need that Thou shouldst grant grace unto my soul, that my spirit may speed to Thee with peace, O King of angels! to pass into thy keeping. I sue to Thee that Thou suffer not the rebel spirits of hell to vex my parting soul!"

With these words he died; but an aged follower, of like spirit, stood over his corpse, and exhorted his fellows. "Our spirit shall be the hardier, and our soul the greater, the fewer our numbers become!" he cried. "Here lies our chief, the brave, the good, the much-loved lord, who has blessed us with many a gift. Old as I am, I will not yield, but avenge his death, or lay me at his side. Shame befall him that thinks to fly from such a field as this!"

Nor did the English warriors fly. Night came down, at last, upon the battlefield, and saved the lives of the few survivors; but they were forced to leave the body of their lord, and the Danes bore away with them his head as a trophy, and with it, alas! ten thousand pounds of silver from the King, who, in his sluggishness and weakness had left Brythnoth to fight and die unaided for the cause of the whole nation. One of the retainers, a minstrel in the happy old days of Hadleigh, who had done his part manfully in the battle, had heard these last goodly sayings of his master, and, living on to peaceful days, loved to rehearse them to the sound of his harp, and dwell on the glories of one who could die, but not be defeated.

Ere those better days had come, another faithful-hearted Englishman had given his life for his people. In the year 1012, a huge army, called from their leader, "Thorkill's Host", were overrunning Kent, and besieging Canterbury. The Archbishop Ælfeg was earnestly entreated to leave the city while yet there was time to escape; but he replied, "None but a hireling would leave his flock in time of danger;" and he supported the resolution of the inhabitants, so that they held out the city for twenty days; and as the wild Danes had very little chance against a well-walled town, they would probably have saved it, had not the gates been secretly opened to them by the traitorous Abbot Ælfman, whom Ælfeg had once himself saved, when accused of treason before the King.

The Danes slaughtered all whom they found in the streets, and the Archbishop's friends tried to keep him in the church, lest he should run upon his fate; but he broke from them, and, confronting the enemy, cried:

"Spare the guiltless! Is there glory in shedding such blood? Turn your wrath on me! It is I who have denounced your cruelty, have ransomed and re-clad your captive." The Danes seized upon him, and, after he had seen his cathedral burnt and his clergy slain, they threw him into a dungeon, whence he was told he could only come forth upon the payment of a heavy ransom.

His flock loved him, and would have striven to raise the sum; but, miserably used as they were by the enemy, and stripped by the exactions of the Danes, he would not consent that they should be asked for a further contribution on his account. After seven months' patience in his captivity, the Danish chiefs, who were then at Greenwich desired him to be brought into their camp, where they had just been holding a great feast. It was Easter Eve, and the quiet of that day of calm waiting was disturbed with their songs, and shouts of drunken revelry, as the chained Archbishop was led to the open space where the warriors sat and lay amid the remains of their rude repast. The leader then told him that they had agreed to let him off for his own share with a much smaller payment than had been demanded, provided he would obtain a largesse for them from the King, his master.

"I am not the man," he answered, "to provide Christian flesh for Pagan wolves;" and when again they repeated the demand, "Gold I have none to offer you, save the true wisdom of the knowledge of the living God." And he began, as he stood in the midst, to "reason to them of righteousness, temperance, and judgment to come."

They were mad with rage and drink. The old man's voice was drowned with shouts of "Gold, Bishop–give us gold!" The bones and cups that lay around were hurled at him, and he fell to the ground, with the cry, "O Chief Shepherd, guard Thine own children!" As he partly raised himself, axes were thrown at him; and, at last, a Dane, who had begun to love and listen to him in his captivity, deemed it mercy to give him a deathblow with an axe. The English maintained that Ælfeg had died to save his flock from cruel extortion, and held him as a saint and martyr, keeping his death day (the 19th of April) as a holiday; and when the Italian Archbishop of Canterbury (Lanfranc) disputed his right to be so esteemed, there was strong opposition and discontent. Indeed, our own Prayer Book still retains his name, under the altered form of St. Alphege; and surely no one better merits to be remembered, for having loved his people far better than himself.

Guzman El Bueno

1293

IN the early times of Spanish history, before the Moors had been expelled from the peninsula, or the blight of Western gold had enervated the nation, the old honour and loyalty of the Gothic race were high and pure, fostered by constant combats with a generous enemy. The Spanish Arabs were indeed the flower of the Mahometan races, endowed with the vigour and honour of the desert tribes, yet capable of culture and civilization, excelling all other nations of their time in science and art, and almost the equals of their Christian foes in the attributes of chivalry. Wars with them were a constant crusade, consecrated in the minds of the Spaniards as being in the cause of religion, and yet in some degree freed from savagery and cruelty by the respect exacted by the honourable character of the enemy, and by the fact that the civilization and learning of the Christian kingdoms were far more derived from the Moors than from the kindred nations of Europe.

By the close of the thirteenth century, the Christian kingdoms of Castille and Aragon were descending from their mountain fastnesses, and spreading over the lovely plains of the south, even to the Mediterranean coast, as one beautiful Moorish city after another yielded to the persevering advances of the children of the Goths; and in 1291 the nephew of our own beloved Eleanor of Castille, Sancho V. called El Bravo, ventured to invest the city of Tarifa.

This was the western buttress of the gate of the Mediterranean, the base of the northern Pillar of Hercules, and esteemed one of the gates of Spain. By it five hundred years previously had the Moorish enemy first entered Spain at the summons of Count Julian, under their leader Tarif-abu-Zearah, whose name was bestowed upon it in remembrance of his landing there. The form of the ground is said to be like a broken punch bowl, with the broken part towards the sea. The Moors had fortified the city with a surrounding wall and twenty-six towers, and had built a castle with a lighthouse on a small adjacent island, called Isla Verde, which they had connected with the city by a causeway. Their fortifications, always admirable, have existed ever since, and in 1811, another five hundred years after, were successfully defended against the French by a small force of British troops under the command of Colonel Hugh Gough, better known in his old age as the victor of Aliwal. The walls were then unable to support the weight of artillery, for which of course they had never been built, but were perfectly effective against escalade.

For six months King Sancho besieged Tarifa by land and sea, his fleet, hired from the Genoese, lying in the waters where the battle of Trafalgar was to be fought. The city at length yielded under stress of famine, but the King feared that he had no resources to enable him to keep it, and intended to dismantle and forsake it, when the Grand Master of the military order of Calatrava offered to undertake the defence with his knights for one year, hoping that some other noble would come forward at the end of that time and take the charge upon himself.

He was not mistaken. The noble who made himself responsible for this post of danger was a Leonese knight of high distinction, by name Alonso Perez de Guzman, already called El Bueno, or "The Good', from the high qualities he had manifested in the service of the late King, Don Alonso VI, by whom he had always stood when the present King, Don Sancho, was in rebellion. The offer was readily accepted, and the whole Guzman family removed to Tarifa, with the exception of the eldest son, who was in the train of the Infant Don Juan, the second son of the late King, who had always taken part with his father against his brother, and on Sancho's accession, continued his enmity, and fled to Portugal.

The King of Portugal, however, being requested by Sancho not to permit him to remain there, he proceeded to offer his services to the King of Morocco, Yusuf-ben-Yacoub, for whom he undertook to recover Tarifa, if 5000 horse were granted to him for the purpose. The force would have been most disproportionate for the attack of such a city as Tarifa, but Don Juan reckoned on means that he had already found efficacious; when he had obtained the surrender of Zamora to his father by threatening to put to death a child of the lady in command of the fortress.

Therefore, after summoning Tarifa at the head of his 5000 Moors, he led forth before the gates the boy who had been confided to his care, and declared that unless the city were yielded instantly, Guzman should behold the death of his own son at his hand! Before, he had had to deal with a weak woman on a question of divided allegiance. It was otherwise here. The point was whether the city should be made over to the enemies of the faith and country, whether the plighted word of a loyal knight should be broken. The boy was held in the grasp of the cruel prince, stretching out his hands and weeping as he saw his father upon the walls. Don Alonso's eyes, we are told, filled with tears as he cast one long, last look at his first-born, whom he might not save except at the expense of his truth and honour.

The struggle was bitter, but he broke forth at last in these words: "I did not beget a son to be made use of against my country, but that he should serve her against her foes. Should Don Juan put him to death, he will but confer honour on me, true life on my son, and on himself eternal shame in this world and everlasting wrath after death. So far am I from yielding this place or betraying my trust, that in case he should want a weapon for his cruel purpose, there goes my knife!"

He cast the knife in his belt over the walls, and returned to the Castle where, commanding his countenance, he sat down to table with his wife. Loud shouts of horror and dismay almost instantly called him forth again. He was told that Don Juan had been seen to cut the boy's throat in a transport of blind rage. "I thought the enemy had broken in," he calmly said, and went back again.

The Moors themselves were horrorstruck at the atrocity of their ally, and as the siege was hopeless they gave it up; and Don Juan, afraid and ashamed to return to Morocco, wandered to the Court of Granada.

King Sancho was lying sick at Alcala de Henares when the tidings of the price of Guzman's fidelity reached him. Touched to the depths of his heart he wrote a letter to his faithful subject, comparing his sacrifice to that of Abraham, confirming to him the surname of Good, lamenting his own inability to come and offer his thanks and regrets, but entreating Guzman's presence at Alcala.

All the way thither, the people thronged to see the man true to his word at such a fearful cost. The Court was sent out to meet him, and the King, after embracing him, exclaimed, "Here learn, ye knights, what are exploits of virtue. Behold your model."

Lands and honours were heaped upon Alonso de Guzman, and they were not a mockery of his loss, for he had other sons to inherit them. He was the staunch friend of Sancho's widow and son in a long and perilous minority, and died full of years and honours. The lands granted to him were those of Medina Sidonia which lie between the Rivers Guadiana and Guadalquivir, and they have ever since been held by his descendants, who still bear the honoured name of Guzman, witnessing that the man who gave the life of his first-born rather than break his faith to the King has left a posterity as noble and enduring as any family in Europe.

Faithful Till Death

1308

ONE of the ladies most admired by the ancient Romans was Arria, the wife of Cæcina Pætus, a Roman who was condemned by the Emperor Claudius to become his own executioner. Seeing him waver, his wife, who was resolved to be with him in death as in life, took the dagger from his hand, plunged it into her own breast, and with her last strength held it out to him, gasping out, "It is not painful, my Pætus."

Such was heathen faithfulness even to death; and where the teaching of Christianity had not forbidden the taking away of life by one's own hand, perhaps wifely love could not go higher. Yet Christian women have endured a yet more fearful ordeal to their tender affection, watching, supporting, and finding unfailing fortitude to uphold the sufferer in agonies that must have rent their hearts.

Natalia was the fair young wife of Adrian, an officer at Nicomedia, in the guards of the Emperor Galerius Maximianus, and only about twenty-eight years old. Natalia was a Christian, but her husband remained a pagan, until, when he was charged with the execution of some martyrs, their constancy, coupled with the testimony of his own wife's virtues, triumphed over his unbelief, and he confessed himself likewise a Christian. He was thrown into prison, and sentenced to death, but he prevailed on his gaoler to permit him to leave the dungeon for a time, that he might see his wife. The report came to Natalia that he was no longer in prison, and she threw herself on the ground, lamenting aloud: "Now will men point at me, and say, 'Behold the wife of the coward and apostate, who, for fear of death, hath denied his God.'"

"Oh, thou noble and strong-hearted woman," said Adrian's voice at the door, "I bless God that I am not unworthy of thee. Open the door that I may bid thee farewell."

But this was not the last farewell, though he duly went back to the prison; for when, the next day, he had been cruelly scourged and tortured before the tribunal, Natalia, with her hair cut short, and wearing the disguise of a youth, was there to tend and comfort him. She took him in her arms saying, "Oh, light of mine eyes, and husband of mine heart, blessed art thou, who art chosen to suffer for Christ's sake."

On the following day, the tyrant ordered that Adrian's limbs should be one by one struck off on a blacksmith's anvil, and lastly his head. And still it was his wife who held him and sustained him through all and, ere the last stroke of the executioner, had received his last breath. She took up one of the severed hands, kissed it, and placed it in her bosom, and escaping to Byzantium, there spent her life in widowhood.

Nor among these devoted wives should we pass by Gertrude, the wife of Rudolf, Baron von der Wart, a Swabian nobleman, who was so ill-advised as to join in a conspiracy of Johann of Hapsburg, in 1308, against the Emperor, Albrecht I, the son of the great and good Rudolf of Hapsburg.

This Johann was the son of the Emperor's brother Rudolf, a brave knight who had died young, and Johann had been brought up by a Baron called Walther von Eschenbach, until, at nineteen years old, he went to his uncle to demand his father's inheritance. Albrecht was a rude and uncouth man, and refused disdainfully the demand, whereupon the noblemen of the disputed territory stirred up the young prince to form a plot against him, all having evidently different views of the lengths to which they would proceed. This was just at the time that the Swiss, angry at the overweening and oppressive behaviour of Albrecht's governors, were first taking up arms to maintain that they owed no duty to him as Duke of Austria, but merely as Emperor of Germany. He set out on his way to chastise them as rebels, taking with him a considerable train, of whom his nephew Johann was one. At Baden, Johann, as a last experiment, again applied for his inheritance, but by way of answer, Albrecht held out a wreath of flowers, telling him they better became his years than did the cares of government. He burst into tears, threw the wreath upon the ground, and fed his mind upon the savage purpose of letting his uncle find out what he was fit for.

By and by, the party came to the banks of the Reuss, where there was no bridge, and only one single boat to carry the whole across. The first to cross were the Emperor with one attendant, besides his nephew and four of the secret partisans of Johann. Albrecht's son Leopold was left to follow with the rest of the suite, and the Emperor rode on towards the hills of his home, towards the Castle of Hapsburg, where his father's noble qualities had earned the reputation which was the cause of all the greatness of the line. Suddenly his nephew rode up to him, and while one of the conspirators seized the bridle of his horse, exclaimed, "Will you now restore my inheritance?" and wounded him in the neck. The attendant fled; Der Wart, who had never thought murder was to be a part of the scheme, stood aghast, but the other two fell on the unhappy Albrecht, and each gave him a mortal wound, and then all five fled in different directions. The whole horrible affair took place full in view of Leopold and the army on the other side of the river, and when it became possible for any of them to cross, they found that the Emperor had just expired, with his head in the lap of a poor woman.

The murderers escaped into the Swiss mountains, expecting shelter there; but the stout, honest men of the cantons were resolved not to have any connection with assassins, and refused to protect them. Johann himself, after long and miserable wanderings in disguise, bitterly repented, owned his crime to the Pope, and was received into a convent; Eschenbach escaped, and lived fifteen years as a cowherd. The others all fell into the hands of the sons and daughters of Albrecht, and woeful was the revenge that was taken upon them, and upon their innocent families and retainers.

That Leopold, who had seen his father slain before his eyes, should have been deeply incensed, was not wonderful, and his elder brother Frederick, as Duke of Austria, was charged with the execution of justice; but both brothers were horribly savage and violent in their proceedings, and their sister Agnes surpassed them in her atrocious thirst for vengeance. She was the wife of the King of Hungary, very clever and discerning, and also supposed to be very religious, but all better thoughts were swept away by her furious passion. She had nearly strangled Eschenbach's infant son with her own bare hands, when he was rescued from her by her own soldiers, and when she was watching the beheading of sixty-three vassals of another of the murderers, she repeatedly exclaimed, "Now I bathe in May dew." Once, indeed, she met with a stern rebuke. A hermit, for whom she had offered to build a convent, answered her, "Woman, God is not served by shedding innocent blood and by building convents out of the plunder of families, but by compassion and forgiveness of injuries."

Rudolf von der Wart received the horrible sentence of being broken on the wheel. On his trial the Emperor's attendant declared that Der Wart had attacked Albert with his dagger, and the cry, "How long will ye suffer this carrion to sit on horseback?" but he persisted to the last that he had been taken by surprise by the murder. However, there was no mercy for him; and, by the express command of Queen Agnes, after he had been bound upon one wheel, and his limbs broken by heavy blows from the executioner, he was fastened to another wheel, which was set upon a pole, where he was to linger out the remaining hours of his life. His young wife, Gertrude, who had clung to him through all the trial, was torn away and carried off to the Castle of Kyburg; but she made her escape at dusk, and found her way, as night came on, to the spot where her husband hung still living upon the wheel. That night of agony was described in a letter ascribed to Gertrude herself. The guard left to watch fled at her approach, and she prayed beneath the scaffold, and then, heaping some heavy logs of wood together, was able to climb up near enough to embrace him and stroke back the hair from his face, whilst he entreated her to leave him, lest she should be found there, and fall under the cruel revenge of the Queen, telling her that thus it would be possible to increase his suffering.

"I will die with you," she said, "tis for that I came, and no power shall force me from you;" and she prayed for the one mercy she hoped for, speedy death for her husband.

In Mrs. Hemans' beautiful words–

> "'And bid me not depart,' she cried,
>   'My Rudolf, say not so;
> This is no time to quit thy side,
>   Peace, peace, I cannot go!
> Hath the world aught for me to fear
>   When death is on thy brow?
> The world! what means it? Mine is here!
>   I will not leave thee now.
> "'I have been with thee in thine hour
>   Of glory and of bliss;
> Doubt not its memory's living power
>   To strengthen me through this.
> And thou, mine honour'd love and true,
>   Bear on, bear nobly on;
> We have the blessed heaven in view,
>   Whose rest shall soon be won.'"

When day began to break, the guard returned, and Gertrude took down her stage of wood and continued kneeling at the foot of the pole. Crowds of people came to look, among them the wife of one of the officials, whom Gertrude implored to intercede that her husband's sufferings might be ended; but though this might not be, some pitied her, and tried to give her wine and confections, which she could not touch. The priest came and exhorted Rudolf to confess the crime, but with a great effort he repeated his former statement of innocence.

A band of horsemen rode by. Among them was the young Prince Leopold and his sister Agnes herself, clad as a knight. They were very angry at the compassion shown by the crowd, and after frightfully harsh language commanded that Gertrude should be dragged away; but one of the nobles interceded for her, and when she had been carried away to a little distance her entreaties were heard, and she was allowed to break away and come back to her husband. The priest blessed Gertrude, gave her his hand and said, "Be faithful unto death, and God will give you the crown of life," and she was no further molested.

Night came on, and with it a stormy wind, whose howling mingled with the voice of her prayers, and whistled in the hair of the sufferer. One of the guard brought her a cloak. She climbed on the wheel, and spread the covering over her husband's limbs; then fetched some water in her shoe, and moistened his lips with it, sustaining him above all with her prayers, and exhortations to look to the joys beyond. He had ceased to try to send her away, and thanked her for the comfort she gave him. And still she watched when morning came again, and noon passed over her, and it was verging to evening, when for the last time he moved his head; and she raised herself so as to be close to him. With a smile, he murmured, "Gertrude, this is faithfulness till death," and died. She knelt down to thank God for having enabled her to remain for that last breath–

> "While even as o'er a martyr's grave
>   She knelt on that sad spot,
> And, weeping, blessed the God who gave
>   Strength to forsake it not!"

She found shelter in a convent at Basle, where she spent the rest of her life in a quiet round of prayer and good works; till the time came when her widowed heart should find its true rest for ever.

What Is Better Than Slaying a Dragon

1332

THE next story we have to tell is so strange and wild, that it would seem better to befit the cloudy times when history had not yet been disentangled from fable, than the comparatively clear light of the fourteenth century.

It took place in the island of Rhodes. This Greek isle had become the home of the Knights of St. John, or Hospitaliers, an order of sworn brethren who had arisen at the time of the Crusades. At first they had been merely monks, who kept open house for the reception of the poor penniless pilgrims who arrived at Jerusalem in need of shelter, and often of nursing and healing. The good monks not only fed and housed them, but did their best to cure the many diseases that they would catch in the toilsome journey in that feverish climate; and thus it has come to pass that the word hospitium, which in Latin only means an inn, has, in modern languages, given birth, on the one hand, to hotel, or lodging house, on the other, to hospital, or house of healing. The Hospital at Jerusalem was called after St. John the Almoner, a charitable Bishop of old, and the brethren were Hospitaliers. By and by, when the first Crusade was over, and there was a great need of warriors to maintain the Christian cause in Jerusalem, the Hospitaliers thought it a pity that so many strong arms should be prevented from exerting themselves, by the laws that forbade the clergy to do battle, and they obtained permission from the Pope to become warriors as well as monks. They were thus all in one–knights, priests, and nurses; their monasteries were both castles and hospitals; and the sick pilgrim or wounded Crusader was sure of all the best tendance and medical care that the times could afford, as well as of all the ghostly comfort and counsel that he might need, and, if he recovered, he was escorted safely down to the seashore by a party strong enough to protect him from the hordes of robber Arabs. All this was for charity's sake, and without reward. Surely the constitution of the Order was as golden as its badge–the eight-pointed cross—which the brethren wore round their neck. They wore it also in white over their shoulder upon a black mantle. And the knights who had been admitted to the full honours of the Order had a scarlet surcoat, likewise with the white cross, over their armour. The whole brotherhood was under the command of a Grand Master, who was elected in a chapter of all the knights, and to whom all vowed to render implicit obedience.

Good service in all their three capacities had been done by the Order as long as the Crusaders were able to keep a footing in the Holy Land; but they were driven back step by step, and at last, in 1291, their last stronghold at Acre was taken, after much desperate fighting, and the remnant of the Hospitaliers sailed away to the isle of Cyprus, where, after a few years, they recruited their forces, and , in 1307, captured the island of Rhodes, which had been a nest of Greek and Mahometan pirates. Here they remained, hoping for a fresh Crusade to recover the Holy Sepulchre, and in the meantime fulfilling their old mission as the protectors and nurses of the weak. All the Mediterranean Sea was infested by corsairs from the African coast and the Greek isles, and these brave knights, becoming sailors as well as all they had been before, placed their red flag with its white cross at the masthead of many a gallant vessel that guarded the peaceful traveller, hunted down the cruel pirate, and brought home his Christian slave, rescued from labouring at the oar, to the Hospital for rest and tendance. Or their treasures were used in redeeming the captives in the pirate cities. No knight of St. John might offer any ransom for himself save his sword and scarf; but for the redemption of their poor fellow Christians their wealth was ready, and many a captive was released from toiling in Algiers or Tripoli, or still worse, from rowing the pirate vessels, chained to the oar, between the decks, and was restored to health and returned to his friends, blessing the day he had been brought into the curving harbour of Rhodes, with the fine fortified town of churches and monastaries.

Some eighteen years after the conquest of Rhodes, the whole island was filled with dismay by the ravages of an enormous creature, living in a morass at the foot of Mount St. Stephen, about two miles from the city of Rhodes. Tradition calls it a dragon, and whether it were a crocodile or a serpent is uncertain. There is reason to think that the monsters of early creation were slow in becoming extinct, or it is not impossible that either a crocodile or a python might have been brought over by storms or currents from Africa, and have grown to a more formidable size than usual in solitude among the marshes, while the island was changing owners. The reptile, whatever it might be, was the object of extreme dread; it devoured sheep and cattle, when they came down to the water, and even young shepherd boys were missing. And the pilgrimage to the Chapel of St. Stephen, on the hill above its lair, was especially a service of danger, for pilgrims were believed to be snapped up by the dragon before they could mount the hill.

Several knights had gone out to attempt the destruction of the creature, but not one had returned, and at last the Grand Master, Helion de Ville-neuve, forbade any further attacks to be made. The dragon is said to have been covered with scales that were perfectly impenetrable either to arrows or any cutting weapon; and the severe loss that encounters with him had cost the Order, convinced the Grand Master that he must be let alone.

However, a young knight, named Dieudonné de Gozon, was by no means willing to acquiesce in the decree; perhaps all the less because it came after he had once gone out in quest of the monster, but had returned, by his own confession, without striking a blow. He requested leave of absence, and went home for a time to his father's castle of Gozon, in Languedoc; and there he caused a model of the monster to be made. He had observed that the scales did not protect the animal's belly, though it was almost impossible to get a blow at it, owing to its tremendous teeth, and the furi-ous strokes of its length of tail. He therefore caused this part of his model to be made hollow, and filled with food, and obtaining two fierce young mastiffs, he trained them to fly at the under side of the monster, while he mounted his warhorse, and endeavoured to accustom it likewise to attack the strange shape without swerving.

When he thought the education of horse and dogs complete, he returned to Rhodes; but fearing to be prevented from carrying out his design, he did not land at the city, but on a remote part of the coast, whence he made his way to the chapel of St. Stephen. There, after having recommended himself to God, he left his two French squires, desiring them to return home if he were slain, but to watch and come to him if he killed the dragon, or were only hurt by it. He then rode down the hillside, and towards the haunt of the dragon. It roused itself at his advance, and at first he charged it with his lance, which was perfectly useless against the scales. His horse was quick to perceive the difference between the true and the false monster, and started back, so that he was forced to leap to the ground; but the two dogs were more staunch, and sprang at the animal, whilst their master struck at it with his sword, but still without reaching a vulnerable part, and a blow from the tail had thrown him down, and the dragon was turning upon him, when the movement left the undefended belly exposed. Both mastiffs fastened on it at once, and the knight, regaining his feet, thrust his sword into it. There was a death grapple, and finally the servants, coming down the hill, found their knight lying apparently dead under the carcass of the dragon. When they had extricated him, taken off his helmet, and sprinkled him with water, he recovered, and presently was led into the city amid the ecstatic shouts of the whole populace, who conducted him in triumph to the palace of the Grand Master.

We have seen how Titus Manlius was requited by his father for his breach of discipline. It was somewhat in the same manner that Helion de

Villeneuve received Dieudonné. We borrow Schiller's beautiful version of the conversation that took place, as the young knight, pale, with his black mantle rent, his shining armour dinted, his scarlet surcoat stained with blood, came into the Knights' Great Hall.

> "Severe and grave was the Master's brow,
> Quoth he, 'A hero bold art thou,
> By valour 't is that knights are known;
> A valiant spirit hast thou shown;
> But the first duty of a knight,
> Now tell, who vows for CHRIST to fight
> And bears the Cross on his coat of mail.'
> The listeners all with fear grew pale,
> While, bending lowly, spake the knight,
>   His cheeks with blushes burning,
> 'He who the Cross would bear aright
>   Obedience must be learning.' "

Even after hearing the account of the conflict, the Grand Master did not abate his displeasure.

> " 'My son, the spoiler of the land
> Lies slain by thy victorious hand—
> Thou art the people's god, but so
> Thou art become thine Order's foe;
> A deadlier foe thine heart has bred
> Than this which by thy hand is dead,
> That serpent still the heart defiling
> To ruin and to strife beguiling,
> It is that spirit rash and bold,
>   That scorns the bands of order;
> Rages against them uncontrolled
>   Till earth is in disorder.
> 'Courage by Saracens is shown,
> Submission is the Christian's own;
> And where our Saviour, high and holy,
> Wandered a pilgrim poor and lowly
> Upon that ground with mystery fraught,
> The fathers of our Order taught
> The duty hardest to fulfil
> Is to give up your own self-will—
> Thou art elate with glory vain.
>   Away then from my sight!

Who can his Saviour's yoke disdain
  Bears not his Cross aright.'
An angry cry burst from the crowd,
The hall rang with their tumult loud;
Each knightly brother prayed for grace.
The victor downward bent his face,
Aside his cloak in silence laid,
Kissed the Grand Master's hand, nor stayed.
The Master watched him from the hall,
Then summoned him with loving call,
'Come to embrace me, noble son,
  Thine is the conquest of the soul;
Take up the Cross, now truly won,
  By meekness and by self-control.' "

The probation of Dieudonné is said to have been some what longer than
the poem represents, but after the claims of discipline had been established,
he became a great favourite with stern old Villeneuve, and the dragon's
head was set up over the gate of the city, where Thèvenot professed to have
seen it in the seventeenth century, and said that it was larger than that of
a horse, with a huge mouth and teeth and very large eyes. The name of
Rhodes is said to come from a Phoenician word, meaning a serpent, and
the Greeks called this isle of serpents, which is all in favour of the truth of
the story. But, on the other hand, such traditions often are prompted by
the sight of the fossil skeletons of the dragons of the elder world, and are
generally to be met with where such minerals prevail as are found in the
northern part of Rhodes. The tale is disbelieved by many, but it is hard
to suppose it an entire invention, though the description of the monster
may have been exaggerated.

Dieudonné de Gozon was elected to the Grand Mastership after the
death of Villeneuve, and is said to have voted for himself. If so, it seems
as if he might have had, in his earlier days, an overweening opinion of his
own abilities. However, he was an excellent Grand Master, a great soldier,
and much beloved by all the poor peasants of the island, to whom he was
exceedingly kind. He died in 1353, and his tomb is said to have been the
only inscribed with these words,

"Here lies the Dragon Slayer."

The Keys of Calais
1347

NOWHERE does the continent of Europe approach Great Britain so closely as at the straits of Dover, and when our sovereigns were full of the vain hope of obtaining the crown of France, or at least of regaining the great possessions that their forefathers has owned as French nobles, there was no spot so coveted by them as the fortress of Calais, the possession of which gave an entrance into France.

Thus it was that when, in 1346, Edward III had beaten Philippe VI at the battle of Crecy, the first use he made of his victory was to march upon Calais, and lay siege to it. The walls were exceedingly strong and solid, mighty defences of masonry, of huge thickness and like rocks for solidity, guarded it, and the king knew that it would be useless to attempt a direct assault. Indeed, during all the Middle Ages, the modes of protecting fortifications were far more efficient than the modes of attacking them. The walls could be made enormously massive, the towers raised to a great height, and the defenders so completely sheltered by battlements that they could not easily be injured and could take aim from the top of their turrets, or from their loophole windows. The gates had absolute little castles of their own, a moat flowed round the walls full of water, and only capable of being crossed by a drawbridge, behind which the portcullis, a grating armed beneath with spikes, was always ready to drop from the archway of the gate and close up the entrance. The only chance of taking a fortress by direct attack was to fill up the moat with earth and faggots, and then raise ladders against the walls; or else to drive engines against the defences, battering-rams which struck them with heavy beams, mangonels which launched stones, sows whose arched wooden backs protected troops of workmen who tried to undermine the wall, and moving towers consisting of a succession of stages or shelves, filled with soldiers, and with a bridge with iron hooks, capable of being launched from the highest story to the top of the battlements. The besieged could generally disconcert the battering-ram by hanging beds or mattresses over the walls to receive the brunt of the blow, the sows could be crushed with heavy stones, the towers burnt by well-directed flaming missiles, the ladders overthrown, and in general the besiegers suffered a great deal more damage than they could inflict. Cannon had indeed just been brought into use at the battle of Crecy, but they only consisted of iron bars fastened together with hoops, and were as yet of little use, and thus there seemed to be little danger to a well-guarded city from any enemy outside the walls.

King Edward arrived before the place with all his victorious army early in August, his good knights and squires arrayed in glittering steel armour, covered with surcoats richly embroidered with their heraldic bearings; his stout men-at-arms, each of whom was attended by three bold followers; and his archers, with their crossbows to shoot bolts, and longbows to shoot arrows of a yard long, so that it used to be said that each went into battle with three men's lives under his girdle, namely, the three arrows he kept there ready to his hand. With the King was his son, Edward, Prince of Wales, who had just won the golden spurs of knighthood so gallantly at Crecy, when only in his seventeenth year, and likewise the famous Hainault knight, Sir Walter Mauny, and all that was noblest and bravest in England.

This whole glittering army, at their head the King's great royal standard bearing the golden lilies of France quartered with the lions of England, and each troop guided by the square banner, swallow-tailed pennon or pointed pennoncel of their leader, came marching to the gates of Calais, above which floated the blue standard of France with its golden flowers, and with it the banner of the governor, Sir Jean de Vienne. A herald, in a rich long robe embroidered with the arms of England, rode up to the gate, a trumpet sounding before him, and called upon Sir Jean de Vienne to give up the place to Edward, King of England, and of France, as he claimed to be. Sir Jean made answer that he held the town for Philippe, King of France, and that he would defend it to the last; the herald rode back again and the English began the siege of the city.

At first they only encamped, and the people of Calais must have seen the whole plain covered with the white canvas tents, marshalled round the ensigns of the leaders, and here and there a more gorgeous one displaying the colours of the owner. Still there was no attack upon the walls. The warriors were to be seen walking about in the leathern suits they wore under their armour; or if a party was to be seen with their coats of mail on, helmet on head, and lance in hand, it was not against Calais that they came; they rode out into the country, and by and by might be seen driving back before them herds of cattle and flocks of sheep or pigs that they had seized and taken away from the poor peasants; and at night the sky would show red lights where farms and homesteads had been set on fire. After a time, in front of the tents, the English were to be seen hard at work with beams and boards, setting up huts for themselves, and thatching them over with straw or broom. These wooden houses were all ranged in regular streets, and there was a marketplace in the midst, whither every Saturday came farmers and butchers to sell corn and meat, and hay for the horses; and the English merchants and Flemish weavers would come by sea and by land to bring cloth, bread, weapons, and everything that could be needed to be sold in this warlike market.

The Governor, Sir Jean de Vienne, began to perceive that the King did not mean to waste his men by making vain attacks on the strong walls of Calais, but to shut up the entrance by land, and watch the coast by sea so as to prevent any provisions from being taken in, and so to starve him into surrendering. Sir Jean de Vienne, however, hoped that before he should be entirely reduced by famine, the King of France would be able to get together another army and come to his relief, and at any rate he was determined to do his duty, and hold out for his master to the last. But as food was already beginning to grow scarce, he was obliged to turn out such persons as could not fight and had no stores of their own, and so one Wednesday morning he caused all the poor to be brought together, men, women, and children, and sent them all out of the town, to the number of 1700. It was probably the truest mercy, for he had no food to give them, and they could only have starved miserably within the town, or have hindered him from saving it for his sovereign; but to them it was dreadful to be driven out of house and home, straight down upon the enemy, and they went along weeping and wailing, till the English soldiers met them and asked why they had come out. They answered that they had been put out because they had nothing to eat, and their sorrowful, famished looks gained pity for them. King Edward sent orders that not only should they go safely through his camp, but that they should all rest, and have the first hearty dinner that they had eaten for many a day, and he sent every one a small sum of money before they left the camp, so that many of them went on their way praying aloud for the enemy who had been so kind to them.

A great deal happened whilst King Edward kept watch in his wooden town and the citizens of Calais guarded their walls. England was invaded by King David II of Scotland, with a great army, and the good Queen Philippa, who was left to govern at home in the name of her little son Lionel, assembled all the forces that were left at home, and crossed the Straits of Dover, and a messenger brought King Edward letters from his Queen to say that the Scots army had been entirely defeated at Nevil's Cross, near Durham, and that their King was a prisoner, but that he had been taken by a squire named John Copeland, who would not give him up to her.

King Edward sent letters to John Copeland to come to him at Calais, and when the squire had made his journey, the King took him by the hand saying, "Ha! welcome, my squire, who by his valour has captured our adversary the King of Scotland."

Copeland, falling on one knee, replied, "If God, out of His great kindness, has given me the King of Scotland, no one ought to be jealous of it, for God can, when He pleases, send His grace to a poor squire as well as to a great Lord. Sir, do not take it amiss if I did not surrender him to the orders of my lady the Queen, for I hold my lands of you, and my oath is to you, not to her."

The King was not displeased with his squire's sturdiness, but made him a knight, gave him a pension of £500 a year, and desired him to surrender his prisoner to the Queen, as his own representative. This was accordingly done, and King David was lodged in the Tower of London. Soon after, three days before All Saint's Day, there was a large and gay fleet to be seen crossing from the white cliffs of Dover, and the King, his son, and his knights rode down to the landing place to welcome plump, fair haired Queen Philippa, and all her train of ladies, who had come in great numbers to visit their husbands, fathers, or brothers in the wooden town. Then there was a great Court, and numerous feasts and dances, and the knights and squires were constantly striving who could do the bravest deed of prowess to please the ladies. The King of France had placed numerous knights and men-at-arms in the neighbouring towns and castles, and there were constant fights whenever the English went out foraging, and many bold deeds that were much admired were done. The great point was to keep provisions out of the town, and there was much fighting between the French who tried to bring in supplies, and the English who intercepted them. Very little was brought in by land, and Sir Jean de Vienne and his garrison would have been quite starved but for two sailors of Abbeville, named Marant and Mestriel, who knew the coast thoroughly, and often, in the dark autumn evenings, would guide in a whole fleet of little boats, loaded with bread and meat for the starving men within the city. They were often chased by King Edward's vessels, and were sometimes very nearly taken, but they always managed to escape, and thus they still enabled the garrison to hold out.

So all the winter passed, Christmas was kept with brilliant feastings and high merriment by the King and his Queen in their wooden palace outside, and with lean cheeks and scanty fare by the besieged within. Lent was strictly observed perforce by the besieged, and Easter brought a betrothal in the English camp; a very unwilling one on the part of the bridegroom, the young Count of Flanders, who loved the French much better than the English, and had only been tormented into giving his consent by his unruly vassals because they depended on the wool of English sheep for their cloth works. So, though King Edward's daughter Isabel was a beautiful fair-haired girl of fifteen, the young Count would scarcely look at her; and in the last week before the marriage day, while her robes and her jewels were being prepared, and her father and mother were arranging the presents they should make to all their Court on the wedding day, the bridegroom, when out hawking, gave his attendants the slip, and galloped off to Paris, where he was welcomed by King Philippe.

This made Edward very wrathful, and more than ever determined to take Calais. About Whitsuntide he completed a great wooden castle upon the seashore, and placed in it numerous warlike engines, with forty men-at-arms and 200 archers, who kept such a watch upon the harbour that not even the two Abbeville sailors could enter it, without having their boats crushed and sunk by the great stones that the mangonels launched upon them. The townspeople began to feel what hunger really was, but their spirits were kept up by the hope that their King was at last collecting an army for their rescue.

And Philippe did collect all his forces, a great and noble army, and came one night to the hill of Sangate, just behind the English army, the knights' armour glancing and their pennons flying in the moonlight, so as to be a beautiful sight to the hungry garrison who could see the white tents pitched upon the hillside. Still there were but two roads by which the French could reach their friends in the town—one along the seacoast, the other by a marshy road higher up the country, and there was but one bridge by which the river could be crossed. The English King's fleet could prevent any troops from passing along the coast road, the Earl of Derby guarded the bridge, and there was a great tower, strongly fortified, close upon Calais. There were a few skirmishes, but the French King, finding it difficult to force his way to relieve the town, sent a party of knights with a challenge to King Edward to come out of his camp and do battle upon a fair field.

To this Edward made answer, that he had been nearly a year before Calais, and had spent large sums of money on the siege, and that he had nearly become master of the place, so that he had no intention of coming out only to gratify his adversary, who must try some other road if he could not make his way in by that before him.

Three days were spent in parleys, and then, without the slightest effort to rescue the brave, patient men within the town, away went King Philippe of France, with all his men, and the garrison saw the host that had crowded the hill of Sangate melt away like a summer cloud.

August had come again, and they had suffered privation for a whole year for the sake of the King who deserted them at their utmost need. They were in so grievous a state of hunger and distress that the hardiest could endure no more, for ever since Whitsuntide no fresh provisions had reached them. The Governor, therefore, went to the battlements and made signs that he wished to hold a parley, and the King appointed Lord Basset and Sir Walter Mauny to meet him, and appoint the terms of surrender.

The Governor owned that the garrison was reduced to the greatest extremity of distress, and requested that the King would be contented with obtaining the city and fortress, leaving the soldiers and inhabitants to depart in peace.

But Sir Walter Mauny was forced to make answer that the King, his lord, was so much enraged at the delay and expense that Calais had cost him, that he would only consent to receive the whole on unconditional terms, leaving him free to slay, or to ransom, or make prisoners whomsoever he pleased, and he was known to consider that there was a heavy reckoning to pay, both for the trouble the siege had cost him and the damage the Calesians had previously done to his ships.

The brave answer was: "These conditions are too hard for us. We are but a small number of knights and squires, who have loyally served our lord and master as you would have done, and have suffered much ill and disquiet, but we will endure far more than any man has done in such a post, before we consent that the smallest boy in the town shall fare worse than ourselves. I therefore entreat you, for pity's sake, to return to the King and beg him to have compassion, for I have such an opinion of his gallantry that I think he will alter his mind."

The King's mind seemed, however, sternly made up; and all that Sir Walter Mauny and the barons of the council could obtain from him was that he would pardon the garrison and townsmen on condition that six of the chief citizens should present themselves to him, coming forth with bare feet and heads, with halters round their necks, carrying the keys of the town, and becoming absolutely his own to punish for their obstinacy as he should think fit.

On hearing this reply, Sir Jean de Vienne begged Sir Walter Mauny to wait till he could consult the citizens, and, repairing to the marketplace, he caused a great bell to be rung, at sound of which all the inhabitants came together in the town hall. When he told them of these hard terms he could not refrain from weeping bitterly, and wailing and lamentation arose all round him. Should all starve together, or sacrifice their best and most honoured after all suffering in common so long?

Then a voice was heard; it was that of the richest burgher in the town, Eustache de St. Pierre. "Messieurs high and low," he said, "it would be a sad pity to suffer so many people to die through hunger, if it could be prevented; and to hinder it would be meritorious in the eyes of our Saviour. I have such faith and trust in finding grace before God, if I die to save my townsmen, that I name myself as the first of the six."

As the burgher ceased, his fellow townsmen wept aloud, and many, amid tears and groans, threw themselves at his feet in a transport of grief and gratitude. Another citizen, very rich and respected, rose up and said, "I will be second to my comrade, Eustache." His name was Jean Daire. After him, Jacques Wissant, another very rich man, offered himself as companion to these, who were both his cousins; and his brother Pierre would not be left behind: and two more, unnamed, made up this gallant band of men willing to offer their lives for the rescue of their fellow townsmen.

Sir Jean de Vienne mounted a little horse–for he had been wounded, and was still lame–and came to the gate with them, followed by all the people of the town, weeping and wailing, yet, for their own sakes and their children's not daring to prevent the sacrifice. The gates were opened, the governor and the six passed out, and the gates were again shut behind them. Sir Jean then rode up to Sir Walter Mauny, and told him how these burghers had voluntarily offered themselves, begging him to do all in his power to save them; and Sir Walter promised with his whole heart to plead their cause. De Vienne then went back into the town, full of heaviness and anxiety; and the six citizens were led by Sir Walter to the presence of the King, in his full Court. They all knelt down, and the foremost said: "Most gallant King, you see before you six burghers of Calais, who have all been capital merchants, and who bring you the keys of the castle and town. We yield ourselves to your absolute will and pleasure, in order to save the remainder of the inhabitants of Calais, who have suffered much distress and misery. Condescend, therefore, out of your nobleness of mind, to have pity on us."

Strong emotion was excited among all the barons and knights who stood round, as they saw the resigned countenances, pale and thin with patiently endured hunger, of these venerable men, offering themselves in the cause of their fellow townsmen. Many tears of pity were shed; but the King still showed himself implacable, and commanded that they should be led away, and their heads stricken off. Sir Walter Mauny interceded for them with all his might, even telling the King that such an execution would tarnish his honour, and that reprisals would be made on his own garrisons; and all the nobles joined in entreating pardon for the citizens, but still without effect; and the headsman had been actually sent for, when Queen Philippa, her eyes streaming with tears, threw herself on her knees amongst the captives, and said, "Ah, gentle sir, since I have crossed the sea, with much danger, to see you, I have never asked you one favour; now I beg as a boon to myself, for the sake of the Son of the Blessed Mary, and for your love to me, that you will be merciful to these men!"

For some time the King looked at her in silence; then he exclaimed: "Dame, dame, would that you had been anywhere than here! You have entreated in such a manner that I cannot refuse you; I therefore give these men to you, to do as you please with."

QUEEN PHILIPPA PLEADS WITH KING EDWARD FOR THE MEN OF CALAIS

Joyfully did Queen Philippa conduct the six citizens to her own apartments, where she made them welcome, sent them new garments, entertained them with a plentiful dinner, and dismissed them each with a gift of six nobles. After this, Sir Walter Mauny entered the city, and took possession of it; retaining Sir Jean de Vienne and the other knights and squires till they should ransom themselves, and sending out the old French inhabitants; for the King was resolved to people the city entirely of English, in order to gain a thoroughly strong hold of this first step in France.

The King and Queen took up their abode in the city; and the houses of Jean Daire were, it appears, granted to the Queen—perhaps, because she considered the man himself as her charge, and wished to secure them for him—and her little daughter Margaret was, shortly after, born in one of his houses. Eustache de St. Pierre was taken into high favour, and placed in charge of the new citizens whom the King placed in the city.

Indeed, as this story is told by no chronicler but Froissart, some have doubted of it, and thought the violent resentment thus imputed to Edward III inconsistent with his general character; but it is evident that the men of Calais had given him strong provocation by attacks on his shipping—piracies which are not easily forgiven—and that he considered that he had a right to make an example of them. It is not unlikely that he might, after all, have intended to forgive them, and have given the Queen the grace of obtaining their pardon, so as to excuse himself from the fulfillment of some over-hasty threat. But, however this may have been, nothing can lessen the glory of the six grave and patient men who went forth, by their own free will, to meet what might be a cruel and disgraceful death, in order to obtain the safety of their fellow townsmen.

Very recently, in the summer of 1864, an instance has occurred of self-devotion worthy to be recorded with that of Eustache de St. Pierre. The City of Palmyra, in Tennessee, one of the Southern States of America, had been occupied by a Federal army. An officer of this army was assassinated, and, on the cruel and mistaken system of taking reprisals, the general arrested ten of the principal inhabitants, and condemned them to be shot, as deeming the city responsible for the lives of his officers. One of them was the highly respected father of a large family, and could ill be spared. A young man, not related to him, upon this, came forward and insisted on being taken in his stead, as a less valuable life. And great as was the distress of his friend, this generous substitution was carried out, and not only spared a father to his children, but showed how the sharpest strokes of barbarity can still elicit light from the dark stone—light that but for these blows might have slept unseen.

The Battle of Sempach
1397

NOTHING in history has been more remarkable than the union of the cantons and cities of the little republic of Switzerland. Of differing races, languages, and, latterly, even religions—unlike in habits, tastes, opinions and costumes—they have, however, been held together, as it were, by pressure from without, and one spirit of patriotism has kept the little mountain republic complete for five hundred years.

Originally the lands were fiefs of the Holy Roman Empire, the city municipalities owning the Emperor for their lord, and the great family of Hapsburg, in whom the Empire became at length hereditary, was in reality Swiss, the county that gave them title lying in the canton of Aargau. Rodolf of Hapsburg was elected leader of the burghers of Zurich, long before he was chosen to the Empire; and he continued a Swiss in heart, retaining his mountaineer's open simplicity and honesty to the end of his life. Privileges were granted by him to the cities and the nobles, and the country was loyal and prosperous in his reign.

His son Albert, the same who was slain by his nephew Johann, as before-mentioned, permitted those tyrannies of his bailiffs which goaded the Swiss to their celebrated revolt, and commenced the long series of wars with the House of Hapsburg—or, as it was now termed, of Austria—which finally established their independence.

On the one side, the Dukes of Austria and their ponderous German chivalry wanted to reduce the cantons and cities to vassalage, not to the Imperial Crown, a distant and scarcely felt obligation, but to the Duchy of Austria; on the other, the hardy mountain peasants and stout burghers well knew their true position, and were aware that to admit the Austrian usurpation would expose their young men to be drawn upon for the Duke's wars, cause their property to be subject to perpetual rapacious exactions, and fill their hills with castles for ducal bailiffs, who would be little better than licensed robbers. No wonder, then, that the generations of William Tell and Arnold Melchthal bequeathed a resolute purpose of resistance to their descendants.

It was in 1397, ninety years since the first assertion of Swiss independence, when Leopold the Handsome, Duke of Austria, a bold but misproud and violent prince, involved himself in one of the constant quarrels with the Swiss that were always arising on account of the insulting exactions of toll and tribute in the Austrian border cities. A sharp war broke out, and the Swiss city of Lucerne took the opportunity of destroying the Austrian castle of Rothemburg, where the tolls had been particularly vexatious, and of admitting to their league the cities of Sempach and Richensee.

Leopold and all the neighbouring nobles united their forces. Hatred and contempt of the Swiss, as low-born and presumptuous, spurred them on; and twenty messengers reached the Duke in one day, with promises of support, in his march against Sempach and Lucerne. He had sent a large force in the direction of Zurich with Johann Bonstetten, and advanced himself with 4000 horse and 1400 foot upon Sempach. Zurich undertook its own defence, and the Forest cantons sent their brave peasants to the support of Lucerne and Sempach, but only to the number of 1300, who, on the 9th of July, took post in the woods around the little lake of Sempach. Meanwhile, Leopold's troops rode round the walls of the little city, insulting the inhabitants, one holding up a halter, which he said was for the chief magistrate; and another, pointing to the reckless waste that his comrades were perpetrating on the fields, shouted, "Send a breakfast to the reapers." The burgomaster pointed to the wood where his allies lay hid, and answered, "My masters of Lucerne and their friends will bring it."

The story of that day was told by one of the burghers who fought in the ranks of Lucerne, a shoemaker, named Albert Tchudi, who was both a brave warrior and a master-singer; and as his ballad was translated by another master-singer, Sir Walter Scott, and is the spirited record of an eyewitness, we will quote from him some of his descriptions of the battle and its golden deed.

The Duke's wiser friends proposed to wait till he could be joined by Bonstetten and the troops who had gone towards Zurich, and the Baron von Hasenburg (i.e. hare-rock) strongly urged this prudent counsel; but–

> " 'O, Hare-Castle, thou heart of hare!'
> Fierce Oxenstiern he cried,
> 'Shalt see then how the game will fare,'
> The taunted knight replied."

"This very noon," said the younger knight to the Duke, "we will deliver up to you this handful of villains."

> "And thus they to each other said,
> 'Yon handful down to hew

> Will be no boastful tale to tell
> The peasants are so few.'"

Characteristically enough, the doughty cobbler describes how the first execution that took place was the lopping off the long-peaked toes of the boots that the gentlemen wore chained to their knees, and which would have impeded them on foot; since it had been decided that the horses were too much tired to be serviceable in the action.

> "There was lacing then of helmets bright,
> And closing ranks amain,
> The peaks they hewed from their boot points
> Might wellnigh load a wain."

They were drawn up in a solid compact body, presenting an unbroken line of spears, projecting beyond the wall of gay shields and polished impenetrable armour.

The Swiss were not only few in number, but armour was scarce among them; some had only boards fastened on their arms by way of shields, some had halberts, which had been used by their fathers at the battle of Morgarten, others two-handed swords and battleaxes. They drew themselves up in the form of a wedge and

> "The gallant Swiss confederates then
> They prayed to God aloud,
> And He displayed His rainbow fair,
> Against a swarthy cloud."

Then they rushed upon the serried spears, but in vain. "The game was nothing sweet ".

The banner of Lucerne was in the utmost danger, the Landamman was slain, and sixty of his men, and not an Austrian had been wounded. The flanks of the Austrian host began to advance so as to enclose the small peasant force, and involve it in irremediable destruction. A moment of dismay and stillness ensued. Then Arnold von Winkelried of Unterwalden, with an eagle glance saw the only means of saving his country, and, with the decision of a man who dares by dying to do all things, shouted aloud: "I will open a passage."

> "'I have a virtuous wife at home,
> A wife and infant son:
> I leave them to my country's care,
> The field shall yet be won!'

He rushed against the Austrian band
  In desperate career,
And with his body, breast, and hand,
  Bore down each hostile spear;
Four lances splintered on his crest,
  Six shivered in his side,
Still on the serried files he pressed,
  He broke their ranks and died!"

The very weight of the desperate charge of this self-devoted man opened a breach in the line of spears. In rushed the Swiss wedge, and the weight of the nobles' armour and length of their spears was only encumbering. They began to fall before the Swiss blows, and Duke Leopold was urged to fly. "I had rather die honourably than live with dishonour," he said. He saw his standard bearer struck to the ground, and seizing his banner from his hand, waved it over his head, and threw himself among the thickest of the foe. His corpse was found amid a heap of slain, and no less then 2000 of his companions perished with him, of whom a third are said to have been counts, barons and knights.

"Then lost was banner, spear and shield
  At Sempach in the flight;
The cloister vaults at Konigsfeldt
  Hold many an Austrian knight."

The Swiss only lost 200; but, as they were spent with the excessive heat of the July sun, they did not pursue their enemies. They gave thanks on the battlefield to the God of victories, and the next day buried the dead, carrying Duke Leopold and twenty-seven of his most illustrious companions to the Abbey of Konigsfeldt, where they buried him in the old tomb of his forefathers, the lords of Aargau, who had been laid there in the good old times, before the house of Hapsburg had grown arrogant with success.

As to the master-singer, he tells us of himself that

"A merry man was he, I wot,
  The night he made the lay,
Returning from the bloody spot,
  Where God had judged the day."

On every 9th of July subsequently, the people of the country have been wont to assemble on the battlefield, around four stone crosses which mark the spot. A priest from a pulpit in the open air gives a thanksgiving sermon on the victory that ensured the freedom of Switzerland, and another reads the narrative of the battle, and the roll of the brave 200, who, after Winkelried's example, gave their lives in the cause. All this is in the face of the mountains and the lake now lying in summer stillness, and the harvest fields whose crops are secure from marauders, and the congregation then proceed to the small chapel, the walls of which are painted with the deed of Arnold von Winkelried, and the other distinguished achievements of the confederates, and masses are sung for the souls of those who were slain. No wonder that men thus nurtured in the memory of such actions were, even to the fall of the French monarchy, among the most trustworthy soldiery of Europe.

The Constant Prince

1433

THE illustrious days of Portugal were during the century and a half of the dynasty termed the House of Aviz, because its founder, Dom João I, had been grand master of the military order of Aviz.

His right to the throne was questionable, or more truly null, and he had only obtained the crown from the desire of the nation to be independent of Castile, and by the assistance of our own John of Gaunt, whose daughter, Philippa of Lancaster, became his wife, thus connecting the glories of his line with our own house of Plantagenet.

Philippa was greatly beloved in Portugal, and was a most noble-minded woman, who infused her own spirit into her children. She had five sons, and when they all had attained an age to be admitted to the order of knighthood, their father proposed to give a grand tournament in which they might evince their prowess. This, however, seemed but play to the high-spirited youths, who had no doubt fed upon the story of the manner in which their uncle, the Black Prince, whose name was borne by the eldest, had won his spurs at Crécy. Their entreaty was, not to be carpetknights dubbed in time of peace, and King João on the other hand objected to entering on a war merely for the sake of knighting his sons. At last Dom Fernando, the youngest of the brothers, a lad of fourteen, proposed that their knighthood should be earned by an expedition to take Ceuta from the Moors. A war with the infidel never came amiss, and was in fact regarded as a sacred duty; moreover, Ceuta was a nest of corsairs who infested the whole Mediterranean coast. Up to the nineteenth century the seaports along the African coast of the Mediterranean were the hives of pirates, whose small rapid vessels were the terror of every unarmed ship that sailed in those waters, and whose descents upon the coasts of Spain, France, and Italy rendered life and property constantly insecure. A regular system of kidnapping prevailed; prisoners had their fixed price, and were carried off to labour in the African dockyards, or to be chained to the benches of the Moorish ships which their oars propelled, until either a ransom could be procured from their friends, or they could be persuaded to become

renegades, or death put an end to their sufferings. A captivity among the
Moors was by no means an uncommon circumstance even in the lives of
Englishmen down to the eighteenth century, and pious persons frequently
bequeathed sums of money for the ransom of the poorer captives.

Ceuta, perched upon the southern Pillar of Hercules, was one of the
most perilous of these dens of robbery, and to seize it might well appear a
worthy action, not only to the fiery princes, but to their cautious father.
He kept his designs absolutely secret, and contrived to obtain a plan of the
town by causing one of his vessels to put in there as in quest of provisions,
while, to cover his preparations for war, he sent a public challenge to the
Count of Holland, and a secret message at the same time, with the assurance
that it was only a blind. These proceedings were certainly underhand, and
partook of treachery; but they were probably excused in the King's own
mind by the notion, that no faith was to be kept with unbelievers, and,
moreover, such people as the Ceutans were likely never to be wanting in
the supply of pretexts for attack.

Just as all was ready, the plague broke out in Lisbon, and the Queen
fell sick of it. Her husband would not leave her, and just before her death
she sent for all her sons, and gave to each a sword, charging them to defend
the widow and orphan, and to fight against the infidel. In the full freshness
of their sorrow, the King and his sons set sail from the Bay of Lagos, in
the August of 1415, with 59 galleys, 33 ships of war, and 120 transports;
the largest fleet ever yet sent forth by the little kingdom, and the first that
had left a Peninsular port with the banners and streamers of which the
more northern armaments were so profuse.

The governor of Ceuta, Zala ben Zala, was not unprepared for the
attack, and had collected 5000 allies to resist the Christians; but a great
storm having dispersed the fleet on the first day of its appearance, he
thought the danger over, and dismissed his friends On the 14th August,
however, the whole fleet again appeared, and the King, in a little boat,
directed the landing of his men, led by his sons, the Infantes Duarte and
Henrique. The Moors gave way before them, and they entered the city
with 500 men, among the flying enemy, and there, after a period of much
danger, were joined by their brother Pedro. The three fought their way to
a mosque, where they defended themselves till the King with the rest of
his army made their way in. Zala ben Zala fled to the citadel, but, after
one assault, quitted it in the night.

The Christian captives were released, the mosque purified and consecrated
as a cathedral, a bishop was appointed, and the King gave the government
of the place to Dom Pedro de Menezes, a knight of such known fidelity
that the King would not suffer him to take the oath of allegiance. An attempt was made by the Moors four years later to recover the place; but the
Infantes Pedro and Henrique hurried from Portugal to succour Menezes,

and drove back the besiegers; whereupon the Moors murdered their King, Abu Sayd, on whom they laid the blame of the disaster.

On the very day, eighteen years later, of the taking of Ceuta, King João died of the plague at Lisbon, on the 14th of August, 1433. Duarte came to the throne; and, a few months after, his young brother, Fernando, persuaded him into fitting out another expedition to Africa, of which Tangier should be the object.

Duarte doubted of the justice of the war, and referred the question to the Pope, who decided against it; but the answer came too late, the preparations were made, and the Infantes Henrique and Fernando took the command. Henrique was a most enlightened prince, a great mathematician and naval discoverer, but he does not appear to have made good use of his abilities on the present occasion; for, on arriving at Ceuta, and reviewing the troops, they proved to have but 8000, instead of 14,000, as they had intended. Still they proceeded, Henrique by land and Fernando by sea, and laid siege to Tangier, which was defended by their old enemy, Zala ben Zala. Everything was against them; their scaling ladders were too short to reach to the top of the walls, and the Moors had time to collect in enormous numbers for the relief of the city, under the command of the kings of Fez and Morocco.

The little Christian army was caught as in a net, and, after a day's hard fighting, saw the necessity of re-embarking. All was arranged for this to be done at night; but a vile traitor, chaplain to the army, passed over to the Moors, and revealed their intention. The beach was guarded, and the retreat cut off. Another day of fighting passed, and at night hunger reduced them to eating their horses.

It was necessary to come to terms, and messengers were sent to treat with the two kings. The only terms on which the army could be allowed to depart were that one of the Infantes should remain as a hostage for the delivery of Ceuta to the Moors. For this purpose Fernando offered himself, though it was exceedingly doubtful whether Ceuta would be restored; and the Spanish poet, Calderon, puts into his mouth a generous message to his brother the King, that they both were Christian princes, and that his liberty was not to be weighed in the scale with their father's fairest conquest.

Henrique was forced thus to leave his brave brother, and return with the remnants of his army to Ceuta, where he fell sick with grief and vexation. He sent the fleet home; but it met with a great storm, and many vessels were driven on the coast of Andalusia, where, by orders of the King, the battered sailors and defeated soldiers were most kindly and generously treated.

Dom Duarte, having in the meantime found out with how insufficient an army his brothers had been sent forth, had equipped a fresh fleet, the arrival of which at Ceuta cheered Henrique with hope of rescuing his brother; but it was soon followed by express orders from the King that

Henrique should give up all such projects and return home. He was obliged to comply, but, unable to look Duarte in the face, he retired to his own estates at the Algarve.

Duarte convoked the States-general of the kingdom, to consider whether Ceuta should be yielded to purchase his brother's freedom. They decided that the place was too important to be parted with, but undertook to raise any sum of money for the ransom; and if this were not accepted, proposed to ask the Pope to proclaim a crusade for his rescue.

At first Fernando was treated well, and kept at Tangier as an honourable prisoner; but disappointment enraged the Moors, and he was thrown into a dungeon, starved, and maltreated. All this usage he endured with the utmost calmness and resolution, and could by no means be threatened into entreating for liberty to be won at the cost of the now Christian city where his knighthood had been won.

His brother Duarte meantime endeavoured to raise the country for his deliverance; but the plague was still desolating Portugal, so that it was impossible to collect an army, and the infection at length seized on the King himself, from a letter which he incautiously opened, and he died, in his thirty-eighth year, in 1438, the sixth year of his reign and the second of his brother's captivity. His successor, Affonso V, was a child of six years old, and quarrels and disputes between the Queen Mother and the Infante Dom Pedro rendered the chance of redeeming the captivity of Fernando less and less.

The King of Castille, and even the Moorish King of Granada, shocked at his sufferings and touched by his constancy, proposed to unite their forces against Tangier for his deliverance; but the effect of this was that Zala ben Zala made him over to Muley Xeque, the King of Fez, by whom he was thrown into a dungeon without light or air. After a time, he was brought back to daylight, but only to toil among the other Christian slaves, to whom he was a model of patience, resignation, and kindness. Even his enemies became struck with admiration of his high qualities, and the King of Fez declared that he even deserved to be a Mahometan!

At last, in 1443, Fernando's captivity ended, but only by his death. Muley Xeque caused a tall tower to be erected on his tomb, in memory of the victory of Tangier; but in 1473, two sons of Muley being made prisoners by the Portuguese, one was ransomed for the body of Dom Fernando, who was then solemnly laid in the vaults of the beautiful Abbey of Batalha on the field of Aljubarota, which had given his father the throne. Universal honour attended the name of the Constant Prince, the Portuguese Regulus; and seldom as the Spanish admire anything Portuguese, a fine drama of the poet Calderon is founded upon that noble spirit which preferred dreary captivity to the yielding up his father's conquest to the enemies of his country and religion. Nor was this constancy thrown away; Ceuta remained a Christian city. It was held by Portugal till the house of Aviz was extinguished in Dom Sebastião, and since that time has belonged to the crown of Spain.

The Carnival of Perth
1435

IT was bedtime, and the old vaulted chambers of the Dominican monastery at Perth echoed with sounds that would seem incongruous in such a home of austerity, but that the disturbed state of Scotland rendered it the habit of her kings to attach their palaces to convents, that they themselves might benefit by the "peace of the Church", which was in general accorded to all sacred spots.

Thus it was that Christmas and Carnival time of 1435-6 had been spent by the Court in the cloisters of Perth, and the dance, the song, and the tourney had strangely contrasted with the grave and self-denying habits to which the Dominicans were devoted in their neighbouring cells. The festive season was nearly at an end, for it was the 20th of February; but the evening had been more than usually gay, and had been spent in games at chess, tables, or backgammon, reading romances of chivalry, harping, and singing. King James himself, brave and handsome, and in the prime of life, was the blithest of the whole joyous party. He was the most accomplished man in his dominions; for though he had been basely kept a prisoner at Windsor throughout his boyhood by Henry IV of England, an education had been bestowed on him far above what he would have otherwise obtained; and he was naturally a man of great ability, refinement, and strength of character. Not only was he a perfect knight on horseback, but in wrestling and running, throwing the hammer, and "putting the stane", he had scarcely a rival, and he was skilled in all the learned lore of the time, wrote poetry, composed music both sacred and profane, and was a complete minstrel, able to sing beautifully and to play on the harp and organ. His Queen, the beautiful Joan Beaufort, had been the lady of his minstrelsy in the days of his captivity, ever since he had watched her walking on the slopes of Windsor Park, and wooed her in verses that are still preserved. They had now been eleven years married, and their Court was one bright spot of civilization, refinement, and grace, amid the savagery of Scotland. And now, after the pleasant social evening, the Queen, with her long fair hair unbound, was sitting under the hands of her tire-women, who were preparing her for the nights rest; and the King, in his furred nightgown, was standing before the bright fire on the hearth of the wide chimney, laughing and talking with the attendant ladies.

Yet dark hints had already been whispered, which might have cast a shadow over that careless mirth. Always fierce and vindictive, the Scots had been growing more and more lawless and savage ever since the disputed succession of Bruce and Balliol had unsettled all royal authority, and led to one perpetual war with the English. The twenty years of James's captivity had been the worst of all,—almost every noble was a robber chief; Scottish Borderer preyed upon English Borderer, Highlander upon Lowlander, knight upon traveller, everyone who had armour upon him who had not; each clan was at deadly feud with its neighbour; blood was shed like water from end to end of the miserable land, and the higher the birth of the offender the greater the impunity he claimed.

Indeed, James himself had been brought next to the throne by one of the most savage and horrible murders ever perpetrated–that of his elder brother, David, by his own uncle; and he himself had probably been only saved from sharing the like fate by being sent out of the kingdom. His earnest words on his return to take the rule of this unhappy realm were these: "Let God but grant me life, and there shall not be a spot in my realm where the key shall not keep the castle, and the bracken bush the cow, though I should lead the life of a dog to accomplish it."

This great purpose had been before James through the eleven years of his reign, and he had worked it out resolutely. The lawless nobles would not brook his ruling hand, and strong and bitter was the hatred that had arisen against him. In many of his transactions he was far from blame-less: he was sometimes tempted to craft, sometimes to tyranny; but his object was always a high and kingly one, though he was led by the horrid wickedness of the men he had to deal with more than once to forget that evil is not to be overcome with evil, but with good. In the main, it was his high and uncompromising resolution to enforce the laws upon high and low alike that led to the nobles' conspiracies against him; though, if he had always been true to his purpose of swerving neither to the right nor to the left, he might have avoided the last fatal offence that armed the murderer against his life.

The chief misdoers in the long period of anarchy had been his uncles and cousins; nor was it till after his eldest uncle's death that his return home had been possible. With a strong hand had he avenged upon the princes and their followers the many miseries they had inflicted upon his people; and in carrying out these measures he had seized upon the great earldom of Strathern, which had descended to one of their party in right of his wife, declaring that it could not be inherited by a female. In this he appears to have acted unjustly, from the strong desire to avail himself by any pretext of an opportunity of breaking the overweening power of the great turbulent nobles; and, to make up for the loss, he created the new earldom of Menteith, for the young Malise Graham, the son of the dispossessed earl. But the proud and vindictive Grahams were not thus to he pacified. Sir Robert Graham, the uncle of the young earl, drew off into the Highlands, and there formed a conspiracy among other discontented men who hated the resolute government that repressed their violence. Men of princely blood joined in the plot, and 300 Highland catherans were ready to accompany the expedition that promised the delights of war and plunder.

Even when the hard-worked King was setting forth to enjoy his holiday at Perth, the traitors had fixed upon that spot as the place of his doom; but the scheme was known to so many, that it could not be kept entirely secret, and warnings began to gather round the King. When, on his way to Perth, he was about to cross the Firth of Forth, the wild figure of a Highland woman appeared at his bridle rein, and solemnly warned him "that, if he crossed that water, he would never return alive". He was struck by the apparition, and bade one of his knights to enquire of her what she meant; but the knight must have been a dullard or a traitor, for he told the King that the woman was either mad or drunk, and no notice was taken of her warning.

There was likewise a saying abroad in Scotland, that the new year, 1436, should see the death of a king; and this same carnival night, James, while playing at chess with a young friend, whom he was wont to call the king of love, laughingly observed that "it must be you or I, since there are but two kings in Scotland–therefore, look well to yourself".

Little did the blithe monarch guess that at that moment one of the conspirators, touched by a moment's misgiving, was hovering round, seeking in vain for an opportunity of giving him warning; that even then his chamberlain and kinsman, Sir Robert Stewart, was enabling the traitors to place boards across the moat for their passage, and to remove the bolts and bars of all the doors in their way. And the Highland woman was at the door, earnestly entreating to see the King, if but for one moment! The message was even brought to him, but, alas! he bade her wait till the morrow, and she turned away, declaring that she should never more see his face!

And now, as before said, the feast was over, and the King stood, gaily chatting with his wife and her ladies, when the clang of arms was heard, and the glare of torches in the court below flashed on the windows. The ladies flew to secure the doors. Alas! the bolts and bars were gone! Too late the warnings returned upon the King's mind, and he knew it was he alone who was sought. He tried to escape by the windows, but here the bars were but too firm. Then he seized the tongs, and tore up a board in the floor, by which he let himself down into the vault below, just as the murderers came rushing along the passage, slaying on their way a page named Walter Straiton.

There was no bar to the door. Yes, there was. Catherine Douglas, worthy of her name, worthy of the cognisance of the bleeding heart, thrust her arm through the empty staples to gain for her sovereign a few moments more for escape and safety! But though true as steel, the brave arm was not as strong. It was quickly broken. She was thrust fainting aside, and the ruffians rushed in. Queen Joan stood in the midst of the room, with her hair streaming round her, and her mantle thrown hastily on. Some of the wretches even struck and wounded her, but Graham called them off, and bade them search for the King. They sought him in vain in every corner of the women's apartments, and dispersed through the other rooms in search of their prey. The ladies began to hope that the citizens and nobles in the town were coming to their help, and that the King might have escaped through an opening that led from the vault into the tennis court. Presently, however, the King called to them to draw him up again, for he had not been able to get out of the vault, having a few days before caused the hole to be bricked up, because his tennis balls used to fly into it and be lost. In trying to draw him up by the sheets, Elizabeth Douglas, another of the ladies, was actually pulled down into the vault; the noise was heard by the assassins, who were still watching outside, and they returned.

There is no need to tell of the foul and cruel slaughter that ensued, nor of the barbarous vengeance that visited it. Our tale is of golden, not of brazen deeds; and if we have turned our eyes for a moment to the Bloody Carnival of Perth, it is for the sake of the King, who was too upright for his bloodthirsty subjects, and, above all, for that of the noble-hearted lady whose frail arm was the guardian of her sovereign's life in the extremity of peril.

In like manner, on the dreadful 6th of October, 1789, when the infuriated mob of Paris had been incited by the revolutionary leaders to rush to Versailles in pursuit of the royal family, whose absence they fancied deprived them of bread and liberty, a woman shared the honour of saving her sovereign's life, at least for that time.

The confusion of the day, with the multitude thronging the courts and park of Versailles, uttering the most frightful threats and insults, had been beyond all description; but there had been a pause at night, and at two o'clock, poor Queen Marie Antoinette, spent with horror and fatigue, at last went to bed, advising her ladies to do the same; but their anxiety was too great, and they sat up at her door. At half-past four they heard musket shots, and loud shouts, and while one awakened the Queen, the other, Madame Auguier, flew towards the place whence the noise came. As she opened the door, she found one of the royal bodyguards, with his face covered with blood, holding his musket so as to bar the door while the furious mob were striking at him. He turned to the lady, and cried, "Save the Queen, madame, they are come to murder her!" Quick as lightning, Madame Auguier shut and bolted the door, rushed to the Queen's bedside, and dragged her to the opposite door, with a petticoat just thrown over her. Behold, the door was fastened on the other side! The ladies knocked violently, the King's valet opened it, and in a few minutes the whole family were in safety in the King's apartments. M. de Miomandre, the brave guardsman, who used his musket to guard the Queen's door instead of to defend himself, fell wounded; but his comrade, M. de Repaire, at once took his place, and, according to one account, was slain, and the next day his head, set upon a pike, was borne before the carriage in which the royal family were escorted back to Paris.

M. de Miomandre, however, recovered from his wounds, and a few weeks after, the Queen, hearing that his loyalty had made him a mark for the hatred of the mob, sent for him to desire him to quit Paris. She said that gold could not repay such a service as his had been, but she hoped one day to be able to recompense him more as he deserved; meanwhile, she hoped he would consider that as a sister might advance a timely sum to a brother, so she might offer him enough to defray his expenses at Paris, and to provide for his journey. In a private audience then he kissed her hand, and those of the King and his saintly sister, Elizabeth, while the Queen gratefully expressed her thanks, and the King stood by, with tears in his eyes, but withheld by his awkward bashfulness from expressing the feelings that overpowered him.

Madame Auguier, and her sister, Madame Campan, continued with their royal lady until the next stage in that miserable downfall of all that was high and noble in unhappy France. She lived through the horrors of the Revolution, and her daughter became the wife of Marshal Ney.

Well it is that the darkening firmament does but show the stars, and that when treason and murder surge round the fated chambers of royalty, their foulness and violence do but enhance the loyal self-sacrifice of such doorkeepers as Catherine Douglas, Madame Auguier, or M. de Miomandre.

> "Such deeds can woman's spirit do,
> O Catherine Douglas, brave and true!
> Let Scotland keep thy holy name
> Still first upon her ranks of fame."

The Crown of St. Stephen
1440

OF all the possessions of the old kingdom of Hungary, none was more valued than what was called the Crown of St. Stephen, so called from one, which had, in the year 1000, been presented by Pope Sylvester II to Stephen, the second Christian Duke, and first King of Hungary. A crown and a cross were given to him for his coronation, which took place in the Church of the Holy Virgin, at Alba Regale, also called in German Weissenburg, where thenceforth the Kings of Hungary were anointed to begin their troubled reigns, and at the close of them were laid to rest beneath the pavement, where most of them might have used the same epitaph as the old Italian leader: "He rests here, who never rested before". For it was a wild realm, bordered on all sides by foes, with Poland, Bohemia, and Austria, ever casting greedy eyes upon it, and afterwards with the Turk upon the southern border, while the Magyars, or Hungarian nobles, themselves were a fierce and untameable race, bold and generous, but brooking little control, claiming a voice in choosing their own Sovereign, and to resist him, even by force of arms, if he broke the laws. No prince had a right to their allegiance unless he had been crowned with St. Stephen's Crown; but if he had once worn that sacred circle, he thenceforth was held as the only lawful monarch, unless he should flagrantly violate the Constitution. In 1076, another crown had been given by the Greek Emperor to Geysa, King of Hungary, and the sacred crown combined the two. It had the two arches of the Roman crown, and the gold circlet of the Constantinopolitan; and the difference of workmanship was evident.

In the year 1439 died King Albert, who had been appointed King of Hungary in right of his wife, Queen Elizabeth. He left a little daughter only four years old, and as the Magyars had never been governed by a female hand, they proposed to send and offer their crown, and the hand of their young widowed Queen, to Wladislas, the King of Poland. But Elizabeth had hopes of another child, and in case it should be a son, she had no mind to give away its rights to its father's throne. How, then, was she to help herself among the proud and determined nobles of her Court? One thing was certain, that if once the Polish king were crowned with St. Stephen's crown, it would be his own fault if he were not King of Hungary as long as he lived; but if the crown were not to be found, of course he could not receive it, and the fealty of the nobles would not be pledged to him.

The most trustworthy person she had about her was Helen Kottenner, the lady who had the charge of her little daughter, Princess Elizabeth, and to her she confided her desire that the crown might be secured, so as to prevent the Polish party from getting access to it. Helen herself has written down the history of these strange events, and of her own struggles of mind, at the risk she ran, and the doubt whether good would come of the intrigue; and there can be no doubt that, whether the Queen's conduct were praiseworthy or not, Helen dared a great peril for the sake purely of loyalty and fidelity. "The Queen's commands", she says, "sorely troubled me; for it was a dangerous venture for me and my little children, and I turned it over in my mind what I should do, for I had no one to take counsel of but God alone; and I thought if I did it not, and evil arose therefrom, I should be guilty before God and the world. So I consented to risk my life on this difficult undertaking; but desired to have someone to help me." This was permitted; but the first person to whom the Lady of Kottenner confided her intention, a Croat, lost his colour from alarm, looked like one half-dead, and went at once in search of his horse. The next thing that was heard of him was that he had had a bad fall from his horse, and had been obliged to return to Croatia, and the Queen remained much alarmed at her plans being known to one so faint-hearted. However, a more courageous confidant was afterwards found in a Hungarian gentleman, whose name has become illegible in Helen's old manuscript.

The crown was in the vaults of the strong Castle of Plintenburg, also called Vissegrad, which stands upon a bend of the Danube, about twelve miles from the twin cities of Buda and Pesth. It was in a case within a chest, sealed with many seals, and since the King's death, it had been brought up by the nobles, who closely guarded both it and the Queen, into her apartments, and there examined and replaced in the chest. The next night, one of the Queen's ladies upset a wax taper, without being aware of it, and before the fire was discovered, and put out, the corner of the chest was singed, and a hole burnt in the blue velvet cushion that lay on the top. Upon this, the lords had caused the chest to be taken down again into the vault, and had fastened the doors with many locks and with seals. The Castle had further been put into the charge of Ladislas von Gara, the Queen's cousin, and Ban, or hereditary commander, of the border troops, and he had given it over to a Burggraf, or seneschal, who had placed his bed in the chamber where was the door leading to the vaults.

The Queen removed to Komorn, a castle higher up the Danube, in charge of her faithful cousin, Count Ulric of Eily, taking with her her little daughter Elizabeth, Helen Kottenner, and two other ladies. This was the first stage on the journey to Presburg, where the nobles had wished to lodge the Queen, and from thence she sent back Helen to bring the rest of the maids of honour and her goods to join her at Komorn. It was early spring, and snow was still on the ground, and the Lady of Kottenner and her faithful nameless assistant travelled in a sledge; but two Hungarian noblemen went with them, and they had to be most careful in concealing their arrangements. Helen had with her the Queen's signet, and keys; and her friend had a file in each shoe, and keys under his black velvet dress.

On arriving in the evening, they found that the Burggraf had fallen ill, and could not sleep in the chamber leading to the vault, because it belonged to the ladies' chambers, and that he had therefore put a cloth over the padlock of the door and sealed it. There was a stove in the room, and the maidens began to pack up their clothes there, an operation that lasted till eight o'clock; while Helen's friend stood there, talking and jesting with them, trying all the while to hide the files, and contriving to say to Helen: "Take care that we have a light." So she begged the old housekeeper to give her plenty of wax tapers, as she had many prayers to say. At last everyone was gone to bed, and there only remained in the room with Helen, an old woman, whom she had brought with her, who knew no German, and was fast asleep. Then the accomplice came back through the chapel, which opened into this same hall. He had on his black velvet gown and felt shoes, and was followed by a servant, who, Helen says, was bound to him by oath, and had the same Christian name as himself, this being evidently an additional bond of fidelity. Helen, who had received from the Queen all the keys to this outer room, let them in, and, after the Burggraf's cloth and seal had been removed, they unlocked the padlock, and the other two locks of the outer door of the vault, and the two men descended into it. There were several other doors, whose chains required to be filed through, and their seals and locks broken, and to the ears of the waiting Helen the noise appeared fatally loud. She says, "I devoutly prayed to God and the Holy Virgin, that they would support and help me; yet I was in greater anxiety for my soul than for my life, and I prayed to God that He would be merciful to my soul, and rather let me die at once there, than that anything should happen against his will, or that should bring misfortune on my country and people."

She fancied she heard a noise of armed men at the chapel door, but finding nothing there, believed—not in her own nervous agitation, a thing not yet invented—that it was a spirit, and returning to her prayers, vowed, poor lady, to make a pilgrimage to St. Maria Zell, in Styria, if the Holy Virgin's intercessions obtained their success, and till the pilgrimage could be made, "to forego every Saturday night my feather bed!" After another false alarm at a supposed noise at the maiden's door, she ventured into the vault to see how her companions were getting on, when she found they had filed away all the locks, except that of the case containing the crown, and this they were obliged to burn, in spite of their apprehension that the smell and smoke might be observed. They then shut up the chest, replaced the padlocks and chains with those they had brought for the purpose, and renewed the seals with the Queen's signet, which bearing the royal arms, would baffle detection that the seals had been tampered with. They then took the crown into the chapel, where they found a red velvet cushion, so large that by taking out some of the stuffing a hiding place was made in which the crown was deposited, and the cushion sewn up over it.

By this time day was dawning, the maidens were dressing, and it was the hour for setting off for Komorn. The old woman who had waited on them came to the Lady of Kottenner to have her wages paid, and be dismissed to Buda. While she was waiting, she began to remark on a strange thing lying by the stove, which, to the Lady Helen's great dismay, she perceived to be a bit of the case in which the crown was kept. She tried to prevent the old woman from noticing it, pushed it into the hottest part of the stove, and, by way of further precaution, took the old woman away with her, on the plea of asking the Queen to make her a bedeswoman at Vienna, and this was granted to her.

When all was ready, the gentleman desired his servant to take the cushion and put it into the sledge designed for himself and the Lady of Kottenner. The man took it on his shoulders, hiding it under an old ox-hide, with the tail hanging down, to the laughter of all beholders. Helen further records the trying to get some breakfast in the marketplace and finding nothing but herrings, also the going to mass, and the care she took not to sit upon the holy crown, though she had to sit on its cushion in the sledge. They dined at an inn, but took care to keep the cushion in sight, and then in the dusk crossed the Danube on the ice, which was becoming very thin, and halfway across it broke under the maidens' carriage, so that Helen expected to be lost in the Danube, crown and all. However, though many packages were lost under the ice, her sledge got safe over, as well as all the ladies, some of whom she took into her conveyance, and all safely arrived at the castle of Komorn late in the evening.

The very hour of their arrival a babe was born to the Queen, and to her exceeding joy it was a son. Count von Eily, hearing "that a king and friend was born to him", had bonfires lighted, and a torchlight procession on the ice that same night, and early in the morning came the Archbishop of Gran to christen the child. The Queen wished her faithful Helen to be godmother, but she refused in favour of some lady whose family it was probably needful to propitiate. She took off the little princess Elizabeth's mourning for her father and dressed her in red and gold, all the maidens appeared in gay apparel, and there was great rejoicing and thanksgiving when the babe was christened Ladislas, after a sainted King of Hungary.

The peril was, however, far from ended; for many of the Magyars had no notion of accepting an infant for their king, and by Easter, the King of Poland was advancing upon Buda, to claim the realm to which he had been invited. No one had discovered the abstraction of the crown, and Elizabeth's object was to take her child to Weissenburg, and there have him crowned, so as to disconcert the Polish party. She had sent to Buda for cloth of gold to make him a coronation dress, but it did not come in time, and Helen therefore shut herself into the chapel at Komorn, and, with doors fast bolted, cut up a rich and beautiful vestment of his grandfather's, the emperor Sigismund, of red and gold, with silver spots, and made it into a tiny coronation robe, with surplice and humeral (or shoulder piece), the stole and banner, the gloves and shoes. The Queen was much alarmed by a report that the Polish party meant to stop her on her way to Weissenburg; and if the baggage should be seized and searched, the discovery of the crown might have fatal consequences. Helen, on this, observed that the King was more important than the crown, and that the best way would be to keep them together; so she wrapped up the crown in a cloth, and hid it under the mattress of his cradle, with a long spoon for mixing his pap upon the top, so, said the Queen, he might take care of his crown himself.

On Tuesday before Whit Sunday the party set out, escorted by Count Ulric, and several other knights and nobles. After crossing the Danube in a large boat, the Queen and her little girl were placed in a carriage, or more probably a litter, the other ladies rode, and the cradle and its precious contents were carried by four men; but this the poor little Lassla, as Helen shortens his lengthy name, resented so much, that he began to scream so loud that she was forced to dismount and carry him in her arms, along a road rendered swampy by much rain.

They found all the villages deserted by the peasants, who had fled into the woods, and as most of their lords were of the other party, they expected an attack, so the little king was put into the carriage with his mother and sister, and the ladies formed a circle round it "that if anyone shot at the carriage we might receive the stroke". When the danger was over the child was taken out again, for he would be content nowhere but in the arms of either his nurse or of faithful Helen, who took turns to carry him on foot nearly all the way, sometimes in a high wind which covered them with dust, sometimes in great heat, sometimes in rain so heavy that Helen's fur pelisse, with which she covered his cradle, had to be wrung out several times. They slept at an inn, round which the gentlemen lighted a circle of fires, and kept watch all night.

Weissenburg was loyal, five hundred armed gentlemen came out to meet them, and on Whitsun Eve they entered the city, Helen carrying her little king in her arms in the midst of a circle of these five hundred holding their naked swords aloft. On Whit Sunday, Helen rose early, bathed the little fellow, who was twelve weeks old that day, and dressed him. He was then carried in her arms to the church, beside his mother. According to the old Hungarian customs, the choir door was closed–the burghers were within, and would not open till the new monarch should have taken the great coronation oath to respect the Hungarian liberties and laws.

This oath was taken by the Queen in the name of her son, the doors were opened, and all the train entered, the little princess being lifted up to stand by the organ, lest she should be hurt in the throng. First Helen held her charge up to be confirmed, and then she had to hold him while he was knighted, with a richly adorned sword bearing the motto "Indestructible", and by a stout Hungarian knight called Mikosch Weida, who struck with such a goodwill that Helen felt the blow on her arm, and the Queen cried out to him not to hurt the child.

The Archbishop of Gran anointed the little creature, dressed him in the red and gold robe, and put on his head the holy crown, and the people admired to see how straight he held up his neck under it; indeed, they admired the loudness and strength of his cries, when, as the good lady records, "the noble king had little pleasure in his coronation for he wept aloud". She had to hold him up for the rest of the service, while Count Ulric of Eily held the crown over his head, and afterwards to seat him in a chair in St. Peter's Church, and then he was carried home in his cradle, with the count holding the crown over his head, and the other regalia borne before him.

And thus Ladislas became King of Hungary at twelve weeks old, and was then carried off by his mother into Austria for safety. Whether this secret robbery of the crown, and coronation by stealth, was wise or just on the mother's part is a question not easy of answer–though of course she deemed it her duty to do her utmost for her child's rights. Of Helen Kottenner's deep fidelity and conscientious feeling there can be no doubt, and her having acted with her eyes fully open to the risk she ran, her trust in Heaven overcoming her fears and terrors, rendered her truly a heroine.

The crown has had many other adventures, and afterwards was kept in an apartment of its own, in the castle of Ofen, with an antechamber guarded by two grenadiers. The door was of iron, with three locks, and the crown itself was contained in an iron chest with five seals. All this, however, did not prevent it from being taken away and lost in the Revolution of 1849.

George the Triller

1455

I

"Why, Lady dear, so sad of cheer?
  Hast waked the livelong night?"
"My dreams foreshow my children's woe,
  Ernst bold and Albrecht bright.

"From the dark glades of forest shades
  There rushed a raging boar,
Two sapling oaks with cruel strokes
  His crooked tusks uptore."

"Ah, Lady dear, dismiss thy fear
  Of phantoms haunting sleep!"
"The giant knight, Sir Konrad hight,
  Hath vowed a vengeance deep.

"My Lord, o'erbold, hath kept his gold,
  And scornful answer spake:
'Kunz, wisdom learn, nor strive to burn
  The fish within their lake.'

"See, o'er the plain, with all his train,
  My Lord to Leipzig riding;
Some danger near my children dear
  My dream is sure betiding."

"The warder waits before the gates,
  The castle rock is steep,
The massive walls protect the halls,
  Thy children safely sleep."

II

'T is night's full noon, fair shines the moon
　On Altenburg's old halls,
The silver beams in tranquil streams
　Rest on the ivied walls.

Within their tower the midnight hour
　Has wrapt the babes in sleep,
With unclosed eyes their mother lies
　To listen and to weep.

What sudden sound is stirring round?
　What clang thrills on her ear?
Is it the breeze amid the trees
　Re-echoing her fear?

Swift from her bed, in sudden dread,
　She to her lattice flies:
Oh! sight of woe, from far below
　Behold a ladder rise:

And from yon tower, her children's bower,
　Lo! Giant Kunz descending!
Ernst, in his clasp of iron grasp,
　His cries with hers is blending.

"Oh! hear my prayer, my children spare,
　The sum shall be restored;
Nay, twenty-fold returned the gold,
　Thou know'st how true my Lord."

With mocking grace he bowed his face:
　"Lady, my greetings take;
Thy Lord may learn how I can burn
　The fish within their lake."

Oh! double fright, a second knight
　Upon the ladder frail,
And in his arm, with wild alarm,
　A child uplifts his wail!

Would she had wings! She wildly springs
　To rouse her slumbering train;

Bolted without, her door so stout
　　Resists her efforts vain!

No mortal ear her calls can hear,
　　The robbers laugh below;
Her God alone may hear her moan,
　　Or mark her hour of woe.

A cry below, "Oh! let me go,
　　I am no prince's brother;
Their playmate I–Oh ! hear my cry
　　Restore me to my mother!"

With anguish sore she shakes the door.
　　Once more Sir Kunz is rearing
His giant head. His errand sped
　　She sees him reappearing.

Her second child in terror wild
　　Is struggling in his hold;
Entreaties vain she pours again,
　　Still laughs the robber bold.

"I greet thee well, the Elector tell
　　How Kunz his counsel takes,
And let him learn that I can burn
　　The fish within their lakes."

III

"Swift, swift, good steed, death's on thy speed,
　　Gain Isenburg ere morn;
Though far the way, there lodged our prey,
　　We laugh the Prince to scorn.

"There Konrad's den and merry men
　　Will safely hold the boys–
The Prince shall grieve long ere we leave
　　Our hold upon his joys.

"But hark! but hark! how through the dark
　　The castle bell is tolling,
From tower and town o'er wood and down,
　　The like alarm notes rolling.

"The peal rings out! echoes the shout!
  All Saxony's astir;
Groom, turn aside, swift must we ride
  Through the lone wood of fir."

Far on before, of men a score
  Prince Ernst bore still sleeping;
Thundering as fast, Kunz came the last,
  Carrying young Albrecht weeping.

The clanging bell with distant swell
  Dies on the morning air,
Bohemia's ground another bound
  Will reach, and safety there.

The morn's fresh beam lights a cool stream,
  Charger and knight are weary,
He draws his rein, the child's sad plain
  He meets with accents cheery.

"Sir Konrad good, be mild of mood,
  A fearsome giant thou!
For love of heaven, one drop be given
  To cool my throbbing brow!"

Kunz' savage heart feels pity's smart,
  He soothes the worn-out child,
Bathes his hot cheeks, and bending seeks
  For woodland berries wild.

A deep-toned bark! A figure dark,
  Smoke grimed and sun embrowned,
Comes through the wood in wondering mood,
  And by his side a hound.

"Oh, to my aid, I am betrayed,
  The Elector's son forlorn,
From out my bed these men of dread
  Have this night hither borne!"

"Peace, if thou 'rt wise," the false groom cries,
  And aims a murderous blow;
His pole-axe long, his arm so strong,
  Must lay young Albrecht low.

See, turned aside, the weapon glide
  The woodman's pole along,
To Albrecht's clasp his friendly grasp
  Pledges redress from wrong.

Loud the hound's note as at the throat
  Of the false groom he flies;
Back at the sounds Sir Konrad bounds:
  "Off hands, base churl," he cries.

The robber lord with mighty sword,
  Mailed limbs of giant strength–
The woodman stout, all arms without,
  Save his pole's timber length–

Unequal fight! Yet for the right
  The woodman holds the field;
Now left, now right, repels the knight,
  His pole full stoutly wields.

His whistle clear rings full of cheer,
  And lo! his comrades true,
All swarth and lusty, with fire poles trusty,
  Burst on Sir Konrad's view.

His horse's rein he grasps amain
  Into his selle to spring,
His gold-spurred heel his stirrup's steel
  Has caught, his weapons ring.

His frightened steed with wildest speed
  Careers with many a bound;
Sir Konrad's heel fast holds the steel,
  His head is on the ground.

The peasants round lift from the ground
  His form in woeful plight,
To convent cell, for keeping well,
  Bear back the robber knight.

"Our dear young lord, what may afford
  A charcoal-burners' store
We freely spread, milk, honey, bread,
  Our heated kiln before!"

IV

Three mournful days the mother prays,
  And weeps the children's fate;
The prince in vain has scoured the plain–
  A sound is at the gate.

The mother hears, her head she rears,
  She lifts her eager finger–
"Rejoice, rejoice, 't is Albrecht's voice,
  Open! Oh, wherefore linger?"

See, cap in hand the woodman stand–
  Mother, no more of weeping–
His hound well tried is at his side,
  Before him Albrecht leaping,

Cries, "Father dear, my friend is here!
  My mother! Oh, my mother!
The giant knight he put to flight,
  The good dog tore the other."

Oh! who the joy that greets the boy,
  Or who the thanks may tell,
Oh how they hail the woodman's tale,
  How he had "trilled[6] him well!"

"I trilled him well," he still will tell
  In homely phrase his story,
To those who sought to know how wrought
  An unarmed hand such glory.

That mother sad again is glad,
  Her home no more bereft;
For news is brought Ernst may be sought
  Within the Devil's Cleft.

That cave within, these men of sin
  Had learnt their leader's fall,
The prince to sell they proffered well
  At price of grace to all.

---

6   Trillen, to shake; a word analogous to our trill, to shake the voice in singing.

Another day and Earnest lay,
  Safe on his mother's breast;
Thus to her sorrow a gladsome morrow
  Had brought her joy and rest.

The giant knight was judged aright,
  Sentenced to death he lay;
The elector mild, since safe his child,
  Sent forth the doom to stay.

But all to late, and o'er the gate
  Of Freiburg's council hall
Sir Konrad's head, with features dread,
  The traitor's eyes appal.

The scullion Hans who wrought their plans,
  And oped the window grate,
Whose faith was sold for Konrad's gold,
  He met a traitor's fate

V

Behold how gay the wood to-day,
  The little church how fair,
What banners wave, what tap'stry brave
  Covers its carvings rare!

A goodly train—the parents twain,
  And here the princess two,
Here with his pole, George, stout of soul,
  And all his comrades true.

High swells the chant, all jubilant,
  And each boy bending low,
Humbly lays down the wrapping gown
  He wore the night of woe.

Beside them lay a smock of grey,
  All grimed with blood and smoke;
A thankful sign to Heaven benign,
  That spared the sapling oak.

"What prize would'st hold, thou 'Triller bold',
  Who trilled well for my son?"
"Leave to cut wood, my Lord, so good,
  Near where the fight was won."

"Nay, Triller mine, the land be thine,
  My trusty giant-killer,
A farm and house I and my spouse
  Grant free to George the Triller!"

Years hundred four, and half a score,
  Those robes have held their place;
The Triller's deed has grateful meed
  From Albrecht's royal race.

The child rescued by George the Triller's Golden Deed was the ancestor of the late Prince Consort, and thus of our future line of kings. He was the son of the Elector Friedrich the mild of Saxony, and of Margarethe of Austria, whose dream presaged her children's danger. The Elector had incurred the vengeance of the robber baron, Sir Konrad of Kauffingen, who, from his huge stature, was known as the Giant Ritter, by refusing to make up to him the sum of 4000 gulden which he had had to pay for his ransom after being made prisoner in the Elector's service. In reply to his threats, all the answer that the robber knight received was the proverbial one, "Do not try to burn the fish in the ponds, Kunz."

Stung by the irony, Kunz bribed the elector's scullion, by name Hans Schwabe, to admit him and nine chosen comrades into the Castle of Altenburg on the night of the 7th of July, 1455, when the Elector was to be at Leipzig. Strange to say, this scullion was able to write, for a letter is extant from him to Sir Konrad, engaging to open the window immediately above the steep precipice, which on that side was deemed a sufficient protection to the castle, and to fasten a rope ladder by which to ascend the crags. This window can still be traced, though thenceforth it was bricked up. It gave access to the children's apartments, and on his way to them, the robber drew the bolt of their mother's door, so that though, awakened by the noise, she rushed to her window, she was a captive in her own apartment, and could not give the alarm, nor do anything but join her vain entreaties to the cries of her helpless children. It was the little son of the Count von Bardi whom Wilhelm von Mosen brought down by mistake for young Albrecht, and Kunz, while hurrying up to exchange the children, bade the rest of his band hasten on to secure the elder prince without waiting for him. He followed in a few seconds with Albrecht in his arms, and his servant Schweinitz riding after him, but he never overtook the main body.

Their object was to reach Konrad's own Castle of Isenburg on the frontiers of Bohemia, but they quickly heard the alarm bells ringing, and beheld beacons lighted upon every hill. They were forced to betake themselves to the forests, and about half-way, Prince Ernst's captors, not daring to go any father, hid themselves and him in a cavern called the Devil's Cleft on the right bank of the River Mulde.

Kunz himself rode on till the sun had risen, and he was within so few miles of his castle that the terror of his name was likely to be a sufficient protection. Himself and his horse were, however, spent by the wild midnight ride, and on the border of the wood of Eterlein, near the monastery of Grunheim, he halted, and finding the poor child grievously exhausted and feverish, he lifted him down, gave him water, and went himself in search of wood strawberries for his refreshment, leaving the two horses in the charge of Schweinitz. The servant dozed in his saddle, and meanwhile the charcoal-burner, George Schmidt, attracted by the sounds, came out of the wood, where all night he had been attending to the kiln, hollowed in the earth, and heaped with earth and roots of trees, where a continual charring of wood was going on. Little Albrecht no sooner saw this man than he sprang to him, and telling his name and rank, entreated to be rescued from these cruel men. The servant awaking, leapt down and struck a deadly blow at the boy's head with his poleaxe, but it was parried by the charcoal-burner, who interposing with one hand the strong wooden pole he used for stirring his kiln, dragged the little prince aside with the other, and at the same time set his great dog upon the servant. Sir Konrad at once hurried back, but the valiant charcoal-burner still held his ground, dangerous as the fight was between the peasant unarmed except for the long pole, and the fully accoutred knight of gigantic size and strength. However, a whistle from George soon brought a gang of his comrades to his aid, and Kunz, finding himself surrounded, tried to leap into his saddle, and break through the throng by weight of man and horse, but his spur became entangled, the horse ran away, and he was dragged along with his head on the ground till he was taken up by the peasants and carried to the convent of Grunheim, whence he was sent to Zwickau, and was thence transported heavily ironed to Freiburg, where he was beheaded on the 14th of July, only a week after his act of violence. The Elector, in his joy at the recovery of even one child, was generous enough to send a pardon, but the messenger reached Freiburg too late, and a stone in the marketplace still marks the place of doom, while the grim effigy of Sir Konrad's head grins over the door of the Rathhaus. It was a pity Friedrich's mildness did not extend to sparing torture as well as death to his treacherous scullion, but perhaps a servant's power of injuring his master was thought a reason for surrounding such instances of betrayal with special horrors.

The party hidden in the Devil's Cleft overheard the peasants in the wood talking of the fall of the giant of Kauffingen, and, becoming alarmed for themselves, they sent to the Governor of the neighbouring castle of Hartenstein to offer to restore Prince Ernst, provided they were promised a full pardon. The boy had been given up as dead, and intense were the rejoicings of the parents at his restoration. The Devil's Cleft changed its name to the Prince's Cleft, and the tree where Albrecht had lain was called the Prince's Oak, and still remains as a witness to the story, as do the moth-eaten garments of the princely children, and the smock of the charcoal-burner, which they offered up in token of thanksgiving at the little forest church of Ebendorff, near the scene of the rescue.

"I trillirt the knaves right well," was honest George's way of telling the story of his exploit, not only a brave one, but amounting even to self-devotion when we remember that the robber baron was his near neighbour, and a terror to all around. The word Triller took the place of his surname, and when the sole reward he asked was leave freely to cut wood in the forest, the Elector gave him a piece of land of his own in the parish of Ebersbach. In 1855 there was a grand celebration of the rescue of the Saxon princes on the 9th of July, the four hundredth anniversary, with a great procession of foresters and charcoal-burners to the "Triller's Brewery", which stands where George's hut and kiln were once placed. Three of his descendants then figured in the procession, but since that time all have died, and the family of the Trillers is now extinct.

Sir Thomas More's Daughter

1535

WE have seen how dim and doubtful was the belief that upbore the grave and beautiful Antigone in her self-sacrifice; but there have been women who have been as brave and devoted in their care of the mortal remains of their friends—not from the heathen fancy that the weal of the dead depended on such rites, but from their earnest love, and with a fuller trust beyond.

Such was the spirit of Beatrix, a noble maiden of Rome, who shared the Christian faith of her two brothers, Simplicius and Faustinus, at the end of the third century. For many years there had been no persecution, and the Christians were living at peace, worshipping freely, and venturing even to raise churches. Young people had grown up to whom the being thrown to the lions, beheaded, or burnt for the faith's sake, was but a story of the times gone by. But under the Emperor Diocletian all was changed. The old heathen gods must be worshipped, incense must be burnt to the statue of the Emperor, or torture and death were the punishment. The two brothers Simplicius and Faustinus were thus asked to deny their faith, and resolutely refused. They were cruelly tortured, and at length beheaded, and their bodies thrown into the tawny waters of the Tiber. Their sister Beatrix had taken refuge with a poor devout Christian woman, named Lucina. But she did not desert her brothers in death; she made her way in secret to the bank of the river, watching to see whether the stream might bear down the corpses so dear to her. Driven along, so as to rest upon the bank, she found them at last, and, by the help of Lucina, she laid them in the grave in the cemetery called Ad Ursum Pileatum. For seven months she remained in her shelter, but she was at last denounced, and was brought before the tribunal, where she made answer that nothing should induce her to adore gods made of wood and stone. She was strangled in her prison, and her corpse being cast out, was taken home by Lucina, and buried beside her brothers. It was, indeed, a favourite charitable work of the Christian widows at Rome to provide for the burial of the martyrs; and as for the most part they were poor old obscure women, they could perform this good work

151

with far less notice than could persons of more mark.

But nearer home, our own country shows a truly Christian Antigone, resembling the Greek lady, both in her dutifulness to the living, and in her tender care for the dead. This was Margaret, the favourite daughter of sir Thomas More, the true-hearted, faithful statesman of King Henry VIII.

Margaret's home had been an exceedingly happy one. Her father, Sir Thomas More, was a man of the utmost worth, and was both earnestly religious and conscientious, and of a sweetness of manner and playfulness of fancy that endeared him to everyone. He was one of the most affectionate and dutiful of sons to his aged father, Sir John More; and when the son was Lord Chancellor, while the father was only a judge, Sir Thomas, on his way to his court, never failed to kneel down before his father in public, and ask his blessing. Never was the old saying, that a dutiful child had dutiful children, better exemplified than in the More family. In the times when it was usual for parents to be very stern with children, and keep them at a great distance, sometimes making them stand in their presence, and striking them for any slight offence, Sir Thomas More thought it his duty to be friendly and affectionate with them, to talk to them, and to enter into their confidence; and he was rewarded with their full love and duty.

He had four children—Margaret, Elizabeth, Cicely, and John. His much-loved wife died when they were all very young, and he thought it for their good to marry a widow, Mrs. Alice Middleton, with one daughter named Margaret, and he likewise adopted an orphan called Margaret Giggs. With this household he lived in a beautiful large house at Chelsea, with well-trimmed gardens sloping down to the Thames; and this was the resort of the most learned and able men, both English and visitors from abroad, who delighted in pacing the shady walks, listening to the wit and wisdom of Sir Thomas, or conversing with the daughters, who had been highly educated, and had much of their father's humour and sprightliness. Even Henry VIII himself, then one of the most brilliant and graceful gentlemen of his time, would sometimes arrive in his royal barge, and talk theology or astronomy with Sir Thomas; or, it might be, crack jests with him and his daughters, or listen to the music in which all were skilled, even Lady More having been persuaded in her old age to learn to play on various instruments, including the flute. The daughters were early given in marriage, and with their husbands, continued to live under their father's roof. Margaret's husband was William Roper, a young lawyer, of whom Sir Thomas was very fond, and his household at Chelsea was thus a large and joyous family home of children and grandchildren, delighting in the kind, bright smiles of the open face under the square cap, that the great painter Holbein has sent down to us as a familiar sight.

But these glad days were not to last for ever. The trying times of the reign of Henry VIII were beginning, and the question had been stirred whether the King's marriage with Katherine of Aragon had been a lawful one. When Sir Thomas More found that the King was determined to take his own course, and to divorce himself without permission from the Pope, it was against his conscience to remain in office when acts were being done which he could not think right or lawful. He therefore resigned his office as Lord Chancellor, and, feeling himself free from the load and temptation, his gay spirits rose higher than ever. His manner of communicating the change to his wife, who had been very proud of his state and dignity, was thus. At church, when the service was over, it had always been the custom for one of his attendants to summon Lady More by coming to her closet door, and saying, "Madam, my lord is gone." On the day after his resignation, he himself stepped up, and with a low bow said, "Madam, my lord is gone," for in good soothe he was no longer Chancellor, but only plain Sir Thomas.

He thoroughly enjoyed his leisure, but he was not long left in tranquillity. When Anne Boleyn was crowned, he was invited to be present, and twenty pounds were offered him to buy a suitably splendid dress for the occasion; but his conscience would not allow him to accept the invitation, though he well knew the terrible peril he ran by offending the King and Queen. Thenceforth there was a determination to ruin him. First, he was accused of taking bribes when administering justice. It was said that a gilt cup had been given to him as a New Year's gift, by one lady, and a pair of gloves filled with gold coins by another; but it turned out, on examination, that he had drunk the wine out of the cup, and accepted the gloves, because it was ill manners to refuse a lady's gift, yet he had in both cases given back the gold.

Next, a charge was brought that he had been leaguing with a half-crazy woman called the Nun of Kent, who had said violent things about the King. He was sent for to be examined by Henry and his Council, and this he well knew was the interview on which his safety would turn, since the accusation was a mere pretext, and the real purpose of the King was to see whether he would go along with him in breaking away from Rome–a proceeding that Sir Thomas, both as churchman and as lawyer, could not think legal. Whether we agree or not in his views, it must always be remembered that he ran into danger by speaking the truth, and doing what he thought right. He really loved his master, and he knew the humour of Henry VIII, and the temptation was sore; but when he came down from his conference with the King in the Tower, and was rowed down the river to Chelsea, he was so merry that William Roper, who had been waiting for him in the boat, thought he must be safe, and said, as they landed and walked up the garden–

"I trust, sir, all is well, since you are so merry?"

"It is so, indeed, son, thank God!"

"Are you then, sir, put out of the bill?"

"Wouldest thou know, son why I am so joyful? In good faith I rejoice that I have given the devil a foul fall; because I have with those lords gone so far that without great shame I can never go back," he answered, meaning that he had been enabled to hold so firmly to his opinions, and speak them out so boldly, that henceforth the temptation to dissemble them and please the King would be much lessened. That he had held his purpose in spite of the weakness of mortal nature, was true joy to him, though he was so well aware of the consequences that when his daughter Margaret came to him the next day with the glad tidings that the charge against him had been given up, he calmly answered her, "In faith, Meg, what is put off is not given up."

One day, when he had asked Margaret how the world went with the new Queen, and she replied, "In faith, father, never better; there is nothing else in the court but dancing and sporting," he replied, with sad foresight, "Never better. Alas, Meg! it pitieth me to remember unto what misery, poor soul, she will shortly come. These dances of hers will prove such dances that she will spurn off our heads like footballs, but it will not be long ere her head will take the same dance."

So entirely did he expect to be summoned by a pursuivant that he thought it would lessen the fright of his family if a sham summons were brought. So he caused a great knocking to be made while all were at dinner, and the sham pursuivant went through all the forms of citing him, and the whole household were in much alarm, till he explained the jest; but the earnest came only a few days afterwards. On the 13th of April of 1534, arrived the real pursuivant to summon him to Lambeth, there to take the oath of supremacy, declaring that the King was the head of the Church of England, and that the Pope had no authority there. He knew what the refusal would bring on him. He went first to church, and then, not trusting himself to be unmanned by his love for his children and grandchildren, instead of letting them, as usual, come down to the water side, with tender kisses and merry farewells, he shut the wicket gate of the garden upon them all, and only allowed his son-in-law Roper to accompany him, whispering into his ear, "I thank our Lord, the field is won."

Conscience had triumphed over affection, and he was thankful, though for the last time he looked on the trees he had planted, and the happy home he had loved. Before the council, he undertook to swear to some clauses in the oath which were connected with the safety of the realm; but he refused to take that part of the oath which related to the King's power over the Church. It is said that the King would thus have been satisfied, but that the Queen urged him further. At any rate, after being four days under the charge of the Abbot of Westminister, Sir Thomas was sent to the Tower of London. There his wife–a plain, dull woman, utterly unable to understand the point of conscience–came and scolded him for being so foolish as to lie there in a close, filthy prison, and be shut up with rats and mice, instead of enjoying the favour of the King. He heard all she had to say, and answered, "I pray thee, good Mrs. Alice, tell me one thing–is not this house as near heaven as my own?" To which she had no better answer than "Tilly vally, tilly vally." But, in spite of her folly, she loved him faithfully; and when all his property was seized, she sold even her clothes to obtain necessaries for him in prison.

His chief comfort was, however, in visits and letters from his daughter Margaret, who was fully able to enter into the spirit that preferred death to transgression. He was tried in Westminster Hall, on the 1st of July, and, as he had fully expected, sentenced to death. He was taken back along the river to the Tower. On the wharf his loving Margaret was waiting for her last look. She broke through the guard of soldiers with bills and halberds, threw her arms round his neck, and kissed him, unable to say any word but "Oh, my father!–oh, my father!" He blessed her, and told her that whatsoever she might suffer, it was not without the will of God, and she must therefore be patient. After having once parted with him, she suddenly turned back again, ran to him, and, clinging round his neck, kissed him over and over again–a sight at which the guards themselves wept. She never saw him again; but the night before his execution he wrote to her a letter with a piece of charcoal, with tender remembrances to all the family, and saying to her, "I never liked your manner better than when you kissed me last; for I am most pleased when daughterly love and dear charity have no leisure to look to worldly courtesy." He likewise made it his especial request that she might be permitted to be present at his burial.

His hope was sure and steadfast, and his heart so firm that he did not even cease from humorous sayings. When he mounted the crazy ladder of the scaffold he said, "Master Lieutenant, I pray you see me safe up; and for my coming down let me shift for myself." And he desired the executioner to give him time to put his beard out of the way of the stroke, "since that had never offended his Highness".

His body was given to his family, and laid in the tomb he had already prepared in Chelsea Church; but the head was set up on a pole on London Bridge. The calm, sweet features were little changed, and the loving daughter gathered courage as she looked up at them. How she contrived the deed, is not known; but before many days had passed, the head was no longer there, and Mrs. Roper was said to have taken it away. She was sent for to the Council, and accused of the stealing of her father's head. She shrank not from avowing that thus it had been, and that the head was in her own possession. One story says that, as she was passing under the bridge in a boat, she looked up, and said, "That head has often lain in my lap; I would that it would now fall into it." And at that moment it actually fell, and she received it. It is far more likely that she went by design, at the same time as some faithful friend on the bridge, who detached the precious head, and dropped it down to her in her boat beneath. Be this as it may, she owned before the cruel-hearted Council that she had taken away and cherished the head of the man whom they had slain as a traitor. However, Henry VIII. was not a Creon, and our Christian Antigone was dismissed unhurt by the Council, and allowed to retain possession of her treasure. She caused it to be embalmed, kept it with her wherever she went, and when, nine years afterwards, she died (in the year 1544), it was laid in her coffin in the "Roper aisle" of St. Dunstan's Church, at Canterbury.

Under Ivan the Terrible

1564

PRINCE Andrej Kourbsky was one of the chief boyards or nobles at the Court of Ivan, the first Grand Prince of Muscovy who assumed the Eastern title of Tzar, and who relieved Russia from the terrible invasions of the Tatars. This wild race for nearly four hundred years had roamed over the country, destroying and plundering all they met with, and blighting all the attempts at civilization that had begun to be made in the eleventh century. It was only when the Russians learnt the use of firearms that these savages were in any degree repressed. In the year 1551 the city of Kazan, upon the River Kazanka, a tributary of the Volga, was the last city that remained in the hands of the Tatars. It was a rich and powerful place, a great centre of trade between Europe and the East, but it was also a nest of robbers, who had frequently broken faith with the Russians, and had lately expelled the Khan Schig Alei for having endeavoured to fulfil his engagements to them. The Tzar Ivan Vassilovitch, then only twenty-two years of age, therefore marched against the place, resolved at any cost to reduce it and free his country from these inveterate foes.

On his way he received tidings that the Crimean Tatars had come plundering into Russia, probably thinking to attack Moscow, while Ivan was besieging Kazan. He at once sent off the Prince Kourbsky with 15,000 men, who met double that number of Tatars at Toula, and totally defeated them, pursuing them to the River Chevorona, where, after a second defeat, they abandoned a great number of Russian captives, and a great many camels. Prince Kourbsky was wounded in the head and shoulder, but was able to continue the campaign.

Some of the boyards murmured at the war, and declared that their strength and resources were exhausted. Upon this the Tzar desired that two lists might be drawn up of the willing and unwilling warriors in his camp. "The first", he said, "shall be as dear to me as my own children; their needs shall be made known to me, and I will share all I have with them. The others may stay at home; I want no cowards in my army." No one of course chose to be in the second list, and about this time was formed the

IVAN THE TERRIBLE.

famous guard called the Strelitzes, a body of chosen warriors who were always near the person of the Tzar.

In the middle of August, 1552, Ivan encamped in the meadows on the banks of the Volga, which spread like a brilliant green carpet around the hill upon which stood the strongly fortified city of Kazan. The Tatars had no fears. "This is not the first time", they said, "that we have seen the Muscovites beneath our walls. Their fruitless attacks always end in retreats, till we have learned to laugh them to scorn;" and when Ivan sent them messengers with offers of peace, they replied, "All is ready; we only await your coming to begin the feast."

They did not know of the great change that the last half-century had made in sieges. One of the Italian condottieri, or leaders of free companies, had made his way to Moscow, and under his instructions, Ivan's troops were for the first time to conduct a siege in the regular modern manner, by digging trenches in the earth, and throwing up the soil in front into a bank, behind which the cannon and gunners are posted, with only small openings made through which to fire at some spot in the enemy's walls. These trenches are constantly worked nearer and nearer to the fortifications, till by the effect of the shot an opening or breach must be made in the walls, and the soldiers can then climb up upon scaling ladders or heaps of small faggots piled up to the height of the opening. Sometimes, too, the besiegers burrow underground till they are just below the wall, then fill the hole with gunpowder, and blow up all above them; in short, instead of, as in former days, a well-fortified city being almost impossible to take, except by starving out the garrison, a siege is in these times almost equally sure to end in favour of the besiegers.

All through August and September the Russians made their approaches, while the Tatars resisted them bravely, but often showing great barbarity. Once when Ivan again sent a herald, accompanied by a number of Tatar prisoners, to offer terms to Yediguer, the present Khan, the defenders called out to their countrymen, "You had better perish by our pure hands than by those of the wretched Christians," and shot a whole flight of arrows at them. Moreover, every morning the magicians used to come out at sunrise upon the walls, and their shrieks, contortions, and waving of garments were believed, not only by the Tatars but by the Russians, and by Andrej Kourbsky himself, to bring foul weather, which greatly harassed the Russians. On this Ivan sent to Moscow for a sacred cross that had been given to the Grand Prince Vladimir when he was converted; the rivers were blessed, and their water sprinkled round the camp, and the fair weather that ensued was supposed to be due to the conteraction of the incantations of the magicians. These Tatars were Mahometans, but they must have retained some of the wind-raising enchantments of their Buddhist brethren in Asia.

A great mine had been made under the gate of Arsk, and eleven barrels of gunpowder placed in it. On the 30th of September it was blown up, and the whole tower became a heap of ruins. For some minutes the consternation of the besieged was such that there was a dead silence like the stillness of the grave. The Russians rushed forward over the opening, but the Tatars, recovering at the sight of them, fought desperately, but could not prevent them from taking possession of the tower at the gateway. Other mines were already prepared, and the Tzar gave notice of a general assault for the next day, and recommended all his warriors to purify their souls by repentance, confession, and communion, in readiness for the deadly strife before them. In the meantime, he sent Yediguer a last offer of mercy, but the brave Tatars cried out, "We will have no pardon! If the Russians have one tower, we will build another; if they ruin our ramparts we will set up more. We will be buried under the walls of Kazan, or else we will make him raise the siege."

Early dawn began to break. The sky was clear and cloudless. The Tatars were on their walls, the Russians in their trenches; the Imperial eagle standard, which Ivan had lately assumed, floated in the morning wind. The two armies were perfectly silent, save here and there the bray of a single trumpet, or beat of a naker drum in one or the other, and the continuous hum of the hymns and chants from the three Russian chapel-tents. The archers held their arrows on the string, the gunners stood with lighted matches. The copper-clad domes of the minarets began to glow with the rising sunbeams; the muezzins were on the roofs about to call the Moslemin to prayer; the deacon in the Tzar's chapel-tent was reading the Gospel–"There shall be one fold and one Shepherd." At that moment the sun's disk appeared above the eastern hills, and ere yet the red orb had fully mounted above the horizon, there was a burst as it were of tremendous thunderings, and the ground shook beneath the church. The Tzar went to the entrance, and found the whole city hill so "rolled in sable smoke", that he could distinguish nothing, and, going back to his place, desired that the service should continue. The deacon was in the midst of the prayer for the establishment of the power of the Tzar and the discomfiture of his enemies, when the crushing burst of another explosion rushed upon their ears, and as it died away another voice broke forth, the shout raised by every man in the Russian lines, "God is with us!" On then they marched towards the openings that the mines had made, but there the dauntless garrison, in spite of the terror and destruction caused by the two explosions, met them with unabated fury, rolling beams or pouring boiling water upon them as they strove to climb the breach, and fighting hand to hand with them if they mounted it. However, by the time the Tzar had completed his devotions and mounted his horse, his eagle could be seen above the smoke upon the citadel.

Still the city had to be won, step by step, house by house, street by street; and even while struggling onwards the Russians were tempted aside by plunder among the rich stores of merchandise that were heaped up in the warehouses of this the mart of the East. The Khan profited by their lack of discipline, and forced them back to the walls; nay, they would have absolutely been driven out at the great gate, but that they beheld their young Tzar on horseback among his grey-haired councillors. By the advice of these old men Ivan rode forward, and with his own hand planted the sacred standard at the gates, thus forming a barrier that the fugitives were ashamed to pass. At the same time he, with half his choice cavalry, dismounted, and entered the town all fresh and vigorous, their rich armour glittering with gold and silver, and plumes of various colours streaming from their helmets in all the brilliancy of Eastern taste. This reinforcement recalled the plunderers to their duty, and the Tatars were driven back to the Khan's palace, whence, after an hour's defence, they were forced to retreat.

At a postern gate, Andrej Kourbsky and two hundred men met Yediguer and 10,000 Tatars, and cut off their retreat, enclosing them in the narrow streets. They forced their Khan to take refuge in a tower, and made signs as if to capitulate. "Listen," they said. "As long as we had a government, we were willing to die for our prince and country. Now Kazan is yours, we deliver our Khan to you, alive and unhurt—lead him to the Tzar. For our own part, we are coming down into the open field to drain our last cup of life with you."

Yediguer and one old councillor were accordingly placed in the hands of an officer, and then the desperate Tatars, climbing down the outside of the walls, made for the Kazanka, where no troops, except the small body under Andrej Kourbsky and his brother Romanus, were at leisure to pursue them. The fighting was terrible, but the two princes kept them in view until checked by a marsh which horses could not pass. The bold fugitives took refuge in a forest, where, other Russian troops coming up, all were surrounded and slain, since not a man of them would accept quarter.

Yediguer was kindly treated by Ivan, and accompanying him to Moscow, there became a Christian, and was baptized by the name of Simeon, in the presence of the Tzar and his whole court, on the banks of the Moskwa. He married a Russian lady, and his whole conduct proved that his conversion was sincere.

But this story has only been told at so much length to show what manner of man Andrej Kourbsky was, and Ivan Vassilovitch had been, and how they had once been brethren in arms; and perhaps it has been lingered over from the melancholy interest there must always be in watching the fall of a powerful nation, and the last struggles of gallant men. Ivan was then a gallant, religious and highly gifted prince, generous and merciful, and with every promise of a glorious reign, full of benefits to his country. Alas! this part of his career was one glimpse of brightness in the course of a long tempestuous day. His reign had begun when he was but three years old. He had had a violent and cruel mother, and had, after her death, been bred up by evil-minded courtiers, who absolutely taught him cruel and dissolute amusements in order to prevent him from attending to state affairs. For a time, the exhortations of the good and fearless patriarch, and the influence of his gentle wife Anastasia, had prevailed, and with great vigour and strong principle he had shaken off all the evil habits of his boyhood, and begun, as it seemed, an admirable reign.

Too soon, a severe illness shook the balance of his mind, and this was quickly followed by the death of the excellent Tzarina Anastasia. Whether grief further unsettled him, or whether the loss of her gentle influence left him a prey to his wicked councillors, from that time forward his conduct was so wildly savage and barbarous as to win for him the surname of the Terrible. Frantic actions, extravagant excesses, and freaks of horrible cruelty looked like insanity; and yet, on the other hand, he often showed himself a clear-headed and sagacious monarch, anxious for the glory and improvement of his people.

But he lived in continual suspicion, and dreaded every eminent man in his dominions. Kourbsky whom he had once loved and trusted, and had charged with the command of his army, as his most able boyard, fell under his suspicion; and, with horror and indignation, learnt that the Tzar was plotting against his life, and intended to have him put to death,. Kourbsky upon this explained to his wife that she must either see him put to a shameful death, or let him leave her for ever. He gave his blessing to his son, a boy of nine years old, and leaving his house at night he scaled the wall of Moscow, and meeting his faithful servant, Vasili Shibanoff, with two horses, he made his escape. This Vasili was his stirrup-bearer, one of those serfs over whom the boyard on whose land they were born possessed absolute power. That power was often abused, but the instinctive faithfulness of the serf towards his master could hardly be shaken, even by the most savage treatment, and a well-treated serf viewed his master's family with enthusiastic love and veneration. Vasili accompanied his master's flight through the birch forests towards the Livonian frontier, the country where but lately Kourbsky had been leading the Tzar's armies. On the way the prince's horse became exhausted by his weight, and Vasili insisted on giving up his own in its stead, though capture in the course of such desertion would have been certain death. However, master and servant safely arrived at Wolmar in Livonia, and there Andrej came to the determination of renouncing the service of the ungrateful Ivan, and entering that of the King of Poland. For this last step there was no excuse. Nothing can justify a man in taking up arms against his country, but in the middle Ages the tie of loyalty was rather to the man than to the state, and Andrej Kourbsky seems to have deemed that his honour would be safe, provided he sent a letter to his sovereign, explaining his grievance and giving up his allegiance. The letter is said to have been full of grave severity and deep, suppressed indignation, though temperate in tone; but no one would consent to be the bearer of such a missive, since the cruel tyrant's first fury was almost certain to fall on him who presented it. Believing his master's honour at stake, Vasili offered himself to be the bearer of the fatal letter, and Kourbsky accepted the offer, tendering to him a sum of money, which the serf rejected, knowing that money would soon be of little service to him, and seeking no reward for what he deemed his duty to his lord.

As Ivan's justice had turned into barbarity, so his religion had turned into foolish fanatic observance. He had built a monastery near Moscow for himself and three hundred chosen boyards, and every morning at three or four o'clock he took his two sons into the belfry with him and proceeded to strike the bells, the Russian mode of ringing them, till all the brethren were assembled. This bell-sounding was his favourite occupation, and in it he was engaged when Vasili arrived. The servant awaited him in the vestibule, and delivered the letter with these words: "From my master and thine exile, Prince Andrej Kourbsky."

Ivan answered by such a blow on the leg with his iron-tipped rod that the blood poured from the wound; but Vasili neither started, cried out, nor moved a feature. At once the Tzar bade him be seized and tortured, to make him disclose whether his master had any partners in guilt, or if any plans were matured. But no extremity of agony could extract aught but praises of the prince, and assurances of his readiness to die for him. From early morning till late at night the torturers worked, one succeeding when another was tired out; but nothing could overcome his constancy, and his last words were a prayer to implore his God to have mercy on his master and forgive his desertion.

His praise came even from the tyrant, who wrote to Kourbsky—"Let thy servant Vaska[7] shame thee. He preserved his truth to thee before the Tzar and the people. Having given thee his word of faith, he kept it, even before the gates of death."

After the flight of Kourbsky, the rage of Ivan continued to increase with each year of his life. He had formed a sort of bodyguard of a thousand ruffians, called the Oprichnina, who carried out his barbarous commands, and committed an infinity of murders and robberies on their own account. He was like a distorted caricature of Henry VIII, and, like him, united violence and cruelty with great exactness about religious worship, carrying his personal observances to the most fanatic extravagance.

In the vacancy of the Metropolitan See, he cast his eyes upon the monastery in the little island of Solovsky, in the White Sea, where the Prior, Feeleep Kolotchof, was noted for his holy life, and the good he had done

---

7   The abbreviation of Vasili or Basil.

among the wild and miserable population of the island. He was the son of a rich boyard, but had devoted himself from his youth to a monastic life, and the fame of his exertions in behalf of the islanders had led the Tzar to send him not only precious vessels for the use of his church, but contributions to the stone churches, piers, and hostelries that he raised for his people; for whom he had made roads, drained marshes, introduced cattle, and made fisheries and salt pans, changing the whole aspect of the place, and lessening even the inclemency of the climate.

On this good man the Tzar fixed his choice. He wrote to him to come to Moscow to attend a synod, and on his arrival made him dine at the palace, and informed him that he was to be chief pastor of the Russian Church. Feeleep burst into tears, entreating permission to refuse, and beseeching the Tzar not to trust "so heavy a freight to such a feeble bark". Ivan held to his determination, and Feeleep then begged him at least to dismiss the cruel Oprichnina. "How can I bless you," he said, "while I see my country in mourning?"

The Tzar replied by mentioning his suspicions of all around him, and commanded Feeleep to be silent. He expected to be sent back to his convent at once, but, instead of this, the Tzar commanded the clergy to elect him Archbishop, and they all added their entreaties to him to accept the office, and endeavour to soften the Tzar, who respected him; and he yielded at last, saying, "The will of the Tzar and the pastors of the church must, then, be done."

At his consecration, he preached a sermon on the power of mildness, and the superiority of the victories of love over the triumphs of war. It awoke the better feelings of Ivan, and for months he abstained from any deed of violence; his good days seemed to have returned and he lived in intimate friendship with the good Archbishop.

But after a time the sleeping lion began to waken. Ivan's suspicious mind took up an idea that Feeleep had been incited by the nobles to request the abolition of the Oprichnina, and that they were exciting a revolt. The spies whom he sent into Moscow told him that wherever an Oprichnik appeared, the people shrank away in silence, as, poor things! they well might. He fancied this as a sign that conspiracies were brewing, and all his atrocities began again. The tortures to which whole families were put were most horrible; the Oprichniks went through the streets with poignards and axes, seeking out their victims, and killing from ten to twenty a day. The corpses lay in the streets, for no one dared to leave his house to bury them. Feeleep vainly sent letters and exhortations to the Tzar–they were unnoticed. The unhappy citizens came to the Archbishop, entreating him to intercede for them, and he gave them his promise that he would not spare his own blood to save theirs.

One Sunday, as Feeleep was about to celebrate the Holy Communion,

Ivan came into the Cathedral with a troop of his satellites, like him, fantastically dressed in black cassocks and high caps. He came towards the Metropolitan, but Feeleep kept his eyes fixed on the picture of our Lord, and never looked at him. Someone said, "Holy Father, here is the prince; give him your blessing."

"No," said the Archbishop, "I know not the Tzar in this strange disguise–still less do I know him in his government. Oh, Prince! we are here offering sacrifice to the Lord, and beneath the altar the blood of guiltless Christians is flowing in torrents... You are indeed on the throne, but there is One above all, our Judge and yours. How shall you appear before his Judgment Seat?–stained with the blood of the righteous, stunned with their shrieks, for the stones beneath your feet cry out for vengeance to Heaven. Prince, I speak as shepherd of souls; I fear God alone."

The Archbishop was within the golden gates, which, in Russian churches, close in the sanctuary or chancel, and are only entered by the clergy. He was thus out of reach of the cruel iron-tipped staff, which the Tzar could only strike furiously on the pavement, crying out, "Rash monk, I have spared you too long. Henceforth I will be to you such as you describe."

The murders went on in their full horrors; but, in spite of the threat, the Archbishop remained unmolested, though broken-hearted at the cruelties around him. At last, however, his resolute witness became more than the tyrant would endure, and messengers were secretly sent to the island of Solovsky, to endeavour to find some accusation against him. They tampered with all the monks in the convent, to induce them to find some fault in him, but each answered that he was a saint in every thought, word, and deed; until at last Payssi, the prior who had succeeded him, was induced, by the hope of a bishopric, to bear false witness against him.

He was cited before an assembly of bishops and boyards, presided over by the Tzar, and there he patiently listened to the monstrous stories told by Payssi. Instead of defending himself, he simply said, "This seed will not bring you a good harvest;" and, addressing himself to the Tzar, said, "Prince, you are mistaken if you think I fear death. Having attained an advanced age, far from stormy passions and worldly intrigues, I only desire to return my soul to the Most High, my Sovereign Master and yours. Better to perish an innocent martyr, than as Metropolitan to look on at the horrors and impieties of these wretched times. Do what you will with me! Here are the pastoral staff, the white mitre, and the mantle with which you invested me. And you, bishops, archimandrites, abbots, servants of the altar, feed the flock of Christ zealously, as preparing to give an account thereof, and fear the Judge of Heaven more than the earthly judge."

He was then departing, when the Tzar recalled him, saying that he could not be his own judge, and that he must await his sentence. In truth, worse indignities were preparing for him. He was in the midst of the Liturgy on the 8th of November, the Greek Michaelmas, when a boyard came in with a troop of armed Oprichniks, who overawed the people, while the boyard read a paper degrading the Metropolitan from his sacred office; and then the ruffians, entering through the golden gates tore off his mitre and robes, wrapped him in a mean gown, absolutely swept him out of the church with brooms, and took him in a sledge to the Convent of the Epiphany. The people ran after him, weeping bitterly, while the venerable old man blessed them with uplifted hands, and, whenever he could be heard, repeated his last injunction, "Pray, pray to God."

Once again he was led before the Emperor, to hear the monstrous sentence that for sorcery, and other heavy charges, he was to be imprisoned for life. He said no reproachful word, only, for the last time, he besought the Tzar to have pity on Russia, and to remember how his ancestors had reigned, and the happy days of his youth. Ivan only commanded the soldiers to take him away; and he was heavily ironed, and thrown into a dungeon, whence he was afterwards transferred to a convent on the banks of the Moskwa, where he was kept bare of almost all the necessaries of life: and in a few days' time the head of Ivan Borissovitch Kolotchof, the chief of his family, was sent to him, with the message, "Here are the remains of your dear kinsman, your sorcery could not save him!" Feeleep calmly took the head in his arms, blessed it, and gave it back.

The people of Moscow gathered round the convent, gazed at his cell, and told each other stories of his good works, which they began to magnify into miracles. Thereupon the Emperor sent him to another convent, at a greater distance. Here he remained till the next year, 1569, when Maluta Skouratof, a Tatar, noted as a favourite of the Tzar, and one of the chief ministers of his cruelty, came into his cell, and demanded his blessing for the Tzar.

The Archbishop replied that blessings only await good men and good works, adding tranquilly, "I know what you are come for. I have long looked for death. Let the Tzar's will be done." The assassin then smothered him, but pretended to the abbot that he had been stifled by the heat of the cell. He was buried in haste behind the altar, but his remains have since been removed to his own cathedral at Moscow, the scene where he had freely offered his own life by confronting the tyrant in the vain endeavour to save his people.

Vain, too, was the reproof of the hermit, who shocked Ivan's scruples by offering him a piece of raw flesh in the middle of Lent, and told him that he was preying on the flesh and blood of his subjects. The crimes of Ivan grew more and more terrible, and yet his acuteness was such that they can hardly be inscribed to insanity. He caused the death of his own son by a blow with that fatal staff of his; and a last, after a fever varied by terrible delirium, in which alone his remorse manifested itself, he died while setting up the pieces for a game at chess, on the 17th of March, 1584.

This has been a horrible story, in reality infinitely more horrible than we have made it; but there is this blessing among many others in Christianity, that the blackest night makes its diamonds only show their living lustre more plainly: and surely even Ivan the Terrible, in spite of himself, did something for the world in bringing out the faithful fearlessness of Archbishop Feeleep, and the constancy of the stirrup-bearer, Vasili.

Fort St. Elmo

1565

THE white cross of the Order of St. John waved on the towers of Rhodes for two hundred and fifty-five years. In 1552, after a desperate resistance, the Turks, under their great Sultan, Solyman the Magnificent, succeeded in driving the Knights Hospitaliers from their beautiful home, and they were again cast upon the world.

They were resolved, however, to continue their old work of protecting the Mediterranean travellers, and thankfully accepted, as a gift from the Emperor Charles V, the little islet of Malta as their new station. It was a great contrast to their former home, being little more than a mere rock rising steeply out of the sea, white, glaring and with very shallow earth, unfit to bear corn, though it produced plenty of oranges, figs, and melons–with little water, and no wood–the buildings wretched, and for the most part uninhabited, and the few people a miserable mongrel set, part Arab, part Greek, part Sicilian, and constantly kept down by the descents of the Moorish pirates, who used to land in the unprotected bays, and carry off all the wretched beings they could catch, to sell for slaves. It was a miserable exchange from fertile Rhodes, which was nearly five times larger than this barren rock; but the Knights only wanted a hospital, a fortress, and a harbour; and this last they found in the deeply indented northern shore, while they made the first two. Only a few years had passed before the dreary Città Notabile had become in truth a notable city, full of fine castle-like houses, infirmaries, and noble churches, and fenced in with mighty wall and battlements–country houses were perched upon the rocks–the harbours were fortified, and filled with vessels of war–and deep vaults were hollowed out in the rock, in which corn was stored sufficient to supply the inhabitants for many months.

Everywhere that there was need was seen the red flag with the eight-pointed cross. If there was an earthquake on the shores of Italy or Sicily, there were the ships of St. John, bringing succour to the crushed and ruined townspeople. In every battle with Turk or Moor, the Knights were among the foremost; and, as ever before, their galleys were the aid of the peaceful merchant, and the terror of the corsair. Indeed, they were nearer Tunis, Tripoli, and Algiers, the great nests of these Moorish pirates, and were better able to threaten them, and thwart their cruel descents, than when so much farther eastward; and the Mahometan power found them quite as obnoxious in Malta as in Rhodes.

Solyman the Magnificent resolved, in his old age, to sweep thes obstinate Christians from the seas, and, only twelve years after the siege of Rhodes, prepared an enormous armament, which he united with those of the Barbary pirates, and placed under the command of Mastafa and Piali, his two bravest pashas, and Dragut, a terrible Algerine corsair, who had already made an attempt upon the island, but had been repulsed by the good English knight, Sir Nicholas Upton. Without the advice of this pirate the Sultan desired that nothing should be undertaken.

The Grand Master who had to meet this tremendous danger was Jean Parisot de la Valette, a brave and resolute man, as noted for his piety and tenderness to the sick in the infirmaries as for his unflinching courage. When he learnt the intentions of the Sultan, he began by collecting a Chaper of his Order, and, after laying his tidings before them, said: "A formidable army and a cloud of barbarians are about to burst on this isle. Brethren, they are the enemies of Jesus Christ. The question is the defence of the Faith, and whether the Gospel shall yield to the Koran. God demands from us the life that we have already devoted to Him by our profession. Happy they who in so good a cause shall first consummate their sacrifice. But, that we may be worthy, my brethren, let us hasten to the altar, there to renew our vows; and may to each one of us be imparted, by the very Blood of the Saviour of mankind, and by faithful participation in His Sacraments, that generous contempt of death that can alone render us invincible."

With these words, he led the way to the church, and there was not an individual knight who did not on that day confess and receive the Holy Communion; after which they were as new men–all disputes, all trivialities and follies were laid aside–and the whole community awaited the siege like persons under a solemn dedication.

The chief harbour of Malta is a deep bay, turned towards the north, and divided into two lesser bays by a large tongue of rock, on the point of which stood a strong castle, called Fort St. Elmo. The gulf to the westward has a little island in it, and both gulf and islet are called Marza Muscat. The gulf to the east, called the Grand Port, was again divided by three fingers of rock projecting from the mainland, at right angles to the tongue that bore Fort St. Elmo. Each finger was armed with a strong talon–the Castle of La Sangle to the east, the Castle of St. Angelo in the middle, and Fort Ricasoli to the west. Between St. Angelo and La Sangle was the harbour where all the ships of war were shut up at night by an immense chain; and behind was il Borgo, the chief fortification in the island. Città

Notabile and Gozo were inland, and their fate would depend upon that of the defences of the harbour. To defend all this, the Grand Master could only number 700 knights and 8500 soldiers. He sent to summon home all those of the Order who were dispersed in the different commanderies in France, Spain, and Germany, and entreated aid from the Spanish king, Philip II, who wished to be considered as the prime champion of Roman Catholic Christendom, and who alone had the power of assisting him. The Duke of Alva, viceroy for Philip in Sicily, made answer that he would endeavour to relieve the Order, if they could hold out Fort St. Elmo till the fleet could be got together; but that if this castle were once lost, it would be impossible to bring them aid, and they must be left to their fate.

The Grand Master divided the various posts to the knights according to their countries. The Spaniards under the Commander De Guerras, Bailiff of Negropont, had the Castle of St. Elmo; the French had Port de la Sangle; the Germans, and the few English knights whom the Reformation had left, were charged with the defence of the Port of the Borgo, which served as headquarters, and the Commander Copier, with a body of troops, was to remain outside the town and watch and harass the enemy.

On the 18th of May, 1565, the Turkish fleet came in sight. It consisted of 159 ships, rowed by Christian slaves between the decks, and carrying 30,000 Janissaries and Spahis, the terrible warriors to whom the Turks owed most of their victories, and after them came, spreading for miles over the blue waters, a multitude of ships of burthen bringing the horses of the Spahis, and such heavy battering cannon as rendered the dangers of a siege infinitely greater than in former days. These Janissaries were a strange, distorted resemblance of the knights themselves, for they were bound in a strict brotherhood of arms, and were not married, so as to care for nothing but each other, the Sultan, and the honour of their troop. They were not dull, apathetic Turks, but chiefly natives of Circassia and Georgia, the land where the human race is most beautiful and nobly formed. They were stolen from their homes, or, too often, sold by their parents when too young to remember their Christian baptism, and were bred up as Mahometans, with no home but their corps, no kindred but their fellow soldiers. Their title, given by the Sultan who first enrolled them, meant New Soldiers, their ensign was a camp kettle, as that of their Pashas was one, two, or three horses' tails, in honour of the old Kurdish chief, the founder of the Turkish empire; but there was no homeliness in their appointments, their weapons—scimitars, pistols, and carabines—were crusted with gold and jewels; their headdress, though made in imitation of a sleeve, was gorgeous, and their garments were of the richest wool and silk, dyed with the deep, exquisite colours of the East. Terrible warriors were they, and almost equally dreaded were the Spahis, light horsemen from Albania and the other Greek and Bulgarian provinces who had entered the Turkish service, and were great plunderers, swift and cruel, glittering, both man and horse, with the jewels they had gained in their forays.

These were chiefly troops for the land attack, and they were set on shore at Port St. Thomas, where the commanders, Mustafa and Piali, held a council, to decide where they should first attack. Piali wished to wait for Dragut, who was daily expected, but Mustafa was afraid of losing time, and of being caught by the Spanish fleet, and insisited on at once laying siege to Fort St. Elmo, which was, he thought, so small that it could not hold out more than five or six days.

Indeed, it could not hold above 300 men, but these were some of the bravest of the knights, and as it was only attacked on the land side, they were able to put off boats at night and communicate with the Grand Master and their brethren in the Borgo. The Turks set up their batteries, and fired their enormous cannon shot upon the fortifications. One of their terrible pieces of ordnance carried stone balls of 160 lb., and no wonder that stone and mortar gave way before it, and that a breach was opened in a few days' time. That night, when, as usual, boatloads of wounded men were transported across to the Borgo, the Bailiff of Negropont sent the knight La Cerda to the Grand Master to give an account of the state of things and ask for help. La Cerda spoke strongly, and, before a great number of knights, declared that there was no chance of so weak a place holding out for more than a week.

"What has been lost," said the Grand Master, "since you cry out for help?"

"Sir," replied La Cerda, "the castle may be regarded as a patient in extremity and devoid of strength, who can only be sustained by continual remedies and constant succour."

"I will be doctor myself," replied the Grand Master, "and will bring others with me who, if they cannot cure you of fear, will at least be brave enough to prevent the infidels from seizing the fort."

The fact was, as he well knew, that the little fort could not hold out long, and he grieved over the fate of his knights; but time was everything, and the fate of the whole isle depended upon the white cross being still on that point of land when the tardy Sicilian fleet should set sail. He was one who would ask no one to run into perils that he would not share, and he was bent on throwing himself into St. Elmo, and being rather buried under the ruins than to leave the Mussulmans free a moment sooner than could be helped to attack the Borgo and Castle of St. Angelo. But the whole Chapter of Knights entreated him to abstain, and so many volunteered for this desperate service, that the only difficulty was to choose among them. Indeed, La Cerda had done the garrison injustice; no one's heart was failing but his own; and the next day there was a respite, for a cannon shot from St. Angelo falling into the enemy's camp, shattered a stone, a splinter of which struck down the Piali Pasha. He was thought dead, and the camp and fleet were in confusion, which enabled the Grand Master to send off his nephew, the Chevalier de la Valette Cornusson, to Messina to entreat the Viceroy of Sicily to hasten to their relief; to give him a chart of the entrance of the harbour, and a list of signals, and to desire in especial that two ships belonging to the Order, and filled with the knights who had hurried from distant lands too late for the beginning of the siege, might come to him at once. To this the Viceroy returned a promise that at latest the fleet should sail on the 15th of June, adding an exhortation to him at all sacrifices to maintain St. Elmo. This reply the Grand Master transmitted to the garrison, and it nerved them to fight even with more patience and self-sacrifice. A desperate sally was led by the Chevalier de Medran, who fought his way into the trenches where the Turkish cannon were planted, and at first drove all before him; but the Janissaries rallied and forced back the Christians out of the trenches. Unfortunately there was a high wind, which drove the smoke of the artillary down on the counter-scarp (the slope of masonry facing the rampart), and while it was thus hidden from the Christians, the Turks succeeded in effecting a lodgment there, fortifying themselves with trees and sacks of earth and wool. When the smoke cleared off, the knights were dismayed to see the horse-tail ensigns of the Janissaries so near them, and cannon already prepared to batter the ravelin, or outwork protecting the gateway.

La Cerda proposed to blow this fortification up, and abandon it, but no other knight would hear of deserting an inch of wall while it could yet be held.

But again the sea was specked with white sails from the south-east. Six galleys came from Egypt, bearing 900 troops–Mameluke horsemen, troops recruited much like the Janissaries and quite as formidable. These ships were commanded by Ulucciali, an Italian, who had denied his faith and become a Mahometan, and was thus regarded with especial horror by the chivalry of Malta. And the swarm thickened for a few days more; like white-winged and beautiful but venomous insects hovering round their prey, the graceful Moorish galleys and galliots came up from the south, bearing 600 dark-visaged, white-turbaned, lithe-limbed Moors from Tripoli, under Dragut himself. The thunders of all the guns roaring forth their salute of honour told the garrison that the most formidable enemy of all had arrived. And now their little white rock was closed in on every side, with nothing but its own firmness to be its aid.

Dragut did not approve of having begun with attacking Fort St. Elmo; he thought that the inland towns should have been first taken, and Mustafa offered to discontinue the attack, but this the Corsair said could not now be done with honour, and under him the attack went on more furiously than ever. He planted a battery of four guns on the point guarding the entrance of Marza Muscat, the other gulf, and the spot has ever since been called Dragut's Point. Strange to say, the soldiers in the ravelin fell asleep, and thus enabled the enemy to scramble up by climbing on one another's shoulders and enter the place. As soon as the alarm was given, the Bailiff of Negropont, with a number of knights, rushed into the ravelin, and fought with the utmost desperation, but all in vain; they never succeeded in dislodging the Turks , and had almost been followed by them into the Fort itself. Only the utmost courage turned back the enemy at last, and, it was believed, with a loss of 3000. The Order had twenty knights and a hundred soldiers killed, with many more wounded. One knight named Abel de Bridiers, who was shot through the body, refused to be assisted by his brethren, saying, "Reckon me no more among the living. You will be doing better by defending our brothers." He dragged himself away, and was found dead before the altar in the Castle chapel. The other wounded were brought back to the Borgo in boats at night, and La Cerda availed himself of a slight scratch to come with them and remain, though the Bailiff of Negropont, a very old man, and with a really severe wound, returned as soon as it had been dressed, together with the reinforcements sent to supply the place of those who had been slain. The Grand Master, on finding how small had been La Cerda's hurt, put him in prison for several days; but he was afterwards released, and met his death bravely on the ramparts of the Borgo.

The 15th of June was passed. Nothing would make the Sicilian Viceroy move, nor even let the warships of the Order sail with their own knights, and the little fort that had been supposed unable to hold out a week, had for full a month resisted every attack of the enemy.

At last Dragut, though severely wounded while reconnoitring, set up a battery on the hill of Calcara, so as to command the strait, and hinder the succours from being sent across to the fort. The wounded were laid down in the chapel and the vaults, and well it was for them that each knight of the Order could be a surgeon and a nurse. One good swimmer crossed under cover of darkness with their last messages, and La Valette prepared five armed boats for their relief; but the enemy had fifteen already in the bay, and communication was entirely cut off. It was the night before the 23rd of June when these brave men knew their time was come. All night they prayed, and prepared themselves to die by giving one another the last rites of the Church, and at daylight each repaired to his post, those who could not walk being carried in chairs, and sat ghastly figures, sword in hand, on the brink of the breach, ready for their last fight.

By the middle of the day every Christian knight in St. Elmo had died upon his post, and the little heap of ruins was in the hands of the enemy. Dragut was dying of his wound, but just lived to hear that the place was won, when it had cost the Sultan 8000 men! Well might Mustafa say, "If the son has cost us so much, what will the father do?"

It would be too long to tell the glorious story of the three months' futher siege of the Borgo. The patience and resolution of the knights was unshaken, though daily there were tremendous battles, and week after week passed by without the tardy relief from Spain. It is believed that Philip II thought that the Turks would exhaust themselves against the Order, and forbade his Viceroy to hazard his fleet; but at last he was shamed into permitting the armament to be fitted out. Two hundred knights of St. John were waiting at Messina, in despair at being unable to reach their brethren in their deadly strait, and constantly haunting the Viceroy's palace, till he grew impatient, and declared they did not treat him respectfully enough, nor call him "Excellency".

"Senor," said one of them, "if you will only bring us in time to save the Order, I will call you anything you please, excellency, highness, or majesty itself."

At last, on the 1st of September, the fleet really set sail, but it hovered cautiously about on the farther side of the island, and only landed 6000 men and then returned to Sicily. However, the tidings of its approach had spread such a panic among the Turkish soldiers, who were worn out and exhausted by their exertions, that they hastily raised the siege, abandoned their heavy artillery, and, removing their garrison from Fort St. Elmo, re-embarked in haste and confusion. No sooner, however, was the Pasha in his ship than he became ashamed of his precipitation, more expecially when he learnt that the relief that had put 16,000 men to flight consisted only of 6000, and he resolved to land and give battle; but his troops were angry and unwilling, and were actually driven out of their ships by blows.

In the meantime, the Grand Master had again placed a garrison in St. Elmo, which the Turks had repaired and restored, and once more the cross of St. John waved on the end of its tongue of land, to greet the Spanish allies. A battle was fought with the newly arrived troops, in which the Turks were defeated; they again took to their ships, and the Viceroy of Sicily, from Syracuse, beheld their fleet in full sail for the East.

Meantime, the gates of the Borgo were thrown open to receive the brethren and friends who had been so long held back from coming to the relief of the home of the Order. Four months' siege, by the heaviest artillery in Europe, had shattered the walls and destroyed the streets, till, to the eyes of the newcomers, the town looked like a place taken by assault, and sacked by the enemy; and of the whole garrison, knights, soldiers, and sailors altogether, only six hundred were left able to bear arms, and they for the most part covered with wounds. The Grand Master and his surviving knights could hardly be recognized, so pale and altered were they by wounds and excessive fatigue; their hair, beards, dress, and armour showing that for four full months they had hardly undressed, or lain down unarmed. The newcomers could not restrain their tears, but all together proceeded to the church to return thanks for the conclusion of their perils and afflictions. Rejoicings extended all over Europe, above all in Italy, Spain, and southern France, where the Order of St. John was the sole protection against the descents of the Barbary corsairs. The Pope sent La Valette a cardinal's hat, but he would not accept it, as unsuited to his office; Philip II presented him with a jewelled sword and dagger. Some thousand unadorned swords a few months sooner would have been a better testimony to his constancy, and that of the brave men whose lives Spain had wasted by her cruel delays.

The Borgo was thenceforth called Città Vittoriosa; but La Valette decided on building the chief town of the isle on the Peninsula of Fort St. Elmo, and in this work he spent his latter days, till he was killed by a sunstroke, while superintending the new works of the city which is deservedly known by his name, as Valetta.

The Order of St. John lost much of its character, and was finally swept from Malta in the general confusion of the Revolutionary wars. The British crosses now float in the harbour of Malta; but the steep white rocks must ever bear the memory of the self-devoted endurance of the beleaguered knights, and, foremost of all, of those who perished in St. Elmo, in order that the signal banner might to the very last summon the tardy Viceroy to their aid.

The Voluntary Convict
1622

IN the early summer of the year 1605, a coasting vessel was sailing along the beautiful Gulf of Lyons, the wind blowing gently in the sails, the blue Mediterranean lying glittering to the south, and the curved line of the French shore rising in purple and green tints, dotted with white towns and villages. Suddenly three light, white-sailed ships appeared in the offing, and the captain's practised eye detected that the wings that bore them were those of a bird of prey. He knew them for African brigantines, and though he made all sail, it was impossible to run into a French port, as on, on they came, not entirely depending on the wind, but, like steamers, impelled by unseen powers within them. Alas! that power was not the force of innocent steam, but the arms of Christian rowers chained to the oar. Sure as the pounce of a hawk upon a partridge was the swoop of the corsairs upon the French vessel. A signal to surrender followed, but the captain boldly refused, and armed his crew, bidding them stand to their guns. But the fight was too unequal, the brave little ship was disabled, the pirates boarded her, and, after a sharp fight on deck, three of the crew lay dead, all the rest were wounded, and the vessel was the prize of the pirates. The captain was at once killed, in revenge for his resistance, and all the rest of the crew and passengers were put in chains. Among these passengers was a young priest named Vincent de Paul, the son of a farmer in Languedoc, who had used his utmost endeavours to educate his son for the ministry, even selling the oxen from the plough to provide for the college expenses. A small legacy had just fallen to the young man, from a relation who had died at Marseilles; he had been thither to receive it, and had been persuaded by a friend to return home by sea. And this was the result of the pleasant voyage. The legacy was the prey of the pirates, and Vincent, severely wounded by an arrow, and heavily chained, lay half-stifled in a corner of the hold of the ship, a captive probably for life to the enemies of the faith. It was true that France had scandalized Europe by making peace with the Dey of Tunis, but this was a trifle to the corsairs; and when, after seven days' further cruising, they put into the harbour of

Tunis, they drew up an account of their capture, calling it a Spanish vessel, to prevent the French Consul from claiming the prisoners.

The captives had the coarse blue and white garments of slaves given them, and were walked five or six times through the narrow streets and bazaars of Tunis, by way of exhibition. They were then brought back to their ship, and the purchasers came thither to bargain for them. They were examined at their meals, to see if they had good appetites; their sides were felt like those of oxen; their teeth looked at like those of horses; their wounds were searched, and they were made to run and walk to show the play of their limbs. All this Vincent endured with patient submission, constantly supported by the thought of Him who took upon Him the form of a servant for our sakes; and he did his best, ill as he was, to give his companions the same confidence.

Weak and unwell, Vincent was sold cheap to a fisherman; but in his new service it soon became apparent that the sea made him so ill as to be of no use, so he was sold again to one of the Moorish physicians, the like of whom may still be seen, smoking their pipes sleepily, under their white turbans, cross-legged, among the drugs in their shop windows–these being small open spaces beneath the beautiful stone lacework of the Moorish lattices. The physician was a great chemist and distiller, and for four years had been seeking the philosopher's stone, which was supposed to be the secret of making gold. He found his slave's learning and intelligence so useful that he grew very fond of him, and tried hard to persuade him to turn Mahometan, offering him not only liberty, but the inheritance of all his wealth, and the secrets that he had discovered.

The Christian priest felt the temptation sufficiently to be always grateful for the grace that had carried him through it. At the end of a year, the old doctor died, and his nephew sold Vincent again. His next master was a native of Nice, who had not held out against the temptation to renounce his faith in order to avoid a life of slavery, but had become a renegade, and had the charge of one of the farms of the Dey of Tunis. The farm was on a hillside in an extremely hot and exposed region, and Vincent suffered much from being there set to field labour, but he endured all without a murmur. His master had three wives, and one of them, who was of Turkish birth,, used often to come out and talk to him, asking him many questions about his religion. Sometimes she asked him to sing, and he would then chant the psalm of the captive Jews: "By the waters of Babylon we sat down and wept;" and others of the "songs" of his Zion. The woman at last told her husband that he must have been wrong in forsaking a religion of which her slave had told her such wonderful things. Her words had such an effect on the renegade that he sought the slave, and in conversation with him soon came to a full sense of his own miserable position as an apostate. A change of religion on the part of a Mahometan is, however, always visited with death, both to the convert and his instructor. An Algerine, who was discovered to have become a Christian, was about this time said to have been walled up at once in the fortifications he had been building; and the story has been confirmed by the recent discovery, by the French engineers, of the remains of a man within a huge block of clay, that had taken a perfect cast of his Moorish features, and of the surface of his garments, and even had his black hair adhering to it. Vincent's master, terrified at such perils, resolved to make his escape in secret with his slave. It is disappointing to hear nothing of the wife; and not to know whether she would not or could not accompany them. All we know is, that master and slave trusted themselves alone to a small bark, and, safely crossing the Mediterranean, landed at Aigues Mortes, on the 28th of June, 1607; and that the renegade at once abjured his false faith, and soon after entered a brotherhood at Rome, whose office it was to wait on the sick in hospitals.

This part of Vincent de Paul's life has been told at length because it shows from what the Knights of St. John strove to protect the inhabitants of the coasts. We next find Vincent visiting at a hospital at Paris, where he gave such exceeding comfort to the patients that all with one voice declared him a messenger from heaven.

He afterwards became a tutor in the family of the Count de Joigni, a very excellent man, who was easily led by him to many good works. M. de Joigni was inspector general of the "Galeres", or Hulks, the ships in the chief harbours of France, such as Brest and Marseilles, where the convicts, closely chained, were kept to hard labour, and often made to toil at the oar, like the slaves of the Africans. Going the round of these prison ships, the horrible state of the convicts, their half-naked misery, and still more their fiendish ferocity went to the heart of the Count and of the Abbé de Paul; and, with full authority from the inspector, the tutor worked among these wretched beings with such good effect that on his doings being represented to the King, Louis XIII, he was made almoner general to the galleys.

While visiting those at Marseilles, he was much struck by the broken-down looks and exceeding sorrowfulness of one of the convicts. He entered into conversation with him, and, after many kind words, persuaded him to tell his troubles. His sorrow was far less for his own condition than for the misery to which his absence must needs reduce his wife and children. And what was Vencent's reply to this? His action was so striking that, though in itself it could hardly be safe to propose it as an example, it must be mentioned as the very height of self-sacrifice.

He absolutely changed places with the convict. Probably some arrangement was made with the immediate jailor of the gang, who, by the exchange of the priest for the convict, could make up his full tale of men to show when his numbers were counted. At any rate the prisoner went free, and returned to his home, whilst Vincent wore a convict's chain, did a convict's work, lived on convict's fare, and, what was worse, had only convict society. He was soon sought out and released, but the hurts he had received from the pressure of the chain lasted all his life. He never spoke of the event; it was kept a strict secret; and once when he had referred to it in a letter to a friend, he became so much afraid that the story would become known that he sent to ask for the letter back again. It was, however, not returned, and it makes the fact certain. It would be a dangerous precedent if prison chaplains were to change places with their charges; and, beautiful as was Vincent's spirit, the act can hardly be justified; but it should also be remembered that among the galleys of France there were then many who had been condemned for resistance to the arbitrary will of Cardinal de Richelieu, men not necessarily corrupt and degraded like the thieves and murderers with whom they were associated. At any rate, M. de Joigni did not displace the almoner, and Vincent worked on the consciences of the convicts with infinitely more force for having been for a time one of themselves. Many and many were won back to penitence, a hospital was founded for them, better regulations established, and, for a time, both prisons and galleys were wonderfully improved, although only for the lifetime of the good inpector and the saintly almoner. But who shall say how many souls were saved in those years by these men who did what they could?

The rest of the life of Vincent de Paul would be too lengthy to tell here, though acts of beneficence and self-devotion shine out in glory at each step. The work by which he is chiefly remembered is his establishment of the Order of Sisters of Charity, the excellent women who have for two hundred years been the prime workers in every charitable task in France, nursing the sick, teaching the young, tending deserted children, ever to be found where there is distress or pain.

But of these, and of his charities, we will not here speak, nor even of his influence for good on the King and Queen themselves. The whole tenor of his life was "golden" in one sense, and if we told all his golden deeds they would fill an entire book. So we will only wait to tell how he showed his remembrance of what he had gone through in his African captivity. The redemption of the prisoners there might have seemed his first thought, but that he did so much in other quarters. At different times, with the alms that he collected, and out of the revenues of his benefices, he ransomed no less then twelve hundred slaves from their captivity. At one time the French Consul at Tunis wrote to him that for a certain sum a large number might be set free, and he raised enough to release not only these, but seventy more, and he further wrought upon the King to obtain the consent of the Dey of Tunis that a party of Christian clergy should be permitted to reside in the consul's house, and to minister to the souls and bodies of the Christian slaves, of whom there were six thousand in Tunis alone, besides those in Algiers, Tangier, and Tripoli!

Permission was gained, and a mission of Lazarist brothers arrived. This, too, was an order founded by Vincent, consisting of priestly nurses like the Hospitaliers, though not like them warriors. They came in the midst of a dreadful visitation of the plague, and nursed and tended the sick, both Christians and Mahometans, with fearless devotion, day and night, till they won the honour and love of the Moors themselves.

The good Vincent de Paul died in the year 1660, but his brothers of St. Lazarus, and sisters of charity still tread in the paths he marked out for them, and his name scarcely needs the saintly epithet that his church as affixed to it to stand among the most honourable of charitable men.

The cruel deeds of the African pirates were never wholly checked till 1816, when the united fleets of England and France destroyed the old den of corsairs at Algiers, which has since become a French colony.

The Housewives of Löwenburg

1631

B RAVE deeds have been done by the burgher dames of some of the German cities collectively. Without being of the first class of Golden Deeds, there is something in the exploit of the dames of Weinsberg so quaint and so touching, that it cannot be omitted here.

It was in the first commencement of the long contest known as the strife between the Guelfs and Ghibellines–before even these had become the party words for the Pope's and the Emperor's friends, and when they only applied to the troops of Bavaria and of Swabia–that, in 1141, Wolf, Duke of Bavaria, was besieged in his castle of Weinberg by Friedrich, Duke of Swabia, brother to the reigning emperor, Konrad III.

The siege lasted long, but Wolf was obliged at last to offer to surrender; and the Emperor granted him permission to depart in safety. But his wife did not trust to this fair offer. She had reason to believe that Konrad had a peculiar enmity to her husband; and on his coming to take possession of the castle, she sent to him to entreat him to give her a safe conduct for herself and all the other women in the garrison, that they might come out with as much of their valuables as they could carry.

This was freely granted, and presently the castle gates opened. From beneath them came the ladies–but in strange guise. No gold nor jewels were carried by them, but each one was bending under the weight of her husband, whom she thus hoped to secure from the vengeance of the Ghibellines. Konrad, who was really a generous and merciful man, is said to have been affected to tears by this extraordinary performance; he hastened to assure the ladies of the perfect safety of their lords, and that the gentlemen might dismount at once, secure both of life and freedom. He invited them all to a banquet, and made peace with the Duke of Bavaria on terms much more favourable to the Guelfs than the rest of his party had been willing to allow.

The castle mount was thenceforth called no longer the Vine Hill, but the Hill of Weibertreue, or woman's fidelity. We will not invidiously translate it woman's truth, for there was in the transaction something of

"EACH WOMAN WAS BENDING UNDER THE WEIGHT OF HER HUSBAND."

a subterfuge; and it must be owned that the ladies tried to the utmost the knightly respect for womankind.

The good women of Löwenburg, who were but citizens' wives, seem to us more worthy of admiration for constancy to their faith, shown at a time when they had little to aid them. It was such constancy as makes martyrs; and though the trial stopped short of this, there is something in the homeliness of the whole scene, and the feminine form of passive resistance, that makes us so much honour and admire the good women that we cannot refrain from telling the story.

It was in the year 1631, in the midst of the long Thirty Years' Was between Roman Catholics and Protestants, which finally decided that each state should have its own religion, Löwenburg, a city of Silesia, originally Protestant, had passed into the hands of the Emperor's Roman Catholic party. It was a fine old German city, standing amid woods and meadows, fortified with strong walls surrounded by a moat, and with gate towers to protect the entrance.

In the centre was a large maketplace, called the Ring, into which looked the Council-house and forteen inns, or places of traffic, for the cloth that was woven in no less than 300 factories. The houses were of stone, with gradually projecting stories to the number of four or five, surmounted with pointed gables. The ground floors had once had trellised porches, but these had been found inconvenient and were removed, and the lower story consisited of a large hall, and strong vault, with a spacious room behind it containing a baking-oven, and a staircase leading to a wooden gallery, where the family used to dine. It seems they slept in the room below, though they had upstairs a handsome wainscoted apartment.

Very rich and flourishing had the Löwenburgers always been, and their walls were quite sufficient to turn back any robber barons, or even any invading Poles; but things were different when firearms were in use, and the bands of mercenary soldiers had succeeded the feudal army. They were infinitely more formidable during the battle or siege from their discipline, and yet more dreadful after it for their want of discipline. The poor Lowneburgers had been greatly misused: their Lutheran pastors had been expelled; all the superior citizens had either fled or been imprisoned; 250 families spent the summer in the woods, and of those who remained in the city, the men had for the most part outwardly conformed to the Roman Catholic Church. Most of these were of course indifferent at heart, and they had found places in the town council which had formerly been filled by more respectable men. However, the wives had almost all remained staunch to their Lutheran confession; they had followed their pastors weeping to the gates of the city, loading them with gifts, and they hastened at every opportunity to hear their preachings, or obtain baptism for their children at the Lutheran churches in the neighbourhood.

The person who had the upper hand in the Council was one Julius, who had been a Franciscan friar, but was a desperate, unscrupulous fellow, not at all like a monk. Finding that it was considered as a reproach that the churches of Löwenburg were empty, he called the whole Council together on the 9th of April, 1631, and informed them that the women must be brought to conformity, or else there were towers and prisons for them. The Burgomaster was ill in bed, but the Judge, one Elias Seiler, spoke up at once. "If we have been able to bring the men into the right path, why should not we be able to deal with these little creatures?"

Herr Mesnel, a cloth factor, who had been a widower six weeks, thought it would be hard to manage, though he quite agreed to the expedient, saying, "It would be truly good if man and wife had one Creed and one Paternoster; as concerns the Ten Commandments it is not so pressing." (A sentiment that he could hardly have wished to see put in practice.)

Another councillor, called Schwob Franze, who had lost his wife a few days before, seems to have had an eye to the future, for he said it would be a pity to frighten away the many beautiful maidens and widows there were among the Lutheran women; but on the whole the men without wives were much bolder and more sanguine of success than the married ones. And no one would undertake to deal with his own wife privately, so it ended by a message being sent to the more distinguished ladies to attend the Council.

But presently up came tidings that not merely these few dames, whom they might have hoped to overawe, were on their way, but that the Judge's wife and the Burgomaster's were the first pair in a procession of full 500 housewives, who were walking sedately up the stairs to the Council Hall below the chamber where the dignitaries were assembled. This was not by any means what had been expected, and the message was sent down that only the chief ladies should come up. "No," replied the Judge's wife, "we will not allow ourselves to be separated," and to this they were firm; they said, as one fared all should fare; and the Town Clerk, going up and down with smooth words, received no better answer than this from the Judge's wife, who, it must be confessed, was less ladylike in language than resolute in faith.

"Nay, nay, dear friend, do you think we are so simple as not to perceive the trick by which you would force us poor women against our conscience to change our faith? My husband and the priest have not been consorting together all these days for nothing; they have been joined together almost day and night; assuredly they have either boiled or baked a devil, which they may eat up themselves. I shall not enter there! Where I remain, my train and following will remain also! Women, is this your will?"

"Yea, yea, let it be so," they said; "we will all hold together as one man." His honour the Town Clerk was much affrighted, and went hastily back, reporting that the Council was in no small danger, since each housewife had her bunch of keys at her side! These keys were the badge of a wife's dignity and authority, and moreover they were such ponderous articles that they sometimes served as weapons. A Scottish virago has been know to dash out the brains of a wounded enemy with her keys; and the intelligence that the good dames had come so well furnished, filled the Council with panic. Dr. Melchior Hubner, who had been a miller's man, wished for a hundred musketeers to mow them down; but the Town Clerk proposed that all the Council should creep quietly down the back stairs, lock the doors on the refractory womankind, and make their escape.

This was effected as silently and quickly as possible, for the whole Council "could confess to a state of frightful terror." Presently the women peeped out, and saw the stairs bestrewn with hats, gloves, and handkerchiefs; and perceiving how they had put all the wisdom and authority of the town to the rout, there was great merriment among them, though, finding themselves locked up, the more tenderhearted began to pity their husbands and children. As for themselves, their maids and children came round the Town Hall, to hand in provisions to them, and all the men who were not of the Council were seeking the magistrates to know what their wives had done to be thus locked up.

The Judge sent to assemble the rest of the Council at his house; and though only four came, the doorkeeper ran to the Town Hall, and called out to his wife that the Council had reassembled, and they would soon be let out. To which, however, that very shrewd dame, the Judge's wife, answered with great composure, "Yea, we willingly have patience, as we are quite comfortable here; but tell them they ought to inform us why we are summoned and confined without trial."

She well knew how much better off she was than her husband without her. He paced about in great perturbation, and at last called for something to eat. The maid served up a dish of crab, some white bread, and butter; but, in his fury, he threw all the food about the room and out the window, away from the poor children, who had had nothing to eat all day, and at last he threw all the dishes and saucepans out of window. At last the Town Clerk and two others were sent to do their best to persuade the women that they had misunderstood–they were in no danger, and were only invited to the preachings of Holy Week: and, as Master Daniel, the joiner, added, "It was only a friendly conference. It is not customary with my masters and the very wise Council to hang a man before they have caught him."

This opprobrious illustration raised a considerable clamour of abuse from the ruder women; but the Judge's and Burgomaster's ladies silenced them, and repeated their resolution never to give up their faith against their conscience. Seeing that no impression was made on them, and that nobody knew what to do without them at home, the magistracy decided that they should be released, and they went quietly home; but the Judge Seiler, either because he had been foremost in the business, or else perhaps because of the devastation he had made at home among the pots and pans, durst not meet his wife, but sneaked out of the town, and left her with the house to herself.

The priest now tried getting the three chief ladies alone together, and most politely begged them to conform; but instead of arguing, they simply answered; "No; we were otherwise instructed by our parents and former preachers."

Then he begged them at least to tell the other women that they had asked for fourteen days for consideration.

"No, dear sir," they replied: "we were not taught by our parents to tell falsehoods, and we will not learn it from you."

Meanwhile Schwob Franze rushed to the Burgomaster's bedside, and begged him, for Heaven's sake, to prevent the priest from meddling with the women; for the whole bevy, hearing that their three leaders were called before the priest, were collecting in the marketplace, keys, bundles, and all; and the panic of the worthy magistrates was renewed. The Burgomaster sent for the priest, and told him plainly, that if any harm befel him from the women, the fault would be his own; and thereupon he gave way, the ladies went quietly home, and their stout champions laid aside their bundles and keys—not out of reach, however, in case of another summons.

However, the priest was obliged, next year, to leave Löwenburg in disgrace, for he was a man of notoriously bad character; and Dr. Melchior became a soldier, and was hanged at Prague.

After all, such a confession as this is a mere trifle, not only compared with martyrdoms of old, but with the constancy with which, after the revocation of the Edict of Nantes, the Huguenots endured persecution—as, for instance, the large number of women who were imprisoned for thirty-eight years at Aigues Mortes; or again, with the steady resolution of the persecuted nuns of Port Royal against signing the condemnation of the works of Jansen. Yet, in its own way, the feminine resistance of these good citizens' wives, without being equally high-toned, is worthy of record, and far too full of character to be passed over.

Fathers and Sons
218-1642-1798

ONE of the noblest characters in old Roman history is the first Scipio Africanus, and his first appearance is in a most pleasing light, at the battle of the River Ticinus, B.C. 219, when the Carthaginians, under Hannibal, had just completed their wonderful march across the Alps, and surprised the Romans in Italy itself.

Young Scipio was then only seventeen years of age, and had gone to his first battle under the eagles of his father, the Consul, Publius Cornelius Scipio. It was an unfortunate battle; the Romans, when exhausted by long resistance to the Spanish horse in Hannibal's army, were taken in flank by the Numidian calvary, and entirely broken. The Consul rode in front of the few equites he could keep together, striving by voice and example to rally his forces, until he was pierced by one of the long Numidian javelins, and fell senseless from his horse. The Romans, thinking him dead, entirely gave way; but his young son would not leave him, and, lifting him on his horse, succeeded in bringing him safe into the camp, where he recovered, and his after days retrieved the honour of the Roman arms.

The story of a brave and devoted son comes to us to light up the sadness of our civil wars between Cavaliers and Roundheads in the middle of the seventeenth century. It was soon after King Charles had raised his standard at Nottingham, and set forth on his march for London, that it became evident that the Parliamentary army, under the Earl of Essex, intended to intercept his march. The King himself was with the army, with his two boys, Charles and James; but the General-in-chief was Robert Bertie, Earl of Lindsay, a brave and experienced old soldier, sixty years of age, godson to Queen Elizabeth, and to her two favourite Earls, whose Christian name he bore. He had been in her Essex's expedition to Cambridge, and had afterwards served in the Low Countries, under Prince Maurice of Nassau; for the long Continental wars had throughout King James' peaceful reign been treated by the English nobility as schools of arms, and a few campaigns were considered as a graceful finish to a gentleman's education. As soon as Lord Lindsay had begun to fear that the disputes between the

King and Parliament must end in war, he had begun to exercise and train his tenantry in Lincolnshire and Northamptonshire, of whom he had formed a regiment of infantry. With him was his son Montagu Bertie, Lord Willoughby, a noble-looking man of thirty-two, of whom it was said, that he was "as excellent in reality as others in pretence," and that, thinking "that the cross was an ornament to the crown, and much more to the coronet, he satisfied not himself with the mere exercise of virtue, but sublimated it, and made it grace." He had likewise seen some service against the Spaniards in the Netherlands, and after his return had been made a captain in the Lifeguards, and a Gentleman of the Bedchamber. Vandyke has left portraits of the father and the son; the one a bald-headed, alert, precise-looking old warrior, with the cuirass and guantlets of elder warfare; the other, the very model of a cavalier, tall, easy, and graceful, with a gentle reflecting face, and wearing the long lovelocks and deep-point lace collar and cuffs characteristic of Queen Henrietta's Court. Lindsay was called General-in-chief, but the King had imprudently exempted the calvary from his command, its general, Prince Rupert of the Rhine, taking orders only from himself. Rupert was only three-and-twenty, and his education in the wild school of the Thirty Years' War had not taught him to lay aside his arrogance and opinionativeness; indeed, he had shown great petulance at receiving orders from the King through Lord Falkland.

At eight o'clock, on the morning of the 23rd of October, King Charles was riding along the ridge of Edgehill, and looking down into the Vale of Red Horse, a fair meadow land, here and there broken by hedges and copses. His troops were mustering around him, and in the valley he could see with his telescope the various Parliamentary regiments, as they poured out of the town of Keinton, and took up their positions in three lines. "I never saw the rebels in a body before," he said, as he gazed sadly at the subjects arrayed against him. "I shall give them battle. God, and the prayers of good men to Him, assist the justice of my cause." The whole of his forces, about 11,000 in number, were not assembled till two o'clock in the afternoon, for the gentlemen who had become officers found it no easy matter to call their farmers and retainers together, and marshal them into any sort of order. But while one troop after another came trampling, clanking, and shouting in, trying to find and take their proper place, there were hot words round the royal standard.

Lord Lindsay, who was an old comrade of the Earl of Essex, the commander of the rebel forces, knew that he would follow the tactics they had both together studied in Holland, little thinking that one day they should be arrayed one against the other in their own native England. He had a high opinion of Essex's generalship, and insisted that the situation of the Royal army required the utmost caution. Rupert, on the other hand, had seen the swift fiery charges of the fierce troopers of the Thirty Years' war, and was backed up by Patrick, Lord Ruthven, one of the many Scots who had won honour under the great Swedish King, Gustavus Adolphus. A sudden charge of the Royal horse would, Rupert argued, sweep the Roundheads from the field, and the foot would have nothing to do but to follow up the victory. The great portrait at Windsor shows us exactly how the King must have stood, with his charger by his side, and his grave, melancholy face, sad enough at having to fight at all with his subjects, and never having seen a battle, entirely bewildered between the ardent words of his spirited nephew and the grave replies of the well-seasoned old Earl. At last, as time went on, and some decision was necessary, the perplexed King, willing at least not to irritate Rupert, desired that Ruthven should array the troops in the Swedish fashion.

It was a greater affront to the General-in-chief than the king was likely to understand, but it could not shake the old soldier's loyalty. He gravely resigned the empty title of General, which only made confusion worse confounded, and rode away to act as colonel of his own Lincoln regiment, pitying his master's perplexity, and resolved that no private pique should hinder him from doing his duty. His regiment was of foot soldiers, and was just opposite to the standard of the Earl of Essex.

The church bell was ringing for afternoon service when the Royal forces marched down the hill. The last hurried prayer before the charge was stout old Sir Jacob Astley's, "O Lord, Thou knowest how busy I must be this day; if I forget Thee, do not Thou forget me;" then, rising, he said, "March on, boys." And, amid prayer and exhortation, the other side awaited the shock, as men whom a strong and deeply embittered sense of wrong had roused to take up arms. Prince Rupert's charge was, however, fully successful. No one even waited to cross swords with his troopers, but all the Roundhead horse galloped headlong off the field, hotly pursued by the Royalists. But the main body of the army stood firm, and for some time the battle was nearly equal, until a large troop of the enemy's cavalry who had been kept in reserve, wheeled round and fell upon the Royal forces just when their scanty supply of ammunition was exhausted.

Step by step, however, they retreated bravely, and Rupert, who had returned from his charge, sought in vain to collect his scattered troopers, so as to fall again on the rebels; but some were plundering, some chasing the enemy, and none could be got together. Lord Lindsay was shot through the thigh bone, and fell. He was instantly surrounded by the rebels on horseback; but his son, Lord Willoughby, seeing his danger, flung himself alone among the enemy, and forcing his way forward, raised his father in his arms thinking of nothing else, and unheeding his own peril. The throng of enemy around called to him to surrender, and, hastily giving up his sword, he carried the Earl into the nearest shed, and laid him on a heap of straw, vainly striving to staunch the blood. It was a bitterly cold night, and the frosty wind came howling through the darkness. Far above, on the ridge of the hill, the fires of the King's army shone with red light, and some way off on the other side twinkled those of the Parliamentary forces. Glimmering lanterns or torches moved about the battlefield, those of the savage plunderers who crept about to despoil the dead. Whether the battle were won or lost, the father and son knew not, and the guard who watched them knew as little. Lord Lindsay himself murmured, "If it please God I should survive, I never will fight in the same field with boys again!"—no doubt deeming that young Rupert had wrought all the mischief. His thoughts were all on the cause, his son's all on him; and piteous was that night, as the blood continued to flow, and nothing availed to check it, nor was any aid near to restore the old man's ebbing strength.

Toward midnight the Earl's old comrade Essex had time to understand his condition, and sent some officers to enquire for him, and promise speedy surgical attendance. Lindsay was still full of spirit, and spoke to them so strongly of their broken faith, and of the sin of disloyalty and rebellion, that they slunk away one by one out of the hut, and dissuaded Essex from coming himself to see his old friend, as he had intended. The surgeon, however, arrived, but too late, Lindsay was already so much exhausted by cold and loss of blood, that he died early in the morning of the 24th, all his son's gallant devotion having failed to save him.

The sorrowing son received an affectionate note the next day from the King, full of regret for his father and esteem for himself. Charles made every effort to obtain his exchange, but could not succeed for a whole year. He was afterwards one of the four noblemen who, seven years later, followed the King's white, silent, snowy funeral in the dismantled St. George's Chapel; and from first to last he was one of the bravest, purest, and most devoted of those who did honour to the Cavalier cause.

We have still another brave son to describe, and for him we must return away from these sad pages of our history, when we were a house divided against itself, to one of the hours of our brightest glory, when the cause we fought in was the cause of all the oppressed, and nearly alone we upheld the rights of oppressed countries against the invader. And thus it is that the battle of the Nile is one of the exploits to which we look back with the greatest exultation, when we think of the triumph of the British flag.

Let us think of all that was at stake. Napoleon Bonaparte was climbing to power in France, by directing her successful arms against the world. He had beaten Germany and conquered Italy; he had threatened England, and his dream was of the conquest of the East. Like another Alexander, he hoped to subdue Asia, and overthrow the hated British power by depriving it of India. Hitherto, his dreams had become earnest by the force of his marvellous genius, and by the ardour which he breathed into the whole French nation; and when he set sail from Toulon, with 40,000 tried and victorious soldiers and a magnificent fleet, all were filled with vague and unbounded expectations of almost fabulous glories. He swept away as it were the degenerate Knights of St. john from their rock of Malta, and sailed for Alexandria in Egypt, in the latter end of June, 1798.

His intentions had not become known, and the English Mediterranean fleet was watching the course of this great armament. Sir Horatio Nelson was in pursuit, with the English vessels, and wrote to the First Lord of the Admirality: "Be they bound to the Antipodes, your lordship may rely that I will not lose a moment in bringing them to action."

Nelson had, however, not ships enough to be detached to reconnoitre, and he actually overpassed the French, whom he guessed to be on the way to Egypt; he arrived at the port of Alexandria on the 28th of June, and saw its blue waters and flat coast lying still in their sunny torpor, as if no enemy were on the seas. Back he went to Syracuse, but could learn no more there; he obtained provisions with some difficulty, and then, in great anxiety, sailed for Greece; where at last, on the 28th of July, he learnt that the French fleet had been seen from Candia, steering to the south-east, and about four weeks since. In fact, it had actually passed by him in a thick haze, which concealed each fleet from the other, and had arrived at Alexandria on the 1st of July, three days after he had left it!

Every sail was set for the south, and at four o'clock in the afternoon of the 1st of August a very different sight was seen in Aboukir Bay, so solitary a month ago. It was crowded with shipping. Great castle-like men-of-war rose with all their proud calm dignity out of the water, their dark port-holes opening in the white bands on their sides, and the tricoloured flag floating as their ensign. There were thirteen ships of the line and four frigates, and, of these, three were 80-gun ships, and one, towering high above the rest, with her three decks, was L'Orient, of 120 guns. Look well at her, for there stands the hero for whose sake we have chose this and no other of Nelson's glorious fights to place among the setting of our Golden Deeds. There he is, a little cadet de vaisseau, as the French call a midshipman, only ten years old, with a heart swelling between awe and exultation at the prospect of his first battle; but, fearless and glad, for is he not the son of the brave Casabianca, the flag-captain? And is not this Admiral Brueys' own ship, looking down in scorn on the fourteen little English ships, not one carrying more than 74 guns, and one only 50?

Why Napoleon had kept the fleet there was never known. In his usual mean way of disavowing whatever turned out ill, he laid the blame upon Admiral Brueys; but, though dead men could not tell tales, his papers made it plain that the ships had remained in obedience to commands, though they had not been able to enter the harbour of Alexandria. Large rewards had been offered to any pilot who would take them in, but none could be found who would venture to steer into that port a vessel drawing more than twenty feet of water. They had, therefore, remained at anchor outside, in Aboukir Bay, drawn up in a curve along the deepest of the water, with no room to pass them at either end, so that the commissary of the fleet reported that they could bid defiance to a force more than double their number. The admiral believed that Nelson had not ventured to attack him when they had passed by one another a month before, and when the English fleet was signalled, he still supposed that it was too late in the day for an attack to be made.

Nelson had, however, no sooner learnt that the French were in sight than he signalled from his ship, the Vanguard, that preparations for battle should be made, and in the meantime summoned up his captains to receive his orders during a hurried meal. He explained that, where there was room for a large French ship to swing, there was room for a small English one to anchor, and, therefore, he designed to bring his ships up to the outer part of the French line, and station them close below their adversary; a plan that he said Lord Hood had once designed, though he had not carried it out.

Captain Berry was delighted, and exclaimed, "If we succeed, what will the world say?"

"There is no if in the case," returned Nelson, "that we shall succeed is certain. Who may live to tell the tale is a very different question."

And when they rose and parted, he said, "before this time to-morrow I shall have gained a peerage or Westminster Abbey."

In the fleet went, through a fierce storm of shot and shell from a French battery in an island in advance. Nelson's own ship, the Vanguard, was the first to anchor within half-pistol-shot of the third French ship, the Spartiate. The Vanguard had six colours flying, in any case any should be shot away; and such was the fire that was directed on her, that in a few minutes every man at the six guns in her forepart was killed or wounded, and this happened three times. Nelson himself received a wound in the head, which was thought at first to be mortal, but which proved but slight. He would not allow the surgeon to leave the sailors to attend to him till it came to his turn.

Meantime his ships were doing their work gloriously. The Bellerophon was, indeed, overpowered by L'Orient, 200 of her crew killed, and all her masts and cables shot away, so that she drifted away as night came on; but the Swiftsure came up in her place, and the Alexander and Leander both poured in their shot. Admiral Brueys received three wounds, but would not quit his post, and at length a fourth shot almost cut him in two. He desired not to be carried below, but that he might die on deck.

About nine o'clock the ship took fire, and blazed up with fearful brightness, lighting up the whole bay, and showing five French ships with their colours hauled down, the others still fighting on. Nelson himself rose and came on deck when this fearful glow came shining from sea and sky into his cabin; and gave orders that the English boars should immediately be put off for L'Orient, to save as many lives as possible.

The English sailors rowed up to the burning ship which they had lately been attacking. The French officers listened to the offer of safety, and called to the little favourite of the ship, the captain's son, to come with them. "No," said the brave child, "he was where his father had stationed him, and bidden him not to move save at his call." They told him his father's voice would never call him again, for he lay senseless and mortally wounded on the deck, and that the ship must blow up. "No," said the brave child, "he must obey his father." The moment allowed no delay–the boat put off. The flames showed all that passed in a quivering flare more intense than daylight, and the little fellow was then seen on the deck, leaning over the prostrate figure, and presently tying it to one of the spars of the shivered masts.

Just then a thundering explosion shook down to the very hold every ship in the harbour, and burning fragments of L'Orient came falling far and wide, plashing heavily into the water, in the dead, awful stillness that followed the fearful sound. English boats were plying busily about, picking up those who had leapt overboard in time. Some were dragged in through the lower portholes of the English ships, and about seventy were saved altogether. For one moment a boat's crew had a sight of a helpless figure bound to a spar, and guided by a little childish swimmer, who must have gone overboard with his precious freight just before the explosion. They rowed after the brave little fellow, earnestly desiring to save him; but in darkness, in smoke, in lurid uncertain light, amid hosts of drowning wretches, they lost sight of him again.

> The boy, oh where was he!
>   Ask of the winds that far around
> With fragments strewed the sea;
>   With mast and helm, and pennant fair
> That well had borne their part:
>   But the noblest thing that perished there
> Was that young faithful heart!

By sunrise the victory was complete. Nay, as Nelson said, "It was not a victory, but a conquest." Only four French ships escaped, and Napoleon and his army were cut off from home. These are the glories of our navy, gained by men with hearts as true and obedient as that of the brave child they had tried in vain to save. Yet still, while giving the full meed of thankful, sympathetic honour to our noble sailors, we cannot but feel that the Golden Deed of Aboukir Bay fell to–

"That young faithful heart."

The Soldiers in the Snow

1672

FEW generals had ever been more loved by their soldiers than the great Viscount de Turenne, who was Marshal of France in the time of Louis XIV. Troops are always proud of a leader who wins victories; but Turenne was far more loved for his generous kindness than for his successes. If he gained a battle, he always wrote in his despatches, "We succeeded," so as to give the credit to the rest of the army; but if he were defeated, he wrote, "I lost," so as to take all the blame upon himself. He always shared as much as possible in every hardship suffered by his men, and they trusted him entirely. In the year 1672, Turenne and his army were sent to make war upon the Elector Frederick William of Brandenburg, in Northern Germany. It was in the depth of winter, and the marches through the heavy roads were very trying and wearisome; but the soldiers endured all cheerfully for his sake. Once when they were wading though a deep morass, some of the younger soldiers complained; but the elder ones answered, "Depend upon it, Turenne is more concerned than we are. At this moment he is thinking how to deliver us. He watches for us while we sleep. He is our father. It is plain that you are but young."

Another night, when he was going the round of the camp, he overheard some of the younger men murmuring at the discomforts of the march; when an old soldier, newly recovered from a severe wound, said: "You do not know our father. He would not have made us go through such fatigue, unless he had some great end in view, which we cannot yet make out." Turenne always declared that nothing had ever given him more pleasure than this conversation.

There was a severe sickness among the troops, and he went about among the sufferers, comforting them, and seeing that their wants were supplied. When he passed by, the soldiers came out of their tents to look at him, and say, " Our father is in good health: we have nothing to fear."

The army had to enter the principality of Halberstadt, the way to which lay over ridges of high hills with narrow defiles between them. Considerable time was required for the whole of the troops to march through a single narrow outlet; and one very cold day, when such a passage was taking place, the Marshal, quite spent with fatigue, sat down under a bush to wait till all had marched by, and fell asleep.

When he awoke, it was snowing fast; but he found himself under a sort of tent made of soldiers' cloaks, hung up upon the branches of trees planted in the ground, and round it were standing, in the cold and snow, all unsheltered, a party of soldiers. Turenne called out to them, to ask what they were doing there. "We are taking care of our father," they said; "that is our chief concern." The general, to keep up discipline, seems to have scolded them a little for straggling from their regiment; but he was much affected and gratified by this sight of their hearty love for him.

Still greater and more devoted love was shown by some German soldiers in the terrible winter of 1812. It was when the Emperor Napoleon I had made his vain attempt to conquer Russia, and had been prevented from spending the winter at Moscow by the great fire that consumed all the city. He was obliged to retreat through the snow, with the Russian army pursuing him, and his miserable troops suffering horrors beyond all imagination. Among them were many Italians, Poles, and Germans, whom he had obliged to become his allies; and the "Golden Deed" of ten of these German soldiers, the last remnant of those led from Hesse Darmstadt by their gallant young Prince Emilius, is best told in Lord Houghton's verses:–

> "From Hessen Darmstadt every step to Moskwa's blazing banks,
> Was Prince Emilius found in flight before the foremost ranks;
> And when upon the icy waste that host was backward cast,
> On Beresina's bloody bridge his banner waved the last.
>
> "His valour shed victorious grace on all that dread retreat–
> That path across the wildering snow, athwart the blinding sleet;
> And every follower of his sword could all endure and dare,
> Becoming warriors, strong in hope, or stronger in despair.
>
> "Now, day and dark, along the storm the demon Cossacks sweep–
> The hungriest must not look for food, the weariest must not sleep.
> No rest but death for horse or man, whichever first shall tire;
> They see the flames destroy, but ne'er may feel the saving fire.
>
> "Thus never closed the bitter night, nor rose the salvage morn,
> But from the gallant company some noble part was shorn;
> And, sick at heart, the Prince resolved to keep his purposed way
> With steadfast forward looks, nor count the losses of the day.

"At length beside a black, burnt hut, an island of the snow,
Each head in frigid torpor bent toward the saddle bow;
They paused, and of that sturdy troop–that thousand banded men–
At one unmeditated glance he numbered only ten!

"Of all that high triumphant life that left his German home–
Of all those hearts that beat beloved, or looked for love to come–
This piteous remnant, hardly saved, his spirit overcame,
While memory raised each friendly face, recalled an ancient name.

"These were his words, serene and firm, 'Dear brothers, it is best
That here, with perfect trust in Heaven, we give our bodies rest;
If we have borne, like faithful men, our part of toil and pain,
Where'er we wake, for Christ's good sake, we shall not sleep in vain.'

"Some uttered, others looked assent–they had no heart to speak;
Dumb hands were pressed, the pallid lip approached the callous cheek.
They laid them side by side; and death to him at last did seem
To come attired in mazy robe of variegated dream.

"Once more he floated on the breast of old familiar Rhine,
His mother's and one other smile above him seemed to shine;
A blessed dew of healing fell on every aching limb;
Till the stream broadened, and the air thickened, and all was dim.

"Nature has bent to other laws if that tremendous night
Passed o'er his frame, exposed and worn, and left no deadly blight;
Then wonder not that when, refresh'd and warm, he woke at last,
There lay a boundless gulf of thought between him and the past.

"Soon raising his astonished head, he found himself alone,
Sheltered beneath a genial heap of vestments not his own;
The light increased, the solemn truth revealing more and more,
The soldiers' corses, self-despoiled, closed up the narrow door.

"That every hour, fulfilling good, miraculous succour came,
And Prince Emilius lived to give this worthy deed to fame.
O brave fidelity in death! O strength of loving will!
These are the holy balsam drops that woeful wars distil."

Gunpowder Perils

1700

THE wild history of Ireland contains many a frightful tale, but also many an action of the noblest order; and the short sketch given by Maria Edgeworth of her ancestry, presents such a chequerwork of the gold and the lead that it is almost impossible to separate them.

At the time of the great Irish rebellion of 1641 the head of the Edgeworth family had left his English wife and her infant son at his castle of Cranallagh in county Longford, thinking them safe there while he joined the royal forces under the Earl of Ormond. In his absence, however, the rebels attacked the castle at night, set fire to it, and dragged the lady out absolutely naked. She hid herself under a furze bush, and succeeded in escaping and reaching Dublin, whence she made her way to her father's house in Derbyshire. Her little son was found by the rebels lying in his cradle, and one of them actually seized the child by the leg and was about to dash out his brains against the wall; but a servant named Bryan Ferral, pretending to be even more ferocious, vowed that a sudden death was too good for the little heretic, and that he should be plunged up to the throat in a bog-hole and left for the crows to pick out his eyes. He actually did place the poor child in the bog , but only to save his life; he returned as soon as he could elude his comrades, put the boy into a pannier below eggs and chickens, and thus carried him straight though the rebel camp to his mother at Dublin. Strange to say, these rebels, who thought being dashed against the wall too good a fate for the infant, extinguished the flames of the castle out of reverence for the picture of his grandmother, who had been a Roman Catholic, and was painted on a panel with a cross on her bosom and a rosary in her hand.

John Edgeworth, the boy thus saved, married very young, and went with his wife to see London after the Restoration. To pay their expenses they mortgaged an estate and put the money in a stocking, which they kept on the top of the bed; and when that store was used up, the young man actually sold a house in Dublin to buy a high-crowned hat and feathers. Still, reckless and improvident as they were, there was sound principle within them, and though they were great favourites, and Charles II insisted on knighting the husband, their glimpse of the real evils and temptations of his Court sufficed them, and in the full tide of flattery and admiration the lady begged to return home, nor did she ever go back to Court again.

Her home was at Castle Lissard, in full view of which was a hillock called Fairymount, or Firmont, from being supposed to be the haunt of fairies. Lights, noises, and singing at night, clearly discerned from the castle, caused much terror to Lady Edgeworth, though her descendants affirm that they were fairies of the same genus as those who beset Sir John Falstaff at Hearne's oak, and intended to frighten her into leaving the place. However, though her nerves might be disturbed, her spirit was not to be daunted; and, fairies or no fairies, she held her ground at Castle Lissard, and there showed what manner of woman she was in a veritable and most fearful peril.

On some alarm which caused the gentlemen of the family to take down their guns, she went to a dark loft at the top of the house to fetch some powder from a barrel that was there kept in store, taking a young maid-servant to carry the candle; which, as might be expected in an Irish household of the seventeenth century, was devoid of any candlestick. After taking the needful amount of gunpowder, Lady Edgeworth locked the door, and was halfway downstairs when she missed the candle, and asking the girl what she had done with it, received the cool answer that "she had left it sticking in the barrel of black salt". Lady Edgeworth bade her stand still, turned round, went back alone to the loft where the tallow candle stood guttering and flaring planted in the middle of the gunpowder, resolutely put an untrembling hand beneath it, took it out so steadily that no spark fell, carried it down, and when she came to the bottom of the stairs dropped on her knees, and broke forth in a thanksgiving aloud for the safety of the household in this frightful peril. This high-spirited lady lived to be ninety years old, and left a numerous family. One grandson was the Abbé Edgeworth, known in France as De Firmont, such being the alteration of Fairymount on French lips. It was he who, at the peril of his own life, attended Louis XVI to the guillotine, and thus connected his name so closely with the royal cause that when his cousin Richard Lovell Edgeworth, of Edgeworthstown, visited France several years after, the presence of a person so called was deemed perilous to the rising power of Napoleon. This latter Mr. Edgeworth was the father of Maria, whose works we hope are well known to our young readers.

The good Chevalier Bayard was wont to mourn over the introduction of firearms, as destructive of chivalry; and certainly the steel-clad knight, with barbed steed, and sword and lance, has disappeared from the battle-field; but his most essential qualities, truth, honour, faithfulness, mercy, and self-devotion, have not disappeared with him, nor can they as long as

Christian men and women bear in mind that "greater love hath no man than this, that he lay down his life for his friend".

And that terrible compound, gunpowder, has been the occasion of many another daring deed, requiring desperate resolution, to save others at the expense of a death perhaps more frightful to the imagination than any other. Listen to a story of the King's birthday in Jersey "sixty years since"—in 1804, when that 4th of June that Eton boys delight in, was already in the forty-fourth year of its observance in honour of the then reigning monarch, George III.

All the forts in the island had done due honour to the birthday of His Majesty, who was then just recovered from an attack of insanity. In each the guns at noon-day thundered out their royal salute, the flashes had answered one another, and the smoke had wreathed itself away over the blue sea of Jersey. The new fort on the hill just above the town of St. Heliers had contributed its share to the loyal thunders, and then it was shut up, and the keys carried away by Captain Salmon, the artillery officer on guard there, locking up therein 209 barrels of gunpowder, with a large supply of bombshells, and every kind of ammunition such as might well be needed in the Channel islands the year before Lord Nelson had freed England from the chance of finding the whole French army on our coast in the flat-bottomed boats that were waiting at Boulogne for the dark night that never came.

At six o'clock in the evening, Captain Salmon went to dine with the other officers in St. Heliers and to drink the King's health, when the soldiers on guard beheld a cloud of smoke curling out at the air-hole at the end of the magazine. Shouting "fire", they ran away to avoid an explosion that would have shattered them to pieces, and might perhaps endanger the entire town of St. Heliers. Happily their shout was heard by a man of different mould. Lieutenant Lys, the signal officer, was in the watch-house on the hill, and coming out he saw the smoke, and perceived the danger. Two brothers, named Thomas and Edward Touzel, carpenters, and the sons of an old widow, had come up to take down a flagstaff that had been raised in honour of the day, and Mr. Lys ordered them to hasten to the town to inform the commander-in-chief, and get the keys from Captain Salmon.

Thomas went, and endeavoured to persuade his brother to accompany him from the heart of the danger; but Edward replied that he must die some day or other, and that he would do his best to save the magazine, and he tried to stop some of the runaway soldiers to assist. One refused; but another, William Ponteney, of the 3rd, replied that he was ready to die with him, and they shook hands.

Edward Touzel then, by the help of a wooden bar and an axe, broke open the door of the fort, and making his way into it, saw the state of the case, and shouted to Mr. Lys on the outside, "the magazine is on fire, it will blow up, we must lose our lives; but no matter, huzza for the King! We must try and save it." He then rushed into the flame, and seizing the matches, which were almost burnt out (probably splinters of wood tipped with brimstone), he threw them by armfuls to Mr. Lys and the soldier Ponteney, who stood outside and received them. Mr. Lys saw a cask of water near at hand; but there was nothing to carry the water in but an earthen pitcher, his own hat and the soldier's. These, however, they filled again and again, and handed to Touzel, who thus extinguished all the fire he could see; but the smoke was so dense, that he worked in horrible doubt and obscurity, almost suffocated, and with his face and hands already scorched. The beams over his head were on fire, large cases containing powder horns had already caught, and an open barrel of gunpowder was close by, only awaiting the fall of a single brand to burst into a fatal explosion. Touzel called out to entreat for some drink to enable him to endure the stifling, and Mr. Lys handed him some spirits-and-water, which he drank, and worked on; but by this time the officers had heard the alarm, dispelled the panic among the soldiers, and come to the rescue. The magazine was completely emptied, and the last smouldering sparks extinguished; but the whole of the garrison and citizens felt that they owed their lives to the three gallant men to whose exertions alone under Providence, it was owing that succour did not come too late. Most of all was honour due to Edward Touzel, who, as a civilian, might have turned his back upon the peril without any blame; nay, could even have pleaded Mr. Lys' message as a duty, but who had instead rushed foremost into what he believe was certain death.

A meeting was held in the church of St. Heliers to consider of a testimonial of gratitude to these three brave men (it is to be hoped that thankfulness to an overruling Providence was also manifested there), when 500l. was voted to Mr. Lys, who was the father of a large family; 300l. to Edward Touzel; and William Ponteney received, at his own request, a life annuity of 20l. and a gold medal, as he declared that he had rather continue to serve the King as a soldier than be placed in any other course of life.

In that same year (1804) the same daring endurance and heroism were evinced by the officers of H.M.S. Hindostan, where, when on the way from Gibraltar to join Nelson's fleet at Toulon, the cry of "Fire!" was heard, and dense smoke rose from the lower decks, so as to render it nearly impossible to detect the situation of the fire. Again and again Lieutenants Tailour and Banks descended, and fell down senseless from the stifling smoke; then were carried on deck, recovered in the free air, and returned to vain endeavour of clearing the powder-room. But no man could long preserve his faculties in the poisonous atmosphere, and the two lieutenants might be said to have many deaths from it. At last the fire gained so much head, that it was impossible to save the vessel, which had in the meantime been brought into the Bay of Rosas, and was near enough to land to enable the crew to escape in boats, after having endured the fire six hours. Nelson himself wrote: "The preservation of the crew seems little short of a miracle. I never read such a journal of exertions in my life."

Eight years after, on the taking of Ciudad Rodrigo, in 1812, by the British army under Wellington, Captain William Jones, of the 52nd Regiment, having captured a French officer, employed his prisoner in pointing out quarters for his men. The Frenchman could not speak English, and Captain Jones–a fiery Welshman, whom it was the fashion in the regiment to term "Jack Jones"–knew no French; but dumb show supplied the want of language, and some of the company were lodged in a large store pointed out by the Frenchman, who then led the way to a church, near which Lord Wellington and his staff were standing. But no sooner had the guide stepped into the building than he started back, crying, "Sacrebleu!" and ran out in the utmost alarm. The Welsh captain, however, went on, and perceived that the church had been used as a powder-magazine by the French; barrels were standing round, samples of their contents lay loosely scattered on the pavement, and in the midst was a fire, probably lighted by some Portuguese soldiers. Forthwith Captain Jones and the sergeant entered the church, took up the burning embers brand by brand, bore them safe over the scattered powder, and out of the church, and thus averted what might have been the most terrific disaster that could have befallen our army.[8]

Our next story of this kind relates to a French officer, Monsieur Mathieu Martinel, adjutant of the 1st Cuirassiers. In 1820 there was a fire in the barracks at Strasburg, and nine soldiers were lying sick and helpless above a room containing a barrel of gunpowder and a thousand cartridges. Everyone was escaping, but Martinel persuaded a few men to return into the barracks with him, and hurried up the stairs through smoke and flame that turned back his companions. He came alone to the door of a room close to that which contained the powder, but found it locked. Catching up a bench, he beat the door in, and was met by such a burst of fire as had almost driven him away; but, just as he was about to descend, he thought that, when the flames reached the powder, the nine sick men must infallibly be blown up, and returning to the charge, he dashed forward, with eyes shut, through the midst, and with face, hands, hair, and clothes singed and burnt, he made his way to the magazine, in time to tear away, and throw to a distance from the powder, the mass of paper in which the cartridges were packed, which was just about to ignite, and appearing at the window, with loud shouts for water, thus showed the possibility of

---

8   The story has been told with some variation, as to whether it was the embers or a barrel of powder that he and the sergeant removed. In the Record of the 52nd it is said to have been the latter; but the tradition the author has received from officers of the regiment distinctly stated that it was the burning brands, and that the scene was a reserve magazine–not, as in the brief mention in Sir William Napier's History, the great magazine of the town.

penetrating to the magazine, and floods of water were at once directed to it, so as to drench the powder, and thus save the men.

This same Martinel had shortly before thrown himself into the River Ill, without waiting to undress, to rescue a soldier who had fallen in, so near a water mill, that there was hardly a chance of life for either. Swimming straight towards the mill dam, Martinel grasped the post of the sluice with one arm, and with the other tried to arrest the course of the drowning man, who was borne by a rapid current towards the mill wheel; and was already so far beneath the surface, that Martinel could not reach him without letting go of the post. Grasping the inanimate body, he actually allowed himself to be carried under the mill wheel, without loosing his hold, and came up immediately after on the other side, still able to bring the man to land, in time for his suspended animation to be restored.

Seventeen years afterwards, when the regiment was at Paris, there was, on the night of the 14th of June, 1837, during the illuminations at the wedding festival of the Duke and Duchess of Orleans, one of those frightful crushes that sometimes occur in an ill-regulated crowd, when there is some obstruction in the way, and there is nothing but a horrible blind struggling and trampling, violent and fatal because of its very helplessness and bewilderment. The crowd were trying to leave the Champ de Mars, where great numbers had been witnessing some magnificent fireworks, and had blocked up the passage leading out by the Military College. A woman fell down in a fainting fit, others stumbled over her, and thus formed an obstruction, which, being unknown to those in the rear, did not prevent them from forcing forward the persons in front, so that they too were pushed and trodden down into one frightful, struggling, suffocating mass of living and dying men, women, and children, increasing every moment.

M. Martinel was passing, on his way to his quarters, when, hearing the tumult, he ran to the gate from the other side, and meeting the crowd tried by shouts and entreaties to persuade them to give back, but the hindmost could not hear him, and the more frightened they grew, the more they tried to hurry home, and so made the heap worse and worse, and in the midst an illuminated yew tree, in a pot, was upset, and further barred the way. Martinel, with imminent danger to himself, dragged out one or two persons; but finding his single efforts almost useless among such numbers, he ran to the barracks, sounded to horse, and without waiting till his men could be got together, hurried off again on foot, with a few of his comrades, and dashed back into the crowd, struggling as vehemently to penetrate to the scene of danger, as many would have done to get away from it.

Private Spenlée alone kept up with him, and, coming to the dreadful heap, these two laboured to free the passage, lift up the living, and remove the dead. First he dragged out an old man in a fainting fit, then a young soldier, next a boy, a woman, a little girl—he carried them to freer air, and came back the next moment, though often so nearly pulled down by the frantic struggles of the terrified stifled creatures, that he was each moment in the utmost peril of being trampled to death. He carried out nine persons one by one; Spenlée brought out a man and a child; and his brother officers, coming up, took their share. One lieutenant, with a girl in a swoon in his arms, caused a boy to be put on his back, and under this double burthen was pushing against the crowd for half and hour, till at length he fell, and was all but killed.

A troop of cuirassiers had by this time mounted, and through the Champ de Mars came slowly along, step by step, their horses moving as gently and cautiously as if they knew their work. Everywhere, as they advanced, little children were held up to them out of the throng to be saved, and many of their chargers were loaded with the little creatures, perched before and behind the kind soldiers. With wonderful patience and forbearance, they managed to insert themselves and their horses, first in single file, then two by two, then more abreast, like a wedge, into the press, until at last they formed a wall, cutting off the crowd behind from the mass in the gateway, and thus preventing the encumbrance from increasing. The people came to their senses, and went off to other gates, and the crowd diminishing, it became possible to lift up the many unhappy creatures, who lay stifling or crushed in the heap. They were carried into the barracks, the cuirassiers hurried to bring their mattresses to lay them on in the hall, brought them water, linen, all they could want, and were as tender to them as sisters of charity, till they were taken to the hospitals or to their homes. Martinel, who was the moving spirit in this gallant rescue, received in the following year one of M. Monthyon's prizes for the greatest acts of virtue that could be brought to light.

Nor among the gallant actions of which powder has been the cause should be omitted that of Lieutenant Willoughby, who, in the first dismay of the mutiny in India, in 1858, blew up the great magazine at Delhi, with all the ammunition that would have armed the sepoys even yet more terribly against ourselves. The "Golden Deed" was one of those capable of no earthly meed, for it carried the brave young officer where alone there is true reward; and all the Queen and country could do in his honour was to pension his widowed mother, and lay up his name among those that stir the heart with admiration and gratitude.

Heroes of the Plague
1576-1665-1721

WHEN our litany entreats that we may be delivered from "plague, pestilence, and famine", the first of these words bears a special meaning, which came home with strong and painful force to European minds at the time the Prayer Book was translated, and for the whole following century.

It refers to the deadly sickness emphatically called "the plague", a typhoid fever exceedingly violent and rapid, and accompanied with a frightful swelling either under the arm or on the corresponding part of the thigh. The East is the usual haunt of this fatal complaint, which some suppose to be bred by the marshy, unwholesome state of Egypt after the subsidence of the waters of the Nile, and which generally prevails in Egypt and Syria until its course is checked either by the cold of winter or the heat in summer. At times this disease has become unusually malignant and infectious, and then has come beyond its usual boundaries and made its way over all the West. These dreadful visitations were rendered more frequent by total disregard of all precautions, and ignorance of laws for preserving health. People crowded together in towns without means of obtaining sufficient air or cleanliness, and thus were sure to be unhealthy; and whenever war or famine had occasioned more than usual poverty, some frightful epidemic was sure to follow in its train, and sweep away the poor creatures whose frames were already weakened by previous privation. And often this "sore judgment" was that emphatically called the plague; and especially during the sixteenth and seventeenth centuries, a time when war had become far more cruel and mischievous in the hands of hired regiments than ever it had been with a feudal army, and when at the same time increasing trade was filling the cities with more closely packed inhabitants, within fortifications that would not allow the city to expand in proportion to its needs. It has been only the establishment of the system of quarantine which has succeeded in cutting off the course of infection by which the plague was wont to set out on its frightful travels from land to land, from city to city.

The desolation of a plague-stricken city was a sort of horrible dream. Every infected house was marked with a red cross, and carefully closed against all persons, except those who were charged to drive carts through the streets to collect the corpses, ringing a bell as they went. These men were generally wretched beings, the lowest and most reckless of the people, who undertook their frightful task for the sake of the plunder of the desolate houses, and wound themselves up by intoxicating drinks to endure the horrors. The bodies were thrown into large trenches, without prayer or funeral rites, and these were hastily closed up. Whole families died together, untended save by one another, with no aid of a friendly hand to give drink or food; and, in the Roman Catholic cities, the perishing without a priest to administer the last rites of the Church was viewed as more dreadful than death itself.

Such visitations as these did indeed prove whether the pastors of the afflicted flock were shepherds or hirelings. So felt, in 1576, Cardinal Carlo Borromeo, Archbishop of Milan, the worthiest of all the successors of St. Ambrose, when he learnt at Lodi that the plague had made its appearance in his city, where, remarkably enough, there had lately been such licentious revelry that he had solemnly warned the people that, unless they repented, they would certainly bring on themselves the wrath of heaven. His council of clergy advised him to remain in some healthy part of his diocese till the sickness should have spent itself, but he replied that a Bishop, whose duty it is to give his life for his sheep, could not rightly abandon them in time of peril. They owned that to stand by them was the higher course. "Well," he said, "is it not a Bishop's duty to choose the higher course?"

So back into the town of deadly sickness he went, leading the people to repent, and watching over them in their sufferings, visiting the hospitals, and, by his own example, encouraging his clergy in carrying spiritual consolation to the dying. All the time the plague lasted, which was four months, his exertions were fearless and unwearied, and what was remarkable was, that of his whole household only two died, and they were persons who had not been called to go about among the sick. Indeed, some of the rich who had repaired to a villa, where they spent their time in feasting and amusement in the luxurious Italian fashion, were there followed by the pestilence, and all perished; their dainty fare and the excess in which they indulged having no doubt been as bad a preparation as the poverty of the starving people in the city.

The strict and regular life of the Cardinal and his clergy, and their home in the spacious palace, were, no doubt, under Providence, a preservative; but, in the opinions of the time, there was little short of a miracle in the safety of one who daily preached in the cathedral–bent over the beds of the sick, giving them food and medicine, hearing their confessions, and administering the last rites of the Church–and then braving the contagion after death, rather than let the corpses go forth unblest to their common grave. Nay, so far was he from seeking to save his own life, that, kneeling before the altar in the cathedral, he solemnly offered himself, like Moses, as a sacrifice for his people. But, like Moses, the sacrifice was passed by– "it cost more to redeem their souls"–and Borromeo remained untouched, as did the twenty-eight priests who voluntarily offered themselves to join in his labours.

No wonder that the chief memories that haunt the glorious white marble cathedral of Milan are those of St. Ambrose, who taught mercy to an emperor, and of St. Carlo Borromeo, who practiced mercy on a people.

It was a hundred years later that the greatest and last visitation of the plague took place in London. Doubtless the scourge called forth–as in Christian lands such judgments always do–many an act of true and blessed self-devotion; but these are not recorded, save where they have their reward: and the tale now to be told is of one of the small villages to which the infection spread–namely, Eyam, in Derbyshire.

This is a lovely place between Buxton and Chatsworth, perched high on a hillside, and shut in by another higher mountain–extremely beautiful, but exactly one of those that, for want of free air, always become the especial prey of infection. At that time lead works were in operation in the mountains, and the village was thickly inhabited. Great was the dismay of the villagers when the family of a tailor, who had received some patterns of cloth from London, showed symptoms of the plague in its most virulent form, sickening and dying in one day.

The rector of the parish, the Rev. William Mompesson, was still a young man, and had been married only a few years. His wife, a beautiful young woman, only twenty-seven years old, was exceedingly terrified at the tidings from the village, and wept bitterly as she implored her husband to take her, and her little George and Elizabeth, who were three and fours years old, away to some place of safety. But Mr. Mompesson gravely showed her that it was his duty not to forsake his flock in their hour of need, and began at once to make arrangements for sending her and the children away. She saw he was right in remaining, and ceased to urge him to forsake his charge; but she insisted that if he ought not to desert his flock, his wife ought not to leave him; and she wept and entreated so earnestly, that he at length consented that she should be with him, and that only the two little ones should be removed while yet there was time.

Their father and mother parted with the little ones as treasures that they might never see again. At the same time Mr. Mompesson wrote to London for the most approved medicines and prescriptions; and he likewise sent a letter to the Earl of Devonshire, at Chatsworth, to engage that his parishioners should exclude themselves from the whole neighbourhood, and thus confine the contagion within their own boundaries, provided the Earl would undertake that food, medicines, and other necessaries, should be placed at certain appointed spots, at regular times, upon the hills around, where the Eyamites might come, leave payment for them, and take them up, without holding any communication with the bringers, except by letters, which could be placed on a stone, and then fumigated, or passed through vinegar, before they were touched with the hand. To this the Earl consented, and for seven whole months the engagement was kept.

Mr. Mompesson represented to his people that, with the plague once among them, it would be so unlikely that they should not carry infection about with them, that it would be selfish cruelty to other places to try to escape amongst them, and thus spread the danger. So rocky and wild was the ground around them, that, had they striven to escape, a regiment of soldiers could not have prevented them. But of their own free will they attended to their rector's remonstrance, and it was not known that one parishoner of Eyam passed the boundary all that time, nor was there a single case of plague in any of the villages around.

The assembling of large congregations in churches had been thought to increase the infection in London, and Mr. Mompesson, therefore, thought it best to hold his services out-of-doors. In the middle of the village is a dell, suddenly making a cleft in the mountainside, only five yards wide at the bottom, which is the pebble bed of a wintry torrent, but is dry in the summer. On the side towards the village, the slope upwards was of soft green turf, scattered with hazel, rowan, and alder bushes, and full of singing birds. On the other side, the ascent was nearly perpendicular, and composed of sharp rocks, partly adorned with bushes and ivy, and here and there rising up in fantastic peaks and archways, through which the sky could be seen from below. One of these rocks was hollow, and could be entered from above–a natural gallery, leading to an archway opening over the precipice; and this Mr. Mompesson chose for his reading-desk and pulpit. The dell was so narrow, that his voice could clearly be heard across it, and his congregation arranged themselves upon the green slop opposite, seated or kneeling upon the grass.

On Wednesdays, Fridays, and Sundays arose the earnest voice of prayer from that rocky glen, the people's response meeting the pastor's voice; and twice on Sundays he preached to them the words of life and hope. It was a dry, hot summer; fain would they have seen thunder and rain to drive away their enemy; and seldom did weather break in on the regularity of these service. But there was another service that the rector had daily to perform; not in his churchyard–that would have perpetuated the infec-tion–but on a heathy hill above the village. There he daily read of "the Resurrection and the Life", and week by week the company on the grassy slope grew fewer and scantier. His congregation were passing from the dell to the heathy mound.

Day and night the rector and his wife were among the sick, nursing, feeding, and tending them with all that care and skill could do; but, in

spite of all their endeavours, only a fifth part of the whole of their inhabitants lived to spend the last Sunday in Cucklet Church, as the dell is still
called. Mrs. Mompesson had persuaded her husband to have a wound
made in his leg, fancying that this would lessen the danger of infection,
and he yielded in order to satisfy her. His health endured perfectly, but
she began to waste under her constant exertions, and her husband feared
that he saw symptoms of consumption; but she was full of delight at some
appearances in his wound that made her imagine that it had carried off
the disease, and that his danger was over.

A few days after, she sickened with symptoms of the plague, and her
frame was so weakened that she sank very quickly. She was often delirious;
but when she was too much exhausted to endure the exertion of taking
cordials, her husband entreated her to try for their children's sake, she
lifted herself up and made the endeavour. She lay peacefully, saying, "she
was but looking for the good hour to come", and calmly died, making the
responses to her husband's prayers even to the last. Her he buried in the
churchyard, and fenced the grave in afterwards with iron rails. There are
two beautiful letters from him written on her death—one to his little children, to be kept and read when they would be old enough to understand
it; the other to his patron, Sir George Saville, afterwards Lord Halifax.
"My drooping spirits", he says, "are much refreshed with her joys, which I
assure myself are unutterable." He wrote both these letters in the belief that
he should soon follow her, speaking of himself to Sir George as "his dying
chaplain", commending to him his "distressed orphans", and begging that
a "humble pious man" might be chosen to succeed him in his parsonage.
"Sire, I thank God that I am willing to shake hands in peace with all the
world; and I have comfortable assurance that He will accept me for the
sake of His Son, and I find God more good than ever I imagined, and wish
that his goodness were not so much abused and contemned", writes the
widowed pastor, left alone among his dying flock. And he concludes, "and
with tears I entreat that when you are praying for fatherless and motherless
infants, you would then remember my two pretty babes".

These two letters were written on the last day of August and first of
September, 1666; but on the 20th of November, Mr. Mompesson was
writing to his uncle, in the lull after the storm. "The condition of this place
hath been so dreadful, that I persuade myself it exceedeth all history and
example. I may truly say our town has become a Golgotha, a place of skulls;
and had there not been a small remnant of us left, we had been as Sodom,
and like unto Gomorrah. My ears never heard such doleful lamentations,
my nose never smelt such noisome smells, and my eyes never beheld such
ghastly spectacles. Here have been seventy-six families visited within my
parish, out of which died 259 persons."

However, since the 11th of October there had been no fresh cases, and he was now burning all woollen cloths, lest the infection should linger in them. He himself had never been touched by the complaint, nor had his maidservant; his man had had it but slightly. Mr. Mompesson lived many more years, was offered the Deanery of Lincoln, but did not accept it, and died in 1708. So virulent was the contagion that, ninety-one years after, in 1757, when five labouring men, who were digging up land near the plague graves for a potato garden, came upon what appeared to be some linen, though they buried it again directly, they all sickened with typhus fever, three of them died, and it was so infectious that no less than seventy persons in the parish were carried off.

The last of these remarkable visitations of the plague, properly so called, was at Marseilles, in 1721. It was supposed to have been brought by a vessel which sailed from Seyde, in the bay of Tunis, on the 31st of January, 1720, which had a clean bill of health when it anchored off the Chateau d'If, at Marseilles, on the 25th of May; but six of the crew were found to have died on the voyage, and the persons who handled the freight also died, though, it was said, without any symptoms of the plague, and the first cases were supposed to be of the fevers caused by excessive poverty and crowding. The unmistakable Oriental plague, however, soon began to spread in the city among the poorer population, and in truth the wars and heavy expenses of Louis XIV had made poverty in France more wretched than ever before, and the whole country was like one deadly sore, festering, and by and by to come to a fearful crisis. Precautions were taken, the infected families were removed to the infirmaries and their houses walled up, but all this was done at night in order not to excite alarm. The mystery, however, made things more terrible to the imagination, and this was a period of the utmost selfishness. All the richer inhabitants who had means of quitting the city, and who were the very people who could have been useful there, fled with one accord. Suddenly the lazaretto was left without superintendents, the hospitals without stewards; the judges, public officers, notaries, and most of the superior workmen in the most necessary trades were all gone. Only the Provost and four municipal officers remained, with 1000 livres in their treasury, in the midst of an entirely disorganized city, and an enormous population without work, without restraint, without food, and a prey to the deadliest of diseases.

The Parliament which still survived in the ancient kingdom of Provence signalized itself by retreating to a distance, and on the 31st of May putting out a decree that nobody should pass a boundary line round Marseilles on pain of death; but considering what people were trying to escape from, and the utter overthrow of all rule and order, this penalty was not likely to have much effect, and the plague was carried by the fugitives to Arles, Aix, Toulon, and sixty-three lesser towns and villages. What a contrast to Mr. Mompesson's moral influence!

Horrible crimes were committed. Malefactors were released from the prisons and convicts from the galleys, and employed for large payment to collect the corpses and carry the sick to the infirmaries. Of course they could only be wrought up to such work by intoxication and unlimited opportunities of plunder, and their rude treatment both of the dead and of the living sufferers added unspeakably to the general wretchedness. To be carried to the infirmary was certain death—no one lived in that heap of contagion; and even this shelter was not always to be had—some of the streets were full of dying creatures who had been turned out of their houses and could crawl no farther.

What was done to alleviate all these horrors? It was in the minority of Louis XV, and the Regent Duke of Orleans, easy, good-natured man that he was, sent 22,000 marks to the relief of the city, all in silver, for paper money was found to spread the infection more than anything else. He also sent a great quantity of corn, and likewise doctors for the sick, and troops to shut in the infected district. The Pope, Clement XI, sent spiritual blessings to the sufferers, and, moreover, three shiploads of wheat. The Regent's Prime Minister, the Abbé Dubois, the shame of his Church and country, fancied that to send these supplies cast a slight upon his administration, and desired his representative at Rome to prevent the sailing of the ships, but his orders were not, for very shame, carried out, and the vessels set out. On their way they were seized by a Moorish corsair, who was more merciful than Dubois, for he no sooner learnt their destination than he let them go unplundered.

And in the midst of the misery there were bright lights "running to and fro among the stubble". The Provost and his five remaining officers, and a gentleman call Le Chevalier Rose, did their utmost in the bravest and most unselfish way to help the sufferers, distribute food, provide shelter, restrain the horrors perpetrated by the sick in their ravings, and provide for the burial of the dead. And the clergy were all devoted to the task of mercy. There was only one convent, that of St. Victor, where the gates were closed against all comers in the hope of shutting out infection. Every other monastic establishment freely devoted itself. It was a time when party spirit ran high. The bishop, Henri François Xavier de Belzunce, a nephew of the Duke de Lauzun, was a strong and rigid Jesuit, and had joined so hotly in the persecution of the Jansenists that he had forbidden the brotherhood called Oratorian fathers to hear confessions, because he suspected them of a leaning to Jansenist opinions; but he and they both alike worked earnestly in the one cause of mercy. They were content to obey his prejudiced edict, since he was in lawful authority, and threw themselves heartily into the lower and more disdained services to the sick, as nurses and tenders of the body alone, not of the soul, and in this work their whole community, Superior and all, perished, almost without exception. Perhaps these men, thus laying aside hurt feeling and sense of injustice, were the greatest conquerors of all whose golden deeds we have described.

Bishop Belzunce himself, however, stands as the prominent figure in the memory of those dreadful five months. He was a man of commanding stature, towering above all around him, and his fervent sermons, aided by his example of severe and strict piety, and his great charities, had greatly impressed the people. He now went about among the plague-stricken, attending to their wants, both spiritual and temporal, and sold or mortgaged all his property to obtain relief for them, and he actually went himself in the tumbrils of corpses to give them the rites of Christian burial. His doings closely resembled those of Cardinal Borromeo, and like him he had recourse to constant preaching of repentance, processions and assemblies for litanies in the church. It is curiously characteristic that it was the English clergyman, who, equally pious, and sensible that only the Almighty could remove the scourge, yet deemed it right to take precautions against the effects of bringing a large number of persons into one building. How Belzunce's clergy seconded him may be gathered from the numbers who died of the disease. Besides the Oratorians, there died eighteen Jesuits, twenty-six of the order called Recollets, and forty-three Capuchins, all of whom had freely given their lives in the endeavour to alleviate the general suffering. In the four chief towns of Provence 80,000 died, and about 8000 in the lesser places. The winter finally checked the destroyer, and then, sad to say, it appeared how little effect the warning had had on the survivors. Inheritances had fallen together into the hands of persons who found themselves rich beyond their expectations, and in the glee of having escaped the danger, forgot to be thankful, and spent their wealth in revelry. Never had the cities of Provence been so full of wild, questionable mirth as during the ensuing winter, and it was remarked that the places which had suffered most severely were the most given up to thoughtless gaiety, and even licentiousness.

Good Bishop Belzunce did his best to protest against the wickedness around him, and refused to leave his flock at Marseilles, when, four years after, a far more distinguished see was offered to him. He died in 1755, in time to escape the sight of the retribution that was soon worked out on the folly and vice of the unhappy country.

The Second of September
1792

THE reign of the terrible Tzar was dreadful, but there was even a more dreadful time, that which might be called the reign of the madness of the people. The oppression and injustice that had for generations past been worked out in France ended in the most fearful reaction that history records, and the horrors that took place in the Revolution pass all thought or description. Every institution that had been misused was overthrown at one fell swoop, and the whole accumulated vengeance of generations fell on the heads of the persons who occupied the positions of the former oppressors. Many of these were as pure and guiltless as their slaughterers were the reverse, but the heads of the Revolution imagined that to obtain their ideal vision of perfect justice and liberty, all the remnants of the former state of things must be swept away, and the ferocious beings who carried out their decrees had become absolutely frantic with delight in bloodshed. The nation seemed delivered up to a delirium of murder. But as

"Even as earth's wild war cries heighten,
The cross upon the brow will brighten",

these times of surpassing horror were also times of surpassing devotion and heroism. Without attempting to describe the various stages of the Revolution, and the different committees that under different titles carried on the work of destruction, we will mention some of the deeds that shine out as we look into that abyss of horror, the Paris of 1792 and the following years.

Think of the Swiss Guards, who on the 10th of August, 1792, the miserable day when the King, Queen, and children were made the captives of the people, stood resolutely at their posts, till they were massacred almost to a man. Well is their fidelity honoured by the noble sculpture near Lucerne, cut out in the living rock of their own Alps, and representing a lion dying to defend the fleur-de-lis.

A more dreadful day still was in preparation. The mob seemed to have

212

imagined that the King and nobility had some strange dreadful power, and that unless they were all annihilated they would rise up and trample all down before them, and those who had the direction of affairs profited by this delusion to multiply executioners, and clear away all that they supposed to stand in the way of the renewal of the nation. And the attempts of the emigrant nobility and of the German princes to march to the rescue of the royal family added to the fury of their cowardly ferocity. The prisons of Paris were crowded to overflowing with aristocrats, as it was the fashion to call the nobles and gentry, and with the clergy who had refused their adhesion to the new state of things. The whole number is reckoned at not less than 8000.

Among those at the Abbaye de St. Germain were M. Jacques Cazotte, an old gentleman of seventy-three, who had been for many years in a government office, and had written various poems. He was living in the country, in Champagne, when on the 18th of August he was arrested. His daughter Elizabeth, a lovely girl of twenty, would not leave him, and together they were taken first to Epernay and then to Paris, where they were thrown into the Abbaye, and found it crowded with prisoners. M. Cazotte's bald forehead and grey looks gave him a patriarchal appearance, and his talk, deeply and truly pious, was full of Scripture language, as he strove to persuade his fellow captives to own the true blessings of suffering.

Here Elizabeth met the like-minded Marie de Sombreuil, who had clung to her father, Charles Viscount de Sombreuil, the Governor of the Invalides, or pensioners of the French army; and here, too, had Madame de Fausse Lendry come with her old uncle the Abbé de Rastignac, who had been for three months extremely ill , and was only just recovering when dragged to the prison, and there placed in a room so crowded that it was not possible to turn round, and the air in the end of August was fearfully close and heated. Not once while there was the poor old man able to sleep. His niece spent the nights in a room belonging to the jailer, with the Princess de Tarente, and Mademoiselle de Sombreuil.

On the 2nd of September these slaughter-houses were as full as they could hold, and about a hundred ruffians, armed with axes and guns, were sent round to all the jails to do the bloody work. It was a Sunday, and some of the victims had tried to observe it religiously, though little divining that, it was to be their last. They first took alarm on perceiving that their jailer had removed his family, and then that he sent up their dinner earlier than usual, and removed all the knives and forks. By and by howls and shouts were heard, and the tocsin was heard, ringing, alarm guns firing, and reports came in to the prisoners of the Abbaye that the populace were breaking into the prisons.

The clergy were all penned up together in the cloisters of the Abbaye, whither they had been brought in carriages that morning. Among them

was the Abbé Sicard, an admirable priest who had spent his whole lifetime
in instructing the deaf and dumb in his own house, where–

> "The cunning finger finely twined
> The subtle thread that knitteth mind to mind;
> There that strange bridge of signs was built where roll
> The sunless waves that sever soul from soul,
> And by the arch, no bigger than a hand,
> Truth travell'd over to the silent land".

He had been arrested, while teaching his pupils, on the 26th of August,
1792, and shut up among other clergy in the prison of the Mayoralty; but
the lads whom he had educated came in a body to ask leave to claim him
at the bar of the National Assembly. Massieu, his best scholar, had drawn
up a most touching address, saying, that in him the deaf and dumb were
deprived of their teacher, nurse, and father. "It is he who has taught us
what we know, without him we should be as the beasts of the field." This
petition, and the gestures of the poor silent beings, went to the heart of
the National Assembly. One young man, named Duhamel, neither deaf
nor dumb, from pure admiration of the good work, went and offered to
be imprisoned in the Abbé 's place. There was great applause, and a decree
was passed that the cause of the arrest should be enquired into, but this
took no effect, and on that dreadful afternoon, M. Sicard was put into
one of a procession of carriages, which drove slowly through the streets
full of priests, who were reviled, pelted, and wounded by the populace till
they reached the Abbaye.

In the turnkey's rooms sat a horrible committee, who acted as a sort
of tribunal, but very few of the priests reached it. They were for the most
part cut down as they stepped out into the throng in the court–consisting
of red-capped ruffians, with their shirt sleeves turned up, and still more
fiendish women, who hounded them on to the butchery, and brought
them wine and food. Sicard and another priest contrived, while their
companions fell, to rush into the committee room, exclaiming, "Messieurs,
preserve an unfortunate!"

"Go along!" they said, "do you wish us to get ourselves massacred?"

But one, recognizing him, was surprised, knowing that his life was to
be spared, and took him into the room, promising to save him as long as
possible. Here the two priests would have been safe but for a wretched
woman, who shrieked out to the murderers that they had been admitted,
and loud knocks and demands for them came from without. Sicard thought
all lost, and taking out his watch, begged one of the committee to give it
to the first deaf mute who should come and ask for him, sure that it would
be the faithful Massieu. At first the man replied that the danger was not

imminent enough; but on hearing a more furious noise at the door, as if the mob were going to break in, he took the watch; and Sicard, falling on his knees, commended his soul to God, and embraced his brother priest.

In rushed the assassins, they paused for a moment, unable to distinguish the priests from the committee, but the two pikemen found them out, and his companion was instantly murdered. The weapons were lifted against Sicard, when a man pushed through the crowd, and throwing himself before the pike, displayed his breast and cried, "Behold the bosom through which you must pass to reach that of this good citizen. You do not know him. He is the Abbé Sicard, one of the most benevolent of men, the most useful to his country, the father of the deaf and dumb!"

The murderer dropped his pike; but Sicard, perceiving that it was the populace who were the real dispensers of life or death, sprang to the window, and shouted, "Friends, behold an innocent man. Am I to die without being heard?"

"You were among the rest," the mob shouted, "therefore you are as bad as the others."

But when he told his name, the cry changed. "He is the father of the deaf and dumb! he is too useful to perish; his life is spent in doing good; he must be saved." And the murderers behind took him up in their arms, and carried him out into the court, where he was obliged to submit to be embraced by the whole gang of ruffians, who wanted to carry him home in triumph; but he did not choose to go without being legally released, and returning into the committee room, he learnt for the first time the name of his preserver, one Monnot, a watchmaker, who, though knowing him only by character, and learning that he was among the clergy who were being driven to the slaughter, had rushed in to save him.

Sicard remained in the committee room while further horrors were perpetrated all round, and at night was taken to the little room called Le Violon, with two other prisoners. A horrible night ensued; the murders on the outside varied with drinking and dancing; and at three o'clock the murderers tried to break into Le Violon. There was a loft far overhead, and the other two prisoners tried to persuade Sicard to climb on their shoulders to reach it, saying that his life was more useful than theirs. However, some fresh prey was brought in, which drew off the attention of the murderers, and two days afterwards Sicard was released to resume his life of charity.

At the beginning of the night, all the ladies who had accompanied their relatives were separated from them, and put into the women's room; but when morning came they entreated earnestly to return to them, but Mademoiselle de Fausse Lendry was assured that her uncle was safe, and they were told soon after that all who remained were pardoned. About twenty-two ladies were together, and were called to leave the prison, but the two who went first were at once butchered, and the sentry called out to the others, "It is a snare, go back, do not show yourselves." They retreated; but Marie de Sombreuil had made her way to her father, and when he was called down into the court, she came with him. She hung round him, beseeching the murderers to have pity on his grey hairs, and declaring that they must strike him only through her. One of the ruffians, touched by her resolution, called out that they should be allowed to pass if the girl would drink to the health of the nation. The whole court was swimming with blood, and the glass he held out to her was full of something red. Marie would not shudder. She drank, and with the applause of the assassins ringing in her ears, she passed with her father over the threshold of the fatal gates, into such freedom and safety as Paris could then afford. Never again could she see a glass of red wine without a shudder, and it was generally believed that it was actually a glass of blood that she had swallowed, though she always averred that this was an exaggeration, and that it had been only her impression before tasting it that so horrible a draught was offered to her.

The tidings that Mademoiselle de Sombreuil had saved her father came to encourage the rest of the ladies, and when calls were heard for "Cazotte", Elizabeth flew out and joined her father, and in like manner stood between him and the butchers, till her devotion made the crowd cry "Pardon!" and one of the men employed about the prison opened a passage for her, by which she, too, led her father away.

Madame de Fausse Lendry was not so happy. Her uncle was killed early in the day, before she was aware that he had been sent for, but she survived to relate the history of that most horrible night and day. The same work was going on at all the other prisons, and chief among the victims of La Force was the beautiful Marie Louise of Savoy, the Princess de Lamballe, and one of the most intimate friends of the Queen. A young widow without children, she had been the ornament of the court, and clever learned ladies thought her frivolous, but the depth of her nature was shown in the time of trial. Her old father-in-law had taken her abroad with him when the danger first became apparent, but as soon as she saw that the Queen herself was aimed at, she went immediately back to France to comfort her and share her fate.

Since the terrible 10th of August, the friends had been separated, and Madame de Lamballe had been in the prison of La Force. There, on the evening of the 2nd of September, she was brought down to the tribunal, and told to swear liberty, equality, and hatred to the King and Queen.

"I will readily swear the two former. I cannot swear the latter. It is not in my heart."

"Swear! If not, you are dead."

She raised her eyes, lifted her hands, and made a step to the door. Murderers closed her in, and pikethrusts in a few moments were the last "stage that carried from earth to heaven" the gentle woman, who had loved her queenly friend to the death. Little mattered it to her that her corpse was soon torn limb from limb, and that her fair ringlets were floating round the pike on which her head was borne past her friend's prison window. Little matters it now even to Marie Antoinette. The worst that the murderers could do for such as these, could only work for them a more exceeding weight of glory.

M. Cazotte was imprisoned again on the 12th of September, and all his daughter's efforts failed to save him. She was taken from him, and he died on the guillotine, exclaiming, "I die as I have lived, faithful to my God and to my King." And the same winter, M. de Sombreuil was also imprisoned again. When he entered the prison with his daughter, all the inmates rose to do her honour. In the ensuing June, after a mock trial, her father and brother were put to death, and she remained for many years alone with only the memory of her past days.

The Vendéens

1793

WHILE the greater part of France had been falling into habits of self-indulgence, and from thence into infidelity and revolution, there was one district where the people had not forgotten to fear God and honour the King.

This was in the tract surrounding the Loire, the south of which is now called La Vendée, and was then termed the Bocage, or the Woodland. It is full of low hills and narrow valleys, divided into small fields, enclosed by high thick hedgerows; so that when viewed from the top of one of the hills, the whole country appears perfectly green, excepting near harvest-time, when small patches of golden corn catch the eye, or where here and there a church tower peeps above the trees, in the midst of the flat red-tiled roofs of the surrounding village. The roads are deep lanes, often in the winter beds of streams, and in the summer completely roofed by the thick foliage of the trees, whose branches meet overhead.

The gentry of La Vendée, instead of idling their time at Paris, lived on their own estates in kindly intercourse with their neighbours, and constantly helping and befriending their tenants, visiting them at their farms, talking over their crops and cattle, giving them advice, and inviting them on holidays to dance in the courts of their castles, and themselves joining in their sports. The peasants were a hardworking, sober, and pious people, devoutly attending their churches, reverencing their clergy, and, as well they might, loving and honouring their good landlords.

But as the Revolution began to make its deadly progress at Paris, a gloom spread over this happy country. The Paris mob, who could not bear to see anyone higher in station than themselves, thirsted for noble blood, and the gentry were driven from France, or else imprisoned and put to death. An oath contrary to the laws of their Church was required of the clergy, those who refused it were thrust out of their parishes, and others placed in their room; and throughout France all the youths of a certain age were forced to draw lots to decide who should serve in the Republican army.

This conscription filled up the measure. The Vendéens had grieved over the flight of their landlords, they had sheltered and hidden their priests, and heard their ministrations in secret; but when their young men were to be carried way from them, and made the defenders and instruments of those who were murdering their King, overthrowing their Church, and ruining their country, they could endure it no longer, but in the spring of 1793, soon after the execution of Louis XVI, a rising took place in Anjou, at the village of St. Florent, headed by a pedlar named Cathelineau, and they drove back the Blues, as they called the revolutionary soldiers, who had come to enforce the conscription. They begged Monsieur de Bonchamp, a gentleman in the neighbourhood, to take the command; and, willing to devote himself to the cause of his King, he complied, saying, as he did so, "We must not aspire to earthly rewards; such would be beneath the purity of our motives, the holiness of our cause. We must not even aspire to glory, for a civil war affords none. We shall see our castles fall, we shall be proscribed, slandered, stripped of our possessions, perhaps put to death; but let us thank God for giving us strength to do our duty to the end."

The next person on whom the peasants cast their eyes possessed as true and strong a heart, though he was too young to count the cost of loyalty with the same calm spirit of self-devotion. The Marquis de la Rochejac-quelein, one of the most excellent of the nobles of Poitou, had already emigrated with his wife and all his family, excepting Henri, the eldest son, who, though but eighteen years of age, had been placed in the dangerous post of an officer in the Royal Guards. When Louis XVI had been obliged to dismiss these brave men, he had obtained a promise from each officer that he would not leave France, but wait for some chance of delivering that unhappy country. Henri had therefore remained at Paris, until after the 10th of August, 1792, when the massacre at the Tuileries took place, and the imprisonment of the royal family commenced; and then every gentleman being in danger in the city, he had come to his father's deserted castle of Durballière in Poitou.

He was nearly twenty, tall and slender, with fair hair, an oval face, and blue eyes, very gentle, although full of animation. He was active and dexterous in all manly sports, especially shooting and riding; he was a man of few words; and his manners were so shy, modest, and retiring, that his friends used to say he was more like an Englishman than a Frenchman.

Hearing that he was alone at Durballière, and knowing that as an of-ficer in the Guards, and also as being of the age liable to the conscription, he was in danger from the Revolutionists in the neighbouring towns, his cousin, the Marquis de Lescure, sent to invite him to his strong castle of Clisson, which was likewise situated in the Bocage. This castle afforded a refuge to many others who were in danger—to nuns driven from their convents, dispossessed clergy, and persons who dreaded to remain at their homes, but who felt reassured under the shelter of the castle, and by the character of its owner, a young man of six-and-twenty, who, though of high and unshaken loyalty, had never concerned himself with politics, but led a quiet and studious life, and was everywhere honoured and respected.

The winter passed in great anxiety, and when in the spring the rising at Anjou took place, and the new government summoned all who could bear arms to assist in quelling it, a council was held among the party at Clisson on the steps to be taken. Henri, as the youngest, spoke first, saying he would rather perish than fight against the peasants; nor among the whole assembly was there one person willing to take the safer but meaner course of deserting the cause of their King and country. "Yes," said the Duchess de Donnissan, mother to the young wife of the Marquis de Lescure, "I see you are all of the same opinion. Better death than dishonour. I approve your courage. It is a settled thing:"–and seating herself in her armchair, she concluded, "Well, then, we must die."

For some little time all remained quiet at Clisson; but at length the order for the conscription arrived, and a few days before the time appointed for the lots to be drawn, a boy came to the castle bringing a note to Henri from his aunt at St. Aubin. "Monsieur Henri, " said the boy, "they say you are to draw for the conscription next Sunday; but may not your tenants rise against it in the meantime? Come with me, sir, the whole country is longing for you, and will obey you."

Henri instantly promised to come, but some of the ladies would have persuaded him not to endanger himself–representing, too, that if he was missing on the appointed day, M. de Lescure might be made responsible for him. The Marquis, however, silenced them, saying to his cousin, "You are prompted by honour and duty to put yourself at the head of your tenants. Follow out your plan, I am only grieved at not being able to go with you; and certainly no fear of imprisonment will lead me to dissuade you from doing your duty."

"Well, I will come and rescue you," said Henri, embracing him, and his eyes glancing with a noble soldier-like expression and an eagle look.

As soon as the servants were gone to bed, he set out with a guide, with a stick in his hand and a pair of pistols in his belt; and travelling through the fields, over hedges and ditches, for fear of meeting with the Blues, arrived at St. Aubin, and from thence went on to meet M. de Bonchamp and his little army. But he found to his disappointment that they had just been defeated, and the chieftains, believing that all was lost, had dispersed their troops. He went to his own home, dispirited and grieved; but no sooner did the men of St. Aubin learn the arrival of their young lord, than they came trooping to the castle, entreating him to place himself at their head.

In the early morning, the castle court, the fields, the village, were thronged with stout hardy farmers and labourers, in grey coats, with broad flapping hats, and red woollen handkerchiefs round their necks. On their shoulders were spits, scythes, and even sticks; happy was the man who could bring an old fowling-piece, and still more rejoiced the owner of some powder, intended for blasting some neighbouring quarry. All had bold true hearts, ready to suffer and to die in the cause of their Church and of their young innocent imprisoned King.

A mistrust of his own powers, a fear of ruining these brave men, crossed the mind of the youth as he looked forth upon them, and he exclaimed, " If my father was but here, you might trust to him. Yet by my courage I will show myself worthy, and lead you. If I go forward, follow me: if I draw back, kill me; if I am slain, avenge me!" They replied with shouts of joy, and it was instantly resolved to march upon the next village, which was occupied by the rebel troops. They gained a complete victory, driving away the Blues, and taking two small pieces of cannon, and immediately joined M. de Bonchamp and Cathelineau, who, encouraged by their success, again gathered their troops and gained some further advantages.

In the meantime, the authorities had sent to Clisson and arrested M. de Lescure, his wife, her parents, and some of their guests, who were conducted to Bressuire, the nearest town, and there closely guarded. There was great danger that the Republicans would revenge their losses upon them, but the calm dignified deportment of M. de Lescure obliged them to respect him so much that no injury was offered to him. At last came the joyful news that the Royalist army was approaching. The Republican soldiers immediately quitted the town, and the inhabitants all came to ask the protection of the prisoners, desiring to send their goods to Clisson for security, and thinking themselves guarded by the presence of M. and Madame de Lescure.

M. de Lescure and his cousin Bernard de Marigny mounted their horses and rode out to meet their friends. In a quarter of an hour afterwards, Madame de Lescure heard the shouts "Long live the King!" and the next minute, Henri de la Rochejacquelein hurried into the room, crying, "I have saved you." The peasants marched in to the number of 20,000, and spread themselves through the town, but in their victory they had gained no taste for blood or plunder–they did not hurt a single inhabitant, nor touch anything that was not their own. Madame de Lescure heard some of them wishing for tobacco, and asked if there was none in the town. "Oh yes, there is plenty to be sold, but we have no money;" and they were very thankful to her for giving the small sum they required. Monsieur de Donnissan saw two men disputing in the street, and one drew his sword, when he interfered, saying, "Our Lord prayed for His murderers, and would one soldier of the Catholic army kill another?" The two instantly embraced.

Three times a day these peasant warriors knelt at their prayers, in the churches if they were near them, if not, in the open field, and seldom have ever been equalled the piety, the humility, the self-devotion alike of chiefs and of followers. The frightful cruelties committed by the enemy were returned by mercy; though such of them as fell into the hands of the Republicans were shot without pity, yet their prisoners were instantly set at liberty after being made to promise not to serve against them again, and having their hair shaved off in order that they might be recognized.

Whenever an enterprise was resolved on, the curates gave notice to their parishioners that the leaders would be at such a place at such a time, upon which they crowded to the spot, and assembled around the white standard of France with such weapons as they could muster.

The clergy then heard them confess their sins, gave them absolution, and blessed them; then, while they set forward, returned to the churches where their wives and children were praying for their success. They did not fight like regular soldiers, but, creeping through the hedgerows and coppices, burst unexpectedly upon the Blues, who, entangled in the hollow lanes, ignorant of the country, and amazed by the suddenness of the attack, had little power to resist. The chieftains were always foremost in danger; above all the eager young Henri, with his eye on the white standard, and on the blue sky, and his hand making the sign of the cross without which he never charged the enemy, dashed on first, fearless of peril, regardless of his life, thinking only of his duty to his king and the protection of his followers.

It was calmness and resignation which chiefly distinguished M. de Lescure, the Saint of Poitou, as the peasants called him from his great piety, his even temper, and the kindness and the wonderful mercifulness of his disposition. Though constantly at the head of his troops, leading them into the most dangerous places, and never sparing himself, not one man was slain by his hand, nor did he even permit a prisoner to receive the least injury in his presence. When one of the Republicans once presented his musket close to his breast, he quietly put it aside with his hand, and only said, "Take away the prisoner". His calmness was indeed well founded, and his trust never failed. Once when the little army had received a consider-able check, and his cousin M. de Marigny was in despair, and throwing his pistols on the table, exclaimed, "I fight no longer", he took him by the arm, led him to the window, an pointing to a troop of peasants kneeling at their evening prayers, he said, "See there a pledge of our hopes, and doubt no longer that we shall conquer in our turn."

Their greatest victory was at Saumur, owing chiefly to the gallantry of Henri, who threw his hat into the midst of the enemy, shouting to his followers, "Who will go and fetch it for me?" and rushing forward, drove all before him, and made his way into the town on one side, while M. de Lescure, together with Stofflet, a gamekeeper, another of the chiefs, made their entrance on the other side. M. de Lescure was wounded in the arm, and on the sight of his blood the peasants gave back, and would have fled had not Stofflet threatened to shoot the first who turned; and in the meantime M. de Lescure, tying up his arm with a handkerchief, declared it was nothing, and led them onwards.

The city was entirely in their hands, and their thankful delight was excessive; but they only displayed it by ringing the bells, singing the Te Deum, and parading the streets. Henri was almost out of his senses with exultation; but at last he fell into a reverie, as he stood, with his arms folded, gazing on the mighty citadel which had yielded to efforts such as theirs. His friends roused him from his dream by their remarks, and he replied, "I am reflecting on our success, and am confounded".

They now resolved to elect a general-in-chief, and M. de Lescure was the first to propose Cathelineau, the pedlar, who had first come forward in the cause. It was a wondrous thing when the nobles, the gentry, and experienced officers who had served in the regular army, all willingly placed themselves under the command of the simple untrained peasant, without a thought of selfishness or of jealousy. Nor did Cathelineau himself show any trace of pride, or lose his complete humility of mind or manner; but by each word and deed he fully proved how wise had been their judgment, and well earned the title given him by the peasants of the "Saint of Anjou".

It was now that their hopes were highest; they were more numerous and better armed than they had ever been before, and they even talked of a march to Paris to "fetch their little king, and have him crowned at Chollet", the chief town of La Vendée. But martyrdom, the highest glory to be obtained on this earth, was already shedding its brightness round these devoted men who were counted worthy to suffer, and it was in a higher and purer world that they were to meet their royal child.

Cathelineau turned towards Nantes, leaving Henri de la Rochejaquelein, to his great vexation, to defend Saumur with a party of peasants. But he found it impossible to prevent these poor men from returning to their homes; they did not understand the importance of garrison duty, and gradually departed, leaving their commander alone with a few officers, with whom he used to go through the town at night, shouting out, "Long live the king!" at the places where there ought to have been sentinels. At last, when his followers were reduced to eight, he left the town, and, rejoicing to be once more in the open field, overtook his friends at Angers, where they had just rescued a great number of clergy who had been imprisoned there, and daily threatened with death. "Do not thank us," said the peasants to the liberated priests; "it is for you that we fight. If we had not saved you, we should not have ventured to return home. Since you are freed, we see plainly that the good God is on our side."

But the tide was now about to turn. The Government in Paris sent a far stronger force into the Bocage, and desolated it in a cruel manner. Clisson was burnt to the ground with the very fireworks which had been prepared for the christening of its master's eldest child, and which had

not been used because of the sorrowful days when she was born. M. de
Lescure had long expected its destruction, but had not chosen to remove
the furniture, lest he should discourage the peasants. His family were with
the army, where alone there was now any safety for the weak and helpless.
At Nantes the attack was unsuccessful, and Cathelineau himself received a
wound of which he died in a few days, rejoicing at having been permitted
to shed his blood in such a cause.

The army, of which M. d'Elbée became the leader, now returned to
Poitou, and gained a great victory at Chatillon; but here many of them
forgot the mercy they had usually shown, and, enraged by the sight of their
burnt cottages, wasted fields, and murdered relatives, they fell upon the
prisoners and began to slaughter them. M. de Lescure, coming in haste,
called out to them to desist. "No, no," cried M. de Marigny; "let me slay
these monsters who have burnt your castle." "Then, Marigny," said his
cousin, "you must fight with me. You are too cruel; you will perish by the
sword." And he saved these unhappy men for the time; but they were put
to death on their way to their own army.

The cruelties of the Republicans occasioned a proclamation on the part
of the Royalists that they would make reprisals but they could never bring
themselves to act upon it. When M. de Lescure took Parthenay, he said to
the inhabitants, "It is well for you that it is I who have taken your town;
for, according to our proclamation, I ought to burn it; but, as you would
think it an act of private revenge for the burning of Clisson, I spare you".

Though occasional successes still maintained the hopes of the Vendéens,
misfortunes and defeats now became frequent; they were unable to save
their country from the devastations of the enemy, and disappointments
began to thin the numbers of the soldiers. Henri, while fighting in a hollow road, was struck in the right hand by a ball, which broke his thumb
in three places. He continued to direct his men, but they were at length
driven back from their post. He was obliged to leave the army for some
days; and though he soon appeared again at the head of the men of St.
Aubin, he never recovered the use of his hand.

Shortly after, both d'Elbée and Bonchamp were desperately wounded;
and M. de Lescure, while waving his followers on to attack a Republican
post, received a ball in the head. The enemy pressed on the broken and
defeated army with overwhelming force, and the few remaining chiefs
resolved to cross the Loire and take refuge in Brittany. It was much against
the opinion of M. de Lescure; but, in his feeble and suffering state, he
could not make himself heard, nor could Henri's representations prevail;
the peasants, in terror and dismay, were hastening across as fast as they
could obtain boats to carry them. The enemy was near at hand, and Stofflet,
Marigny, and the other chiefs were only deliberating whether they should
not kill the prisoners whom they could not take with them, and, if set at

liberty, would only add to the numbers of their pursuers. The order for their death had been given; but, before it could be executed, M. de Lescure had raised his head to exclaim, "It is too horrible!" and M. de Bonchamp at the same moment said, almost with his last breath, "Spare them!" The officers who stood by rushed to the generals, crying out that Bonchamp commanded that they should be pardoned. They were set at liberty; and thus the two Vendéen chiefs avenged their deaths by saving five thousand of their enemies!

M. de Bonchamp expired immediately after; but M. de Lescure had still much to suffer in the long and painful passage across the river, and afterwards, while carried along the rough roads to Varades in an armchair upon two pikes, his wife and her maid supporting his feet. The Bretons received them kindly, and gave him a small room, where, the next day, he sent for the rest of the council, telling them they ought to choose a new general, since M. d'Elbée was missing. They answered that he himself alone could be commander. "Gentlemen," he answered: "I am mortally wounded; and even if I am to live, which I do not expect, I shall be long unfit to serve. The army must instantly have an active chief, loved by all, known to the peasants, trusted by everyone. It is the only way of saving us. M. de la Rochejaquelein alone is known to the soldiers of all the divisions. M. de Donnissan, my father-in-law, does not belong to this part of the country, and would not be as readily followed. The choice I propose would encourage the soldiers; and I entreat you to choose M. de la Rochejaquelein. As to me, if I live, you know I shall not quarrel with Henri; I shall be his aide-de-camp."

His advice was readily followed, Henri was chosen; but when a second in command was to be elected, he said no, he was second, for he should always obey M. de Donnissan, and entreated that the honour might not be given to him, saying that at twenty years of age he had neither weight nor experience, that his valour led him to be first in battle, but in council his youth prevented him from being attended to; and, indeed, after giving his opinion, he usually fell asleep while others were debating. He was, however, elected; and as soon as M. de Lescure heard the shouts of joy with which the peasants received the intelligence, he sent Madame de Lescure to bring him to his bedside. She found him hidden in a corner, weeping bitterly; and when he came to his cousin, he embraced him, saying earnestly, again and again, that he was not fit to be general, he only knew how to fight, he was too young and could never silence those who opposed his designs, and entreated him to take the command as soon as he was cured. "That I do not expect," said M. de Lescure; "but if it should happen, I will be your aide-de-camp, and help you to conquer the shyness which prevents your strength of character from silencing, the murmurers and the ambitious."

Henri accordingly took the command; but it was a melancholy office

that devolved upon him of dragging onward his broken and dejected peasants, half-starved, half-clothed, and followed by a wretched train of women,
children, and wounded; a sad change from the bright hopes with which,
not six months before, he had been called to the head of his tenants. Yet still
his high courage gained some triumphs, which for a time revived the spirits
of his forces and restored their confidence. He was active and undaunted,
and it was about this time, when in pursuit of the Blues, he was attacked
by a foot soldier when alone in a narrow lane. His right hand was useless,
but he seized the man's collar with his 1eft, and held him fast, managing
his horse with his legs till his men came up. He would not allow them to
kill the soldier, but set him free, saying "Return to the Republicans, and
tell them that you were alone with the general of the brigands, who had but
one hand and no weapons, yet you could not kill him". Brigands was the
name given by the Republicans, the true robbers, to the Royalists, who, in
fact, by this time, owing to the wild life they had so long led, had acquired
a somewhat rude and savage appearance. They wore grey cloth coats and
trousers, broad hats, white sashes with knots of different colours to mark
the rank of the officers, and red woollen handkerchiefs. These were made
in the country, and were at first chiefly worn by Henri, who usually had
one round his neck, another round his waist, and a third to support his
wounded hand; but the other officers, having heard the Blues cry out to
aim at the red handkerchief, themselves adopted the same badge, in order
that he might be less conspicuous.

In the meantime a few days' rest at Laval had at first so alleviated the
sufferings of M. de Lescure, that hopes were entertained of his recovery;
but he ventured on greater exertions of strength than he was able to bear,
and fever returned, which had weakened him greatly before it became
necessary to travel onwards. Early in the morning, a day or two before their
departure, he called to his wife, who was lying on a mattress on the floor,
and desired her to open the curtains, asking, as she did so, if it was a clear
day. "Yes," said she. "Then," he answered, "I have a sort of veil before my
eyes, I cannot see distinctly; I always thought my wound was mortal, and
now I no longer doubt. My dear, I must leave you, that is my only regret,
except that I could not restore my king to the throne; I leave you in the
midst of a civil war, that is what afflicts me. Try to save yourself. Disguise
yourself, and attempt to reach England." Then seeing her choked with tears,
he continued: "Yes, your grief alone makes me regret life; for my own part,
I die tranquil; I have indeed sinned, but I have always served God with
piety; I have fought, and I die for Him, and I hope in His mercy. I have
often seen death, and I do not fear it I go to heaven with a sure trust, I
grieve but for you; I hoped to have made you happy; if I ever have given
you any reason to complain, forgive me." Finding her grief beyond all
consolation, he allowed her to call the surgeons, saying that it was possible

he might be mistaken. They gave some hope, which cheered her spirits, though he still said he did not believe them. The next day they left Laval; and on the way, while the carriage was stopping, a person came to the door and read the details of the execution of Marie Antoinette which Madame de Lescure had kept from his knowledge. It was a great shock to him, for he had known the Queen personally, and throughout the day he wearied himself with exclamations on the horrible crime. That night at Ernée he received the Sacrament, and at the same time became speechless, and could only lie holding his wife's hand and looking sometimes at her, sometimes toward heaven. But the cruel enemy were close behind, and there was no rest on earth even for the dying. Madame de Lescure implored her friends to leave them behind; but they told her she would be exposed to a frightful death, and that his body would fall into the enemy's hands; and she was forced to consent to his removal. Her mother and her other friends would not permit her to remain in the carriage with him; she was placed on horseback and her maid and the surgeon were with him. An hour after, on the 3rd of November, he died, but his wife did not know her loss till the evening when they arrived at Fougères; for though the surgeon left the carriage on his death, the maid, fearing the effect which the knowledge might have upon her in the midst of her journey, remained for seven hours in the carriage by his side, during two of which she was in a fainting fit.

When Madame de Lescure and Henri de la Rochejaquelein met the next morning, they sat for a quarter of an hour without speaking, and weeping bitterly. At last she said "You have lost your best friend," and he replied, "Take my life, if it could restore him."

Scarcely anything can be imagined more miserable than the condition of the army, or more terrible than the situation of the young general, who felt himself responsible for its safety, and was compelled daily to see its sufferings and find his plans thwarted by the obstinacy and folly of the other officers, crushed by an overwhelming force, knowing that there was no quarter from which help could come, yet still struggling on in fulfilment of his sad duty. The hopes and expectations which had filled his heart a few months back had long passed away; nothing was around him but misery, nothing before him but desolation; but still he never failed in courage, in mildness, in confidence in Heaven.

At Mans he met with a horrible defeat; at first, indeed, with a small party he broke the columns of the enemy, but fresh men were constantly brought up, and his peasants gave way and retreated, their officers following them. He tried to lead them back through the hedges, and if he had succeeded, would surely have gained the victory. Three times with two other officers he dashed into the midst of the Blues; but the broken, dispirited peasants would not follow him, not one would even turn to fire a shot. At last, in leaping a hedge, his saddle turned, and he fell, without indeed being hurt, but the sight of his fall added to the terror of the miserable Vendéens. He struggled long and desperately through the long night that followed to defend the gates of the town, but with the light of morning the enemy perceived his weakness and effected their entrance. His followers had in the meantime gradually retired into the country beyond, but those who could not escape fell a prey to the cruelty of the Republicans. "I thought you had perished," said Madame de Lescure, when he overtook her. "Would that I had," was his answer.

He now resolved to cross the Loire, and return to his native Bocage, where the well-known woods would afford a better protection to his followers. It was at Craon, on their route to the river, that Madame de Lescure saw him for the last time, as he rallied his men, who had been terrified by a false alarm.

She did not return to La Vendée, but, with her mother, was sheltered by the peasants of Brittany throughout the winter and spring until they found means to leave the country.

The Vendéens reached the Loire at Ancenis, but they were only able to find two small boats to carry them over. On the other side, however, were four great ferry boats loaded with hay; and Henri, with Stofflet, three other officers, and eighteen soldiers crossed the river in their two boats, intending to take possession of them, send them back for the rest of the army, and in the meantime protect the passage from the Blues on the Vendéen side. Unfortunately, however, he had scarcely crossed before the pursuers came down upon his troops, drove them back from Ancenis, and entirely prevented them from attempting the passage, while at the same time Henri and his companions were attacked and forced from the river by a body of Republicans on their side. A last resistance was attempted by the retreating Vendéens at Savenay, where they fought nobly but in vain; four thousand were shot on the field of battle, the chiefs were made prisoners and carried to Nantes or Angers, where they were guillotined, and a few who succeeded in escaping found shelter among the Bretons, or one by one found their way back to La Vendée. M. de Donnissan was amongst those who were guillotined, and M. d'Elbée, who was seized shortly after, was shot with his wife.

Henri, with his few companions, when driven from the banks of the Loire, dismissed the eighteen soldiers, whose number would only have attracted attention without being sufficient for protection; but the five chiefs crossed the fields and wandered through the country without meeting a single inhabitant—all the houses were burnt down, and the few remaining peasants hidden in the woods. At last, after four-and-twenty hours, walking, they came to an inhabited farm, where they lay down to sleep on the straw. The next moment the farmer came to tell them the Blues were coming; but they were so worn out with fatigue, that they would not move. The Blues were happily, also, very tired, and, without making any search, lay down on the other side of the heap of straw, and also fell asleep. Before daylight the Vendéens rose and set out again, walking miles and miles in the midst of desolation, until, after several days, they came to Henri's own village of St. Aubin, where he sought out his aunt, who was in concealment there, and remained with her for three days, utterly overwhelmed with grief at his fatal separation from his army, and only longing for an opportunity of giving his life in the good cause.

Beyond all his hopes, the peasants no sooner heard his name, than once more they rallied round the white standard, as determined as ever not to yield to the Revolutionary government; and the beginning of the year 1794 found him once more at the head of a considerable force, encamped in the forests of Vésins, guarding the villages around from the cruelties of the Blues. He was now doubly beloved and trusted by the followers who had proved his worth, and who even yet looked forward to triumphs beneath his brave guidance; but it was not so with him, he had learnt the lesson of disappointment, and though always active and cheerful, his mind was made up, and the only hope he cherished was of meeting the death of a soldier. His headquarters were in the midst of a forest, where one of the Republican officers, who was made prisoner, was much surprised to find the much-dreaded chieftain of the Royalists living in a hut formed of boughs of trees, dressed almost like a peasant, and with his arm still in a sling. This person was shot, because he was found to be commissioned to promise pardon to the peasants, and afterwards to massacre them; but Henri had not learnt cruelty from his persecutors, and his last words were of forgiveness.

It was on Ash Wednesday that he had repulsed an attack of the enemy, and had almost driven them out of the wood, when, perceiving two soldiers hiding behind a hedge, he stopped, crying out, "Surrender, I spare you." As he spoke one of them levelled his musket, fired, and stretched him dead on the ground without a groan. Stofflet, coming up the next moment, killed the murderer with one stroke of his sword; but the remaining soldier was spared out of regard to the last words of the general. The Vendéens wept bitterly, but there was no time to indulge their sorrow, for the enemy were returning upon them; and, to save their chieftain's corpse from insult, they hastily dug a grave, in which they placed both bodies, and retreated as the Blues came up to occupy the ground. The Republicans sought for the spot, but it was preserved from their knowledge; and the high-spirited, pure-hearted Henri de la Rochejaquelein sleeps beside his enemy in the midst of the woodlands where be won for himself eternal honour. His name is still loved beyond all others; the Vendéens seldom pronounce it without touching their hats, and it is the highest glory of many a family that one of their number has served under Monsieur Henri.

Stofflet succeeded to the command, and carried on the war with great skill and courage for another year, though with barbarities such as had never been permitted by the gentle men; but his career was stained by the death of Marigny, whom, by false accusations, he was induced to sentence to be shot. Marigny showed great courage and resignation, himself giving the word to fire–perhaps at that moment remembering the warning of M. de Lescure. Stofflet repented bitterly, and never ceased to lament his death. He was at length made prisoner, and shot, with his last words declaring his devotion to his king and his faith.

Thus ends the tale of the Vendéen war, undertaken in the best of causes, for the honour of God and His Church, and the rescue of one of the most innocent of kings, by men whose saintly characters and dauntless courage have seldom been surpassed by martyrs or heroes of any age. It closed with blood, with fire, with miseries almost unequalled; yet who would dare to say that the lives of Cathelineau, Bonchamp, Lescure, La Rochejaquelein, with their hundreds of brave and pious followers, were devoted in vain? Who could wish to see their brightness dimmed with earthly rewards ?

And though the powers of evil were permitted to prevail on earth, yet what could their utmost triumph effect against the faithful, but to make for them, in the words of the child king for whom they fought, one of those thorny paths that lead to glory!

The Faithful Slaves of Haiti
1793

MOURNFUL as are in general the annals of slavery, yet even this cloud is not without its silver lining; and noble deeds of fidelity and self-devotion are on record even from those whom their masters have been accustomed to look on as so degraded as to be incapable of more than an animal species of loyalty.

The French are not in general bad slave-masters. Excitement does indeed stir their Keltic blood into a state in which they will perpetrate horrible ferocities; but in ordinary life their instinct of courtesy and amiability makes them perhaps the least obnoxious of all nations to those whom they believe their inferiors, whether in the bondage of conquest or of slavery.

No doubt, however, there was a fearful arrear of wrongs in the beautiful West Indian island of Hispaniola, or St. Domingo, as it was called when it was shared between France and Spain, with the boundary between them of a river, now known by the portentous name of Massacre. One of the most fertile of all the lovely isles whose aspect had enchanted their discoverer, St. Domingo was a region of rapid wealth to the French Creoles, who lived at ease, and full of luxury and enjoyment, on their rich plantations of sugar, cotton, and coffee, and, often men of high birth, further formed, in right of their white skins, a jealous aristocracy, holding their heads high above the dark population below them, alike of free mulattoes of mixed descent and of negro slaves. Little were they prepared for the decree of the French National Convention, which at one sweep levelled all distinctions–placing the black and brown of every tint on an equality with the whites. The consequence was that the tricoloured cockade was trampled on by the indignant Creoles, who refused obedience to the decree of the mother country, and proceeded to elect a General Assembly of their own; while the aggrieved mulattoes collected on their side in armed bodies for the defence of their newly granted privileges.

In the midst a more terrible enemy arose. The slaves, with the notes of freedom ringing in their ears, rose in a body, and began to burn the plantations and to massacre the whites. Fugitives came rushing into

Capetown, the capital, from all quarters; and at each plantation reached by the insurgents, the slaves, even if previously contented, were gathered into the flood of savagery, and joined in the war of extermination. In less than two months, 2000 white persons, of all ranks, sexes, and ages, had perished, 480 sugar plantations, and 900 coffee, indigo, and cotton settlements had been destroyed. With the horrors and the bloodshed of those days, however, we are not concerned, nor need we trace the frightful and protracted war that finally established negro supremacy over the island that now bears the name of Haiti. It is with the bright spots in the dark picture that we are to deal.

Count de Lopinot, an old officer in the army, who had settled with his wife upon the island, had been so uniformly kind to his slaves, that their hearts were with him; they rose for the protection of him and his family, and when the way of escape was open, entreated him to take them all with him, to live and die in his service. The place chosen for his retreat was the English island of Trinidad, where he obtained from Government a grant of waste land among the mountains, to be selected by himself. The centre of Trinidad is so mountainous, as to be still uncultivated and unsettled, and the Count was forced to take with him his bodyguard of faithful negroes, to cut a passage for him through the tropical forest.

The spot he selected was beautifully situated, fertile, and. well watered; but the best road he could make to it was so rugged as to be unfit for the transport of sugar, and he therefore laid it out for cocoa—upon a design peculiar to himself. The outline of his grounds represented a gigantic French general officer; epaulettes and all, upon whose prostrate form were ranged cocoa plants, at about fifteen or twenty feet apart, each about the size of a gooseberry bush; and at intervals, the forest tree, known by the negroes as Cocoa-Mammy because it is supposed to shade, nourish, and even gather dew for the cocoa plants under its charge. It is from sixty to eighty feet high, and bears brilliant flame-coloured blossoms, so that the hills of Trinidad seem all in a blaze in its flowering season. To this curiously planned estate the grateful count gave the surname of La Reconnaissance, and on the first day when he brought his countess, and installed the negro families in their new abodes, he celebrated a solemn thanksgiving. So much was he beloved, that twenty years after his death the negroes of La Reconnaissance still kept a holiday in his memory.

These negroes were loyal in a body; but on another estate in St. Domingo there was a single loyal exception, a genuine African, not born on the estate, but brought thither by the slave trade. The whole of his master's family were massacred, excepting two little boys, of five and three years old, whom he contrived to hide, and afterwards to escape with to the coast, where he put them on board ship, and succeeded in conveying them to Carolina. Happily, in those days, slavery was apparently on the decline, even in the Southern States, and free negroes were allowed to be at large in the streets of Charleston, so that the faithful man was able to maintain the children by his labour; and not only this, but to fulfil his earnest purpose of educating them consistently with their parents' station in life. He placed them at a good boarding-school, and, while living a hard and frugal life himself, gave them each a dollar a week for pocket money.

The elder of the two went to sea, rose to be captain of a merchant-ship, and married a Spanish heiress in Cuba, when, on settling upon her estate, he at once sent for his good old guardian, built him a house, and made him an overseer, giving him, in memory of old times, a dollar every week for pocket money, and treating him with great affection. The old man lived to a great age, and, on his death, his master was surprised to find that, though a devout Christian, and an intelligent man, he still wore round his neck a little African amulet, which no doubt his affectionate spirit retained as the only memory of his native land.

Another negro, named Eustache, who was born in 1773, on the sugar plantation of Monsieur Belin de Villeneuve, in the northern part of the island, had been always a remarkably intelligent man, though entirely ignorant, and not even able to read. When the bloody attacks on the houses of the whites took place he is said, by his timely warnings and ingenious contrivances, to have at different times saved the lives of no less than 400 white persons without betraying the negroes; and, lastly, he was enabled to place his master safely on board an American vessel with a sufficient cargo of sugar to secure him from destitution. Eustache himself embarked at the same time, considering himself as still M. Belin's slave as completely as though they were still on the plantation. On the voyage the vessel was captured by an English privateer; but, while all the Americans and French were put under hatches, the negro was left at large to profit by the liberty the English sailors fancied they had conferred upon him. They were a drunken, undisciplined set, and while they were carousing Eustache played all sorts of antics for their amusement, until they were so completely off their guard, that he succeeded in releasing and arming the prisoners and carrying off the prize, with the English as prisoners in their turn, safe into the roads of Baltimore. He there hired himself out to work, and applied all his earnings to the assistance of the many ruined French from St. Domingo, who had taken refuge there. After a time it was supposed that the French power was re-established in the island, and M. Belin ventured back, with a number of his friends, in hopes of recovering his property; but he found himself in greater danger than ever. The town of Fort Dauphin was occupied by the Spaniards, and 20,000 negroes, commanded by a black called Jean Français, were encamped on the heights near the town, and massacred every Frenchman they encountered. The Spaniards gave the unhappy French no arms nor assistance, and M. Belin fled for his life to the seashore, pursued by a party of blacks. He saw a Spanish guard before him, and, throwing off his coat, ran in among them, giving his name to the officer. A Spanish uniform was thrown over him, and he was saved.

Eustache had been separated from his master in the crowd, and, uncertain whether he were still alive, resolved at least to save his property. He actually persuaded Jean Français' wife to let him hide some boxes of valuables under her bed, by telling her that, if his master had been massacred, they would belong to himself; and then, going to the place of slaughter, examined all the corpses, but happily in vain. After much enquiry, he discovered M. Belin, and succeeded in getting both him and his property on board ship, and bringing all safely a second time to Baltimore.

M. Belin afterwards resided at Port au Prince, where he became president of the council. Eustache continued in his service as attached and devoted as ever, and after a time observing that he was distressed by the increasing dimness of his eyesight, this devoted slave went secretly at four o'clock every morning to get himself taught to read, overcame all difficulties, and, when he thought himself perfect in the art, came to his master with a book, and thenceforth kept the old man occupied and amused.

M. Belin took care to emancipate his faithful servant before his death, and left him a considerable legacy, which he regarded as a trust for his master's distressed countrymen, and spent from day to day in acts of beneficence, gaining his own livelihood by hiring himself out as a cook at great dinners, for he was admirable in that line, and obtained constant employment. In 1831 he was still alive, and was sought out to receive the prize for which ten years before M. Monthyon had left an endowment, to serve as an acknowledgment of the noblest action that could each year be discovered. Eustache's exertions were then made known, and in the words of the discourse made on that occasion, his daily deeds were thus described: "Every moment some new instance of his incorrigible generosity comes to light. Sometimes it is poor children whom he has put out to nurse, or others whose apprentice fee he has paid. Sometimes he buys tools or agricultural implements for workmen without means. Here, relations of his master obtain from him large sums which they will not restore and that he will never demand; there he is left unpaid by persons who have employed him and whom he does not press because they have fallen into misfortune, and he respects distress." When he found, to his great surprise, how much his doings were admired, he answered one of the committee who had sought him out, "Indeed, sir, I am not doing this for men but for the Master above."

Eustache was not the only negro who received a "prize of virtue". In 1848 the French liberated all the slaves in their various colonies, without having given sufficient time for preparation. The blacks made instant use of their freedom by deserting their masters and setting up little huts for themselves with gardens, where the tropical climate enabled them to grow all their wants required without any need for exertion. This was, of course, ruin to the owners of the large plantations hitherto entirely dependent on slave labour. Among those thus deserted was one in French Guiana, named La Parterre, and belonging to a lady, a widow with a large family. Out of seventy negro slaves, not one remained on the estate except Paul Dunez, who had become a sort of foreman, and who promised his mistress that he would do his utmost for her. He tried at first to obtain some hired labour; but not succeeding, he tried to keep as much as possible under cultivation, though he had no one to help him but his wife and young sons. The great difficulty was in keeping up the dykes which fence out the coast from the sea on that low, marshy coast of northern South America, a sort of tropical Holland. Day after day was Paul labouring at the dykes, and at every spring tide he would watch for two or three nights together, so as to be ready to repair any breach in the embankment. This went on for thirty-two months, and was labour freely given without hire, for faithful loyalty's sake; but at last the equinoctial tides of 1851 were too much for Paul's single arm, he could not be at every breach at once, and the plantation was all laid under water!

To work he set again to repair the damage as best he might, and the government at Cayenne, hearing of his exertions, resolved to assign to him a prize which had been founded for the most meritorious labour in the colony; namely, the sum of 600 francs and admission for his son into the college at the capital. But Paul's whole devotion was still for his mistress. Her son, not his own, was sent to the college, and the 600 francs were expended in fitting the boy out as became the former circumstances of his family, on whose service Paul continued to spend himself.

The next year his name was sent up to Paris, and the first prize of virtue was decreed to him for his long course of self-denying exertions.

The Petitioners For Pardon

1720 AND ABOUT 1805

NO one in our own country has deserved warmer or more loving esteem than Helen Walker, the Scottish maiden who, though she would not utter a word of untruth to save her sister from being sentenced to death, yet came on foot from Edinburgh to London, made her way to the Duke of Argyle, and being introduced by him, by her entreaties obtained that sister's pardon from Queen Caroline, who was acting as Regent in the absence of George II. It is hard to say which was the more glorious, the God-fearing truth that strengthened this peasant girl to risk a life so dear to her, or the trustful courage and perseverance that carried her through a journey, which in the early part of the eighteenth century was both tedious and full of danger; and it is satisfactory to know that her after life, though simple and homely, by no means was unworthy of the high excellence of her youth. Her sister, Tibbie, for whom she had done so much, married and left her, and she lived on to be remembered by her neighbours as a religious, quiet old woman, gaining her living by knitting new feet to old stockings, teaching little children, and keeping chickens. Her neighbours respected her, and called her a "lofty body". They used to tell that in a thunderstorm, she used to move herself with her work and her Bible to the front of the house, saying that the Almighty could smite as well in the city as in the field. Sir Walter Scott made her the model of the most beautiful character he ever drew, and afterwards placed a monument to her honour in her own village church.

In the beginning of this century, a girl younger than Helen Walker was impelled to a journey beside which that from Edinburgh to London seems only like a summer stroll, and her motive was in like manner deep affection, love truly stronger than death. As Helen Walker served to suggest the Jeanie Deans of the *Heart of Midlothian* so Prascovia Lopouloff was the origin of Elizabeth, the heroine of Madame Cottin's *Exiles of Siberia*, but in both cases the real facts have been a good deal altered in the tales, and we may doubt whether the Russian lady appears to so much advantage, when dressed up by the French authoress, as does the Scottish lassie in the hands of her countryman.

Prascovia was the daughter of a captain in the Russian army, who for some unknown reason had undergone the sentence of exile to Siberia, from the capricious and insane Czar Paul I. The Russian government, being despotic, is naturally inclined to be suspicious, and it has long been the custom to send off persons supposed to be dangerous to the state, to live in the intensely cold and remote district of Siberia. Actual criminals are marched off in chains, and kept working in the mines; but political offenders are permitted to live with their families, have a weekly sum allowed for their support, and when it is insufficient, can eke it out by any form of labour they prefer, whether by hunting, or by such farming as the climate will allow.

The miseries of the exiles have been much mitigated in these later times, many more comforts are permitted them, and though closely watched, and suffering from many annoying regulations, those of higher rank receive a sufficient sum out of their own revenues to enable them to live in tolerable ease, and without actual drudgery; and at Tobolsk, the capital of Siberia, there is a highly educated and accomplished society of banished Poles and of Russians who have incurred suspicion.

Under the Czars who reigned before the kind-hearted Alexander I, the banishment was far more terrible. It was not only the being absent from home and friends, but it was a fall from all the luxuries of civilized life to the utmost poverty, and that in a climate of fearful severity, with a winter lasting nine months, and the sun unseen for many weeks of that time. Captain Lopouloff was condemned for life, was placed in the village of Ischim, far to the north of Tobolsk, and only obtained an allowance of ten kopeks a day. His wife, and their little girl of about three years old, accompanied him, and the former adapted herself patiently to her situation, working hard at the common domestic cares for which she had been used to trust to servants; and as the little Prascovia grew older, she not only helped her mother, but gained employment in the village, going out to assist in the late and scanty rye harvest, and obtaining a small bundle of the rye as her wages. She was very happy, even in this wild dreary home, amid all the deep snows, iron frosts, and long darkness, until she was nearly fifteen, when she began to understand how wretched her father was in his banishment. He had sent a petition to the Governor of Siberia, in the charge of an officer, who had promised to represent his case strongly, and the watching for the answer, and continued disappointment, whenever a courier arrived from Tobolsk, rendered him so restless, that he no longer tried to put on a cheerful countenance before his daughter, but openly lamented his hard fate, in seeing her growing up untaught and working with her hands like the meanest serf.

His despair awoke Prascovia from her childish enjoyments. She daily prayed that he might be brought home and comforted, and, as she said herself, it one day darted into her mind like a flash of lightning, just as she finished saying her prayers, that she might go to Petersburg and obtain his pardon. Long did she dwell upon the thought, going alone among the pine trees to dream over it, and to pray that grace and strength might be given her for this great work—this exceeding bliss of restoring her father to his home. Still she durst not mention the project; it seemed so impossible, that it died away upon her lips whenever she tried to ask her father's permission, till at last she set herself a time, at which nothing should prevent her from speaking. The day came; she went out among the whispering pines, and again prayed for strength to make her proposal, and that her father might be led to listen to it favourably. But prayers are not always soon answered. Her father listened to her plan in silence, then called out to his wife, "Here is a fine patroness! Our daughter is going off to Petersburg to speak for us to the Emperor," and he related all the scheme that had been laid before him, with such a throbbing heart, in a tone of amusement.

"She ought be attending to her work instead of talking nonsense," said the wife; and when poor Prascovia, more mortified at derision than by anger, began to cry bitterly, her mother held out a cloth to her, saying in a kind, half-coaxing tone, "Here, my dear, dust the table for dinner, and then you may set off to Petersburg at your ease."

Still day after day Prascovia returned to the charge, entreating that her scheme might at least be considered, till her father grew displeased, and severely forbade her to mention it again. She abstained; but for three whole years she never failed to add to her daily prayers a petition that his consent might be gained. During this time her mother had a long and serious illness, and Prascovia's care, as both nurse and housewife, gave her father and mother such confidence in her, that they no longer regarded her as a child; and when she again ventured to bring her plan before them, they did not laugh at her, but besought her not to leave them in their declining years to expose herself to danger on so wild a project. She answered by tears, but she could not lay it aside.

Another difficulty was, that without a passport she would have been immediately sent back to Ischim, and so many petitions from her father had been disregarded, that there was little chance that any paper sent by him to Tobolsk would be attended to. However, she found one of their fellow exiles who drew up a request in due form for a passport for her, and after six months more of waiting the answer arrived. She was not herself a prisoner, she could leave Siberia whenever she pleased, and the passport was enclosed for her. Her father, however, seized upon it, and locked it up, declaring that he had only allowed the application to go in the certainty that it would be refused, and that nothing would induce him to let a girl of eighteen depart alone for such a journey.

Prascovia still persevered, and her disappointment worked upon her mother to promise not to prevent her from going, provided her father consented; and at last he yielded. "What shall we do with this child?" he said: "we shall have to let her go." Still he said, "Do you think, poor child, that you can speak to the Emperor as you speak to your father in Siberia? Sentinels guard every entrance to his palace and you will never pass the threshold. Poor even to beggary, without clothes or introductions, how could you appear, and who will deign to present you?" However, Prascovia trusted that the same Providence that had brought her the passport would smooth other difficulties; she had boundless confidence in the Power to whom she had committed herself, and her own earnest will made obstacles seem as nothing. That her undertaking should not be disobedient was all she desired. And at length the consent was won, and the 8th of September fixed for her day of departure.

At dawn she was dressed, with a little bag over her shoulder, and her father was trying to make her take the whole family store of wealth, one silver rouble, though, as she truly said, this was not enough to take her to Petersburg, and might do some good at home, and she only took it at last when he laid his strict commands on her. Two of the poorest of the exiles tried to force on her all the money they had–thirty copper kopeks and a silver twenty-kopek piece; and though she refused these, she affectionately promised that the kind givers should share in any favour she should obtain.

When the first sunbeam shone into the room, there was, according to the beautiful old Russian custom, a short, solemn silence, for private prayer for the traveller. Then, after a few words, also customary, of indifferent conversation, there was a last embrace, and Prascovia, kneeling down, received her parents' blessing, rose up, and set her face upon her way–a girl of nineteen, with a single rouble in her pocket, to walk through vast expanses of forest, and make her way to the presence of her sovereign.

The two poor exiles did their utmost for her by escorting her as far as they were allowed to go from Ischim, and they did not leave her till she had joined a party of girls on their way to one of the villages she had to pass. Once they had a fright from some half-tipsy lads; but they shook them off, and reached the village, where Prascovia was known and hospitably lodged for the night. She was much tired in the morning, and when she first set forth on her way, the sense of terror at her loneliness was almost too much for her, till she thought of the angel who succoured Hagar, and took courage; but she had mistaken the road, and by and by found herself at the last village she had passed the night before. Indeed, she often lost her way; and when she asked the road to Petersburg, she was only laughed at. She knew the names of no nearer places in the way, but fancied that the sacred town of Kief, where the Russian power had first begun, was on the route; so, if people did not know which was the road to Petersburg, she would ask for Kief. One day, when she came to a place where three roads branched off, she asked some travellers in a carriage that passed her, which of them led to Kief. "Whichever you please," they answered, laughing; "one leads as much as the other either to Kief, Paris, or Rome." She chose the middle one, which was fortunately the right, but she was never able to give any exact account of the course she had taken, for she confused the names of the villages she passed, and only remembered certain incidents that had impressed themselves on her memory. In the lesser hamlets she was usually kindly received in the first cottage where she asked for shelter; but in larger places, with houses of a superior order, she was often treated as a. suspicious-looking vagabond. For instance, when not far from a place called Kamouicheff, she was caught in a furious storm at the end of a long day's march. She hurried on in hopes of reaching the nearest houses; but a tree was blown down just before her, and she thought it safer to hasten into a thicket, the close bushes of which sheltered her a little against the wind. Darkness came on before the storm abated enough for her to venture out, and there she stayed, without daring to move, though the rain at length made its way through the branches, and soaked her to the skin. At dawn, she dragged herself to the road, and was there offered a place in a cart driven by a peasant, who set her down in the middle of the village at about eight o'clock in the morning. She fell down while getting out, and her clothes were not only wet through with the night's drenching, but covered with mire; she was spent with cold and hunger, and felt herself such a deplorable object, that the neatness of the houses filled her with alarm. She, however, ventured to approach an open window, where she saw a woman shelling peas, and begged to be allowed to rest and dry herself, but the woman surveyed her scornfully, and ordered her off; and she met with no better welcome at any other house. At one, where she sat down at the door, the mistress drove her off, saying that she harboured neither thieves nor vagabonds. "At least," thought the poor wanderer, "they cannot hunt me from the church," but she found the door locked, and when she sat down on its stone steps, the village boys came round her, hooting at her, and calling her a thief and runaway; and thus she remained for two whole hours, ready to die with cold and hunger, but inwardly praying for strength to bear this terrible trial.

At last, however, a kinder woman came up through the rude little mob, and spoke to her in a gentle manner. Prascovia told what a terrible night she had spent in the wood, and the starost, or village magistrate, examined her passport, and found that it answered for her character. The good woman offered to take her home, but on trying to rise, she found her limbs so stiff that she could not move; she had lost one of her shoes, and her feet were terribly swollen; indeed, she never entirely recovered the effects of that dreadful night of exposure. The villagers were shocked at their own inhospitality, they fetched a cart and lodged her safely with the good woman, with whom she remained several days, and when she was again able to proceed, one of the villagers gave her a pair of boots. She was often obliged to rest for a day or two, according to the state of her strength, the weather, or the reception she met with, and she always endeavoured to requite the hospitality she received by little services, such as sweeping, washing, or sewing for her hosts. She found it wiser not to begin by telling her story, or people took her for an impostor; she generally began by begging for a morsel of food; then, if she met with a kind answer, she would talk of her weariness and obtain leave to rest, and when she was a little more at home with the people of the house, would tell them her story; and when, if nothing else would do, she was in urgent need, the sight of her passport secured attention to her from the petty authorities, since she was there described as the daughter of a captain in the army. But she always said that she did not, comparatively, often meet with rebuffs, whilst the acts of kindness she had received were beyond counting. "People fancy," she used afterwards to say, "that my journey was most disastrous, because I tell the troubles and adventures that befel me, and pass over the kind welcomes I received, because nobody cares to hear them."

Once she had a terrible fright. She had been refused an entrance at all the houses in the village street, when an old man, who had been very short and sharp in his rejection, came and called her back. She did not like his looks, but there was no help for it, and she turned back with him. His wife looked even more repulsive than himself, and no sooner had they entered the miserable one-roomed cottage, than she shut the door and fastened it with strong bolts, so that the only light in the place came from oak slips which were set on fire and stuck into a hole in the wall. By their flicker Prascovia thought she saw the old people staring at her most unpleasantly, and presently they asked her where she came from.

"From Ischim. I am going to Petersburg."

"And you have plenty of money for the journey?"

"Only eighty copper kopeks now," said Prascovia, very glad just then to have no more.

"That's a lie," shouted the old woman; "people don't go that distance without money."

She vainly declared it was all she had; they did not believe her, and she could hardly keep back her tears of indignation and terror. At last they gave her a few potatoes to eat, and told her to lie down on the great brick stove, the wide ledges of which are the favourite sleeping places of the poorer Russians. She laid aside her upper garments, and with them her pockets and her pack, hoping within herself that the smallness of the sum might at least make her not worth murdering; then praying with all her might, she lay down. As soon as they thought her asleep, they began whispering.

"She must have more money," they said; "she certainly has notes."

"I saw a string round her neck," said the old woman, "and a little bag hanging to it. The money must be there."

Then after some lower murmurs, they said, "No one saw her come in here. She is not known to be still in the village."

And next the horrified girl saw the old woman climbing up the stove. She again declared that she had no money, and entreated for her life, but the woman made no answer, only pulled the bag from off her neck, and felt her clothes all over, even taking off her boots, and opening her hands, while the man held the light; but, at last, finding nothing in the bag but the passport, they left her alone, and lay down themselves. She lay trembling for a good while, but at last she knew by their breathing that they were both asleep, and she, too, fell into a slumber, from which she did not waken till the old woman roused her at broad daylight. There was a plentiful breakfast of peasant fare prepared for her, and both spoke to her much more kindly, asking her questions, in reply to which she told them part of her story. They seemed interested, and assured her that they had only searched her because they thought she might be a dishonest wanderer, but that she would find that they were far from being robbers themselves. Prascovia was heartily glad to leave their house; but when she ventured to look into her little store, she found that her eighty kopeks had become 120. She always fully believed that these people had had the worst intentions, and thanked God for having turned their hearts. Her other greatest alarm was one morning, when she had set out from her night's lodging before anyone was up, and all the village dogs flew at her. Running and striking with her stick only made them more furious, and one of them was tearing at the bottom of her gown, when she flung herself on her face, recommending her soul to God, as she felt a cold nose upon her neck; but the beast was only smelling her, she was not even once bitten, and a peasant passing by drove them off.

Winter began to come on, and an eight days' snowstorm forced her to stop till it was over; but when she wanted to set off again, the peasants declared that to travel on foot alone in the snow would be certain death even to the strongest men, for the wind raises the drifts, and makes the way undistinguishable, and they detained her till the arrival of a convoy of sledges, which were taking provisions to Ekatherinenburg for the Christmas feasts. The drivers, on learning her story, offered her a seat in a sledge, but her garments were not adapted for winter travelling, and though they covered her with one of the wrappers of their goods, on the fourth day, when they arrived at the kharstina, or solitary posting-station, the intense cold had so affected her, that she was obliged to be lifted from the sledge, with one cheek frost-bitten. The good carriers rubbed it with snow, and took every possible care of her; but they said it was impossible to take her on without a sheepskin pelisse, since otherwise her death from the increasing cold was certain. She cried bitterly at the thought of missing this excellent escort, and on the other hand, the people of the kharstina would not keep her. The carriers then agreed to club together to buy her a sheepskin, but none could be had; no one at the station would spare theirs, as they were in a lonely place, and could not easily get another. Though the carriers even offered a sum beyond the cost to the maid of the inn, if she would part with hers, she still refused; but at last an expedient was found. "Let us lend her our pelisses by turns," said one of the carriers. "Or rather, let her always wear mine, and we will change about every verst." To this all agreed; Prascovia was well wrapped up in one of the sheepskin pelisses, whose owner rolled himself in the wrapper, curled his feet under him, and sung at the top of his lungs. Every verst-stone there was a shifting of sheepskins, and there was much merriment over the changes, while all the way Prascovia's silent prayers arose, that these kind men's health might suffer no injury from the cold to which they thus exposed themselves.

At the inn at which they put up at Ekaterinenburg, the hostess told Prascovia the names of the most charitable persons in the town, and so especially praised a certain Madame Milin, that Prascovia resolved to apply to her the next day for advice how to proceed farther. First, as it was Sunday, however, she went to church. Her worn travelling dress, as well as her fervent devotion, attracted attention, and as she came out, a lady asked her who she was. Prascovia gave her name, and further requested to be directed where to find Madame Milin, whose benevolence was everywhere talked of. "I am afraid," said the lady, "that this Madame Milin's beneficence is a good deal exaggerated; but come with me, and I will take care of you."

Prascovia did not much like this way of speaking; but the stranger pointed to Madame Milin's door, saying that if she were rejected there, she must return to her. Without answering, Prascovia asked the servants whether Madame Milin were at home, and only when they looked at their mistress in amazement, did she discover that she had been talking to Madame Milin herself all the time.

This good lady kept her as a guest all the rest of the winter, and strove to remedy the effects of the severe cold she had caught on the night of the tempest. At the same time, she taught Prascovia many of the common matters of education becoming her station. Captain Lopouloff and his wife had been either afraid to teach their daughter anything that would recall their former condition in life, or else had become too dispirited and indifferent for the exertion, and Prascovia had so entirely forgotten all she had known before her father's banishment, that she had to learn to read and write over again. She could never speak of Madame Milin's kindness without tears, but the comfort and ease in which she now lived, made her all the more distressed at the thought of her parents toiling alone among the privations of their snowy wilderness. Madame Milin, however, would not allow her to leave Ekatherinenburg till the spring, and then took a place for her in a barge upon the River Khama, a confluent of the Volga; and put her under the care of a man who was going to Nishni Novgorod, with a cargo of iron and salt.

Unfortunately this person fell sick, and was obliged to be left behind at a little village on the banks of the Khama, and Prascovia was again left unprotected. In ascending the Volga, the barge was towed along by horses on the bank, and in a short sharp storm, the boatmen, in endeavouring to keep the barge from running against the bank, pushed Prascovia and two other passengers overboard with a heavy oar. They were instantly rescued, but there was no privacy on the barge, and as Prascovia could not bear to undress herself in public, her wet clothes increased the former injury to her health. Madame Milin, trusting to the person to whom she had confided her young friend, to forward her on from Novgorod, had given her no introductions to anyone there, nor any directions how to proceed, and the poor girl was thus again cast upon the world alone, though, thanks to her kind friend, with rather more both in her purse and in her bundle than when she had left Ischim; but, on the other hand, with a far clearer knowledge of the difficulties that lay before her, and a much greater dread of cities.

The bargemen set her ashore at the foot of a bridge at the usual landing-place. She saw a church on a rising ground before her, and, according to her usual custom, she went up to pray there before going to seek a lodging. The building was empty, but behind a grating she heard the voices of women at their evening devotions. It was a nunnery, and these female tones refreshed and encouraged her. "If God grants my prayers," she thought, "I shall hide myself under such a veil as theirs, for I shall have nothing to do but to thank and praise Him." After the service, she lingered near the convent, dreading to expose herself to the rude remarks she might meet at an inn, and at last, reproaching herself for this failure in her trust, she returned into the church to renew her prayers for faith and courage. One of the nuns who had remained there told her it was time to close the doors, and Prascovia ventured to tell her of her repugnance to enter an inn alone, and to beg for a night's shelter in the convent. The sister replied that they did not receive travellers, but that the abbess might give her some assistance. Prascovia showed her purse, and explained that the kind friends at Ekatherinenburg had placed her above want, and that all she needed was a night's lodging; and the nun, pleased with her manner, took her to the abbess. Her artless story, supported by her passport, and by Madame Milin's letters, filled the good sisterhood with excitement and delight; the abbess made her sleep in her own room, and finding how severely she was suffering from the effects of her fall into the Volga, insisted on her remaining a few days to rest. Before those few days were over, Prascovia was seized with so dangerous an illness that the physicians themselves despaired of her life; but even at the worst she never gave herself up; "I do not believe my hour is come," she said. "I hope God will allow me to finish my work." And she did recover, though so slowly that all the summer passed by before she could continue her journey, and then she was too weak for rough posting vehicles, and could only wait among the nuns for the roads to be fit for sledges.

At last she set off again for Moscow in a covered sledge, with a letter from the abbess to a lady, who sent her on again to Petersburg, under the care of a merchant, with a letter to the Princess de T—, and thus at length she arrived at the end of her journey, eighteen months after she had set off from Ischim with her rouble and her staff. The merchant took her to his own house, but before he had found out the Princess, he was obliged to go to Riga, and his wife, though courteous and hospitable, did not exert herself to forward the cause of her guest. She tried to find one of the ladies to whom she had been recommended, but the house was on the other side of the Neva, and as it was now February, the ice was in so unsafe a state that no one was allowed to pass. A visitor at the merchant's advised her to get a petition to the Senate drawn up, begging for a revision of her father's trial, and offered to get it drawn up for her. Accordingly, day after day, for a whole fortnight, did the poor girl stand on the steps of the Senate-house, holding out her petition to everyone whom she fancied to be a senator, and being sometimes roughly spoken to, sometimes waved aside, sometimes offered a small coin as a beggar, but never attended to. Holy Week came on, and Prascovia's devotions and supplications were addressed entirely to her God. On Easter-day, that day of universal joy, she was unusually hopeful; she went out with her hostess in the carriage, and told her that she felt a certainty that another time she should meet with success.

"I would trouble myself no more with senates and senators," said the lady. "It is just as well worth while as it would be to offer your petition to yonder iron man," pointing to the famous statue of Peter the Great.

"Well," said Prascovia, "God is Almighty, and if He would, He could make that iron man stoop and take my petition." The lady laughed carelessly; but as they were looking at the statue, she observed that the bridge of boats over the Neva was restored, and offered to take Prascovia at once to leave her letter with Mde. de L—. They found this lady at home, and already prepared to expect her; she received her most kindly, and looked at the petition, which she found so ignorantly framed and addressed, that it was no wonder that it had not been attended to. She said that she had a relation high in office in the Senate who could have helped Prascovia, but that unfortunately they were not on good terms.

Easter-day, however, is the happy occasion when, in the Greek Church, all reconciliations are made. Families make a point of meeting with the glorious greeting, "Christ is risen," and the response, "He is risen indeed;" and the kiss exchanged at these glad tidings seals general pardon for all the bickerings of the year. And while Prascovia was at dinner with her friends, this very gentleman came in, with the accustomed words, and, without further delay, she was introduced to him, and her circumstances explained. He took great interest in her, but assured her that applications to the Senate were useless; for even if she should prevail to have the trial revised, it would be a tedious and protracted affair, and very uncertain; so that it would be far better to trust to the kind disposition of the Czar Alexander himself.

Prascovia went back to the merchant's greatly encouraged, and declaring that, after all, she owed something to the statue of Peter the Great, for but for him they might not have observed that the Neva was open! The merchant himself now returned from Riga, and was concerned at finding her affairs no forwarder. He took her at once to the Princess de T—, a very old lady, who received her kindly, and let her remain in her house; but it was full of grand company and card-playing, and the Princess herself was so aged and infirm, that she, as well as all her guests, forgot all about the young stranger, who, with a heart pining with hope deferred, meekly moved about the house-finding that every opening of promise led only to disappointment. Still she recollected that she had been advised to present a request to M. V—, one of the secretaries of the Empress Mary, widow of the last, and mother of the present Czar. With this, she went to his house. He had heard of her, but fancying hers a common case of poverty, had put out fifty roubles to be given to her. He was not at home when she called; but his wife saw her, was delighted with her, drew from her the whole history of her perseverance in her father's cause, and kept her to see M. V—. He, too, was warmly interested, and going at once to the Empress-mother, who was one of the most gentle and charitable women in the world, he brought back her orders that she should be presented to the Empress that very evening.

Poor child, she turned pale, and her eyes filled with tears at this sudden brightening of hope. Instead of thanking M. V—, her first exclamation was, "My God, not in vain have I put my trust in thee." Then kissing Mme. V—'s hands, she cried, "You, you alone can make my thanks acceptable to the good man who is saving my father!"

She never disturbed herself as to her dress, or any matter of court etiquette: her simple heart was wrapped up in its one strong purpose. Mme. V— merely arranged the dress she had on, and sent her off with the Secretary. When she really saw the palace before her, she said, "Oh, if my father could see me now, how glad he would be. My God, finish Thy work!"

The Empress Mary was a tender-hearted woman of the simplest manners. She received Prascovia in her private room, and listened most kindly to her story; then praised her self-devotion and filial love, and promised to speak in her behalf to the Emperor–giving her 300 roubles for her present needs. Prascovia was so much overcome by her kindness, that when afterwards Mme. V— asked how she had sped in her interview, she could only weep for gladness.

Two days after, the Empress-mother herself took her to a private audience of the Emperor himself and his wife, the Empress Elizabeth. No particulars are given of this meeting, except that Prascovia was most graciously received, and that she came away with a gift of 5000 roubles, and the promise that her father's trial should be at once revised.

And now all the persons who had scarcely attended to Prascovia vied with each other in making much of her: they admired her face, found out that she had the stamp of high birth, and invited her to their drawing-rooms. She was as quiet and unmoved as ever; she never thought of herself, nor of the effect she produced, but went on in her simplicity, enjoying all that was kindly meant. Two ladies took her to see the state apartments of the Imperial palace. When they pointed to the throne, she stopped short, exclaiming, "Is that the throne? Then that is what I dreaded so much in Siberia!" And as all her past hopes and fears, her dangers and terrors, rushed on her, she clasped her hands, and exclaiming, "The Emperor's throne!" she almost fainted. Then she begged leave to draw near, and, kneeling down, she kissed the steps, of which she had so often dreamt as the term of her labours, and she exclaimed aloud, "Father, father! see whither the Divine power has led me! My God, bless this throne–bless him who sits on it–make him as happy as he is making me!" The ladies could hardly get her away from it, and she was so much exhausted by the strength of her feelings, that she could not continue her course of sight-seeing all that day.

She did not forget the two fellow exiles who had been so kind to her; she mentioned them to everyone, but was always advised not to encumber her suit for her father by mentioning them. However, when, after some delay, she received notice that a ukase had been issued for the father's pardon, and was further told that His Majesty wished to know if she had anything to ask for herself, she replied, that he would overwhelm her with his favours if he would extend the same mercy that he had granted to her father to these two poor old banished gentlemen; and the Emperor, struck by this absence of all selfishness, readily pardoned them for their offence, which had been of a political nature, and many years old.

Prascovia had always intended to dedicate herself as a nun, believing that this would be her fullest thank-offering for her father's pardon, and her heart was drawn towards the convent at Nishnï, where she had been so tenderly nursed during her illness. First, however, she went to Kief, the place where the first Christian teaching in Russia had begun, and where the tombs of St. Olga, the pious queen, and Vladimir, the destroyer of

IN HER LAST LONG SLEEP.

idols, were objects of pilgrimage. There she took the monastic vows, a step which seems surprising in so dutiful a daughter, without her parents' consent; but she seems to have thought that only thus could her thankfulness be evinced, and to have supposed herself fulfilling the vows she had made in her distress. From Kief, she returned to Nishnï, where she hoped to meet her parents. She had reckoned that about the time of her arrival they might be on their way back from Siberia, and as soon as she met the abbess, she eagerly asked if there were no tidings of them. "Excellent tidings," said the abbess. "I will tell you in my rooms." Prascovia followed her in silence, until they reached the reception room, and there stood her father and mother! Their first impulse, on seeing the daughter who had done so much for them, was to fall on their knees; but she cried out with dismay, and herself kneeling, exclaimed, "What are you doing? It is God, God only, who worked for us. Thanks be to His providence for the wonders He has wrought in our favour."

For one week the parents and child were happy together; but then Captain Lopouloff and his wife were forced to proceed on their journey. The rest of Prascovia's life was one long decline, her health had been fatally injured by the sufferings that she had undergone; and though she lived some years, and saw her parents again, she was gently fading away all the time. She made one visit to Petersburg, and one of those who saw her there described her as having a fine oval face, extremely black eyes, an open brow, and a remarkable calmness of expression, though with a melancholy smile. It is curious that Scott has made this open-browed serenity of expression a characteristic of his Jeanie Deans.

Prascovia's illness ended suddenly on the 9th of December, 1809. She had been in church on that same morning, and was lying on her bed, with the sisters talking round her, when they observed that they were tiring her. They went away for one of their hours of prayer, leaving one who began to chant the devotions aloud, but Prascovia begged her to read instead of singing, as the voice disturbed her prayers. Still she did not complain, and they left her at night without alarm, but in the morning they found her in her last long sleep, her hands forming the sign of the cross.

The Children of Blentarn Ghyll
1807

BLENTARN Ghyll is the name of a little narrow gorge in those Westmorland mountains, called Langdale Pikes, at whose feet lie the lovely green vale and lake of Grasmere. The lake is fed by mountain streamlets, called in the north becks. One of these becks comes down another beautiful valley called Easedale, sheltered by mountains and green with grass, as smooth and soft as on a lawn, from being cropped short by the sheep, which can be turned out here earlier in the spring than on the other mountainsides. At one end, Easedale opens on the village of Grasmere, at the other is a steep ascent, leading to a bare stony ravine, shut in on all sides by high mountains, and with no outlet except the rough descent into Easedale, and likewise a dangerous winding path about six miles over the mountains to Langdale Head. This lonely ravine is called Far Easedale, and at the upper end there formerly stood a cottage named Blentarn Ghyll. Ghyll means a cleft worn in the rock by water; and just above the cottage there is such a cleft, opening from a basin in the rock that must once have been a tarn, or mountain lakelet, but the pool is now dry, and for want of the living eye of sparkling water, it is termed Blentarn or Blind Pool.

The cottage was the dwelling of an honest old soldier named George Green, who had taken the little mountain farm and married an active, bustling woman, who kept her home in great order, and regularly sent her children, tidily dressed, to school at Grasmere whenever the weather did not make the long wild mountain walk impossible for them.

It was in the winter of the year 1807 that there was an auction of furniture at a farmhouse at Langdale Head. These sales are great occasions among the people of these hills; everyone attends them for a considerable distance round, and there is much friendly hospitality, much business of all sorts transacted, and many meetings of old friends, who scarcely ever see each other at other times. To this gathering George and Sarah Green set off early in the forenoon of a bright winter day, leaving their cottage and six little ones in the charge of the eldest sister, a girl of nine years old, named Agnes, for they had neither indoor nor outdoor servant, and no neighbour nearer than Grasmere.

Little Agnes was, however, a remarkably steady and careful child, and all went well through the day, but towards night the mist settled down heavily upon the hills, and the heavy sighing in the air told that a storm was working up; the children watched anxiously for their parents, but the fog cut off their view, flakes of snow began to fall, and darkness closed in early on them.

Agnes gave the others their supper of milk and oatmeal porridge, and they sat down waiting and watching, and fancying they heard sounds in the hills; but the clock struck one hour after another, and no step was on the threshold, no hand at the latch, no voice at the door, only the white silent flakes fell thicker and thicker, and began to close up the door, and come in white clinging wreaths through the crevices of the windows. Agnes tried to cheer the others up, but there was a dread on them all, and they could not bear to move away from the peat fire on the hearth, round which they were nestled. She put the two youngest, who were twins, to bed in their cradle, and sat on with the others, two boys and another girl, named Catherine, till the clock struck twelve, when she heard them one by one say their prayers, and doing the same herself, lay down to rest, trusting to her Heavenly Father's care.

The morning came, and no father and mother; only the snow falling thicker than ever, and almost blocking them in; but still Agnes did not lose hope; she thought her father and mother might have taken shelter at night in some bield, as she would have termed a sheepfold, or that the snow might have prevented them from setting out at all, and they might come home by Grasmere in the morning. She cheered herself up, and dressed the others, made them say their prayers, and gave them their breakfast, recollecting as she saw the lessening stores that her mother must know how little was provided for them, and be as anxious to get home as they were to see her there. She longed to go down to Grasmere to enquire; but the communication was entirely cut off by the snow, for the beck was, in the winter, too wide for a child to leap, and too rapid to be waded, and the crazy wooden bridge that crossed it had so large a hole in it, that, when concealed with snow, it was not safe to attempt the passage. She said afterwards that she could not help being terrified at the loneliness and desolateness, but that she recollected that at least if she could not get out, no bad men could get in to hurt them; and she set herself resolutely to comfort and help the lesser creatures who depended on her. She thought over all that could be done for the present, and first wound up the clock, a friend that she could not allow to be silent; next she took all the remaining milk and scalded it, to prevent it turning sour; then she looked into the meal chest, and made some porridge for breakfast, but the store was so low that she was forced to put all except the babies upon short allowance; but to reconcile the others to this, she made cakes of a small hoard of flour, and baked them on the hearth. It was snowing so fast that she feared that the way to the peat stack would be blocked up, and therefore her next work was, with the help of the two boys, to pull down as much fuel as would last for a week, and carry it indoors; and she examined the potatoes laid up in bracken leaves, but fancying that if she brought them in, the warmth of the cottage would spoil them, she only took enough for a single meal. Milking the cow was the next office performed by this orderly little maid, but the poor thing was half-starved and had little to give. Agnes saw that more hay must be given to her, and calling the boys, scrambled with them into the loft, and began to pull down the hay; but this was severe work for such young children, and darkness came on in the midst, frightening the two little fellows, so that it required all the sister's steady resolution and perseverance to finish supplying the poor cow with even that night's supper and bed. Suppertime came, and after it the motherly child undressed the twins and found voice to sing them to sleep, after which she joined the huddle of the other three, nestled on the hearth, and hour after hour they listened for the dear voices, till they fancied they heard sounds on the howling blast, held their breath, and then, as it died away, were conscious of the silence of the lull. So fierce was the snowdrift that Agnes had to guard the door and window from admitting long wreaths of it, and protect the fire from being put out as it came hissing down the chimney. Again her watch lasted till midnight, and no parents, no help came; again she went to bed, and awoke to find the snow falling thicker than ever, and hope failing within her. Her fond, active mother, her strong, brave father, a noted climber, would surely long ago have found the way home to their children had all been well with them. Agnes described herself as getting through this third lonely day by keeping her little flock together on the hearth, and making them say their prayers aloud by turns.

By the following morning the snow was over, and the wind had changed, so sweeping away the drifts, that though the treacherous bridge might not be attempted, a low stone wall had been exposed, which these little mountaineers knew would serve as a guide into Grasmere, by a circuit, which would avoid crossing the brook. It would be needful to force some gaps, that is, to push down the loose stones of the uncemented stone walls that divided the fields, and the little boys came with Agnes to help her in this as far as the ridge of the hill; but the way was long and unsafe for small children, and Agnes sent them back, while she made her way alone, a frail little being in the vast slopes of snow, to the house nearest in Grasmere.

She knocked at the door and was made kindly welcome, but no sooner did she ask for her father and mother than smiles turned to looks of pity and dismay. In half an hour the news that George and Sarah Green were missing had spread through the valley, and sixty strong men had met at

Kirktown, the hamlet close to the parish church, to seek for them. The last that was known of them was, that after the auction, some of their friends had advised them not to try the dangerous path so late; but when they had gone no one knew. Some of the people of Langdale likewise had heard wild shrieks at midnight on the night after the sale, but had fancied them merely the moans of the wind.

One day after another the search continued, but still in vain. The neighbours patiently gave up their work day after day to turn over the deep snow around the path from Langdale, but for three–or some say five–days no trace of them was found. At last dogs were used, and guided the seekers far away from the path, until a loud shout from the top of a steep precipice told that the lost was found. There lay Sarah Green, wrapped in her husband's greatcoat, of course quite dead, and at the foot of the rock his body was found, in a posture that seemed to show that he had been killed by the fall without a struggle. The neighbours thought that the mist and snow must have bewildered them till they had wandered thus far in the darkness, and that George had been making a few steps forward to make out the road when the fall took place, but that his wife had very possibly been unconscious of his fall, and stood still where he had left her, uttering those sad cries that had been so little regarded at Langdale, until she was unable to move and was benumbed by the sleep of cold. Those who knew them best, thought that the poor woman's grief and terror for her lonely little ones had probably so overpowered her as to disturb the husband's coolness and presence of mind, and that if he had been alone, he would probably have easily saved himself. The brave little girl keeping her patient watch and guard over the five younger ones, and setting out on her lonely way through the snow, must have had more of the spirit of her soldier-father than of her mother. It was to Dorothy Wordsworth, the sister of the poet, that little Agnes was persuaded to tell the history of this calm, resolute, trustful waiting time, which, simple as it is, we think our readers will own as truly worthy to be counted among Golden Deeds. The father and mother were buried on a lovely spring day at St. Oswald's Churchyard at Kirktown, and Wordsworth wrote–

"Now do these sternly featured hills
  Look gently on this grave,
And quiet now the depths of air
  As sea without a wave.

"But deeper lies the heart of peace,
  In quiet more profound;
The heart of quietness is here,
  Within this churchyard bound.

"And from all agony of mind
It keeps them safe and far
From fear, and grief, and from all need
Of sun or guiding star."

After the funeral, the farm folk of the neighbourhood were all pressing forward to beg to adopt one or other of the little orphans. The twins were kept together, Catherine was taken by the Wordsworth family, Agnes and her brothers found separate but comfortable homes among their parents' friends. Help came pouring in, Queen Charlotte and her daughters were greatly touched by the mountain child's tender motherliness, and sent a handsome donation for the benefit of the orphans, and so many subscriptions were offered, that at last Miss Wordsworth declined receiving any more, lest the children should be injured by having too much wealth for the station to which they were growing up.

Agostina of Zaragoza
1808

ONE of the most unjustifiable acts of Napoleon's grasping policy was the manner in which he entrapped the poor, foolish, weak Spanish royal family into his power, and then kept them in captivity, and gave their kingdom to his brother Joseph. The whole Spanish people were roused to resistance by this atrocious transfer, and the whole of the peasantry rose as one man to repel this shameful aggression. A long course of bad government had done much to destroy the vigour of the nation, and as soldiers in the open field they were utterly worthless; but still there were high qualities of patience and perseverance among them, and these were never more fully shown than in their defence of Zaragoza, the ancient capital of the kingdom of Aragon.

This city stands in an open plain, covered with olive grounds, and closed in by high mountains. About a mile to the south-west of the city was some high ground called the Torrero, upon which stood a convent, and close beside the city flowed the Ebro, crossed by two bridges, one of which was made of wood, and said to be the most beautiful specimen of the kind of fabric in Europe. The water is of a dirty red, but grows clear when it has stood long enough, and is then excellent to drink. There were no regular fortifications, only a brick wall, ten or twelve feet high, and three feet thick, and often encroached upon by houses. Part of it was, however, of old Roman workmanship, having been built under Augustus, by whom the town was called Cæsarea Augusta, a name since corrupted into Zaragoza (both z 's pronounced as softly as possible). Four of the twelve gates were in this old wall, which was so well built as to put to shame all the modern buildings and their bad bricks. These were the material of even the churches and convents, all alike with the houses, and so bad was the construction that there were cracks in most of the buildings from top to bottom. The houses were generally three stories high, the streets very narrow and crooked, except one wide and long one, called sometimes the Calle Santa, sometimes the Cozo. Zaragoza was highly esteemed as the first seat of Christianity in Spain; indeed, legend declared that St. James the

Great had preached there, and had beheld a vision of the Blessed Virgin, standing upon a marble pillar, and bidding him there build a church in honour of her. The pillar was the great object of veneration in Aragon, and there was a double cathedral, with service performed alternately in the two parts. So much venerated was our Lady of the Pillar, that Pilar became a girl's name in the surrounding country, and this was the centre of pilgrimages to the Aragonese, as St. James's shrine at Compostella was to the Castilians. As is well said by Southey, in the fiery trial of the Zaragozans, "the dross and tinsel of their faith disappeared, and its pure gold remained". The inhabitants appeared, like most Spaniards since the blight of Philip II's policy had fallen on them, dull, apathetic beings, too proud and indolent for exertion, the men smoking cigaritos at their doors, the women only coming out with black silk mantillas over their heads to go to church. The French on first seizing it, with the rest of Spain, thought it the dullest place they had ever yet entered and greatly despised the inhabitants.

General Lefebvre Desnouettes was sent to quiet the insurrection against the French in Aragon; and on the 13th and 14th of June, 1808, he easily routed the bodies of Spaniards who tried to oppose him. The flying Spanish troops were pursued into Zaragoza by the French cavalry, but here the inhabitants were able from their houses to drive back the enemy. Don Jose Palafox, a Spanish nobleman, who had been equerry to the King, took the command of the garrison, who were only 220 soldiers, and endeavoured to arm the inhabitants, about 60,000 in number, and all full of the most determined spirit of resistance to the invaders. He had only sixteen cannon and a few muskets, but fowling-pieces were collected, and pikes were forged by all the smiths in the town.

The siege began on the 27th of June. The French army was in considerable force, and had a great supply of mortars and battering cannon; such as could by their shells and shot rend the poor brick city from end to end. The Torrero quickly fell into their hands, and from that height there was a constant discharge of those terrible shells and grenades that burst in pieces where they fall, and carry destruction everywhere. Not one building within the city could withstand them, and they were fired, not at the walls but into the town. All that could be done was to place beams slanting against the houses, so that there might be a shelter under them from the shells. The awnings that sheltered the windows from the summer sun were taken down, sewn up into sacks, and filled with earth, then piled up before the gates, with a deep trench dug before them; the houses on the walls were pulled down, and every effort made to strengthen the defences, the whole of the lately quiet, lazy population toiling earnestly together, in the midst of the deadly shower that was always falling from the Torrero, and striking down numbers as they worked.

The same spirit animated everyone. The Countess Burita, a beautiful young lady, formed the women into an organised company for carrying wine, water, and food to the soldiers on guard, and relieving the wounded, and throughout the whole siege her courage and perseverance never failed; she was continually seen in the places most exposed to the enemy's fire, bringing help and refreshment wherever she appeared among the hard-pressed warriors. The nuns became nurses to the sick and wounded, and made cartridges, which were carried to the defenders by the children of the place. The monks attended the sick and dying, or else bore arms, feeling that this—the cause of their country, their king, and their faith—had become to them a holy war. Thus men, women, and children alike seemed full of the same loyal spirit; but some traitor must have been among them, for on the night of the 28th, the powder magazine in the centre of the town was blown up, destroying fourteen houses and killing 200 people. At the same time, evidently prepared to profit by the confusion thus caused, the French appeared before three of the gates, and a dreadful fire began from the Torrero, shells bursting everywhere among the citizens, who were striving in the dark to dig their friends out of the ruined houses.

The worst of the attack was at the gate called Portillo, and lasted the whole day. The sand-bag defence was frequently destroyed by the fire, and as often renewed under this dreadful shot by the undaunted Spaniards. So dreadful was the carnage, that at one moment every man of the defenders lay dead. At that moment one of the women who were carrying refreshments came up. Her name was Agostina Zaragoza; she was a fine-looking woman of two-and-twenty, and was full of a determined spirit. She saw the citizens hesitate to step forward to man the defences where certain death awaited them. Springing forward, she caught the match from the hand of a dead gunner, fired his twenty-six-pounder, and seating herself on it, declared it her charge for the rest of the siege. And she kept her word. She was the heroine of the siege where all were heroines. She is generally called the Maid of Zaragoza, but she seems to have been the widow of one of the artillerymen who was here killed, and that she continued to serve his gun—not solely as a patriot, but because she thus obtained a right to provisions for her little children, who otherwise might have starved in the famine that began to prevail. If this lessens the romance, it seems to us to add to the beauty and womanliness of Agostina's character, that for the sake of her children she should have run into the hottest of the peril, and taken up the task in which her husband had died.

Her readiness in that critical moment saved the Portillo for that time, but the attacks were renewed again and again with equal fury and fearful bloodshed. The French General had fancied that he could easily take such an unfortified place, and finding it so difficult, had lost his temper, and was thus throwing away his men's lives; but after several such failures, he began to invest the city regularly. Gunpowder was failing the besieged until they supplied its place by wonderful ingenuity. All the sulphur in the place was collected, nitre was obtained by washing it out of the soil of the streets, and charcoal by charring the stalks of the very large variety of hemp that grows in that part of Spain. At the end of forty-six days the city was entirely surrounded, provisions were falling short, and there was not a single place safe from shot and shell. On the 2nd of August a hospital caught fire, and the courage of the women was again shown by their exertions in carrying out the sick and wounded from the flames in spite of the continued shot from the enemy's batteries; indeed, throughout the siege the number of women and boys who were killed was quite as great in proportion as that of men; the only difficulty was to keep them from running needlessly into danger.

On the 4th of August, the French opened a battery within pistol-shot of the gate called after the great Convent of St. Engracia. The mud walls were levelled at the first discharge, and after a deadly struggle the besiegers forced their way into the convent, and before the end of the day had gained all that side of the city, up to the main central street, the Cozo. General Lefebvre thought all was now over with his enemies, and summoned Palafox to surrender, in a note containing only these words–"Headquarters, St. Engracia. Capitulation." The answer he received was equally brief–"Headquarters, Zaragoza. War to the knife."

There they were! A street about as wide as Pall-Mall was all that lay between besiegers and besieged, to whom every frail brick house had become a fortress, while the openings of the narrow cross streets were piled up with sand-bags to form batteries. Soon the space was heaped with dead bodies, either killed on the spot or thrown from the windows, and this was enough to breed a pestilence among the survivors. The French let them lie, knowing that such a disease would be the surest destruction to the garrison, and they fired on the Spanish whenever they ventured out to bury them. Upon this Palafox devised tying ropes to his French prisoners, and driving them out to bring in the corpses for burial. The enemy would not fire on their own countrymen, and thus this danger was lessened, although not entirely removed, and sickness as well as famine was added to the misery of the brave Aragonese. The manufacture of powder, too, could no longer be carried on, but happily Don Francisco, the brother of Palafox, was able to make his way into the city with 3000 men, and a convoy of arms and ammunition. Padre Santiago Sass, the curate of one of the parishes of Zaragoza, showed himself one of the bravest of all the brave, fighting at every hazardous point, and at other times moving about among the sick and dying to give them the last rites of the Church. No one's heart failed in that eleven days of one continual battle from house to house, from room to room, when the nights were times of more dreadful conflict than the days. Often under cover of the darkness, a party would rush across to seize a battery; and once a Spaniard made his way under cover of the corpses, which filled the whole space between the combatants, and fastened a rope to one of the French guns. It had almost been dragged across the street, and was only lost by the breaking of the rope.

On the 8th of August, the Spaniards agreed that if they could not hold their ground in the city, they must retire across the Ebro, break down the bridge, and defend the suburbs as they had defended the streets. Only an eighth part of their city now remained to them; and on the night of the 13th the enemy's fire was more destructive and constant than ever. The great Convent of St. Engracia was blown up, the whole of the French part of the city glared with flaming houses, the climax of the horrors of the siege seemed to be come! But the reports of the batteries gradually ceased, and, with the early morning light, the garrison beheld the road to Pamplona filled with French troops in full retreat.

In effect, intelligence had been received of reverses to the invaders, and of extended movements among the Spaniards, which had led the French to decide on quitting Zaragoza ere these desperate defenders should be reinforced by the army which was collecting to relieve them.

Their fortitude had won the day. The carnage had ended, and it remained for them to clear their streets from the remains of the deadly strife, and to give thanks for their deliverance. Agostina, in testimony of her courage, was to receive for life the pay of an artilleryman, and to wear a little shield of honour embroidered on her sleeve.

So ended the wonderful siege of Zaragoza. It is sad to know that when the French forces came in full numbers into Spain, the brave town shared the fate of the rest of the country. But the resistance had not been in vain; it had raised a feeling for the gallant Spaniards throughout Europe, and inspired a trust in their constancy which contributed to bring them that aid from England by which their country was, after six years, finally freed from the French usurpation.

Casal Novo

1811

THERE is something exceedingly interesting in knowing what a brave and generous man, who had never flinched from any danger, looked back upon in his last days as the one Golden Deed of his life; and therefore, among the many noble and spirited actions during the war by which the British arms chased the usurping French out of the Peninsula, that one is selected of which the doer spoke thus, forty-seven years later, when he thought himself upon his deathbed.

"As I lie here and think of my past life," said Sir William Napier, "I feel small—very small indeed. I try to remember if I have done any good, but the evil far overbalances it. We shall all be weighed in the balance, and found wanting. In the eye of the great good God, earthly goodness can have no positive existence, yet He sees and makes allowances for us all, giving more credit for good and less blame for evil than our fellow creatures' harsh judging would have done. Men should strive after those priceless virtues of patience, wisdom, charity, self-sacrifice. In looking back on my life, it would be a comfort to me now if I could remember to have done a perfectly self-sacrificing act—if I could think I had been ready and willing at any moment to lay down my life for another person's good. I try to remember, but I can't remember that I ever did. I have often run into danger, and exposed myself to pain sometimes, to save others. Yes, I have done that! but there was always a springing hope, a sort of conviction that I should escape; and that being so, away flies the merit. The nearest thing I ever did to absolute self-sacrifice was at Casal Novo, when I received in my back the ball that lies there still."

The old soldier's deliberate judgment of all the noblest deeds of a long life was the realising of the truth that "all our righteousnesses are as filthy rags", and no eye but his own would have looked at them so critically. But let us see the manner of the one thing that "came nearest to self-sacrifice".

It was in the year 1811, when Wellington had entrenched his army on the slopes of Torres Vedras, in Portugal, and there, by his patience and sagacity, had repulsed the French army under Marshal Massena, and was following up his retreat out of the kingdom of Portugal. The English and Portuguese troops used to rise at three in the morning, and march at four; and on the 14th of March, when the army was setting out in the morning twilight, there was a heavy fog covering all the valley in front. Sir William Erskine, the general in command of the Light Division, consisting of the 52nd and 43rd Regiments and the Rifles, all the very flower of the army, was an incompetent man, and fancying the French were in full retreat, ordered his troops to move forward on their march. Some of the officers objected to the rashness of plunging into the mist without precaution; but they were not heeded, and the order to advance was given.

The 52nd moved forward first, in a column of sections, and were to be followed by the Rifles. Down the hillside they went, then across a narrow ravine at the bottom, and were mounting the steep road on the other side, when there was a sudden hail of round shot and bullets close upon them. The fog cut off their view, but the bugles continued to sound the advance, and they pushed on through walled fields, the enemy giving way before them, till they gained the ridge of the hill, though with loss of men, and with three captains wounded–one of them George Napier, and another "Jack Jones", afterwards the hero of the powder-magazine at Ciudad Rodrigo.

The mist suddenly drew up, and displayed to the English troops the hillside covered with dark masses of the blue-clad French soldiers, and in the midst what looked like a red pimple on the ridge, being in fact the 52nd in the very middle of Marshal Ney's division–so near the Marshal himself, the bravest of the brave, that if they had only been able to see him, they might have made him prisoner by his own bivouac fire.

The rest of the Light Division were put in motion to support them, and Captain William Napier was sent forward, with six companies of his regiment, the 43rd, to aid them on the left. When he came to a round hill, he halted, and left four companies to watch, while, with the other two, he descended into one of the narrow ravines to join the left of the 52nd, whom he heard, though he could not see over the ridge of the hill. Part of the regiment had charged, but not the whole, and thus Napier, coming up into a walled field where he expected to join the left side of the 52nd, found only Captain Dobbs and two men of the 52nd cut off from the rest of their regiment.

The French came gathering fast about them, and cutting off their retreat. The two officers agreed that the boldest course would be the safest, so they called to the two companies behind them to follow, and sprang over the wall in front, meaning to force their way on to the 52nd in front. But only the two 52nd men followed, both the companies of the 43rd held back; and when the two captains had reached a second wall, they found merely this pair of men with them, and a great body of the enemy in front, closing upon them and firing.

The wall gave a moment's protection, and Napier declared he would either save Dobbs or lose his own life by bringing up his two companies. Dobbs entreated him not to attempt it, saying that it was impossible to make two steps from the wall and live. Still, however, Napier, who was stung by the backwardness of his men, dashed back unhurt. His men were crouching under the wall; they had perhaps failed before from being out of breath, from their charge up the hill with their heavy knapsacks on their backs, and still more from the mismanagement of the two lieutenants in command of them, both dull, rude men, tyrannical in their behaviour. One, who was noted for his fighting duels, was lying down with his face to the ground, and when the captain called–shouted to him, and bade him remember his uniform, and come on with the men–he did not stir, till, in extremity of provocation, Napier threw a stone at his head. This made him get up, and scramble over the wall with his men; but on the other side he was wild with terror–eyes staring and hands spread out–and when Napier ordered the men on to where Dobbs was, and ran forward himself, they, under their lieutenant's cowardly leading, all edged away to the right, out of the fire, and again Napier reached his friend alone.

Maddened at the failure, he again sprang back to lead them, but ere he could reach them was struck by a bullet in the spine, and fell. The French most ungenerously continued to fire at him as he lay, and his legs had been paralysed by the effect of his wound, so that he could only drag himself by his hands towards a heap of stones, behind which he sheltered his head and shoulders. No less than twenty shots struck the heap in the moment before Captain Lloyd with his own company of the 43rd, and some of the 52nd, came up, and drove off the enemy. Napier was carried away from this spot, and laid for a time under an olive tree, while the fight lasted, and the French were driven on from ridge to ridge.

While he was lying there, helpless and exhausted, the grenadier company of Royal Scots were hastening forward, and their captain seeing the wounded man, ran up, and said, "I hope you are not seriously wounded." He could not speak, but only shook his head; and being asked again, "Can I be of any service to you?" made the same sign; but when Captain Wilson offered him some cold tea, and brandy from his flask, he raised his head with a sudden flash of pleasure, and gladly drank two tumblerfuls; then thanked with his eyes and hands. "Heaven protect you," the captain said, and hurried on to overtake his men. Napier was a singularly handsome, noble-looking man, with perfect features, jet-black hair and dark-grey eyes, and though now deadly pale, the remarkably beautiful outline of his features and the sweet and noble expression of his countenance made a great impression on Captain Wilson; but among the numbers of the army, they were never again thrown together, and did not know each other's names.

Napier was thought to be mortally wounded, and his brother Charles, who, half-recovered from a wound, had ridden ninety miles to join the army, met a litter of branches, covered by a blanket, and borne by the soldiers. He asked who it was? "Captain Napier, of the 52nd–broken arm." Then came another litter–"Captain Napier, of the 43rd–mortally wounded." Charles Napier looked at his brothers, and passed on to the battle.

The brothers were placed in a house at Condeixa, but, besides their wounds, they, like all the army, suffered terribly from famine, for the French had destroyed everything before them, and the villagers themselves were absolutely starving. A tallow candle that the brothers found in the house was eaten up with the utmost relish! By some chance a loaf of bread came into the hands of Captain Light, a cavalry officer, at the end of a long day's march. Hungry as he was, he would not look at it, but mounted again, and rode twenty miles to Condeixa, over the mountains, and there, fearing a refusal, he flung the loaf into the room where the brothers lay, and rode back to his regiment.

William Napier soon partially recovered, but the bullet could never be extracted, and caused him agonies at intervals throughout the rest of his life. The story of the combat, which he felt as that of his greatest deed, was told by him in his great history of the Peninsular war, but without a hint of his own concern in the matter. Sixteen years after the battle, he met at a dinner party a gentleman, who, àpropos to some mention of handsome men, said that the very handsomest he had ever seen, was one whom he had found lying speechless under an olive tree at Casal Novo, and had succoured as above described. Sir William Napier sprang from his chair, exclaiming, "My dear Wilson! that was you–that glass of tea and brandy saved my life." He had already become acquainted with Sir John Morillyon Wilson, but till that moment neither had known that the other was his partner in the adventure of the olive tree.

Assuredly that stony field was a scene to look back on from old age with thankful satisfaction. And no less worthy of honour was, it seems to us, that twenty miles' ride by the hungry, weary officer, to bring his wounded comrades the loaf of bread.

The Mad Dog

1816

SIR Thomas Fowell Buxton was well known in the early part of the nineteenth century as one of the most earnest assistants of William Wilberforce in freeing England from the crimes inseparable from slave-holding. It is not, however, of his public career, nor of his deep piety, that we are about to speak, but of one incident in his life, which shows how a really religious and intrepid man will face a sudden and frightful peril for the sake of others. The event took place in the summer of 1816, when he was thirty years old, a capital sportsman and a man of remarkable personal strength and great height (six foot four). He was not as yet a baronet, and was at the time living at Hampstead, and daily riding into Spitalfields to attend to the affairs of a brewery in which he was a partner. During a visit that his wife and children were making at a distance, he had been staying with his brother-in-law, Mr. Hoare, not far from his home. When his servant brought his horse to him there, it was with the intelligence that his dog, Prince, was in a strange state, had killed the cat, almost killed another dog, and had tried to bite some of the servants. Mr. Buxton desired that the creature should be tied up and taken care of, and then rode off to his business in the town; but as he returned he saw Prince, evidently mad, covered with mud, running furiously and biting at everything.

Mr. Buxton tried to ride him down or drive him into some outhouse, but in vain; and he bit at least a dozen dogs, two boys, and a man, springing at a boy and seizing him by the breast, but this time his master was near enough to knock him down with his whip. He then changed his course, setting off for London, and Mr. Buxton rode by his side, waiting for some opportunity of stopping him, and constantly calling to him; but the poor animal was past attending to the well-known voice, whether coaxing or scolding. He was getting near more closely inhabited places, and considering the fearful damage he might effect, Mr. Buxton thought, "if ever there was an occasion that justified a risk of life, this was it", and determined to catch him himself. Prince ran to a garden-door, and Mr. Buxton, leaping from his horse, grasped him by the neck. His struggles were so desperate, that it seemed at first almost impossible—even for so powerful a man—to hold him (he was evidently a large dog); but lifting him up from the ground, he was more easily managed, and Mr. Buxton contrived to ring the bell; but for a long time no one came to his help, and being afraid lest the foam which was pouring from the poor beast's jaws might get into some scratch on his fingers, and be as dangerous as an actual bite, he with great difficulty held Prince with one hand while he worked the other into the glove in his pocket, then changed hands, and thus put on the other glove. At last the gardener opened the door, and asked what he wanted. "I've brought you a mad dog," was the answer; and desiring him to get a strong chain, Mr. Buxton walked into the yard carrying Prince by the neck. He was determined not to kill the dog at once, thinking that if it should prove not to be a case of hydrophobia, it would be a great relief to the persons who had been bitten, and this could only be determined by letting the disease take its course. The gardener was in great terror, but had sense enough to obey directions, and was able to secure the collar round the dog's neck, and fasten the other end of the chain to a tree. Mr. Buxton then walked to the utmost bound of the chain, and with all his force, "which," he says, "was nearly exhausted" by the dog's "frantic struggles", threw the creature as far away from him as he could, and sprang back in time to avoid poor Prince's desperate bound after him, which was followed by "the most fearful yell he ever heard".

All day the unhappy creature, in the misery of that horrible disease to which our faithful companions are sometimes subject, rushed round and round the tree, champing the foam that gushed from his jaws, and when food was thrown to him, snatched at it with fury, but could not eat it. The next day, Mr. Buxton thought the chain in danger of giving way, so, renewing his act of bravery, he obtained a stronger chain, and a pitchfork. Between the prongs of this he contrived to get the dog's body, without piercing it, and thus held him pinned to the ground, while fastening a much larger chain round his neck. On the pitchfork being removed, the dog sprang up and dashed after his master with such violence that the old chain snapped in two. However, the frenzy soon spent his strength, and he died only forty-eight hours after the first symptoms of madness had appeared. All the dogs and cats he had bitten were killed by Mr. Buxton himself, knowing that for such a painful business it was wiser to trust to no one's resolution and humanity but his own. The man and boys had the bitten parts cut out and the wounds burnt, and it was hoped that the horrid consequences might be averted from them. He himself expressed great thankfulness both for his own escape and his children's absence from home, and thus wrote to his wife a day or two after:—"What a terrible business it was. You must not scold me for the risk I ran. What I did I did from a conviction that it was my duty, and I never can think that an over-cautious care of self in circumstances where your risk may preserve others, is so great a virtue as you seem to think it. I do believe that if I had shrunk from the danger, and others had suffered in consequence, I should have felt more pain than I should have done had I received a bite."

The perfect coolness and presence of mind shown in the whole adventure are, perhaps, some of its most remarkable features—all being done from no sudden impulse, no daring temper, but from the grave, considerate conviction of the duty of encountering the peril on the part of the person most likely to be able to secure others; and no one who has shuddered at the accounts of the agonies of hydrophobia can fail to own how deadly that peril was.

As a pendant to our countryman's battle with a mad dog, let us see a combat between one of these frenzied creatures and a French weaver, named Simon Albony, a poor man of the town of Rhodes, who was the bread-winner for his aged father. Coming home from his work, in the summer of the year 1830, at about seven o'clock in the evening, he encountered a mad dog, who had already greatly injured several of the townspeople. The creature was advancing slowly, but suddenly turned upon him. Setting his back against a wall, he courageously waited for it, and laid hold of it, though not without being severely bitten. He kept it with a firm hand, shouting that he would not let it go to do further mischief, but that someone must bring him an axe, and break its back.

Monsieur Portat, a mounted gendarme, heard him, and, hastening to his help, found him struggling with this large hound, holding him by the neck and ears, and constantly asking for an axe to kill him with. The gendarme struck the dog with his stick, but it was not strong enough to kill it; and another person came up with a heavier club, and gave it a fin-ishing stroke. Albony had received fourteen wounds on the body, thighs, and hands; but they were immediately operated upon, and at the time his name was brought forward, seven months afterwards, to receive a prize from the Monthyon fund for his heroism, it was hoped that the danger of any bad effects had passed away.

The Monthyon Prizes

1820

THE Baron de Monthyon was a French lawyer, greatly devoted to all that could do good to his fellow creatures. Little of his personal history is known; but what made his name celebrated was the endowments that he left by his will at his death, in 1820. The following is a translation of certain clauses in his will:–

"12. I bequeath the sum of 10,000 francs to provide an annual prize for whosoever shall discover any mode of rendering any mechanical art less unhealthy.

"13. A like sum of 10,000 francs as an annual prize for whosoever shall invent any means of perfecting medical science or surgical art.

"14. A like sum of 10,000 francs for an annual prize to the poor French person, who, in the course of the year, shall have performed the most virtuous action.

"15. A like sum of 10,000 francs for the French person who shall have composed and published in France the book most beneficial to morals. "

The two former prizes to be distributed by the Academy of Sciences; the two latter by the French Academy.

Besides these, there were large legacies to hospitals. All the prizes, we believe, continue to be given; but it is with the "Prize of Virtue", as it is called, that we are concerned. The French Academy, which is a society of all the most distinguished literary personages in France, has the office of bestowing this prize, which may either be given entire, or divided into lesser portions among a number of claimants, at the option of the Academy. The recommendation for such a prize must be sent up by the authorities of the town or village where it has taken place, and must contain a full account of the action itself, attested by witnesses, and likewise of the life of the person recommended, going back at least two years, and countersigned by all the chief persons in the place. Those to whom the prize is adjudged must appear in person, or by an authorized proxy, at the meeting of the Academy, where a discourse upon virtue in general is delivered by one of the members, and the meritorious deeds to which the prize is awarded are described in detail.

We are not sure that it suits our English tastes to have "golden deeds" thus paid for in gold; and we are quite sure that most English folks capable of such actions would much rather hide themselves than hear their praises trumpeted forth by an Academician. Nevertheless, there is something noble in M. de Monthyon's intention; and as almost all the "virtuous actions" were done perfectly irrespective of the prize, we cannot but be grateful for having had them brought to our knowledge.

Faithful servants, peasant women devoted to charity, and heroic pre-servers of life, are the chief objects selected by the Academy, with here and there an instance of extraordinary exertions of filial piety; as, for instance, Jeanne Parelle, to whom a prize was given in 1835.

She was one of the eight children of a labourer at Coulange, near Montrésor, and was born in 1786. She was in service when, in 1812, her mother became paralytic, and she came home and thenceforth devoted herself to the care of her parents. A few years after, her father had a sort of fit, in which his teeth were closely locked together, but his mouth filled with blood, and he would have been choked but for Jeanne's readiness in forcing them apart with her hands, at the cost of being severely bitten. The attack came on every night, and as regularly did Jeanne expose her hands to the dreadful bites of her unconscious father, until sometimes the flesh was torn almost to the bone, and yet she cheerfully went about her work all day, endeavouring to prevent her father from perceiving her injuries. This lasted ten years, during which time the poor people only once con-sulted a doctor, who could do nothing for them. The poor old man grew blind, sold his little house, and at last died, leaving his wife deaf, blind, unable to move from her chair, or to do anything but tell her beads. Jeanne spun, made hay, and tended her with the utmost care and cheerfulness; but, at length, the mother and daughter accepted an invitation from an elder married sister to come to Blois. They moved accordingly; but the sister was unable to do much for them, and they were obliged to hire a room, where they were supported by Jeanne's exertions, together with an allowance from the Bureau de Charité of three loaves and three pounds of meat in a month.

Of Jeanne's patience and sweetness with the poor old childish woman, the following testimony was given:–One festival-day, Mère Parelle wished to go to church, and Jeanne, now a hard-working woman of forty-five, made no difficulties, but petted and caressed her, promising that she should go; and on a hot August day she was seen with a great arm-chair on one arm, and her mother on the other. She dragged the old woman three steps, then set her down in the chair to rest; then lifted her up, led her a little farther, and put the chair down again. They were three-quarters of an hour in going the distance Jeanne would have walked in five minutes; and after the return was effected, Jeanne was full of delight. "Well, dearest, did you say your prayers well? Are you glad? You are not tired!" And this laborious journey was cheerfully renewed on the old woman's least wish. Sometimes Jeanne was advised to send her to the hospital, the last refuge of poverty in France, analogous to a workhouse.

"It breaks my heart when they say so," she said.

"But, Jeanne, your mother would be well cared for."

"I know that; I do not say so from contempt for the hospital. She would be taken care of. But tenderness, who would give her that?" And another time she added, "God leaves us our parents, that we may take care of them. If I forsook my poor patient, I should deserve that God should forsake me."

Jeanne and her mother lived on a ground floor, and many persons thus had the opportunity of observing that her tenderness never relaxed. She herself lived on the inferior bread provided by the charity, with a few turnips and potatoes, whilst she kept her mother on white bread, and, if possible, procured butter, cheese, and milk for her. Once when the curate had sent her a pie, which had been scarcely touched, her friends were surprised to see how long it lasted. "Yes, I make the most of it for my mother; I cut off nice little bits for her at her meals, it gives them a relish."

"Do not you eat it, then!"

"It would be a great pity for me to eat it, and nibble away her share, poor thing–it is her treat, and she has so few pleasures, poor sufferer!–neither hearing, nor seeing, and always in pain."

In a great frost, when it was bitterly cold, she was found trying to cover her mother with an old worn-out pelisse, and looking quite melancholy, so a good thick woollen wrapper was sent to her. On the next visit the old woman was found tied up in it, with strings over her shoulders, and the daughter beaming with delight. "Bless those who have warmed my mother," she said; "God will warm them in paradise." A pair of old warm flannel sleeves were given her for herself, but she was seen again with bare arms in the extreme cold. "Did not the sleeves fit you?" "Oh, I picked them to pieces. My mother bad pains in her knees, so I sewed the flannel on to her under-petticoat; it is warm, you see; she likes it, poor thing." And there the pieces were, laid out neatly so as to thicken the petticoat. Amid all her infirmities the delicate neatness and fresh cleanliness of the Mère Parelle were a continual wonder. One of the visiting ladies said, "Really your mother looks quite fresh and bright;" and the good daughter smiled, looking like a young mother complimented upon her child's beauty. "You think her so?" she said. "Ah, poor thing! she is fresher than I am, for she does not drudge so much;" and then with a sigh, "Ah, if she could but hear me!" For the poor sufferer had at last grown so entirely deaf, that she did not hear her daughter at all, and was constantly calling Jeanne without knowing that she was answered. For two months in the winter the daughter had never gone to bed, and though her own health began to suffer, she never complained. For five-and-twenty years, when the prize was given in 1830, had Jeanne Parelle been the unwearied nurse and bread-winner of first two, then one parent. It seems a small thing that man should attempt to reward such exertions, yet, on the other hand, there is something touching in this hard-handed, untaught, toiling, moiling elderly charwoman being chosen out to receive honour due by the first men in intellect and position in her country, and all for the simple, homely virtues of humble life.

Madame Vigier, a bourgeoise of Aurillac, originally in easy circumstances, and at one time rich, was left a widow with four sons, and gradually fell into a state of extreme distress. Two kind gentlemen, M. Sers, the Préfet of Cantal, and M. Azémard, curate of Nôtre Dame, were interested in the family, and three of the sons were placed in good situations, but the youngest, Jean, being a particularly clever, promising boy, they wished him to receive a superior education; and finding themselves unable both to keep him at school, and support his mother, they decided on sending Madame Vigier to the hospital. Jean was at this time nine and a half years old, and, at his boarding-school, scarcely knew of his mother's condition. Intending to break the matter to him, the curate invited him to his house for a holiday, and he came in his best clothes, but just as he had arrived M. Azémard was called away for a few minutes, and telling the boy not to meddle with his breviary, he went downstairs.

Little Jean was naughty boy enough to be incited to meddle by the prohibition itself! As he took up the breviary, out fell a paper. It was an order for the hospital, and his mother's name was on it! The first thing the boy did was to run downstairs, and back to the school, there to change his clothes for his everyday ones. When he reappeared, the curate said, "Ah! poor child, curiosity led you astray, but the fault has brought its own punishment, and you have been hiding yourself to cry over it."

"No, Monsieur le Curé, I have not been crying. I know it all. My mother shall not go to the hospital, she would die of vexation. I will not return to school. I will stay with her. I will support her."

The curate, though struck with his manner, tried to reason him out of his resolution, and took him to several friends, who represented to him that by finishing his education, he would enable himself, by and by, to provide far better for his mother than if he broke it off at once; but his one idea was to save her from the hospital, and he was not to be persuaded. He consulted his brothers, who were making their way in the world, and begged them to assist him in maintaining her; then when they refused, he asked them at least to lend him a small sum, promising to repay them. Still they refused, and all that was left for him to do, was to sell his clothes and a watch that the prefect had given him as a reward for some success at school. With this capital, the little fellow set up as a hawker of cakes and children's toys, and succeeded in earning enough to support his mother. At the time his name was brought forward for a "prix de vertu" he had been nineteen years solely devoted to her, refusing every offer that would separate him from her, and making her happy by his attentions. He was at that time porter at an inn at Aurillac, a situation which must have been a great contrast with those which he might have obtained but for his love of his mother.

It may be said, however, that to show "piety at home" is the very first and most natural of duties. Let us pass on, then, to see what devoted affection has done where the tie was only that of servant to master.

The faithful statesman of the great Henri IV, the Duc de Sully, was amply rewarded by his grateful master, and left a princely estate to his family, but after a few generations the male line became extinct, and the heiress, named Maximilienne de Bethune, after her great ancestor, carried the property into the house of Aubespine.

Bad management, together with the reverses of the Revolution, gradually destroyed the riches of this family, and at last the Marquis d'Aubespine was obliged to sell the castle of Villebon, with all the memorials of the great Sully, and the only estate that remained to him. Out of the price, he could only save enough from his creditors to purchase for himself an annuity of 6000 francs, another of 2400 francs for his son, and a third of 400 for Alexandre Martin, a servant who had lived with him thirty-five years, and had been educated at his expense. Soon after the poor old Marquis died, and the creditors immediately came down upon Martin, and seized his annuity. There was no redress, and Martin returned to his native village of Champrond-en-Gatinais, and took up the trade of a carpenter, which he had learnt at the Marquis's expense before becoming his servant. On the 16th of June, 1830, his cottage door opened, and there stood his old master's son, the Comte d'Aubespine, with his three little motherless children, Angelique, five years old, Josephine, four, and Louis little more than a year. The Count said that his affairs obliged him to leave France for a short time, and he had no one to whom to entrust his little ones but to good Alexandre. The charge was willingly accepted as an honour, though the carpenter knew the family secrets too well to wonder that nothing was said about paying their expenses, and perhaps he also guessed that this short absence was only to last for the Count's life.

At any rate, he accepted the children. He had three of his own, of whom the eldest was able to work. She and her mother earned twenty-four sous a day, and he earned thirty, and upon this the little Count and his sisters were maintained, as far as possible, according to their rank. At their meals they were seated at the cottage table, and waited on as respectfully by Martin, as if they had been at the grand salon in the château, and he their footman. He never sat down with them, but kept them distinct in all ways from his own children, who ate scanty brown bread with him, that the little guests might eat white; wore their coarse clothes to rags, that the young d'Aubespines might be dressed neatly; and slept on the floor, while the little nobles had comfortable beds. There were no murmurs; all came naturally out of the grateful loyalty of the family towards their master's grandchildren. No more was heard of the father till his death, six years after. The news of this event excited the attention of the neighbourhood, and it became known that the last descendants of Sully were growing up in the cottage of a poor carpenter, and owing their education to the curate of the parish. Some ladies at Chartres offered to take charge of the two little girls, and though the parting was most painful, Martin was glad to enable them to be brought up as ladies. As to the boy, the first help that came for his education was from a charitable foundation, endowed by his great ancestor, at Nogent de Rotrou, and thus the only portion of the wealth of Sully that ever reached his young descendant, was that which had been laid up in the true treasure-house of charity. Afterwards a scholarship was presented to him by Louis Philippe at the College of Henri IV, and in 1838 he and Alexandre Martin were both present at a meeting of the Academy, when a discourse was made by M. Salvandi, part of which deserves to be recorded.

"Martin, your task is over. You have deserved well from all good men. You have shown our age a sight only too rare—gratitude, fidelity, respect. The Academy awards to your virtue a prize of 3000 francs. And you, Louis d'Aubespine, since you are present at this solemnity, may it make a deep and lasting impression on your young heart. You are entering life, as persons are now and then forced to appear at a later age, with all eyes on you. Learn that the first of earthly blessings is to be honoured by one's country, and pray the God who has watched over your infancy to enable you to win that blessing that depends on ourselves, and that no event can rob us of. One day you will be told that illustrious blood flows in your veins, but never forget that you must trace your line as far back as to Sully, before you can find a name worthy to stand beside that of Martin. Grow up then to show yourself worthy of the memory of your ancestor, the devotion of your benefactor, and the patronage of the King!"

A maid-servant, called Rose Pasquer, at Nantes, during the worst years of the Revolution, entirely maintained her master and mistress after they had been ruined by the loss of their estates in St. Domingo. She was eighty years in the service of the same family, and received a prize in her hundredth year, in 1856.

Another woman, named Madeleine Blanchet, who lost her husband at the end of the first year of her marriage, was taken into the service of an old lady at Buzançais, called Madame Chambert, who put out the widow's baby to nurse, and was very kind to her. In this house, Madeleine had been for nine years, when, in the winter of 1852, there was a tremendous riot in the town, on account of the high price of bread. For some time beforehand, reports had been flying about that the Red Republicans intended to rise against all persons of property, whom they called bourgeois, and there was a story that an old man had said, "I have seen two Revolutions already, at the third I shall fix my scythe crosswise, and then woe to the bourgeois." These rumours filled the town with alarm, and certain rich persons were known to be marked out for the fury of the mob, and among them were Madame Chambert and her son. On the night before the affray, their servants received a warning that if they tried to defend their master and mistress, they would be killed; but there were at least two who disregarded the threat, a man-servant named Bourgeau and Madeleine Blanchet.

On the morning of the 14th of January was heard that sound of dread–the tocsin. The Republicans were already collected, and began by sacking a great manufactory, and then falling upon the various obnoxious establishments in the town, becoming more savage with every success. There was no resistance; the citizens shut themselves up in their houses, without attempting to unite to defend themselves, and in a short time the whole town was at the mercy of the insurgents. After many acts of plunder and cruelty had taken place, the raging populace came to M. Chambert's house, and speedily breaking in, a man named Venin led the way into the drawing-room, where M. Chambert was trying to encourage his aged mother, and the two servants were with them. Madeleine was so much terrified that she fainted away, upon hearing Venin speak insolently to her master; Bourgeau went up to him and knocked him down; but as others of the furious mob came rushing in, Bourgeau's courage forsook him, and he fled. His master had fetched his gun, and shot Venin, who had risen for another attack; but this was the signal for the whole rage of the multitude to be directed against him, and he too fled, only to be followed by the savage populace, who hunted him from room to room, even to the next house, where he fell under a multitude of blows, crying out, "Mercy, friends!" "You have no friends," answered a voice from the crowd, the last sound that met the ears of the dying man.

Madeleine had, in the meantime, recovered from her swoon, recalled by the shrieks and sobs of her poor old mistress, mingled with the oaths, imprecations, and abusive threats of the murderous crowd. She saw the room thronged with these wild figures, their blouses stained with wine and blood, weapons of all sorts in their hands, triumphant fury in their faces. Her first endeavour, on regaining her senses, was to push through them to the side of the old lady, whom they had not yet personally attacked, and whose terror seemed for the moment lessened by the sight of her maid's kindly face. Then, as there was no certainty that even age and womanhood would long be a protection, Madeleine tried to remove her, and supporting her with one arm, she made her way with the other, struggling on through blows, pushes, and trampling feet, till she had rather carried than led Madame Chambert into the court; but here was the greatest danger of all. Seeing the lady escaping, the mob outside fell upon her, blows were aimed at the two defenceless women, and the mistress fell down, while the ruffians rushed at them with cries of "Death! death!"–the same shouts with which they had hunted the son.

"Go–go, my poor girl!" faintly murmured Madame Chambert. "I must die here! Go away!"

No, indeed! Madeleine knelt over her, calling out, "You shall not kill my mistress till you have killed me!"

A man brandished a Cutlass over her, and several frantic women struck her, even whilst, with outstretched arms, she parried all the strokes at her mistress, all the time appealing to their better feelings, and showing them the cowardly barbarity of thus wreaking their vengeance on a helpless old woman. Her words, and still more her self-devotion; touched two of the men, whose human hearts returned to them sufficiently to make them assist her in withstanding the ferocity of the rest. They helped her to lift up Madame Chambert, and guarded her on her way to a friend's house, where a hiding place was found for the mistress. But the maid would not stay there; she recollected her mistress's property, and hurried back into the midst of the mob to save all she could, seizing on the plate and other valuables whenever she saw them–sometimes snatching them out of the hands of the plunderers, or pouncing on their heaps of spoil–and then, whenever she had rescued anything, depositing it in the friendly house, and then going back for another prize. She continued to go and come for several hours, until all that she had not been able to save had been entirely destroyed. All this she considered as the simplest duty, and mere fulfilment of her trust as a servant.

When order was restored, and the rioters were tried for their atrocities, she was called in as a witness, and asked what she had seen. She replied shortly and clearly, but said not a word of herself.

"But," said the President, "witnesses tell us that you covered your mistress with your own body, and saved her from the blows of the murderers. Is it true?"

"Yes, sir," she answered, quietly.

"You were heard to declare, that they should kill you before they should kill your mistress. Is it true?"

"Yes, sir," again she said; and that was all–not a sentence of self-exaltation, or of the false modesty of self-depreciation, passed her lips.

"If," said the President, after hearing all the evidence, "there had been only twenty men at Buzançais with the heart of that woman, none of the disasters we deplore would have taken place."

And yet Madeleine had begun by fainting; thus showing how little sensibility of nerves has to do with that true moral courage whose source is in the soul alone—as the Academician said who had the pleasant task of relating her exploits, when, at the next meeting of the Academy, she received a gold medal, and an extra prize of 5000 francs.

Almost at the same time there came to light an act of generosity, of the most unusual description, on the part of a servant, and not even towards her own master. Fanny Muller, a young girl in one of the semi-German departments of France, was betrothed to Jean Pierre Wat, a youth in her native village, before they parted, in order to go into service, and save enough to marry upon. Fanny became a maid at an hotel at Paris, and was there much esteemed for the modesty and propriety of her conduct. In 1830, an Italian officer came to the inn—an elderly man, exiled from his country for political causes, arid suffering acutely from a frightful wound received sixteen years previously, when he was serving under Napoleon I. Every day Fanny was called in to assist the surgeon in dressing the wound, and her tender heart made her a kindly nurse, until the poor soldier had exhausted all his means, and the landlord was about to turn him out in a state of utter destitution. Shocked at his condition, Fanny offered him her savings out of her wages of thirty-five francs a month, with which he took a lodging, and there tried to maintain herself by giving music lessons. He was joined by his son, a young boy, but soon after fell so ill again, that he could no longer give lessons. Fanny came again to the rescue; and when her little hoard was exhausted, she borrowed. Just then her betrothed, Wat, came to Paris, with his savings of 2000 francs, and claimed her promise. She told him all, and—wonderful to relate—he was a like-minded man; he freely gave his little fortune into her hands to pay the debt, and, putting off the marriage, he further assisted her in supporting the invalid and the boy. At last, after fifteen years of this patient generosity, the poor old officer died of the effects of the amputation of the injured limb; and the clergyman of the district, knowing the circumstances, recommended the betrothed pair for the Monthyon prize, as a dowry that might at length enable them to enjoy the happiness that they had so generously deferred.

Hosts of other deeds of pure charity and beneficence among the poorest of the poor have come to light among the records of these prizes. Here is a memorial sent in 1823 by the curate of the parish of St. Jean and St. François, at Paris:—

The wife of Jacquemin, a water-carrier, living at No. 17, Rue de Quatre Fils, au Marais, father of three children, one aged five years, dumb and infirm, only earning from thirty-five to forty sous a day, came, some days ago, to ask help for a helpless, indigent woman, maimed of two fingers, and incapable of gaining a livelihood.

"Where does the woman live?" I asked.

"With us."

"How long has she been with you?"

"Ten months: this is the eleventh."

"What does she pay you by the day or month?"

"Nothing."

"What! nothing?"

"Not as much as you could put in your eye."

"Has she relief?"

"Yes; and so have I. I get bread for my children. Since she has been with us, I weaken the porridge, and she eats it with us."

"You have no means of helping others, unless she has promised to make it up to you."

"She never promised me anything but her prayers."

"Does not your husband complain?"

"My husband is a man of few words. He says nothing; he is so kind."

"Does he not go to the public-house?"

"Never; he works himself to death for his children."

"Ten months is a long time."

"She was out in the street, and begged me to shelter her for two or three days; and Jacquemin and I could never have the heart to turn her out. He says, besides, that one must do as one would be done by."

"But, my good woman, what is your lodging?"

"Two rooms."

"What is your rent?"

"It was a hundred and twenty francs; but it has been raised twenty, which makes it eight sous a day."

"I think you should be asking charity for yourself."

"I have already told you, M. le Curé, that I have bread for my children. I ask for nothing for myself. Thank God, as long as my husband and I can work, I should be ashamed to beg for ourselves!"

"Well, good woman, here are ten francs for–"

"Oh, how happy poor Madame Petrel will be!"

Tears of joy came into this charitable woman's eyes. I had meant the ten francs for herself; but I did not undeceive her–the mistake was such an honour to her.

"Go and tell the widow Petrel, who owes you so much, to get two petitions drawn up; one for the Grand Almoner, the other for the Prefect, for a place in the hospital. I will present them."

And the widow was placed in the hospital, while the good Jacquemins received a prize.

There was a more heroic touch in the story of Madeleine Saunier, who was born in 1802, at St. Etienne de Varenne, in the department of the Rhone. This girl had, even when a child, sent out to watch cattle in the fields, been in the habit of sharing the meals she carried out with her with the poor, only begging them to keep the secret. The privations she imposed on herself had a serious effect on her health and growth; but still, when she grew up, her whole soul was fixed on charity; and though she had to work for her own support, she still contrived to effect marvels for others.

A poor blind widow, with an idiot daughter, lived a mile and a half from her cottage; but for fifteen years Madeleine never failed to walk to them, to feed them, set their house in order, and cheer them up to wait for her coming the next day. About as far off in another direction was a poor girl in such a horrible state of leprosy, that–shocking to relate–her own family had abandoned her, and for eighteen months she lay in an outhouse, where no one came near her but Madeleine Saunier, who came twice a day to give her the little nourishment she could take, and to dress her frightful wounds; and at last she died in the arms of this her only friend.

In 1840, Madeleine was nearly drowned in trying to cross a swelling torrent that lay between her and one of her daily pensioners, and when she was blamed for the rashness, she only said, "I could not help it; I could not go yesterday, I was obliged to go to-day."

In the course of a cold winter, Madeleine was nursing a dying woman named Mancel, who lived on the hillside, in a hovel more like a wild beast's den than the home of a human creature. Towards the end of a long night, Madeleine had lighted a few green sticks to endeavour to lessen the intense cold, when the miserable door, which was only closed by a stone on the floor, was pushed aside, and through the smoke, against the snow, the dark outline of a wolf was seen, ready to leap into the room. All Madeleine could do was to spring to the door, and hold it fast, pulling up everything she could to keep it shut, as the beast bounded against it, while she shouted and called in all the tones she could assume, in hopes that the wolf would fancy the garrison more numerous. Whether he were thus deceived or not, he was hungry enough to besiege her till her strength was nearly exhausted, and then took himself off at daylight.

A few hours after, the sick woman died, but Madeleine could not bear to leave the poor corpse to the mercy of the wolf, and going to the nearest cottage implored permission to place it there till the burial could take place. Then again, over the snow into the wolf-haunted solitude, back she went; she took the body on her shoulders, and, bending under her burthen, she safely brought it to the cottage, where she fell on her knees, and thanked God for her safety. The next day, the wolf's footsteps on the snow showed that he had spent the night in prowling round the hut, and that its frail defence had not excluded him from entering it.

France, with all its faults, has always been distinguished for the pure, disinterested honour it shows to high merit for its own sake, and Madeleine had already received a testimony of respect from good Queen Amélie, before the Monthyon prize was decreed to her.

One of the prizes was given to Étienne Lucas, a little boy of six and a half, who saw a child of two fall into the river Eure. He knew the danger, for one of his sisters had lately been drowned; but running to the spot, he waded about fifteen paces in the stream, caught the little one, and drew him to the bank, keeping his head carefully above water. But the bank was too steep for the little fellow to climb, and he could only stand screaming till a man came and lifted out both. A gold medal was given to him and a scholarship at an educational establishment. Indeed, the rescuers from water, from fire, and all the accidents to which human life is liable, would be too many to attempt to record, and having described a few, we must leave our readers to seek the rest for themselves in that roll of golden deeds, the records of the Prix de Vertu.

The Loss of The Magpie Schooner
1826

AMONG those men who have performed the most gallant and self-devoted deeds in the most simple and natural way, we should especially reckon captains in the navy. With them it is an understood rule, that, happen what may, the commanding officer is to be the last to secure his own life–the last to leave the ship in extremity. Many and many a brave life has thus been given, but the spirit nurtured by such examples is worth infinitely more than ever the continued service of the persons concerned could have been. And for themselves–this world is not all, and have we not read, that "He who will save his life shall lose it, and he who will lose his life shall save it"?

The Newfoundland coast is a peculiarly dangerous one, from the dense fogs that hang over the water, caused by the warm waters of the Gulf stream; which, rushing up from the equator, here come in contact with the cold currents from the pole, and send up such heavy vapour, that day can sometimes scarcely be discerned from night, and even at little more than arm's length objects cannot be distinguished, while from without the mist looks like a thick sheer precipice of snow.

In such a fearful fog, on the morning of the 20th of June, 1822, the small schooner, Drake, struck suddenly upon a rock, and almost immediately fell over on her side, the waves breaking over her. Her commander, Captain Baker, ordered her masts to be cut away, in hopes of lightening her so that she might right herself, but in vain. One boat was washed away, another upset as soon as she was launched, and there only remained the small boat called the captain's gig. The ship was fast breaking up, and the only hope was that the crew might reach a small rock, the point of which could be seen above the waves, at a distance that the fog made it difficult to calculate, but it was hoped might not be too great. A man named Lennard seized a rope, and sprang into the sea, but the current was too strong for him, he was carried away in an opposite direction, and was obliged to be dragged on board again. Then the boatswain, whose name was Turner, volunteered to make the attempt in the gig, taking a rope fastened round his body. The crew cheered him after the gallant fashion of British sea-men,. though they were all hanging on by ropes to the ship, with the sea breaking over them, and threatening every moment to dash the vessel to pieces. Anxiously they watched Turner in his boat, as he made his way to within a few feet of the rock. There it was lifted high and higher by a huge wave, then hurled down on the rock and shattered to pieces; but the brave boatswain was safe, and contrived to keep his hold of the rope and to scramble upon the stone.

Another great wave, almost immediately after, heaved up the remains of the ship, and dashed her down close to this rock of safety, and Captain Baker, giving up the hope of saving her, commanded the crew to leave her and make their way to it. For the first time he met with disobedience. With one voice they refused to leave the wreck unless they saw him before them in safety. Calmly he renewed his orders, saying that his life was the last and least consideration; and they were obliged to obey, leaving the ship in as orderly a manner as if they were going ashore in harbour. But they were so benumbed with cold, that many were unable to climb the rock, and were swept off by the waves, among them the lieutenant. Captain Baker last of all joined his crew, and it was then discovered that they were at no great distance from the land, but that the tide was rising, and that the rock on which they stood would assuredly be covered at high water, and the heavy mist and lonely coast gave scarcely a hope that help would come ere the slowly rising waters must devour them.

Still there was no murmur, and again the gallant boatswain, who still held the rope, volunteered to make an effort to save his comrades. With a few words of earnest prayer, he secured the rope round his waist, struggled hard with the waves, and reached the shore, whence he sent back the news of his safety by a loud cheer to his comrades.

There was now a line of rope between the shore and the rock, just long enough to reach from one to the other when held by a man at each end. The only hope of safety lay in working a desperate passage along this rope to the land. The spray was already beating over those who were crouched on the rock, but not a man moved till called by name by Captain Baker, and then it is recorded that not one, so summoned, stirred till he had used his best entreaties to the captain to take his place; but the captain had but one reply–"I will never leave the rock until every soul is safe."

Forty-four stout sailors had made their perilous way to shore. The forty-fifth looked round and saw a poor woman lying helpless, almost lifeless, on the rock, unable to move. He took her in one arm, and with the other clung to the rope. Alas! the double weight was more than the much-tried rope could bear; it broke halfway, and the poor woman and the sailor were both swallowed in the eddy. Captain Baker and three seaman remained, utterly cut off from hope or help. The men in best condition hurried off in search of help, found a farmhouse, obtained a rope, and hastened back; but long ere their arrival, the waters had flowed above the head of the brave and faithful captain. All the crew could do was, with full hearts, to write a most touching letter to an officer, who had once sailed with them in the Drake, to entreat him to represent their captain's conduct to the Lords of the Admiralty. "In fact," said the letter, "during the whole business he proved himself a man, whose name and last conduct ought ever to be held in the highest estimation, by a crew who feel it their duty to ask, from the Lords Commissioners of the Admiralty, that which they otherwise have not the means of obtaining; that is, a public and lasting record of the lion-hearted, generous, and very unexampled way in which our late noble commander sacrificed his life, in the evening of the 23rd of June." This letter was signed by the whole surviving crew of the Drake, and in consequence, a tablet in the dockyard chapel at Portsmouth commemorates the heroism of Captain Charles Baker.

No wonder that the newly escaped crew, who had watched the grave, resolute face, and heard the calm, firm answers, felt as if such bravery were unexampled, and yet–thanks to Him, who braced the hearts of our seamen–it is such fortitude as has been repeated again and again upon broken ships, and desolate rocks, and freezing icebergs, among wild winds and wilder waves.

From the cold fogs of Newfoundland, let us turn to one of the most beautiful of all the tracts of old ocean, that of the Caribbean sea, where the intense blue of the tropical sky is reflected in a sea of still deeper blue, sparkling and dimpling under the full power of the sunbeams, and broken by the wooded islands, forming the most exquisite summer scenery in the world.

But these most beautiful of seas are also the most treacherous. This is the especial home of the hurricane, and of brief furious squalls, that rise almost without warning, except from slight indications in the sky, which only an experienced eye can detect; and from the sudden sinking of the mercury in the barometer; but this often does not take place till so immediately before the storm, that there is barely a minute in which to prepare a vessel for an encounter with this most terrific of her enemies.

In these seas, in the August of 1826, the little schooner, Magpie, was cruising, under the command of a young lieutenant named Edward Smith, in search of a piratical vessel, which had for some time been the terror of the western shores of the island of Cuba. The 26th had been a remarkably sultry day, and towards evening the Magpie lay becalmed off the Colorados rocks, when, at about eight o'clock, a slight breeze sprung up from the west, and the sails were spread, but in less than an hour, the wind shifted to the southward, and a small dark lurid vapour was seen under the moon. This was the well-known signal of coming peril, and instantly Mr. Smith was summoned on deck, the sails furled, and the vessel made as ready as human skill could make her for her deadly encounter. The cloud was rapidly increasing, and for a few seconds there was a perfect stillness, till upon this came a rushing, roaring sound, distant at first, but in the space of a breath, nearer and nearer; while the sea, still as a lake elsewhere, was before the black wall that moved headlong on, lashed into one white sheet of foam, flying up like flakes of snow. It was upon them! The lieutenant's voice was heard calling to cut away the masts; but even then the ship was on her side, and in a few seconds more she was gone from beneath the crew! A gunner's mate, named Meldrum, saw for one moment, by the light of a vivid flash of lightning, the faces of his comrades struggling in the water, then he swam clear of the eddy made by the sinking ship, and found something floating, and grasping at it, obtained first one oar and then another. The gust, having done its work, had rushed upon its way, and the sea was as still and calm as if its late fury had been only a dream.

Meldrum listened breathlessly for some sign of his shipmates, and presently, to his great relief, heard a voice asking if anyone was near. It was that of Mr. Smith, who, with six more, was clinging to a boat, which had floated up clear of the ship. So many rushed to her in their first joy, that she at once capsized, and though all the ship's company, twenty-four in number, were clinging to her, some were stretched across the keel, and she was thus of course utterly useless except as a float.

Mr. Smith ordered them all to quit their position, and allow her to be righted. They obeyed, and he then placed two in her to bale out the water with their hats, directing the others to support themselves by hanging round the gunwales till the boat could be lightened enough to admit them. Just as the baling commenced, one of the men cried out that he saw the fin of a shark, and the horror of becoming a prey to the monster made the men forget everything; they struggled to get into the boat, and upset it again! Again, however, the lieutenant's firmness prevailed, the boat was righted, and he bade the men splash the water with their legs by way of frightening away the enemy. All went on well, and at length the boat was able to hold four men—morning had come, and hope with it, when at about ten o'clock, the cry "A shark! a shark!" was renewed, and at least fifteen of these creatures were among them. Once more, in the panic, the boat was overturned, but after the first moment, the calm, unflinching voice of Edward Smith recalled the men to their resolution; the boat was righted, the two men replaced, and the others still hung outside, where the sharks, at first in a playful mood, came rubbing against the men, and even passing over the boat. At last a cry of agony came from one of the men, whose leg had been seized by a shark, and blood once tasted, there was little more hope; yet still Smith kept his men steady, as, holding by the stern, he cheered the balers, and exhorted the rest to patience till the boat could safely hold them. But the monsters closed on their prey; shriek after shriek and reddening water showed when one after another was torn from the boat, and at last but six remained, when, as the lieutenant looked into the boat for a second, he ceased splashing, and at that moment one leg was bitten off. Still, in order not to startle his men, he endured the anguish without a cry or moan, and they were not aware of what had happened till the other limb was seized by the ravenous teeth, when with a groan he could not repress, his hands quitted their hold. Two of the men were in time to grasp him and to lift him into the boat, and there, mangled and convulsed with agony as he lay, he still turned his whole mind to the safety of his crew. Calling to him a lad named Wilson, whom, as the youngest and therefore the most sheltered from danger, he thought the most likely to survive, he desired him to tell the admiral that he was going to Cape Ontario in search of the pirate when the disaster occurred. "Tell him," he added, "that my men have done their duty, and that no blame is attached to them. I have but one favour to ask, and that is, that he will promote Meldrum to be a gunner."

He then shook each man by the hand and bade him farewell, with a cheering word for all as long as he could speak; but, as the long day of burning sun, without food or water, passed by, his strength failed, and he had lost the power of speech, when at sunset, on another alarm of the sharks, a startled movement of the men caused the boat to be again upset, and his sufferings were ended in the waves.

The brief grave records of courts-martial speak only of the facts that concern the service, and they do not tell us of the one anchor of hope that could alone have braced that dying sailor's soul to that unmurmuring patience through the anguish, thirst, and heat of that tropical day; but no one can doubt that a man, who thought so much of others, so little of himself, whose soul was on his duty, and who bore the extremity of agony so long and uncomplainingly, must have been upheld by that which alone can give true strength. Indeed, we know that Edward Smith was one of the best loved and most promising of the sons of a Hampshire family, brought up by a widowed mother, and that he was especially valued by the Admiral on the station, Sir Lawrence Halstead.

The only officer now left was a young mate named Maclean, who, with the spirit of his lieutenant, again persuaded the men to right the boat, which was now able to hold them all, for only four were left, himself, the gunner's mate, Meldrum, the boy Wilson, and one more. Twenty hours of struggling in the water, with, latterly, the sun broiling their heads, and not a morsel of food nor a drop of drink, had, however, nearly worn them out; the oars were lost, and though the approach of night rendered the air cooler, yet the darkness was unwelcome, as it took away all chance of being seen and picked up by some passing vessel. At about three o'clock at night, poor young Wilson and the other man lost their senses from the sufferings they had undergone, and both jumped overboard and perished.

Maclean and Meldrum collected themselves after the shock, and steadily continued to bale out the water, till the boat was so nearly dry, that they could lie down in her; and so spent were they, that deep sleep came to them both; nor did they wake till the sun was glaring upon them far above the horizon. What a wakening!–alone in a frail boat, their companions gone, water all round, and swarming with the cruel sharks–the sun burning overhead, and themselves now thirty-six hours without food, and parched with the deadly thirst, which they had the resolution not to attempt to slake with salt water, well knowing that the momentary relief would be followed by worse suffering, perhaps by frenzy. They durst not even speak to one another, but sat, one in the bow, one in the stern, in silent patience, waiting for death.

Hours passed away in this manner; but towards eight in the morning a white speck was seen in the distance, and both opened their parched lips to shout "A sail!–a sail!" They shook hands, with tears of joy and hope, and strained their eyes as the vessel came nearer, and the dark hull could be seen above the horizon. Nearer, nearer–scarcely half a mile from them was the vessel, when, alas! she altered her course: she was sailing away. They shouted their loudest, and waved their jackets; but in vain–they were unseen, and were being left to perish!

The gunner's mate now rose up. He was the elder and the stronger man, and he quietly announced his intention of swimming to the vessel. It was a long, fearfully long distance for a man fasting for so many hours; and more terrible still than drowning was the other danger that was hidden under the golden ripples of those blue waters. But to remain was certain death to both, and this attempt gave the one last hope. The brave man gave his last wishes in charge to his officer, made the one entreaty, that if Mr. Maclean saw a shark in pursuit, he would not let him know, shook hands, and, with a brief prayer for the protection of the Almighty, sprang overboard.

Maclean was strongly tempted to swim with this last companion, but conquered the impulse as only leading to a needless peril, cheered and waved his jacket. Once he thought he saw the fin of a shark, and made a splashing, in hopes of scaring it from pursuit, then watched the swimmer with earnest hope. Meldrum swam, straining every nerve, splashing as he went to keep away the sharks, and shouting, but no one appeared on deck; and when he had accomplished about two-thirds of the way, his strength failed him, and he was about to resign himself to float motionless, all easy prey to the sharks, when a head was seen in the vessel. He raised his arms, jumped himself up in the water, and was seen! The brig was hove-to, a boat was put out, and he was taken into it, still able to speak and point the way to his companion.

The brig was American; and, at first, the history of the last day and night was thought so incredible, that the destitute pair were taken for escaped pirates; but they were, at last, set on shore at Havannah, and thence conveyed to Port Royal by the first man-of-war that touched there.

At the court-martial held by Sir Lawrence Halstead these facts came out. Meldrum could not be prevailed on to tell his own story; but when his young officer had related it, both burst into tears, and embraced before the court. Not an officer present but was deeply affected; and Meldrum was, of course, at once promoted, according to the dying request of Lieutenant Smith. He died in the year 1848, but the name of the Magpie schooner will ever remain connected with the memory of undaunted resolution and unwearied patience.

The Fever At Osmotherly

1825

OSMOTHERLY IS a small village in Yorkshire, not far from North Allerton. It had been much neglected, the houses were ill-built, and there had been little attention to the means of cleanliness, so that the place was exceedingly unhealthy, and the people were in the state of dullness and ignorance, that was sure to be the result of possessing a clergyman who unhappily cared neither for their souls nor bodies, and did not even reside among them, but only came over from time to time to read the service in the church.

No wonder that a deadly low fever broke out in this unfortunate place, in the autumn of 1825, and went creeping on from house to house, laying one person low after another, so that the healthy could hardly be found to nurse the sick. Among the families upon whom it fell very heavily was that of an old widow, who had seen better days, but had become nearly destitute, and had for many years past been chiefly supported by an allowance from her brother, who had settled as a merchant in America. This brother had died in the previous year, and his only child, Mary Lovell Pickard, at that time twenty-five years of age, had, after her long nursing of him, been persuaded to cross the Atlantic, and make acquaintance with her English relations.

She had spent many happy months with aunts and cousins in prosperous circumstances, but she was not going to neglect the poor old aunt in the North, and taking advantage of the escort of some friends who were going to Scotland, she travelled with them as far as to Penrith, and then went by coach to North Allerton, and by post-chaise to Osmotherly, where she intended to pay a three weeks' visit at Brush Farm, and be picked up again at Penrith on their return.

Her first letter from this place, written on the 2nd of September, 1825, describes her hostess as "a small, thin old lady, with a pale complexion, and the very brightest black eyes, which sparkle when she speaks with a degree of animation almost amusing in such an old lady. She lives in a comfortable little two-story cottage, of four rooms, which far exceeds anything I ever saw for neatness,"–though it seems to have had a clay floor. "I find," added kind-hearted Mary, "that I could not have come at a better time to do good, or a worse for gaining spirits." She found the poor old lady nearly worn out with the care of two little grandsons, one of whom was dreadfully ill with whooping-cough, but could not be nursed at home, as his younger brother, a baby of a fortnight old, was equally ill with the same complaint, and his father was in great danger with the fever, and had just lost a brother in smallpox. And worse than all, a son of the old lady had been just brought home in a melancholy state, that was almost madness.

Many would have thought only of flying from the fever. Mary Pickard only thought how she could help the sufferers. First she took charge of the sick child, who was soon very fond of her, and took a fancy to call her "Uncle Mady", and she likewise went about among the other poor, teaching them the care of their sick, and giving them every kind of nourishment they needed, aiding them with hand and head, till no wonder they were always declaring, "they never saw such a lady as Miss Pickard". What she gave away among them was never known, probably not even to herself; but it is plain that she must have been at the expense of their medical advice, since her aunt was totally dependent on her, and the daughter's husband had hitherto lived solely by his daily labour, while the rest of the parish was extremely poor, and the destitution caused by sickness was dreadful. She says herself that the "good little doctor" was her only helper, and no doubt she must have called him in, since in those days unions and union doctors were not, and though parish doctors were appointed, they were a benefit only in name to the poor, who depended almost entirely on private charity, where they were within reach of it, or else upon old women, cunning men, and herbalists. She had a hard fight with the village superstitious fancies, and a harder one with the cottagers' habits of uncleanliness; and such was the panic that prevailed, that she could hardly rouse them into exertion to remove the dirt that was probably the cause of the sickness, and certainly much increased it. Whole families seem to have owed their food to her, while their breadwinner was laid by; but there is no record of the details of her general doings; she said in after years, that she should like to write down an account of the curious things that had befallen her at Osmotherly, but she never had time to do so, and we only have her letters written to her American friends at the time, which speak of little but what concerned her relations, and for them the work she did would have seemed in itself sufficient.

Her cousin "Bessy's" husband died of the fever on the 8th of September, and Mary it was who closed his eyes, and the next day stood godmother to the poor little month-old baby, which was christened at its father's funeral, with little hope of its living, for its cough was bringing on fits. Two nights after she says: "I had been up with the little boy the greater part of the night before . . . but, (in the true spirit of Polly Pickard, attempting to do more than anyone would have thought reasonable), I was quite persuaded that, as I was to sit up, it was as well to do all I could; and as poor Bessy had not had a quiet night since her child was born, and was going to sleep alone in her house for the first time since her husband's death, I thought it would do her good, and me no harm, to sit up in her parlour, and take care of the baby in the cradle, that she might have a little sleep, and not feel alone. The dear little baby had been better than for some time during the day, and I doubted not that it would lie in the cradle or on my knee very quietly, except during its coughing fits. Bessy went to bed; but the poor little creature grew worse, and coughed itself into a fit, in which it lay so long, that I thought it dead, and awoke its mother. But its little heart began to beat again, and it seemed to be reviving, though slowly, and I sent her off again. It appeared for some time to be recovering; but all at once it sunk away and died in my arms, so peacefully and sweetly, that I could scarcely be persuaded that it had not fallen into a still slumber, or had another fit. But it was indeed gone; and when I could bring myself to give it up, I arranged its little body for its last home. I don't know when I have had my feelings more excited. It was a lovely little creature, and I have nursed it so much since I have been here, that I found it had become an object of great interest to me: not a day has passed that I have not given three or four hours to it, and it was always so quiet with me, that it seemed almost to know when I took it." As to her own danger in the midst of infection: "Don't fear for me; I don't think I am going to be sick, and it will be for some good purpose if I am."

She took up her quarters with the poor bereaved mother, and was able to be a great comfort to her, by long talks at night, when all was still, showing her the way to the only true comfort, of which the poor, ill-taught young woman had hitherto known little. At the week's end, however, poor Bessy sickened of the worst form of typhus; and the next day the favourite little Jamie fell ill also. The villagers thought the house doomed, and Mary saw not a creature but the doctor, day after day. The illness lasted eleven days, during which Mary never left her night or day, except to run back to her grandmother's for a change of clothes; for the sufferer did not like to be touched by any other person, and it was best that as few should be exposed to the infection as possible. "Her senses never forsook her for a moment, nor her deep sense of gratitude to God for the mercies which He had bestowed on her amid all her sufferings. It seemed to her that His immediate Providence had sent me to them just at this time; and her expressions of affection and thankfulness were indeed most delightful to me." She died on the 30th of September; and Mary returned to the care of the little Jamie, who was still extremely ill. The elder boy was seven years old, and able to understand the desolateness of his home, and, as he sat by the fire, kept on repeating at intervals the entreaty, "Cousin Mary, you will let me live with you, won't you?" Poor little fellow! he did not long need an earthly home; he, too, fell ill, and, after a most patiently borne sickness, watched constantly by this loving friend, died on the 30th of October.

Still, Mary's nursing was not ended. On the 2nd of November, she wrote: "There are very many cases of the fever in the village, and as I am almost the only person in it who is not afraid of infection, I still have full employment in assisting the poor sufferers. My cousin's little niece is still very ill. I have indeed been wonderfully preserved and strengthened. Heaven save me from presumption, but I cannot help feeling that I could not have lived through all that I have, unless God had protected me!"

By the end of the month, however, the fever had abated sufficiently for Mary to comply with the earnest entreaties of her friends, and come to them at Penrith; but it was a cruel parting with poor little Jamie, who had grown so fond of her, that his screams of agony at her departure long echoed in her ears. The welcome and quiet she enjoyed among her friends made the stay with them "like the rest of the Sabbath to the weary labourer", though she was very weak and weary, and needed much rest and care. But before December was at an end, came a letter from the doctor, telling her the poor old aunt herself was at the point of death, with the same malignant fever. Vainly did Mary's friends assure her that the danger of returning into the infected air was far greater than even all she had gone through before, in her present weakened state. She knew it was her duty to go, and took leave of them "with many solemn thoughts, though hid by cheerful looks", and feeling as if it was for ever that she parted with them.

After an eight hours' solitary journey, she arrived, and had the pleasure of the most ecstatic greeting from poor little Jamie. "He ran round me, jumped up in my lap, stroked and kissed my face, as if he could not trust to the evidence of one sense, and at last burst out a-crying, 'Uncle Mady won't go away again! Uncle Mady live with Jamie every day, won't you, Uncle Mady?'"

Again she had to be sole nurse and servant in the sick house, "acting in a fourfold capacity ", as she called it. She put up a little bed in a corner of her aunt's room, and devoted herself to her. It was less lonely than before; for the doctor had brought his sister to keep house for him, and Mary was able to see much of her. Moreover, the old aunt began to recover from the time of her arrival; and her American heart was rejoiced by the snow—"it looked so homeish, and so much like your happy home the last time I saw it, that I have been enjoying the sight highly".

But the cold and wet, at last, broke down her strength. One night, when alone, such a dreadful cramp seized her, that she fell on the floor, and for a considerable time could neither move nor make anyone hear. For many days after, she lay on her bed, in a state of extreme weakness, from which she could hardly be recovered, but with unfailing brightness. It was always remarked, that, "her worst days were her gayest ones"; and at length she recovered, and left the place where she had been for so many months truly a ministering angel. She returned to that home in America which had, during her toils, seemed to her, "like the dreams one has of heaven, in the twilight hours, between sleeping and waking". There she became a happy wife and mother, and continued to send remittances to the old aunt, as long as they were needed; but she lost sight of little Jamie, and had no further intercourse with him. He, however, did not forget her, and, early in 1849, sent a long affectionate letter to her, dwelling gratefully on all she had done for his dying parents and himself. But, alas! the letter came too late. Mary–now the widowed Mrs. Ware–had long been sinking under a fatal malady, so endured, that "her sick chamber was always the happiest room in the house", and had died on a lovely April day, in which she looked up and said, with a smile, "What a beautiful day to go home! "

Surely, if it be a glorious deed to save life at the risk of our own, Mary Lovell Pickard, standing alone among the dead and dying, in her cheerful resolution and strong trust, deserves honour as much as any hero who braved death in battle or in wreck.

Miss Pickard's noble action, and another similar one suggested a beautiful sketch by Miss Martineau, entitled "The Sickness and Health of the People of Bleaburn , in Nos. 9, 10, 11, 12 of *Household Words.*

Let us add to this a parallel from Saint Remi Bosrecourt, near Dieppe, where, in 1824, there was a terrible attack of typhus, extremely infectious. It broke out in a house where there were eleven persons: and such were its ravages, that, at last, only the father remained with four little children all ill; and such was the general alarm, that no one would go near the cottage. All the nurses whom the authorities of the village endeavoured to employ, replied that they would not run after death. At last, a lady, Mademoiselle Celestine Détrimont, offered herself; and when the fearful risk was set before her, she answered, "In the service of God and the poor there is no fear of death". To the cottage then she went. One more child died, and she herself prepared it for burial, placing the coffin in the courtyard, where alone anyone dared to come. The other three and the father were saved by her care; and this is said to have been only one instance in a whole life of self-devotion and charity.

The Chieftainess and the Volcano
1825

FEW regions in the world are more beautiful than those islands far away in the Pacific which we have been used to call the Sandwich Isles. They are in great part formed by the busy little coral worms, but in the midst of them are lofty mountains, thrown up by the wonderful power that we call volcanic. In sailing up to the islands the first thing that becomes visible are two lofty peaks, each two miles and a half high. One is white with perpetual snow, the other is dark–dark with lava and cinders, on which the inward heat will not permit the snow to cast a white mantle. The first of these has been tranquil for many years, the other is the largest and most terrible active volcano in the world, and is named Kilauea. The enormous crater is a lake of liquid fire, from six to nine miles in circumference. Over it plays a continual vapour, which hangs by day like a silvery cloud, but at dusk is red and glowing like the Aurora Borealis, and in the night is as a forest in flames. Rising into this lurid atmosphere are two black cones, in the midst of a sea of fused lava, in which black and pink rocks are tossed wildly about as in a seething cauldron. The edge of this huge basin of burning matter is a ledge of hard lava, above which rises a mighty wall of scoria or cinder; in one place forming an abrupt precipice 4000 feet high, but in others capable of being descended, by perilous paths, by those who desire to have a closer view of the lake of flame within. Upon the bushes that grow on the mountaintop is found a curious fibrous substance formed by the action of the air upon the vapour rising from the molten minerals beneath; it is like cobwebs of spun glass. Tremendous is the scene at all times, but at the periods of eruption, the terrific majesty is beyond all imagination, when rivers of boiling lava, blood-red with heat, rush down the mountainside, forming cascades of living fire, or spreading destruction over the plains, and when reaching the sea, struggling, roars, thundering, in bubbling flames and dense smoke for the mastery with the other element.

Heathen nations living among such wonderful appearances of nature cannot fail to connect them with divine beings. The very name of Volcano testifies to the old classical fancy that the burning hills of the Mediterranean were the workshops of the armourer-god Vulcan and his Cyclops; and in the Sandwich Islands, the terrible Kilauea was supposed to be the home of the goddess Pele, whose bath was in the mighty crater, and whose hair was supposed to be the glassy threads that covered the hills. Fierce goddess as she was, she permitted no woman to touch the verge of her mountain, and her wrath might involve the whole island in fiery destruction.

At length, however, the islanders were delivered from their bondage of terror into a clearer light. Missionaries came among them, and intercourse with Europeans made them ashamed of their own superstitious fancies. Very gradually the faith of the people detached itself from the savage deities they had worshipped, and they began to revere the One true Maker of heaven and earth. But still their superstitions hung round Kilauea. There the fiery goddess still revelled in her fearful gambols, there the terrible sights and sounds, and the desolating streams that might at any moment burst from her reservoir of flame were as tokens of anger that the nation feared to provoke. And after the young King Liholiho, with all his court, had made up their minds to abandon their idols, give up their superstitious practices, and seek instruction from Christian teachers, still the priests of Pele, on her flaming mountain, kept their stronghold of heathenism, and threatened her wrath upon those who should forsake the ancient worship.

Then it was that a brave Christian woman, strong in faith and courage, resolved to defy the goddess in her fastness, and break the spell that bound the trembling people to her worship. Her name was Kapiolani, wife of Naihe, the public orator of Hawaii. There was no common trust and resolution needed to enable her to carry out her undertaking. Not only was she outraging the old notions that fearful consequences must follow the transgression of the tabu, or setting apart. Not only was the ascent toilsome and leading into cold regions, which were dreadful to a delicate Hawaiian, but the actual danger of the ascent was great. Wild crags and slippery sheets of lava, or slopes of crumbling cinders, were strangers to the feet of the tender coast-bred woman. And the heated soil, the groanings, the lurid atmosphere, the vapour that oozed up from the crevices of the half-cooled lava, must have filled any mind with awe and terror, above all, one that had been bred up in the faith that these were the tokens of the fury of a vindictive and powerful deity, whose precincts she was transgressing. Very recently a large body of men had been suffocated on the mountainside by the mephitic gases of the volcano—struck dead, as it must have seemed, by the breath of the goddess.

But Kapiolani, strong in the faith that He, as whose champion she came, was all-sufficient to guard her from the perils she confronted, climbed resolutely on, bearing in her hand the sacred berries, which it was sacrilege for one of her sex to touch. The enraged priests of Pele came forth from their sanctuary among the crags, and endeavoured to bar her way with threats of the rage of their mistress; but she heeded them not. She made her way to the summit, and gazed into the fiery gulf below, then descended the side of the terrible crater, even to the margin of the boiling sea of fire, and hurling into it the sacred berries, exclaimed: "If I perish by the anger of Pele, then dread her power; but, behold, I defy her wrath. I have broken her tabus; I live and am safe, for Jehovah the Almighty is my God. His was the breath that kindled these flames; His is the Hand which restrains their fury. Oh! all ye people, behold how vain are the gods of Hawaii, and turn and serve the Lord!"

Safely the brave woman descended the mountain, having won her cause, the cause of Faith.

In classic times, the philosopher Empedocles had leapt into the burning crater of Mount Etna, thereby to obtain an imperishable name. How much more noble is the name that Kapiolani gained for herself, by the deed that showed forth at whose command alone it is that the mountains quake and flow down, and the hills melt like wax.

Discipline

Perhaps there have never been occasions, when the habit of instantaneous obedience to the voice of duty has produced more touching instances of forbearance and unselfishness than in the confusion and despair of a ship-wreck. What a wreck can be without such qualities, has been but too well proved by the horrible scenes that took place after the loss of the French ship Meduse, when brutal selfishness was followed by savage violence and cannibalism too shocking to be dwelt upon; though memorable as an example, that "every man for himself", is the most fatal of all policies, even were self-preservation the primary object.

In British ships of war, unshrinking obedience, heeding nothing but the one matter in hand, is the rule. "As a landsman," says Colonel Fisher, an engineer officer, who was on board the Plover gunboat in the hottest fire on the Peiho River, "I was much struck with the coolness with which the navigation of the vessel was attended to; the man in the chains cries the soundings, the master gives his orders to the man at the helm and the engineers below; the helmsman has no eyes or ears but for the master's directions and signals .... All seem intent on what is their duty at the time being, and utterly unmindful of the struggle raging round them." And this when not only were they being shot down every moment, but when each comparatively harmless ball rocked the gunboat, sent splinters flying, or brought the yards down upon their heads. Where such conduct is regarded as a mere matter of course, from the grey-headed admiral down to the cadet and the cabin-boy, no wonder that multitudes of deeds have been done, glorious because they placed duty far above self, and proved that Nelson's signal is indeed true to the strongest instinct of the English sailor.

The only difficulty is to choose among the instances of patient obedi-ence on record; and how many more are there, unknown to all but to Him who treasures up the record, until the day when "the sea shall give up her dead!" Let us cast a glance at the Atalante, bewildered in a fog upon the coast of Nova Scotia, and deceived by the signal guns of another ship in distress, till she struck upon the formidable reefs, known by the name of the Sisters Rocks, off Sambro Island. The wreck was complete and hope-less, and a number of men scrambled at once into the pinnace; but the captain, seeing that she could never float so loaded, ordered twenty of them out, and was implicitly obeyed, so entirely without a murmur, that as the men hung clinging to the weather gunwale of the ship, they drowned the crashing of the falling masts with their cheers.

As soon as the pinnace was lightened, she floated off, but immediately turned bottom upwards. Still the crew never lost their self-possession for one moment, but succeeded in righting her, and resuming their places, without the loss of a man. They then waited beyond the dash of the break-ers on the reef, for Captain Hickey and their companions, who were still clinging to the remains of the ship. There were two other boats, but too small to hold the whole number, and an attempt was made to construct a raft, but the beating of the waves rendered this impossible, so the men already in the pinnace were directed to lie down in the bottom, and pack themselves like herrings in a barrel, while the lesser boats returned through the surf to pick off the rest–a most difficult matter, and indeed some had to be dragged off on ropes, and others to swim, but not one was lost. The captain was of course the last man to quit the wreck, though several of the officers were most unwilling to precede him even for a moment, and by the time he reached the boat, the last timbers had almost entirely disappeared, amid the loud cheers of the brave-hearted crew.

Nothing was saved but the admiral's despatches, which the captain had secured at the first moment, and the chronometer. This last was the special charge of the captain's clerk, who had been directed always to hold it in his hand when the guns were fired, or the ship underwent any shock, so as to prevent the works from being injured. On the first alarm he had caught up the chronometer and run on deck, but being unable to swim, was forced to cling to the mizen mast. When the ship fell over, and the mast became nearly horizontal, he crawled out to the mizen top, and sat there till the spar gave way and plunged him into the waves, whence he was dragged into one of the boats, half-drowned but grasping tight his precious trust. A poor merry negro, who held fast to his fiddle to the last moment, as he clung to the main chains, was obliged to let his instrument go, amid the laughter and fun of his messmates, who seem to have found food for merriment in every occurrence. No one had a full suit of clothes, but an old quartermaster, named Samuel Shanks, who had comported himself throughout as composedly as if shipwrecks befell him every day, and did not even take off his hat, except for a last cheer to the Atalante as she sunk. He recollected that he had a small compass seal hanging to his watch, and this being handed to the captain, in his gig, and placed on the top of the chronometer, it proved steady enough to steer by, as the three boats crept carefully along in the dense fog. They landed, after a few hours, on the coast, about twenty miles from Halifax, at a fishing station, where they were warmed and fed.

Thence the captain took the most exhausted and least clothed of the party in the boats to Halifax, leaving the others to march through the half-cleared country. Before night the whole ship's company assembled, without one man missing, in as complete order as if nothing had happened.

Here perfect discipline had proved the means of safety, and hope had never failed for a moment; but we have still fresh in our memories an occasion where such forbearing obedience led to a willing self-sacrifice, when safety might have been possible to the strong at the expense of certain destruction to the weak.

The Birkenhead, a war steamer used as a transport, was on her way to Algoa Bay with about 630 persons on board, 132 being her own crew, the rest detachments from the 12th, 74th, and 91st Regiments, and the wives and children of the soldiers. In the dead of the night between the 25th and 28th of February, the vessel stuck on a reef of sunken rocks on the African coast, and from the rapidity with which she was moving, and the violence of the waves, became rapidly a hopeless wreck. On the shock, the whole of the men and officers hurried on deck, and the commanding officer, Lieutenant-Colonel Seton, calling the other officers about him, impressed on them the necessity of preserving order and silence among the men, and placed them at the disposal of the commander of the vessel.

Sixty were placed at the pumps, others to disengage the boats, and others to throw the poor horses overboard, so as to lighten the ship, while the rest were sent to the poop to ease the forepart of the ship. Everyone did as directed, and not a murmur nor cry was heard. They were as steady as if on parade, as ready as though embarking in a British harbour.

The largest boat was unhappily too much encumbered to be got at quickly enough, but the cutter was filled with the women and children, and pushed off, as did two other small boats. The other two large ones were, one capsized, the other stove in by the fall of the funnel, which took place immediately after the cutter was clear of the ship, only twelve or fifteen minutes after the ship had struck. At the same time the whole vessel broke in two parts, crosswise, and the stern part began to sink and fill with water. The commander called out, "All those that can swim jump overboard and swim for the boats."

But Colonel Seton and the officers with him besought their men to forbear, showing them that if they did so, the boats with the women must be swamped. And they stood still. Not more than three made the attempt. Officers and men alike waited to face almost certain death rather than endanger the women and children. Young soldiers, mostly but a short time in the service, were as patiently resolute as their elders. In a few moments the whole of these brave men were washed into the sea, some sinking, some swimming, some clinging to spars. The boats picked up as many as was possible without overloading them, and then made for the shore, which was only two miles off, hoping to land these and return for more, but the surf ran so high that landing was impossible, and after seeking till daylight for a safe landing place, they were at last picked up by a schooner, which then made for the wreck, where thirty or forty were still hanging to the masts in a dreadful state of exhaustion.

A few, both of men and horses, had succeeded in swimming to the shore, but some were devoured by the sharks on the way, and out of the whole number in the ship, only 192 were saved. But those who were lost, both sailors and soldiers, have left behind them a memory of calm, self-denying courage as heroic as ever was shown on battlefield.

The Rescuers

We have had a glimpse of the horrors on board a wrecked ship, and the resolution with which they can be endured and conquered. Let us now look at the shore, and at the spirit that has prompted even women to become their rescuers.

Here, then, is a portion of a "Night Scene by the Sea", namely, the dangerous coast near Cromer, in the country of Norfolk. It is taken from a poem by Joanna Baillie, and is literally and exactly true. There, amid

"The roar of winds and waves
As strong contention loudly raves,
A fearful sound of fearful commotion
The many angry voices of the ocean",

the foremost in affording aid to the shipwrecked seamen was a crippled lady,

"One with limbs nerve-bound,
Whose feet have never touched the ground,
Who loves in tomes of Runic lore
To scan the curious tales of yore,
Of gods and heroes dimly wild,
And hath intently oft beguiled
Her passing hours with mystic rhymes,
Legends by bards rehearsed of other times;
Learned, and loving learning well,
For college hall or cloistered cell
A student meet, yet all the while
As meet, with repartee or smile,
'Mid easy converse, polished, blithe, and boon,
To join the circles of a gay saloon;
From childhood reared in wealth and ease,
The daily care herself to please–
For selfish nature here below
A dangerous state, I trow".

That crippled lady was Anna Gurney, one of a gifted family, surpassing them perhaps in mental powers and attainments, certainly not inferior to any in Christian benevolence, and (which is the strangest thing of all), absolutely more than a match for the soundest and healthiest among them in personal activity, though unable through her whole life to stand or move without mechanical aid. Her intellect was of the highest order. After learning all the more accessible languages, she betook herself to the ancient Teutonic branches, and in 1819 translated the Anglo-Saxon Chronicle. As invalid and as scholar, she would, as the verses above quoted observe, have seemed in especial danger of dwelling on nothing beyond her own constant and severe sufferings, and the studies that beguiled her attention from them.

Yet she was full of the warmest, brightest sympathy. Her conversation was not only delightful from her brilliant powers, but from her ready perception of the wants and wishes of others. Not only was her wheeled chair propelled in a moment to her bookshelves when she wanted a volume to illustrate her thought, but the moment she caught a friend's eye in search of any article at a little distance, her chair was turned in that direction, and the object was presented with infinite grace. She made young people exceedingly fond of her, and delighted to assist them in their studies. She would help boys to prepare their Greek and Latin tasks with infinite zest, and would enliven a lesson with comical and original allusions. Other children of a lower rank were also taught by her, and from her home at North Repps Cottage, she won by her kindness and helpfulness, the strongest influence over the fisherfolk upon the coast, who looked upon her as a superior being.

At her own expense she procured a lifeboat and apparatus for rescuing the shipwrecked, and to secure the right use of these, she would be wheeled down to the shore in her chair to give orders and superintend their execution. Surely there can be no more noble picture than this infirm woman, constantly in pain, whose right it would have seemed to be shielded from a rough blast or the very knowledge of suffering, coming forth in the dead of night, amid the howling storm, beating spray, and drenching rain, to direct and inspirit its rugged, seafaring men, and send them on errands of life or death. Which was most marvellous, it is hard to say, the force of will that actuated her, or the force of understanding that gave value to such presence and commands.

Truly may Miss Baillie say–

> "But no, my words her words may not express,
> Their generous import your own hearts must guess".

And when half-drowned sailors were brought ashore, she remained to give care and directions for their treatment, or took them to her own home, where they were so welcomed, that it was a saying on the coast that it was worth while to be wrecked to be received by Miss Gurney.

> "The lady returns to her home again,
> With the sound of blessings in her ear,
> From young and old, her heart to cheer;
> Sweet thoughts within her secret soul to cherish,
> The blessings of those who were ready to perish;
> And there lays her down on her peaceful pillow,
> Bless'd by the Lord of the wind and the billow."

When at the age of sixty-one, she laid her down on her last pillow, she was carried to her rest, in the seaside church of Overstrand, by old fishermen–rugged, loving men who knew and valued her–and when they had lowered the coffin down the stone steps of the open vault, they formed a knot at the foot and wept bitterly. More than a thousand persons from the coast had gathered to show their respect and gratitude; most were in mourning, many in tears. "I never", said one who was present, "saw so many men weeping, at one time, it seemed a general wail." The service was read by the clergyman of the parish (who could not but feel that he had lost his most precious earthly helper) simply and calmly; with cheerful brightness, which showed that his faith had realised her gain, he gave thanks for her.

The cripple gave what she had–her vigorous mind, her means, and her spirit. Let us turn to one who had neither silver nor gold, nothing but her resolute heart and brave skilful hands. Grace Darling, the daughter of the keeper of one of the lighthouses upon the Fern Islands, a perilous cluster of rocks off Northumberland, was wakened towards the morning of the 6th of September, 1838, by shrieks of distress; and when dawn came, perceived the remains of a wreck upon Longstone Island, the outermost of the group.

Grace awoke her father and urged him to launch his boat and go to the rescue of anyone who might still be alive in the stranded vessel, but the tide was rising, wind and sea were wild, and the old man hung back. Grace, however, was sure that she discerned a movement on the wreck, as though living beings were still there, and seizing an oar, placed herself in the boat, which she was well able to manage. Her father could not let her go alone, and they rowed off together in a tremendous sea, encouraged by perceiving that nine persons were still clinging to the forepart of the ship. The father, after many vain attempts, succeeded in landing on the rock, and making his way to the wreck, while Grace rowed off and on among the breakers, dexterously guiding her little boat, which but for her excellent management would have been dashed to pieces among the rocks.

One by one, with the utmost care and skill, the nine survivors were placed in the boat and carried to the lighthouse, where Grace lodged, fed, and nursed them for two whole days before the storm abated enough for communication with the mainland. One of them was a Mrs. Dawson, whose two children, of eleven and eight years old, had actually been buffeted to death by the waves while she held them in her arms, and who was so much injured herself, that it was long before she could leave her bed.

The vessel was the Forfarshire, a large steamer plying between Hull and Dundee. Her boilers had been out of order, their leakage had rendered the engines useless, and when the storm arose, the ship was unmanageable without her steam, and was driven helplessly upon the Fern Islands. The only boat had been lowered by eight of the sailors, who were pushing off in her when one gentleman rushed on deck, seized a rope, and swung himself in after them. These nine were picked up by a sloop and saved. Of the others, the whole number had either been drowned in their berths or washed off the wreck, except four of the crew and five passengers, whom Grace Darling's valour had rescued. The entire amount of the lost was not known, but more than forty had certainly gone on board at Hull. Some sailors at Sunderland went out to the wreck during the storm at the peril of their lives, but found only corpses to bring away. Grace's noble conduct rang throughout England, and every testimonial that could be offered was sent to her. We believe that this brave girl soon after died of decline.

The Rescue Party

1853

THE Arctic seas have been the scene of some of the most noted instances of daring and patience shown by mariners. Ever since the reign of Edward VI, when the brave Sir Hugh Willoughby and his crew all perished frozen at their posts among the rocks of Spitzbergen, the relentless ice, and soft though fatal snows of those dreary realms, have formed the grave of many a gallant sailor. Many a life has been lost in the attempt to discover the North-west passage, between Davis's and Behring's Straits, and to trace the outline of the northern coast of America. Whether those lives were wasted, or whether their brave example was not worth more to the world than a few years more of continuance, is not the question here to be asked. The later Arctic voyagers had a nobler purpose than that of completing the survey of the barren coast, namely, the search for Sir John Franklin, who, in 1845, had gone forth with two tried vessels, the Erebus and Terror, on his second polar expedition, and had been seen and heard of no more.

Voyage after voyage was undertaken, in the hope at first of relieving and rescuing the lost ships' companies, and then of ascertaining their fate, until the Admiralty decided that to send forth more exploring parties was a vain risking of valuable lives, and it was only the earnest perseverance of Sir John Franklin's wife and the chivalrous adventure of individuals that carried on the search, until, at the end of fourteen years, Captain, now Sir Leopold M'Clintock, in the Fox yacht, discovered the last records, which placed it beyond all doubt that the gentle and courageous Franklin had died peacefully, before evil days had come on his party, and that the rest had more gradually perished under cold and hunger, in the fearful prison of icebergs.

Gallant and resolute as were all these northern travellers, there are two names that perhaps deserve, above the others, to be recorded, because their free offer of themselves was not prompted by the common tie of country. One was the French Lieutenant Bellot, who sailed in the Albertin 1851, and after most manful exertions, which gained the respect and love of all who sailed with him, was drowned by the breaking of the ice in Wellington

Sound. The other was Dr. Elisha Kane, an American naval surgeon, who in 1853 volunteered to command an American expedition in search of the lost vessels, which were supposed to be shut up by the ice in a basin of clearer, warmer water, such as it was thought might exist round the North Pole, and the way to which might be opened or closed, according to the shifting of the icebergs.

His vessel was the brig Advance, and his course was directed through Davis's Straits, and on the way past the Danish settlements in Greenland, they provided themselves with a partially educated young Esquimaux as a hunter, and with a team of dogs, which were to be used in drawing sledges over the ice in explorations.

The whole expedition was one Golden Deed, but there is not space to describe it in all its details: we must confine ourselves to the most striking episode in their adventures, hoping that it may send our readers to the book itself. The ship was brought to a standstill in Renfaelner Bay, on the west side of Smith's Strait, between the 79th and 80th degrees of latitude. It was only the 10th of September when the ice closed in so as to render further progress of the ship impossible. On the 7th of November the sun was seen for the last time, and darkness set in for 141 days—such darkness at times as was misery even to the dogs, who used to contend with one another for the power of lying within sight of the crack of light under the cabin door.

Before the light failed, however, Dr. Kane had sent out parties to make caches, or stores of provisions, at various intervals. These were to be used by the exploring companies whom he proposed to send out in sledges, while the ice was still unbroken, in hopes of thus discovering the way to the Polynia, or polar basin, in which he thought Franklin might be shut up. The same work was resumed with the first gleams of returning light in early spring, and on the 18th of March a sledge was dispatched with eight men to arrange one of these depots for future use. Towards midnight on the 29th, Dr. Kane and those who had remained in the ship, were sewing moccasins in their warm cabin by lamplight, when steps were heard above, and down came three of the absent ones, staggering, swollen, haggard, and scarcely able to speak. Four of their companions were lying under their tent frozen and disabled, "somewhere among the hummocks, to the north and east, it was drifting heavily". A brave Irishman, Thomas Hickey, had remained at the peril of his life to feed them, and these three had set out to try to obtain aid, but they were so utterly exhausted and bewildered, that they could hardly be restored sufficiently to explain themselves.

Instantly to set out to the rescue, was of course Dr. Kane's first thought, and as soon as the facts had been ascertained, a sledge, a small tent, and some pemmican, or pounded and spiced meat, were packed up; Mr. Ohlsen, who was the least disabled of the sufferers, was put into a fur bag, with his legs rolled up in dogskins and eiderdown, and strapped upon the sledge, in the hope that he would serve as a guide, and nine men, with Dr. Kane, set forth across the ice in cold seventy-eight degrees below the freezing-point.

Mr. Ohlsen, who had not slept for fifty hours, dropped asleep as soon as the sledge began to move, and thus he continued for sixteen hours, during which the ten proceeded with some knowledge of their course, since huge icebergs of noted forms, stretching in "long beaded lines" across the bay, served as a sort of guide-posts. But just when they had come beyond their knowledge, except that their missing comrades must be somewhere within forty miles round, he awoke, evidently delirious and perfectly useless. Presently, they came to a long level floe, or field of ice, and Dr. Kane thinking it might have been attractive to weary men unable to stagger over the wild hummocks and rugged surface of the other parts, he decided to search it thoroughly. He left the sledge, raised the tent, buried the pemmican, and took poor Ohlsen out of his bag, as he was just able to keep his legs, and the thermometer had sunk three degrees lower, so that to halt would have been certain death. The thirst was dreadful, for there was no waiting to melt the snow, and in such a temperature, if it be not thawed before touching the mouth, it burns like caustic, and leaves the lips and tongue bleeding. The men were ordered to spread themselves, so as to search completely; but though they readily obeyed, they could not help continually closing up together, either, Dr. Kane thought, from getting bewildered by the forms of the ice, or from the invincible awe and dread of solitude, acting on their shattered nerves in that vast field of intense lonely whiteness, and in the atmosphere of deadly cold. The two strongest were seized with shortness of breath and trembling fits, and Dr. Kane himself fainted twice on the snow. Thus they had spent two hours, having been nearly eighteen without food or water, when Hans, their Esquimaux hunter, thought he saw a sledge track in the snow, and though there was still a doubt whether it were not a mere rift made by the wind, they followed it for another hour, till at length they beheld the stars and stripes of the American flag fluttering on a hummock of snow, and close behind it was the tent of the lost.

Dr. Kane was among the last to come up; his men were all standing in file beside the tent, waiting in a sort of awe for him to be the first to enter it and see whether their messmates still lived. He crawled into the darkness, and heard a burst of welcome from four poor helpless figures lying stretched on their backs. "We expected you! We were sure you would come!" and then burst out a hearty cheer outside, and for the first time Dr. Kane was wellnigh overcome by strong feelings.

Here were fifteen souls in all to be brought back to the ship. The newcomers had travelled without rest for twenty-one hours, and the tent would barely hold eight men, while outside, motion was the only means of sustaining life. By turns, then, the rescue party took two hours of sleep each, while those who remained awake paced the snow outside, and food having been taken, the homeward journey began, but not until all the sick had been undressed, rubbed, and newly packed in double buffalo skins, in which–having had each limb swathed in reindeer skins–they were laid on their own sledge, and sewn up in one huge bale, with an opening over each mouth for breathing. This took four hours, and gave almost all the rescuers frostbitten fingers, and then, all hands standing round, a prayer was said, and the ten set out to drag the four in their sledge over ice and snow, now in ridges, now hummocks, up and down, hard and wild beyond conception. Ohlsen was sufficiently restored to walk, and all went cheerfully for about six hours, when everyone became sensible of a sudden failure of their powers.

"Bonsall and Morton, two of our stoutest men, came to me, begging permission to sleep; they were not cold, the wind did not enter them now, a little sleep was all that they wanted." Presently Hans was found nearly stiff under a drift, and Thomas, bolt upright, had his eyes closed, and could hardly articulate. At last John Blake threw himself on the snow and refused to rise. They did not complain of feeling cold; but it was in vain that I wrestled, boxed, ran, argued, jeered, or reprimanded, an immediate halt could not be avoided." So the tent was pitched again with much difficulty, for their hands were too powerless to strike a light, and even the whisky, which had been put under all the coverings of the sledge at the men's feet, was frozen. Into the tent all the sick and failing were put, and James M'Gary was left in charge of them, with orders to come on after a halt of four hours, while Dr. Kane and William Godfrey pushed on ahead, meaning to reach the tent that had been left halfway, and thaw some food by the time the rest came up.

Happily, they were on a level tract of ice, for they could hardly have contended with difficulties in the nine miles they had still to go to this tent. They were neither of them in their right sense, but had resolution enough to keep moving, and imposing on one another a continued utterance of words; but they lost all count of time, and could only remember having seen a bear walking leisurely along, and tearing up a fur garment that had been dropped the day before. The beast rolled it into a ball, but took no notice of them, and they proceeded steadily, so "drunken with cold", that they hardly had power to care for the sight of their halfway tent undergoing the same fate. However, their approach frightened away the bear, after it had done no worse than overthrowing the tent. The exhausted pair raised it with much difficulty, crawled in, and slept for three hours. When they awoke, Dr. Kane's beard was frozen so fast to the buffalo-skin over him, that Godfrey had to cut him out with his jack-knife; but they had recovered their faculties, and had time to make a fire, thaw some ice, and make some soup with the pemmican, before the rest of the party arrived.

After having given them this refreshment, the last stage of the journey began, and the most severe; for the ice was wild and rough, and exhaustion was leading to the most grievous of losses–that of self-control. In their thirst, some could no longer abstain from eating snow–their mouths swelled, and they became speechless; and all were overpowered by the deadly sleep of cold, dropping torpid upon the snow. But Dr. Kane found that, when roused by force at the end of three minutes, these snatches of sleep did them good, and each in turn was allowed to sit on the runners of the sledge, watched, and awakened. The day was without wind and sunshiny, otherwise they must have perished; for the whole became so nearly delirious; that they retained no recollection of their proceedings, they only traced their course afterwards by their footmarks. But when perception and memory were lost, obedience and self-devotion lived on–still these hungry, frostbitten, senseless men tugged at the sledge that bore their comrades–still held together, and obeyed their leader, who afterwards continued the soundest of the party. One was sent staggering forward, and was proved by the marks in the snow to have repeatedly fallen; but he reached the brig safely, and was capable of repeating with perfect accuracy the messages Dr. Kane had charged him with for the surgeon.

A dog team, with a sledge and some restoratives, was at once sent out to meet the others, with the surgeon, Dr. Hayes, who was shocked at the condition in which he encountered them–four lying, sewn up in furs, on the sledge, which the other ten were drawing. These ten, three days since, hardy, vigorous men, were covered with frost, feeble, and bent. They gave not a glance of recognition, but only a mere vacant, wild stare, and still staggered on, every one of them delirious. It was one o'clock in the afternoon of the third day that they arrived, after sixty-six hours' exposure, during which they had been almost constantly on foot. Most of those who still kept their footing stumbled straight on, as if they saw and heard nothing, till they came to the ship's side, where, on Dr. Kane giving the word to halt, they dropped the lines, mounted the ship's side, and each made straight for his own bed, where he rolled in, just as he was, in all his icy furs, and fell into a heavy sleep.

There were only the seven who had been left with the ship (five of them being invalids), to carry up the four helpless ones, and attend to all the rest. Dr. Kane, indeed, retained his faculties, assisted in carrying them in, and saw them attended to; after which he lay down in his cot, but after an hour or two, he shouted, "Halloo, on deck there!" and when Dr. Hayes came to him, he gave orders "to call all hands to lay aft, and take two reefs in the stove-pipe!" In like manner, each of the party, as he awoke, began to rave; and for two days the ship was an absolute madhouse, the greater part of its inmates frantic in their several cots. Dr. Kane was the first to recover—Ohlsen the last, his mind constantly running upon the search for his comrades in the tent, which he thought himself the only person able to discover. Of those whom the party had gone to assist, good "Irish Tom" soon recovered; but two died in the course of a few days, and the rest suffered very severely.

The rest of Dr. Kane's adventures cannot here be told; suffice it to say, that his ship remained immovable, and, after a second winter of terrible suffering from the diseases induced by a want of fresh meat and vegetables—the place of which was ill-supplied by rats, puppies, and scurvy-grass—it was decided to take to the boats; and between these and sledges, the ship's company of the Advance, at last, found their way to Greenland, after so long a seclusion from all European news, that when they first heard of the Crimean war, they thought an alliance between England and France a mere hallucination of their ignorant informant. Dr. Kane—always an unhealthy man—did not live long after his return, but he survived long enough to put on record one of the most striking and beautiful histories of patience and unselfishness that form part of the best treasury this world has to show.

The Children in the Wood of the Far South
1864

OUR roll of Golden Deeds is nearly at an end, not indeed that acts of self-devotion are exhausted, but that full and authentic particulars have not reached us of more than we have related. We have not ventured to tell the stories of the gentlemen who, in the Indian mutiny, rode for miles through an enemy's country, under a burning sun, with the young child of a friend in their arms. One of these little creatures, still under three years old, whose protector had had to fight his way through the natives with her on his horse's neck, was too young to know what she owed to him, and only remembered the horrors of her ride, so that when he was at length able to restore her to her mother, she shrank from him, and would not even look at him. The other little girl, a little Miss Christian, not four years old, was only rescued for the time to fall with her protector into the possession of a native prince, who retained them in his power while besieging Lucknow. The child pined and died before the time of release came, but her illness was the occasion of an unlooked-for comfort to her companions in captivity. A native doctor, who was allowed to prescribe for her, sent some powders for her wrapped in a chance bit of printed paper. It proved to be the leaf of a torn Bible, and these were the words that it bore; "I, even I, am He that comforteth you: who art thou, that thou shouldst be afraid of a man that shall die, and of the son of man that shall be made as grass; and forgettest the LORD thy Maker, that hath stretched forth the heavens, and laid the foundation of the earth; and hast feared continually every day because of the fury of the oppressor? and where is the fury of the oppressor? The captive exile hasteneth that he may be loosed, and that he should not die in the pit, nor that his bread should fail. But I am the LORD thy God, that divided the sea, whose waves roared: the LORD of hosts is His Name." (Isa., li. 12-15.)

The few survivors of that band of "captive exiles" have declared that these words were to them a message of exceeding joy and hope of deliverance from the fury of the oppressor, and that they were thus greatly strengthened to endure unto the end. Neither the child nor her rescuer were among them. They had both been set free by sickness from captivity and all other ills of this mortal life.

Neither can we here pause upon the story of Arthur Cheek, the young ensign of only sixteen years old, who at Allahabad, sorely wounded and dying of thirst, not only was steadfast in confessing his own faith, but by his exclamation, "Oh, my friend, come what may, do not deny the LORD JESUS", prevented the apostasy of a convert from Mahometanism, whom the Sepoys were cruelly torturing. A sudden attack of the Madras fusiliers saved the convert, but it was too late to save the martyr boy, who had sunk to rest ere his countrymen had made their way into the city.

We must turn from these, and speak of those little elder sisters, almost mothers in their love and devotion. We see such little heroines oftener than we think dragging about babies as big as themselves, to whom they often give the last morsel when they are hungry enough themselves, or rushing almost under horses' hoofs, or carriage wheels, to snatch some unlucky brother from the destruction into which he is just big enough to toddle. Perhaps the most notable of all these sisters was Françoise Marie, of Roche-beaucour, who, at eleven years old, was left an orphan with a little brother of four, to whom she fully did a mother's part for three years, maintaining him entirely by her knitting and spinning, until, in a severe winter, a wolf with five whelps burst into the cottage, attracted by the smell of the hot loaves that Françoise had been baking.

She had almost driven the she-wolf off with a heavy stick, when seeing one of the cubs about to attack her brother, she seized the boy, thrust him into a cupboard, and buttoned the door. That moment gave the wolf time to fly on her throat, and the next moment she was the prey of the wild beasts. Her brother remained safe, though unable to get out of the cupboard till released by the neighbours. He was an old man in 1796, still cherishing the memory of the mother-like sister who had died to save him.

Nor may we forget the little Scottish sister, who, when lost with her little brother on the mountainside, was saved by the good collie dog, who sped home to call help, and guided the father to the spot, where, buried far under a snowdrift, lay the two children, the younger wrapped in all the warmer garments of the elder. Both survived, thanks to the good dog's timely sagacity. Indeed, we believe that a chapter of canine deeds, almost deserving the name of golden, might be brought together in honour of our faithful comrades. There was Delta, the dog whose skeleton was disinterred at Herculaneum, stretched over that of a boy of twelve years old, with an inscription on his collar, telling that he had three times saved the life of his master—from the sea, from robbers, and from wolves; there was Phileros, the dog of Athens, who broke his leg by leaping after his young master when he had fallen out at the window, and finally died of grief on his grave; there was the dog who is commemorated in Vandyke's picture of the Duke of Richmond, whom his sagacity and courage had saved from assassins; there was the dog who awoke his master, Lord Forbes, at Castle Forbes, in Ireland, and dragged him, half-suffocated and helpless, from his burning bedroom; there was the well-known dog who daily carried bannocks to the shepherd's child lost in the cave behind the waterfall; there was the Newfoundland dog who won a silver collar by saving, first the postman, and then his letter bag from the water of a swelled ford. Gellert must be given up, since his story proves to be only a Western version of an Indian legend of a serpent and mungoose, instead of a wolf and a hound, but there is no passing by the dog of Montargis, who, under Charles VI of France, vainly defended his master, Aubri de Montdidier, when sent upon by his mortal foe, Macaire; then lay day and night on the forest grave where Macaire hoped his crime was hidden, before going to the house of his master's chief friend in Paris, for his daily meal, until at length he was followed, the ground searched, the murder discovered, and the corpse freshly buried. Afterwards, the dog's furious attacks upon Macaire were deemed an accusation, and the matter was put to the proof by the ordeal of combat in the Isle de Notre Dame. The dog had a tub into which he might retire, the man a club and a shield. The combat was so lengthy that Macaire, no doubt from the force of conscience, was so worn out that he fainted away, and on coming to himself owned the deed. Dogs of St. Bernard and Newfoundland dogs rise before us by scores when we think of these gallant doings–among them the strange black dog who came to the lone widow's house the night she had with her all the proceeds of the sale of her effects, fought manfully till he drove off the thieves who assailed the house, and disappeared so mysteriously next morning, that she always regarded him as a special messenger of Providence for her protection. The touching story of "Rab and his friends" is no unique incident; it is only that in Dr. John Brown it met with a spectator and biographer able to appreciate and regard the beautiful affection and fidelity that our Maker has embodied before our eyes in these His good creatures. If, as some wise men have deemed, the brutes are created to show us in living shape, figures and emblems of our own qualities, the dog, with his master taking to him the place of our Great Master, is most certainly the living type of that heart-whole devotion which is the root of Golden Deeds.

But we must pass on to the latest of which we have heard, and then turn aside from the roll that has truly been a labour of love and refreshment.

It was in Australia–that great and somewhat repulsive southern island, or rather continent, that has deranged the convenient old geographical arrangment of four quarters of the world, and, willingly or unwillingly, has received a large proportion of the English population, before whom the poor feeble native race are fast dwindling away.

Under English management, Australia is excellent for sheep farms; but the "bush", as colonists everywhere call uncleared forest land, is particularly desolate and dreary. And it was into such bush that, in the winter of 1864, the three little children of a carpenter, named Duff, at a station near Melbourne, were often sent out to gather broom. The eldest was a boy of nine years old; Jane, his sister, was seven, and little Frank was five. One evening they did not come back, and their parents became alarmed. There are, indeed, in Australia no dangerous wild beasts, such as the bears that two little lost Canadian babes once called to as their father's oxen, "Buck" and "Bell"; but on the other hand, there are no raspberries, such as sustained those little wanderers–not even the "blackberries" that "dyed the pretty lips" of our own "Babes in the Wood"–only dull gum trees, with oddly shaped cones and blue upright leaves, and bark that they shed instead of changing leaves–she-oak trees, with hard joints, like over-grown English horse-tails–monstrous nettle trees, like a bad dream of our English stinging-nettle–all growing in such similar shapes and clusters, that it is a most difficult, nay, impossible, thing for a person once lost to recover his bearings; and, worse than all, the drought is terrible, so that thirst will cause a more painful death than even hunger. Stout men, sturdy explorers, have been known to lie down, famished, to die in this unhospitable forest; and what could be the fate of the poor little children?

The father and his neighbours in vain shouted "Cooee!" (the bush call), and sought the country day after day, until a week had passed; when he obtained the aid of some of the natives, who, despised as they are by the colonists, have a wonderful power of tracking the faintest trail in their forests. They soon made out signs where the children had been, from the bendings of the twigs or the tramplings of the grass. "Here litttle one tired," they said; "sit down. Big one kneel down; carry him along. Here travel all night; dark–not see that bush; her fall on him." Then came: "Here little one tired again; big one kneel down; no get up–fall flat on face."

The children had been lost on Friday afternoon. On the Saturday week, the blacks led the father up to a clump of broom, where lay three little figures, the least in the middle, with his sister's frock over his own clothes. Duff went up to them, comforted, at least, that he could carry home the little corpses to their mother. But the eldest boy roused himself, sat up, and said, "Father!" then fell back from sheer weakness; and indeed, his lips were so shrunk, that they could no longer cover his teeth. Little Frank awoke as if from a quiet sleep. "Father, why didn't you come before?" he said; "we were cooeeing for you." Jane was scarcely alive; when she was lifted up, she only made a murmur of "Cold–cold!" If neither had lived to tell the tale, little Frank's condition, so much better than that of his elders, would have told how free from selfishness their behaviour must have been through all that dreadful week. When the elder brother was carried past the places that the blacks had pointed out, his account of their wanderings and adventures exactly agreed with what the natives had inferred. He said that this whole time they had been without food, and had only had one drink of water–perhaps from the "pitcher plant", which is a native of those woods, and has a wonderfully shaped cup, which retains water for many weeks. A man had been known to live eleven days in the bush upon nothing but water; but the endurance of these little ones was even more wonderful.

They were all fast recovering; and the feeling of admiration for little Jane was so strong in the colony, that a subscription was being raised for her, which soon amounted to several hundred pounds. May it be well and wisely laid out on her behalf, and may her further life be worthy of the Golden Deed of her childhood!